HARVARD STUDIES IN MONOPOLY AND COMPETITION

1. CORPORATE SIZE AND EARNING POWER
William Leonard Crum

2. THE CONTROL OF COMPETITION IN CANADA
Lloyd G. Reynolds

HARVARD STUDIES IN
MONOPOLY AND COMPETITION

LONDON : HUMPHREY MILFORD
OXFORD UNIVERSITY PRESS

CORPORATE SIZE AND EARNING POWER

BY

WILLIAM LEONARD CRUM
PROFESSOR OF ECONOMICS IN HARVARD UNIVERSITY

CAMBRIDGE, MASSACHUSETTS
HARVARD UNIVERSITY PRESS
1939

PRINTED AT THE HARVARD UNIVERSITY PRESS
CAMBRIDGE, MASSACHUSETTS, U.S.A.

THIS IS THE FIRST of a series of monographs on selected aspects of the general problem of monopoly and competition, reporting specific studies in the research program of a special committee of the Harvard Department of Economics. The analytical investigation leading to the present monograph was financed in part by a grant from the A. W. Shaw Fund. The second and third monographs in this series will be "The Control of Competition in Canada," by Lloyd G. Reynolds, and "Unfair Competition," by John P. Miller, and will appear under the editorship of Edward S. Mason.

PREFACE

Upon completion, just over ten years ago, of my manuscript for *Corporate Earning Power*,[1] I wrote in the Preface that three controlling reasons led to publication then of a volume which was fairly called a first report of the results of my analysis of Treasury data on corporate profits. These reasons were:

> Certain of these results seem clearly established by the investigation; and, as these results have large practical import, it is desirable to make them available promptly. Early publication will bring the materials, in readily available form, before numerous active business men and students of finance or economics in general, who are competent to re-examine and develop the many points on which I may have erred or treatment of which I may have omitted. Finally, as this volume indicates some of the inadequacies in the data as now tabulated and published by the Treasury, it may furnish an incentive to the fuller and more serviceable reporting of corporation statistics to the end that later investigations shall rest upon data more readily adapted to the uses of the analytical statistician.

I am happy to believe that subsequent achievement, especially with reference to the second and third purposes, has been truly remarkable. The book did stimulate — I should by no means suggest that it was the sole or chief stimulus — active further investigation of corporate profits, and a notable improvement in the fundamental data. Other investigators have devoted their skill and energy to the problem of measuring and explaining variations, over time or at any one time, in corporate earning power. Some investigators have disclosed or corrected errors in my own analyses or interpretations; some have carried much further the study of the questions raised by the book, or examined additional questions; all have made helpful contribu-

[1] Stanford University Press, 1929.

tions to a now rapidly expanding knowledge of an exceedingly important but also exceedingly intricate aspect of economic science. Notable improvement has occurred also in the statistical data: Treasury tabulations of corporate accounts are today vastly more satisfactory for scientific study than ten years ago. Indeed, the present monograph could not have been attempted had the statistics remained in the form known to us in 1929. Most of the credit for this extraordinary improvement in the tabulations belongs to present and former officers of the Division of Research and Statistics in the Treasury and of the Statistical Section of the Income Tax Unit in the Bureau of Internal Revenue.

The present monograph is not a revised edition of *Corporate Earning Power*; it is concerned almost entirely with a very elaborate examination of a single aspect of corporate earning power, an aspect upon which the earlier book could at best give only inadequate and indeed superficial results because of inappropriate data. The great improvement in the form of the published data since 1929, coupled with a mere lengthening of the historical record with the passage of time, has rendered possible now such a study of the highly important relation of corporate size to earning power as could not have been undertaken a decade ago. I am confident also that the author comes to the task with much better qualifications: continuing study of the profits problem and related financial and economic matters has given me a deeper insight which ought to be reflected in the pages of this new book. Needless to say, I have derived much benefit from criticisms of the earlier book, and from the splendid work of other investigators.

The purposes of publishing the present volume might well be stated in exactly the words quoted above. I believe some of the results here presented are of great and immediate importance, and I hope their presentation will prove helpful to economists and others interested in profits. I am sure the book makes only a beginning in the interpretation of the facts presented, though I have sought to develop or suggest those points which seem to me most important. I doubt not that some of my interpretations and even some of my numerical analyses are in error, and that I have suffered from various misapprehensions. It is my hope that this book will stimulate a new wave of investigation, that critics will reveal and correct my errors, that other investigators will share with me the task of drawing more numerous and more complete inferences from the rich mine of fact here made available, and that the book will suggest other entirely different approaches to this and related problems. I trust also that this book, benefiting greatly though it does from improvements already made in the basic data, will suggest points at which still further improvement can be undertaken.

An individual almost never has the means or time and energy to carry out alone so vast a task as the investigation reported in this book. I am grateful to the A. W. Shaw Fund for a grant which covered a substantial fraction of the out-of-pocket costs. Mrs. Eleanor Crum, Mr. F. L. Hall, Miss Althea MacDonald, Mrs. Harriet Ross, and Mrs. Anna Thorpe have assisted me in various parts and at various stages of the research investigation and the preparation of the book. Each has devoted patient and painstaking effort to meeting the exacting demands of an unpredictable and sometimes erratic taskmaster, and to insuring so far as possible technical perfection of the completed book. To each I here make a wholly inadequate expression of my deep gratitude.

W. L. C.

Cambridge
June 9, 1939

CONTENTS

TABLES

CHARTS

CORPORATE SIZE AND EARNING POWER

I

INTRODUCTION

THE ANALYSIS reported in the following chapters centers about one basic question: To what extent is corporate earning power related to the size of corporate enterprise? That various aspects of this question and various other questions more or less closely connected therewith should receive attention in the course of the analysis must be taken for granted. That any relations or apparent relations found in examining the basic question need to be subjected to critical analyses somewhat disconnected from the general outline of study is also evident. But always the basic question is kept in mind: Are variations in profit rates associated with variations in size?

The entire study is concerned with the *corporate* entity. This means not only that non-corporate types of business are ignored, and that the findings of the study do not necessarily reach to such types. It means also that the unit of size under consideration is the entire enterprise operated by a single corporation, and not a single plant or other operating unit; although in many cases the business of a particular corporation may in fact be limited to a single plant. Likewise the concept of profit, or rate of return, is one pertinent to the whole enterprise of a corporate legal entity, and not to a plant or process or operation having unity in a technological sense. In other words, the concepts of size and of profit are not those in mind when an economist examines the relation between profits and the *scale* of operations.

Without doubt some of the findings of the present study are influenced by, and reflect in some degree, existing relationships between profits and scale of operations. This should follow because in very numerous cases the business operation of a particular corporate entity is identifiable with a plant or other production unit, and because in numerous other cases in which a single corporation operates several production units which are separate or isolated in the technological sense the economic ties between these units are such as to modify our concepts of scale. But, however important the bearing of the scale of operations upon profit rates as examined herein, no satisfactory basis appears for inferences about relations between scale and profits from the findings as to relations between corporate size and rates of return. The data examined do not admit of analyses leading safely to such inferences; and no other body of data, covering industry broadly and not merely specific narrow types of industry, supplies, so far as I know, the basis for such inferences. Possibly one may identify one or more lines of industry, among those studied below, for which general knowledge suggests that corporate size is associated approximately with scale of production unit; but I fail to note any such case. Even in lines of industry, such as trade and clothing manufacturing, for which general knowledge tells us that vast numbers of corporations own and operate one plant each, general knowledge also tells us that numerous companies — not separable from the others in our data — have chains or groups of plants. We are forced to conclude that this investigation can give little if any definitive information on the existence and identity of an optimum scale of operations.

OBJECTIVES OF THE ANALYSIS

The study is, instead, designed to answer questions concerning the relation between profit and size from the point of view of the corporate legal and financial entity, and in particular from the point of view of its equity owners. Even for this purpose the available data are not wholly satisfactory: where several corporate entities are linked together by intercorporate investments or other means, our object might well require considering the whole system as a single entity. The data actually used are in an important degree of a sort appropriate for such treatment, of interrelated systems of corporations, for the years 1931–33; although the so-called consolidated returns filed under revenue acts prior to that of 1934 cover by no means all cases of such systems which we might properly wish to treat as units. After 1933, with one important exception (the railroad industry), the data available pertain strictly to corporations as legal entities — each such legal entity is counted separately, regardless of intercorporate ties. At least for 1934–36, therefore, the analysis here reported does not consider a system of corporations, however closely linked by intercorporate ties, as a unit: the size-and-profit relationships pertain, not to the system, but to the several corporate members thereof.

Even if we had data throughout the six-year period which invariably treated as a single entity each system of corporations linked together by intercorporate investments, and by such control of financial and operating policy as might result therefrom, we should still find the data not wholly satisfactory for our purpose. Other forms of control may be of large, if not equal, importance; and so little is known about these forms of control, except that they manifestly are not reflected in accounting records, that data on profits and size could not be reconstructed with a view to allowing for them. For the present we must be content with an analysis, based on the available tabulations of accounting records, which overlooks these defects; and I am of opinion that the defects, serious though they may be, do not prevent our analysis from having very great significance.

With the limitations on the analysis as outlined above, we may fairly hold that the findings are significant mainly from the investment point of view: rate of profit is an indicator of the appropriateness or successfulness of investment and is an important criterion which, in the sense of the economist, guides the flow of investment. Correspondingly, if we find rate of return differing with size of enterprise, we infer that the incentive — ignoring other incentives than profits — to making new investment or to withdrawing old investment varies with size of enterprise. The analysis places its emphasis upon the rate of return on owners' equity, and hence upon the risk-taking portion of investment; and this is in accord with the major problems concerning the allocation of capital to industry, though the economist can by no means neglect factors influencing the flow of creditors' capital. I present a partial and tentative analysis, in Chapter XXIII, of the return on both borrowed and owned capital; and a more incisive and elaborate study from this point of view may have large significance to the economist, particularly when he is interested in the general problem of allocation of capital to industry. But the allocation of risk-taking capital remains of central importance from several points of view, and on this subject the findings of my main analysis should prove highly informing.

Other questions than those relating to the allocation of capital to industry can helpfully be considered in the light of the findings here reported. The form of industrial organization, and changes or tendencies therein, come under this head. That differential rates of return — real or expected — among enterprises of different size exert a powerful influence upon industrial organization can not be doubted. This suggests a list of problems relating to monopoly, control, and concentration in industry. The analysis clearly bears directly, with some limitations, upon industrial concentration and some of its consequences and manifestations. With respect to control, I have already indicated that the data leave much to be desired; though I suspect some helpful indications are afforded by the analysis. On questions of monopoly, as defined in the strict sense of the economist, I fear this study makes little progress; though I doubt not that specialists in the theory of monopoly can explain or interpret some of my findings on the ground of monopoly or partial monopoly. My belief is that other types of data than those used here, or at least in addition to them, are required for a scientific appraisal of the existence and effects of monopoly.

But the term *monopoly*, regardless of definition by careful economists, has become an epithet in the hands of practical politicians or less careful "economists," and I fear my findings will promptly be cited as evidence concerning monopoly in this sense. In the popular mind, monopoly is often identified with mere size of enterprise; and the very fact that mere size *may* have a decisive bearing upon monopoly in the strict sense renders the task of dislodging this notion from the thought of masses of people exceedingly difficult. Politicians seldom have the stoutness of character, if indeed the intelligence, to refrain from accepting the popular connotations of a technical term; and therefore we need not be surprised if, in discussions of public policy, monopoly is identified with size. And whether mere size of enterprise is called monopoly or not, public policy may concern itself therewith; although intelligent public policy will not find size objectionable and deserving of punitive treatment without careful examination of the evidence.

I believe my findings clearly show that, on the average, large enterprise — in all or nearly all broad lines of industry, and in different stages of the economic cycle — is more profitable than small enterprise, especially very small enterprise. I fail to see that this suggests the wisdom of imposing punitive restraints on large industrial enterprise. From the public point of view — granting that the public does not wish to take the long and hazardous step of securing its industrial capital and enterprise-leadership by some other means than offering a reward in the form of profits — the maintenance and development of an economic productive mechanism requires that *some* at least of the capital required receive a reward. A public policy which largely destroys the chance of reward by punishing large enterprise, which on the average is now most successful in securing such rewards, might well do irreparable harm to the productive mechanism. I gladly grant that the profit showing of smaller enterprise *might* be more satisfactory if large enterprise were eliminated or restricted, but I find no clear evidence in support of this view. Indeed, my analysis shows experience quite as unfavorable for small enterprise in certain lines of industry for which no high degree of concentration in large enterprises exists as in other lines. I further admit that wise public policy *may* need to encourage small enterprise, on the ground that new industrial developments often and perhaps generally start small; and it might thus be held that such a policy of encouragement would facilitate initiating new developments, and so promote the long-run progress of the economy. But one should not overlook the contrary possibility that such encouragement might facilitate an undue survival of wasteful — or at least less efficient — operating entities, with a corresponding less good use of some of society's limited store of capital. And it might also facilitate participation in an industry by firms which do serious damage, through unwise competitive methods, to the industry as a whole.

THE LOT OF SMALL BUSINESS

I present evidence indicating that *some* small enterprises earn profits at handsome rates; and this necessarily implies, as the evidence shows, that other small enterprises suffer losses at even greater rates than the average rate of loss for all small enterprises. It is in the field of small enterprise that the great mortality of concerns must occur; the public press and other sources of information bring to our notice instances of expiration of life of some huge enterprises, and these have great importance because of the mere magnitude of the resources involved and of the wide ramifications marking the business relationships of a giant concern. But not sufficiently spectacular, and perhaps too frequent to constitute news, is the demise of the small concern with but a few thousand dollars of assets. Yet these concerns must constantly be passing out of active life in large numbers each year: the very fact that considerable groups of such enterprises can, in a single year, have losses on the average of 50 per cent and even much higher proportions of their equity can spell but one outcome. Unfortunately, our data do not enable us to trace the experience of particular corporations — small or larger (except the prominent listed companies) — through successive years; and no empirical study is as yet possible of the cumulative effect of several years of losses upon the solvency and the chance of survival of corporations. But the annual figures, studied in isolation, are sufficiently indicative: no possible doubt can remain that many small corporate enterprises must succumb in a period of severe depression, and that some can not survive even in times of prosperity.

Small concerns which fail may indeed be absorbed by other concerns — which are already larger or become larger through such absorptions — and one of the foundations of prosperity of certain larger concerns may be this acquisition of assets on bargain-counter terms. Small concerns which do not fail may frequently become large, through expansion of their own activities or the acquisition of other concerns. In any case, despite the undoubted persistence over a long interval of numerous companies as small concerns, probability is high that small concerns do not long remain small: they succeed and expand, or they fail and are absorbed or merely disappear. The small size class includes the sector of corporate industry, then, in which the test of survival of the fittest operates with greatest force. Whether public policy should aim to accelerate or delay the application of this test in particular cases is perhaps debatable, and I suspect any prompt answer to this question would be superficial. I raise the question to emphasize the necessity of avoiding a determination of public policy by mere reference to some political slogan like "equality of opportunity," or "the small competitive business." Economically competent and publicly desirable small concerns may well shudder at what politicians may do to ("for") them in the name of equality or of competition.

OTHER FUNDAMENTAL PROBLEMS

Another series of questions, on which this analysis affords helpful information, concerns the internal organization — especially the capital structure — of a corporate enterprise. The relation between the return on owners' equity and the return on borrowed capital, and differences if any in that relation among lines of industry and among size classes, may be of high significance. Without doubt many other factors influence capital structure, but this factor is of great importance. The evidence presented below is only partial, and is not conclusive on the points at issue; but I hope the analysis will suggest lines along which further inquiry may prove fruitful. It may be remarked that the distinction between owned capital and borrowed capital, with a subdivision of the latter into long-term and short-term, is not a sufficiently fine classification. But, despite prominent instances of complicated capital structures, good reason exists for believing that the typical structure is fairly simple; and we may hope that further analysis of available data, with perhaps a slightly finer classification, will yield important findings.

Questions of taxation, in matters of both policy and practice, bristle through the book. In a few cases I have raised such questions, and the reader will discover many more. That taxation is now one of the dominant factors in corporate experience can not be doubted; and the study of the effects of taxation, actual or proposed, upon corporate experience in its profits and other manifestations may well be more important than a study of corporate indebtedness or even in some cases prices and costs. I trust some readers will be inclined to locate these tax questions with reference to my analysis, and examine them on theoretical or empirical grounds. I have in the main refrained from pursuing these questions, because the subject of business taxation appears to require consideration in all its aspects, and in connection with other types of taxation and indeed other aspects of fiscal policy. Nevertheless, the present analysis does include numerous important results which will be greatly helpful in such a general study of taxation.

The analysis as reported places emphasis, secondary only to that upon size, upon cyclical variations and industrial differences in earning power. The second of these is in a sense incidental to the size study, which required testing of the results to disclose whether they were pertinent to various lines of activity; but mere industrial differences in the level of profits have significance for their own sake, and much more informing inferences can be drawn from these comparisons than are presented in the book.

The evidence presented on cyclical variations was less clearly required as an incident to the main issue, though one of the objects of studying time variations was to test whether findings with respect to size were independent of the trade cycle. The cyclical record is probably of great interest on its own account: the rate of profit is one factor in the economy about which more precise and more detailed knowledge has long been desired by cycle theorists. The evidence here presented, though (except in Chapter XX) restricted to a six-year period having exceptional cyclical characteristics and to a concept of profit rate which is rather narrow, can not fail to supply important fragments of the desired information.

The book makes only a very limited beginning in searching

beneath the record of rates revealed by the main analysis, to disclose possible explanations of the results found. Three of the important factors which may bear upon the results, and might be expected to explain them in some part, are examined in Chapters XXII–XXIV. Although the tests there applied are restricted to limited portions of the general body of data under study in the book, and are seriously hampered by imperfections and uncertainties in definitions or data or methods of testing, I find tentatively that the major conclusions of the book — with respect to the relation of rate to size — are not explained by these factors. Inventory profits, though having large influence upon the level of profits at various stages of the cycle, seem not to vary among size classes in such way as to account for the observed correlation of rate of return with size. Interest on the borrowed portion of capital can, apparently, be described in similar terms. The case is less clear for salaries of officers, and decision in this case rests upon highly uncertain assumptions as to the degree to which such salaries include a distribution of what is truly profit in the economic sense. Other factors may perhaps be similarly tested, and more extensive and careful tests may be applied to these three factors; but I have preferred to leave such problems, along with other problems which are abundantly suggested by the book, to later analytical study in which many specialists can helpfully cooperate.

DEFINITIONS AND STATISTICS

The analyses of the book center about a specially defined rate of profit. For many purposes a measure of the *rate* of profit, rather than of the amount of profit, is desirable; and for the special objectives of this study, as amount of profit is likely to be somewhat associated with size, a rate figure is essential. Issues at once arise, however, concerning the specification of that rate — as respects both its numerator and its denominator. The uncertainties concerning the specification of the numerator would arise in any case: even if we were studying merely amount of profit, issues would need to be met in defining profit. Clearly, for a study of return from the point of view of risk-taking owners, a definition of profit must cover only the residual profit available — actually or constructively — to such owners after prior claims have been met.

This point of view seems clearly to warrant the exclusion of corporation taxes on profits — normal taxes, excess-profits taxes, and undistributed-profits taxes — from the profits figure to be used in our definition of rate. I am aware that, for some purposes, arguments may be advanced in favor of not deducting taxes to arrive at profits. For example, in the study of tax policy, especially if graduated rates are to be applied, profits before taxes may be the more significant figure; though framers of tax policy ought not to ignore the figure for profits after taxes. Or, in the study of earning power involving comparisons of profits among classes of corporations, wherein emphasis is not placed upon the point of view of the equity owners, something might be said for not excluding taxes. Thus, it might be held that exclusion of taxes would lead to unfair comparisons by reducing indicated profits of successful companies and not making corresponding alterations in the indicated losses of other companies. Or, it might be held that a corporation income tax is designed to be — and is, though here perplexing questions of incidence appear — a tax upon the incomes of individual owners rather than upon the income of the corporation. None of these arguments, or any others which have come to mind, seems to bear significantly upon the purpose of the present investigation. That purpose is to study the profits — residual earnings — to which the owners have a legal claim; and it seems tolerably clear that no such claim takes precedence over the public claim asserted, however wisely or unwisely, by the taxing authority in the lawful exercise of its powers. To deny the exclusion of taxes from profits, for such a purpose as that of this book, strikes me as no more defensible than to deny the exclusion of interest on funded debt or any other prior claim against earnings.

Other issues relative to the definition of profits were found of such little importance or so ill-adapted to study that they were largely or wholly ignored. With respect to capital gains and losses, which constitute part of profits as tabulated by the Treasury, strong theoretical reasons exist for exclusion. The data do not admit of a general test of the effect of this element; but some consideration of the evidence appears in Chapter XXIV, where it appears that capital gains or losses can result in only moderate distortion of our results. Except for this element, the definition of profits in Treasury tabulations is close to that suited to our measurement of return, as soon as correction is made for taxes. Questions concerning the precision with which tabulated data fit this definition are commented upon below.

Decision as to the appropriate denominator for the rate of return is less obviously reached. The possible advantage in stating the base with which the amount of return is compared — with reference to which it is expressed as a rate — in a form reflecting actual capital invested by the owners (with allowances for withdrawals and additions) is apparent, particularly for certain practical and theoretical inquiries. As explained in the following chapter, determination of invested capital — separately for lines of industry and size classes — does not seem feasible even on an approximate basis; and the data therefore enforce the use of another definition. Even if this were not true, however, I might have decided to use book value of the equity as the denominator of rate of return. As the object of study is the rate of return on proprietors' capital, with a view — among other purposes — to examination of forces affecting the allocation of new capital or withdrawal of old capital, much may be gained by expressing current return with reference to a current appraisal of the owners' stake in the enterprise.

II

RATE OF RETURN FOR ALL CORPORATIONS IN THE AGGREGATE

THE BROAD FACTS concerning earning power of corporate equity, as revealed for the aggregate of all corporations covered by Treasury compilations from tax returns accompanied by balance sheets, are so striking that we are tempted to accept their apparent implications as conclusive. In each of the six years, 1931–36, shown in Chart 1, the average rate of return on equity is, with negligible irregularities, progressively better as we pass to the right — that is, pass upward on the scale of size. Even in 1932, the year of poorest return for the entire aggregate without regard to size, the largest size class had a positive return, whereas all other classes and the aggregate had negative returns (losses). Even in 1936, the year of best return for the entire aggregate, the smallest size class had a negative return, whereas all other classes and the aggregate had positive returns. Chart 1 suggests an unmistakable tendency for large corporations to enjoy greater earning power than small corporations; but this chart is based upon data covering all corporations, without regard to type of industry or other possibly significant bases of classification. We shall in the following pages examine the evidence more closely and note several significant qualifications to temper this broad first finding.

RETURN ON EQUITY

In order to examine critically Chart 1 and related evidence, we must note certain departures, which have proved necessary or desirable, from the procedure used in my earlier studies of

CHART I

Rate of Return Compared with Size, for all Corporate Industry *

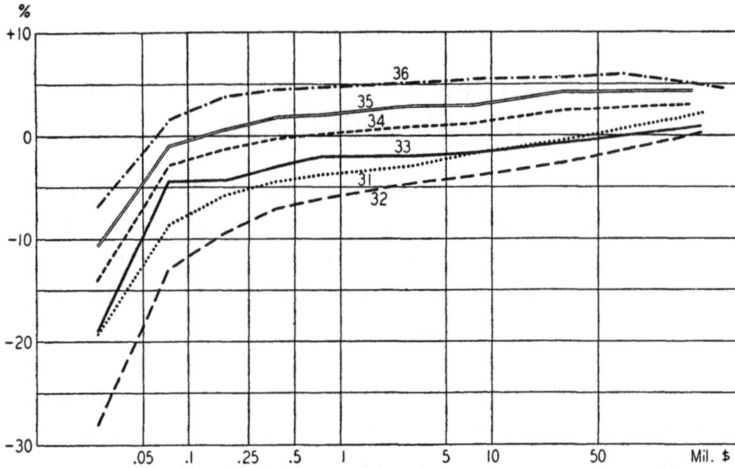

* Horizontal scale logarithmic. Data in Table II.

An arithmetical error, discovered in proofreading, led to incorrect figures for the deficit category and both categories combined in 1935 for the 50,000-thousand-dollar class. The incorrect figures (−7.74 for the deficit category, and −.98 for both categories combined) have been replaced by the correct figures (−11.77, and −1.24 respectively) in Table II, but no corresponding correction has been made in Chart I or other charts affected by the error in this table. The error also rendered the corresponding six-year averages incorrect (Table B). These incorrect figures (−13.59 for the deficit category, and −4.68 for both categories combined) have been replaced in Table B by the correct figures (−14.26, and −4.73 respectively), but no corresponding correction has been made in Chart IV or other charts affected by the error in this table. All other tables affected by this error (upon which no charts are based) have been corrected.

return on invested capital and on corporate equity.[1] The return on equity as used in the present analysis is a ratio, of profits to equity of stockholders, in which both numerator and denominator differ from those used in one or both of the earlier

[1] W. L. Crum, "Corporate Earnings on Invested Capital," *Harvard Business Review*, XVI, 3, Spring, 1938; and "Earning Power with Respect to the Size of Corporations," *ibid.*, XVII, 1, Autumn, 1938.

studies. A specimen computation of the rate of return on equity, as herein defined, appears in Table I. Here the numerator is aggregate profits defined as follows: the figure for compiled net profits after Federal taxes, as given in *Statistics of Income*.[2]

TABLE I

SPECIMEN CALCULATION OF RATE OF RETURN, ENTIRE MANUFACTURING DIVISION IN 1935 *

	Income corps.		Deficit corps.
a. Preferred stock	3,603,143		1,999,410
b. Common stock	13,037,225		7,242,269
c. Surplus and undivided profits	10,519,464		3,529,830
d. Sum	27,159,832		12,771,509
e. Deficit	317,351		2,002,790
f. Equity, end of year	26,842,481		10,768,719
g. Net profits after taxes	2,606,697		−467,738
h. Difference	24,235,784		11,236,457
i. Cash dividends paid	1,840,952		342,837
j. Equity, beginning of year, estimated	26,076,736		11,579,294
k. Sum of two equities	52,919,217		22,348,013
l. Average equity	26,459,609		11,174,006
m. Rate of return, %	9.85		−4.18
n. Combined average equity		37,633,615	
o. Combined net profits after taxes		2,138,959	
p. Rate of return, entire division, %		5.68	

* Unit: $1000, except for *m* and *p*.

Sources and derivation of data: *a*, *b*, *c*, *e*, *i* are transcribed from *Statistics of Income for 1935, Part 2*, p. 53 or pp. 67–68; *d* is sum of *a*, *b*, *c*; *f* is *d* minus *e*; *g* is transcribed from p. 53 of source for this illustration — and in general from pp. 52–59 for each *entire* division and group, from pp. 62–65 for the size classes of the entire corporate list without regard to industrial type, and from pp. 66–83 for the size classes of the *deficit* category in each division and group — but must be estimated for the size classes of the *income* category in each division and group (see method of estimate below, Chapter XXVI); *h* is *f* minus *g*; *j* is sum of *h* and *i*; *k* is sum of *f* and *j*; *l* is half of *k*; *m* is *g* divided by *l*; *n* combines the *l* items of the two columns; *o* likewise combines the *g* items; *p* is *o* divided by *n*. Income corporations are those "with net income," deficit corporations are those "with no net income."

[2] The annual publication in which the Treasury presents tabulations compiled from tax returns. See, for example, page 72 of *Statistics of Income for 1934, Part 2*. Washington: U.S. Treasury, 1937.

The denominator of the ratio here used is estimated from the aggregate equity, at the end of the calendar year,[3] comprising the sum of preferred stock, common stock, and surplus, as tabulated, minus the tabulated deficit. The estimate consists of (1) applying to this year-end aggregate two adjustments which *partially* record the changes in equity during the year, and application of which *partially* converts the year-end figure to a beginning-year figure; and (2) averaging these two figures — that for the end of the year and that for the beginning — to obtain an estimated average equity for the year. The two adjustments are subtraction of the year's net profits after taxes, and addition of the year's cash dividends paid. The resulting average equity for the year — an imperfect estimate of the average, because the adjustments only partially account for changes in equity during the year — is the denominator of the ratio. This denominator differs from the basic concept previously used in two important respects.[4] The compiled figure is *not* here adjusted to the estimated "amount owned outside the corporate system," because, with the size-class and other groupings examined in the present analysis, no satisfactory allowance — even by estimate — for corporate holdings in the equity of other corporations appears to be possible. Moreover, the estimated average-for-the-year equity, as here derived from the year-end balance-sheet figures, does *not* make even an estimated allowance for net new issues of equity securities during the year; because, in nearly all of the groups of classified data here studied, fully comparable balance-sheet figures for the be-

[3] Fiscal year returns, however, include balance sheets for dates other than December 31, and these dates may range from the preceding July to the succeeding June. Likewise the income statistics as tabulated, though pertaining predominantly to the calendar year, include figures for each corporation having the major fraction of its fiscal year falling in the stated calendar year. This imperfect time classification of the data is not serious for the present analysis. Both sets of statistics also include part-year returns.

[4] See "Corporate Earnings on Invested Capital," pp. 344, 345, and 347.

ginning and end of a year cannot be secured for any one group of identical corporations. The allowance, however, for the year's changes in equity due to earnings and dividend payments does render the denominator as used preferable to straight year-end figures.

The foregoing comments explain largely why the over-all results of the present study (Chart 1) differ from those of the earlier study.[5] They indicate also important limitations on the present results, as precise measures of the rate of return on equity. But these qualifications do not appear to damage seriously the comparisons among groups or size-classes of corporations, which constitute the main object of the present analysis. A further qualification — pertaining to differences among corporations, or from time to time, in the valuation of assets and in particular different practices respecting revaluation of assets — should be noted as impairing somewhat the comparisons made below among groups of corporations in any year or among different years. No adequate basis exists for appraising the degree of this impairment. Comments on this limitation on the data, and certain other limitations, appear in Chapter XXVIII.

RATE OF EARNINGS, SPECIFIC SIZE CLASSES

The data as tabulated in *Statistics of Income* are given separately for groups of corporations classified according to their size and on various other bases of classification. The criterion of size is total assets, as reported on the balance sheets accompanying the corporation tax returns.[6] Although certain ob-

[5] *Ibid.*, p. 346, Exhibit V, Column 5.

[6] Not all corporations filing tax returns submit balance sheets; but the great majority do so, and those which do not are mainly corporations having small net incomes or deficits. See "Corporate Earnings on Invested Capital," p. 340, footnote 10, and p. 347. The present analysis is necessarily confined to corporations filing balance sheets.

jections can be raised to a size classification based on this criterion, total assets can be accepted as a tolerably close measure of what is ordinarily implied by the size of an enterprise. The nine specific classes are of unequal width: under 50, 50–100, 100–250, 250–500, 500–1,000, 1,000–5,000, 5,000–10,000, 10,000–50,000, and 50,000 and over (by exception, in 1936, 50,000–100,000, and a tenth class, 100,000 and over), in thousands of dollars. We will hereafter generally refer to each class, except the lowest and highest, by its lower limit. In plotting Chart 1, points pertaining to each size class were located midway between the limits of that class; but for the top class, which has no stated upper limit, points were located at the approximate average total assets per corporation for the corporations in that class in each particular year.[7]

A striking feature of the chart is that the six curves run nearly parallel through most of their course. This implies that the progressive relationship — by which the rate of return on equity rises as size increases — is not peculiar to any one year or stage of the business cycle. The chart includes years of substantial business recovery as well as deep depression, although it shows no year of high prosperity. For the six years shown, the progression of earning power with size is unmistakable. Notable also is the systematic record of losses for the smallest size class, and a slightly less systematic adverse record for the next three classes in the scale of size. For none of the six years did the corporations with total assets below $50,000 show a net profit on equity in their class aggregates, but we must not forget that many particular corporations within this class earned profits (see below, Chapter XXV). Other striking

[7] The chart is plotted on a logarithmic horizontal scale, which shows the class widths not greatly differing from each other (on a percentage or ratio basis), whereas they are widely different on an actual dollar basis. Moreover, such a scale results in plotting the "mid-point" — for example, 75,000 for the 50,000–100,000 class — somewhat nearer the right than the left boundary of the class.

features of the curves include the very small advance in rate of return from the 10-million-dollar class to the top class for 1934 and 1935, whereas the former class shows a fairly sharp advance above the next lower class; and the very slow advance in rate for 1936 above $250,000, with an actual decline in the top class. These observations must not be supposed to imply, however, that mere possession of assets somewhat below the top size offers a special opportunity for corporate success; the observed tendencies presumably reflect partly differences between size classes as to their dominant lines of industry, upon which more will be said in following chapters.

The differences in level of the six curves, together with their approximate parallelism, indicate that cyclical changes in business affect corporations of various sizes about equally. The cyclical decline from 1931, already depressed, to 1932 left its stamp on the earnings rate for every size class; and the successive cyclical advances in 1933, 1934, 1935, and 1936 benefited all size classes. The close approach to parallelism, moreover, implies that these changes were approximately uniform in amount for most classes: a given cyclical change in business contributed an approximately uniform percentage of their total equity to the earnings rates of the various size classes.

Exceptions to parallelism can indeed be found; for example, the curves diverge at the left end, and thus indicate that the earnings experience is somewhat more variable for the smallest corporations than for others. Only once in the chart do the curves cross: the 1933 rate is below the 1931 rate for the two largest size classes, but the reverse holds for all smaller classes. Thus 1933 had brought revival to a level above 1931 for all classes except the two largest; for the two largest size classes 1933 remained less favorable than 1931, though better than 1932. This peculiarity also can probably be traced to those types of industry which predominate in the largest size classes; for those types of industry — chiefly railroads, banks, oil companies, and certain manufacturers of heavy durable goods — the benefits of the cyclical revival were delayed until after 1933.

TIME VARIATIONS

Another view of the time comparisons is presented in Chart II, which shows figures from Chart I (the six-year record of rate of return on equity) for the 50-thousand-dollar class, the 10-million-dollar class, and all nine (ten in 1936) classes combined.[8] The selection of the two size classes is somewhat arbitrary; but is intended, while avoiding the lowest and highest classes, to yield a contrast between very large and very small corporations.

Each curve in Chart II reflects the cyclical changes from 1931 to 1936: a deepening of the depression in 1932, successive recoveries in 1933, 1934, 1935, and 1936. Nowhere do the curves cross; the curve for the large size class is in all years above the general curve for all classes combined, and the curve for the small size class is much lower. The 10-million-dollar class curve is in 1931–33 below the zero line, and the 50-thousand-dollar class curve is except in 1936 below the zero line. The giant corporations as a group — the top class, for which no curve is shown — had no net loss, even in the worst year of the depression; and the smallest corporations as a group (under 50 thousand dollars) had no net profit, even in the best year of the six.

A surprising approach to uniformity between the two upper curves, in the annual amount of shift from one year to the next, bears upon a point already noted in connection with the approximate parallelism of the curves of Chart I. The cyclical decline into still deeper depression from 1931 to 1932 brought

[8] To have shown all size-class curves on the chart would have confused the comparisons, without adding significant information.

a reduction of about two points (2 per cent of their respective equity) for the two curves. For these same curves, the 1932–33 advance yielded a gain of about 1.5 points, the 1934–35 ad-

CHART II

TIME VARIATIONS IN RATE OF RETURN, FOR ALL CORPORATE INDUSTRY AND SELECTED SIZE CLASSES *

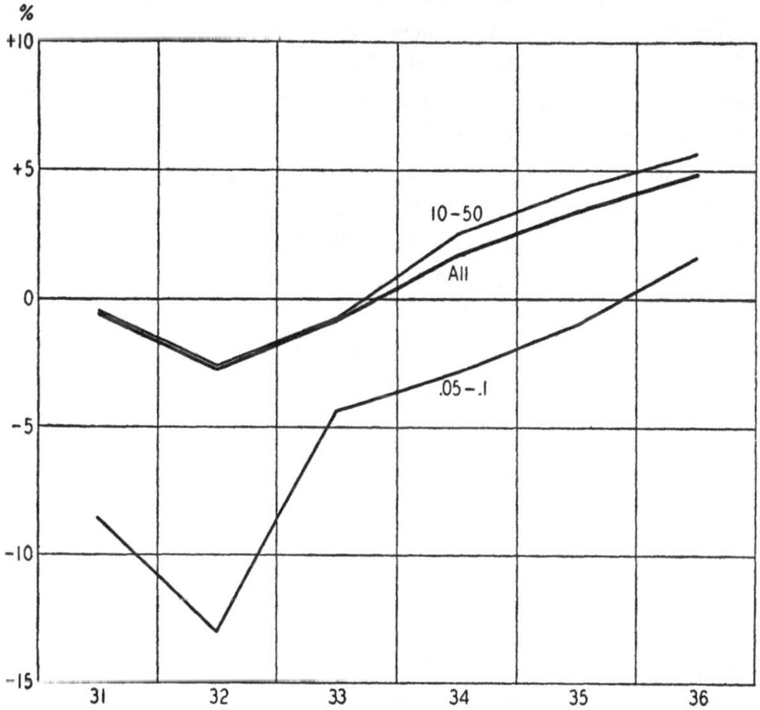

* Data in Table II. See footnote to Chart I.

vance yielded a somewhat larger gain, and the 1935–36 advance likewise yielded a gain, of nearly the same magnitude. In all but one of these annual movements the bottom curve showed wider shifts; and, in the 1933–34 movement, diversity rather than uniformity appears among the three curves. These observations concerning approach to uniformity among the classes in their response to cyclical change are supported by the near parallelism in Chart I; but they should not be emphasized unduly. They do strongly suggest, however, that cyclical fluctuations in business have about equal impact upon corporations of all sizes except the smallest.

In studying the record of time changes in Chart II and the shifts over time — differences in level — of the curves of Chart I, we must note that the figures for successive years are not exactly comparable; hence the year-to-year changes in the computed rate are not precise measures of the actual changes which would be reflected by strictly homogeneous data. In ordinary cases of the change from one year to another, this lack of comparability flows from the fact that the corporations in any one size class do not remain identical from year to year. Changes in the total assets of a particular corporation — through the earning of a surplus or deficit (after dividends and all charges) in the second year, issuance of new securities or any increase in debt, revaluation of assets or merger, or any other operation affecting total assets — may shift it from one size class to another. In ordinary years, such shifts are perhaps fairly numerous, but probably do not seriously impair the percentage figures.

The case is much more serious for 1934 and, to a less extent, for 1935. The Revenue Act of 1934 denied the privilege of filing consolidated tax returns for all corporations except railroads.[9] On this account, most of the corporations which had filed consolidated returns for 1933 were obliged to file a separate return for each subsidiary in 1934. The number of consolidated returns in 1933 and previous years had not been

[9] The effect of this change in the law was reflected mainly in the data of 1934; but, as the change did not apply until their 1935 returns for certain fiscal-year corporations, some effect was reflected also in 1935. See below, Chapter XXVII.

large; but, as the consolidated corporations were mainly huge companies, the amount of assets involved in the 1934 change was very great. Under the former law, the single return of a consolidated corporation would fall in a single size class, presumably large; under the new law, the separate returns of its subsidiaries would fall in various size classes according to the respective amounts of their total assets. Moreover, the aggregate total assets of the subsidiaries as separately tabulated would be likely to exceed the total assets on a consolidated basis (see below, page 360). As a result, large changes from 1933 to 1934, and to a less extent from 1934 to 1935, occurred in the make-up of the several size classes. As this set of changes was marked by shifts in the industrial make-up of the various size classes, the impairment of the percentages and other computed results — for comparisons of 1934 and later years with 1933 and earlier years, and for certain other comparisons — may be rather serious.[10]

PROFITABLE AND UNPROFITABLE CORPORATIONS

The broad facts disclosed by Charts I and II can not be accepted as conclusive, but must be criticized by examination of further classifications of the data. Two such classifications yield helpful information: that according to type of industry (discussed in detail in later chapters), and that according to whether a taxable net income was or was not realized. The latter classification, which appears as a sub-classification in most of the Treasury data as classified on other bases (for example, with respect to size), divides corporations into two groups which we shall call *income* corporations and *deficit* corporations.[11] Large shifts between these two categories can and do occur from year to year.

[10] See "Corporate Earnings on Invested Capital," p. 338, footnote 5.

[11] The criterion of classification here is the statutory net income — the figure on which the corporation's normal tax was reckoned before the Act

The rates of return on equity for income corporations, as shown in Chart III for each size class in the several years, present a strikingly different picture from that shown graphically

CHART III

RATE OF RETURN COMPARED WITH SIZE, FOR INCOME CATEGORY OF ALL CORPORATE INDUSTRY *

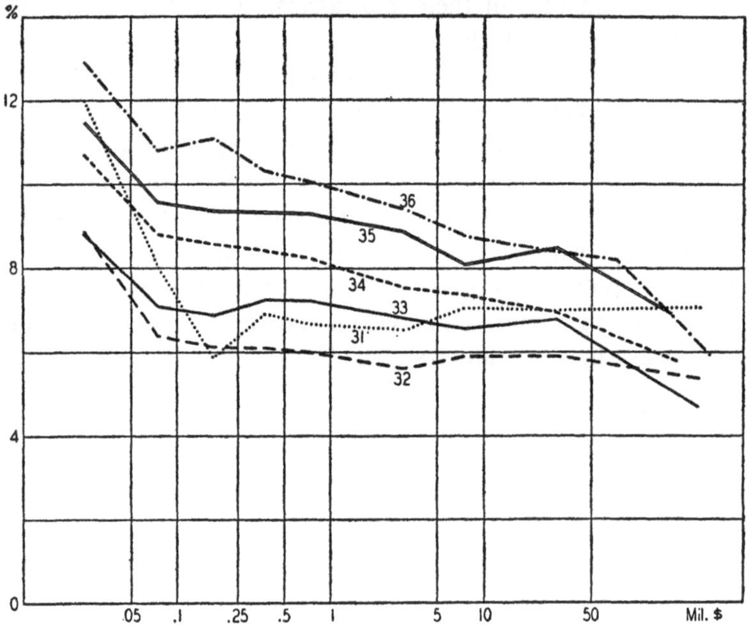

* Horizontal scale logarithmic. Data in Table II.

in Chart I for income and deficit corporations combined. The systematic upward course of the curves there, as size increases, is replaced here by a much less regular *downward* tendency. For the income corporations, the rate of return tends to de-

---

of 1936 — and, as this differs somewhat from our definition of net profits as used in the numerator of the ratio of profits to equity, some deficit corporations may have had net profits in our sense, and some income corporations may have had negative profits. These disparities are, however, unimportant in the present analysis. Note, however, that the "deficit"

crease — though somewhat irregularly — as size increases. In all years the maximum rate for income corporations appears in the smallest size class; and in all years but 1931 the minimum rate appears for the largest size class. No such range of variation between maximum and minimum, however, appears in these positive ratios for the income corporations as for the general ratios of Chart I. (The scale of this chart exaggerates the variations, for income corporations.) We are forced to conclude that the systematic upward course of the curves of Chart I is due entirely to the experience of the deficit corporations.

This aspect of the situation is brought out in Chart IV, which presents rates of return obtained by taking simple averages of the six annual rates, for each size class (the top two classes for 1936 being combined).[12] The upward course of the general curve, covering all corporations (income and deficit) combined, is fully accounted for, and more, by the striking and persistent advance in rate of return (reduction in *negative* rate of return) for the deficit corporations as we pass up the scale of size. This figure advances from below −39 per cent for the smallest size class to about −1.5 per cent for the largest; whereas the corresponding figure for the *income* corporations *declines* from nearly 11 per cent to nearly 6 per cent.[13]

---

corporations actually had a positive rate of return, in the top size class in 1934 and 1935 (Table II).

[12] The use of simple averages of the annual rates implies that the list of corporations actually falling in any size class in any one year — and this is true separately for the income category and the deficit category, as well as for both combined — is an acceptable sample for appraising the earning power in that class in that year. Shifts of specific corporations from size class to size class, and from (to) the income category to (from) the deficit category, from year to year result in shifts in the make-up of the sample. See below, p. 389, for discussion of this point, and for reasons why weighting was not used.

[13] A somewhat similar comparison, based upon a considerably different definition of rate of return, appears in *The Effect of Size on Corporate Earnings and Condition*, Harvard Business School, Business Research Studies, 8, 1934, pp. 14–17.

The full set of ratios, for all size classes separately, is not here presented graphically for the deficit corporations in specific years; but Table II, giving the full set of rates, yields comparisons similar to that of Chart IV for each of the six years.

CHART IV

SIX-YEAR AVERAGE OF RATES OF RETURN COMPARED WITH SIZE, FOR ALL CORPORATE INDUSTRY AND INCOME AND DEFICIT CATEGORIES *

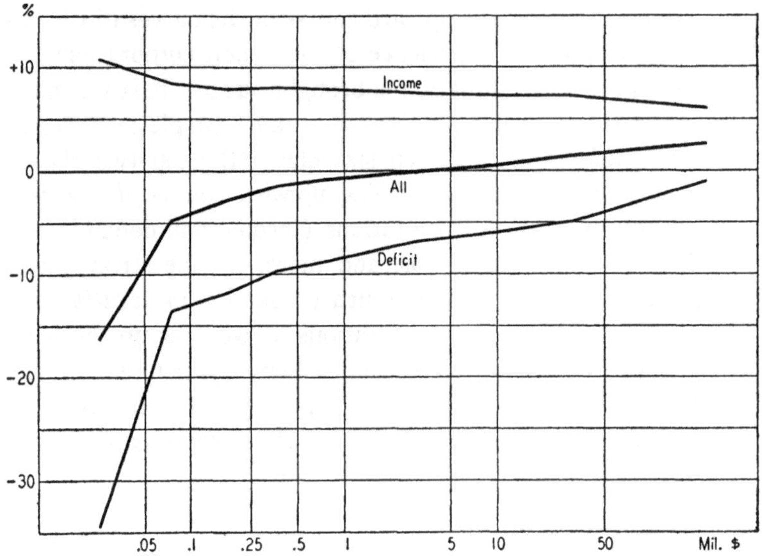

* Horizontal scale logarithmic. Data in Table B. See footnote to Chart I.

Despite irregularities, the same broad indication appears: the upward course of the curves of Chart I results from a systematic tendency for the losses of deficit corporations to be far more severe — in terms of equity — for the small than for the large size classes. The joint effect of the tendencies observed in Chart III for the income corporations, and in Chart IV and Table II for the income and deficit corporations, is a very wide spread between the rates of return of income and of deficit

TABLE II

Rates of Return for all Corporate Industry *

Class †	1931	1932	1933	1934	1935 ‡	1936
0	**−19.31**	**−28.09**	**−18.94**	**−14.04**	**−10.77**	**−6.89**
	11.98	8.88	8.81	10.69	11.48	12.90
	−40.96	*−37.53*	*−31.58*	*−33.26*	*−29.98*	*−33.78*
50	**−8.58**	**−12.97**	**−4.37**	**−2.83**	**−1.24**	**1.62**
	8.04	6.37	7.10	8.80	9.58	10.81
	−20.59	*−18.73*	*−8.86*	*−12.75*	*−11.77*	*−12.86*
100	**−5.74**	**−9.36**	**−4.25**	**−1.22**	**.70**	**3.79**
	5.85	6.12	6.89	8.57	9.36	11.11
	−15.77	*−14.31*	*−10.96*	*−10.03*	*−9.50*	*−10.17*
250	**−4.48**	**−7.03**	**−2.99**	**−.22**	**1.81**	**4.52**
	6.91	6.10	7.27	8.41	9.32	10.32
	−12.33	*−11.69*	*−9.39*	*−8.37*	*−7.49*	*−8.49*
500	**−3.74**	**−6.08**	**−2.07**	**.24**	**2.07**	**4.76**
	6.64	5.99	7.23	8.23	9.29	10.05
	−10.29	*−10.49*	*−8.13*	*−7.53*	*−6.99*	*−8.76*
1,000	**−2.91**	**−4.59**	**−1.86**	**.97**	**2.87**	**5.24**
	6.52	5.60	6.82	7.54	8.88	9.43
	−8.39	*−8.24*	*−7.22*	*−5.36*	*−4.65*	*−7.02*
5,000	**−1.74**	**−3.88**	**−1.66**	**1.21**	**2.90**	**5.48**
	7.07	5.91	6.56	7.38	8.11	8.78
	−7.24	*−8.25*	*−7.39*	*−5.00*	*−3.47*	*−5.86*
10,000	**−.46**	**−2.59**	**−.73**	**2.50**	**4.29**	**5.66**
	6.98	5.91	6.77	6.95	8.50	8.40
	−6.02	*−6.54*	*−6.61*	*−2.46*	*−1.59*	*−6.32*
50,000	**2.13**	**.30**	**.88**	**3.03**	**4.33**	**5.99**
	7.03	5.34	4.65	5.76	6.91	8.18
	−1.50	*−2.37*	*−1.95*	*.08*	*1.54*	*−4.55*
100,000	. . .	. . .	. . .	. . .	. . .	**4.62**
	. . .	. . .	. . .	. . .	. . .	5.96
	. . .	. . .	. . .	. . .	. . .	*−1.34*
Entire range of size	**−.60**	**−2.76**	**−.81**	**1.72**	**3.42**	**4.83**
	7.03	5.56	5.77	6.75	7.94	7.81
	−5.94	*−6.57*	*−5.48*	*−3.13*	*−1.90*	*−5.99*

* Expressed in per cent; ratio of profit (or loss) after taxes to estimated average equity, as explained in text, p. 18. Figures in boldface type are for income and deficit categories of corporations combined, in ordinary type for the income category, in italics for the deficit category.

† Lower limit of class interval, in thousands of dollars of total assets. The 50,000-thousand-dollar class has no stated upper limit, 1931–35; the 100,000-thousand-dollar class has no stated upper limit, 1936.

‡ See footnote to Chart 1.

corporations for the smallest size class, and a progressive narrowing of this spread with increasing size of assets until the spread is very small for the top class. Suggested explanations of this narrowing spread have been given elsewhere,[14] but a full understanding of the situation is by no means readily available. A highly important implication, however, may be mentioned now and will be treated in some detail below (Chapter XXV): the wide spread between the income and deficit curves for the lowest size class reflects a much greater dispersion in earning power — range from very large rates of loss to very large rates of gain — among the corporations within that class than in the larger size classes.

SUMMARY

The foregoing analysis has brought out a remarkable apparent correlation between rate of return on equity and the size of corporations, as reflected by total assets. The larger the corporation the higher is the rate of return, on the average; and this relation holds, with surprising constancy, in each of the six years 1931–1936. The extreme variability in rate of return from the smallest size class to the largest is, however, approximately accounted for by the deficit corporations. These corporations by themselves show an even wider range in the rates of return (negative) from the smallest size class to the largest; whereas the income corporations have a remarkably steady rate of return (positive) from size class to size class, with some indication that the rate for income corporations is ordinarily higher for the small size classes than for the large.

A considerable, but unknown, part of the variation in rate of return from size class to size class is almost surely accounted for by the fact that particular size classes are dominated by particular types of industry. The diversity in average rate of return among industries is strikingly wide, as we shall see,

[14] *The Effect of Size on Corporate Earnings and Condition*, p. 15.

though these comparisons are somewhat impaired by the imperfect industrial classification of corporations. These wide differences among industries, coupled with the considerable concentration of certain industries in particular size classes, perhaps explain an important fraction of the variation in rate among the size classes as disclosed by the record for the entire corporate system as presented in this chapter. Whether, for a given industry, variation in size is also accompanied by variation in rate of return is the central topic of Chapters IV–XVIII.

III

LINES OF INDUSTRY

The corporation statistics tabulated and published by the Treasury in *Statistics of Income* are, with few exceptions, classified according to the major income-producing activity of each reporting corporation. The classification distinguishes — within the comprehensive total which covers all corporations without regard to type of industry — nine broad industrial divisions; and all but one of these are listed in the stubs of Table III, which shows the comparative importance of the divisions. A further breakdown separates the corporations of the manufacturing division into groups — twelve in 1931–32, thirteen in 1933–35, and sixteen in 1936 — and these are listed in the stubs of the similar Table IV. The availability of these separate data for the industrial divisions and manufacturing groups renders possible a more detailed study than that of Chapter II, with a view to ascertaining whether the relations between size and earning power there found are characteristic of various types of industry.

NATURE OF THE CLASSIFICATION

The present and succeeding chapters apply, in fact, the methods of Chapter II to the analysis for each industrial division and manufacturing group. Before proceeding with this specific analysis of various lines of industry, however, we may well pause to inquire concerning the precision and validity of the industrial classification of Treasury data on corporations. The main question at issue is whether the tabulated data for some industrial class — for example, textile manufacturing — truly represent the nation's corporate business of that category. Do the published data cover all corporate business of that type and no corporate business of any other type?[1] The actual assignment of a particular corporation to a specific

TABLE III

IMPORTANCE OF EACH INDUSTRIAL DIVISION, EXPRESSED AS PERCENTAGE OF TOTAL FOR ALL NINE DIVISIONS COMBINED, IN TERMS OF (A) TOTAL ASSETS AND (R) TOTAL COMPILED RECEIPTS *

		1931	1932	1933	1934	1935	1936
Agriculture	A	.7	.8	.7	.8	.7	.6
	R	.4	.4	.5	.5	.5	.6
Mining	A	3.4	3.4	3.4	3.4	3.1	3.0
	R	2.1	2.1	2.4	2.4	2.2	2.2
Manufacturing	A	21.5	21.1	21.5	17.4	17.4	17.9
	R	41.4	40.0	42.5	41.0	42.4	43.9
Construction	A	.8	.8	.7	.6	.5	.6
	R	2.0	1.7	1.3	1.2	1.3	1.5
Public utilities † ..	A	24.4	25.8	25.7	22.7	21.9	20.7
	R	12.6	13.5	12.3	11.1	10.1	9.4
Trade	A	6.0	5.6	5.8	5.8	5.8	6.0
	R	28.1	28.4	28.8	32.5	32.7	32.1
Service	A	2.2	3.0	2.8	2.6	2.8	3.6
	R	3.3	3.7	3.2	3.3	3.2	3.4
Finance	A	40.8	39.5	39.3	46.7	47.8	47.5
	R	10.0	10.2	9.0	8.1	7.7	6.9

* A small nondescript "division" called "nature not given" is not shown in the table.

The percentages are calculated from data in *Statistics of Income*, for corporations filing balance sheets.

† Includes transportation.

industrial class is determined by the "main income-producing business" of that corporation. The reporting corporation classifies itself, in response to a query in the form on which its tax

[1] We say "corporate business" because these statistics pertain only to corporations and obviously do not yield trustworthy indications for business done by partnerships or individual proprietorships. A separate ex-

return is filed. The main query of this sort on the form consists (except in 1931, when an equivalent type of query was used) of a schedule including the names of various lines of business activity, and requests the reporting corporation to check the name of that line in which its main income-producing business falls. A second query, on the face of the tax-return form, calls for the "kind of business"; and the response here is sometimes a supplementary guide to the Treasury in classifying the corporation according to industrial type. In general, however, we may say with accuracy that each corporation classifies itself.

We shall assume what is broadly true, that this reporting of classification is correct. But the issue, for analytical purposes, is not concerned with the question of accuracy of a statement of fact. It is concerned rather with the implication of the fact as stated. If each corporation in the entire corporate system were in truth engaged in only one line of business, there would be no issue — our tabulated data would then yield a tolerably accurate picture of corporate affairs in each separate line of business. The truth is, however, that many corporations are engaged in several lines of business and some corporations are engaged in many lines of business. And yet, if a corporation is engaged in more than one line of business, *all* of its accounting data reported on its tax return — both income account and balance sheet — are assigned to the *single* line of business reported as its main income-producing activity.

Thus, even a small incorporated enterprise may be operating a filling station, a storage garage, an automobile repair shop, a taxi service, and an automobile sales agency. These activities, although somewhat related, obviously do not fall in one industrial class; and yet the tax return of that corporation would be assigned entirely to *one* class — the class in which the principal line falls. Or, consider a great corporation manufacturing

amination of records for such businesses would be needed to show whether the findings here reported apply also outside the corporate area.

the industrial classification of corporate industry with which we are here concerned.

The former great importance of the consolidated returns in the entire structure of corporations is brought out in Tables v and vi. Despite the small number of these returns — less than

TABLE V

Percentage Relation of Consolidated Corporations to all Corporations, for Each Division *

	In terms of gross income			In terms of total assets
	1931	1932	1933	1933
Agriculture	33.0	31.1	32.0	24.6
Mining	60.8	56.1	59.3	54.1
Manufacturing	56.7	49.2	46.3	56.0
Construction	15.5	15.6	13.7	27.4
Public utilities	84.9	68.9	69.0	72.8
Trade	27.6	21.5	19.1	24.9
Service	34.3	27.9	26.7	28.0
Finance	21.7	19.0	17.2	21.3
All combined †	46.7	39.6	37.9	43.6

* Calculated from data in *Statistics of Income* for 1931–33, for columns 1–3; same, issues for 1933–34, for column 4. Gross income is for all income tax returns, total assets for those with balance sheets.

† Includes "nature not given," which is not shown here separately.

10,000 out of a total of nearly a half million for the entire corporate structure — their share of corporate gross business, as roughly measured by gross income 1931–33, and of total assets in 1933 was strikingly large. For all lines of industry combined this share ran above one third in each year shown, and the share was much higher for some divisions and manufacturing groups.[6] When we bear in mind that *all* the business of the

[6] I have discussed the importance of the consolidated returns for earlier years elsewhere, from a somewhat different point of view. See *Quarterly Journal of Economics*, May, 1933, pp. 414–448.

Gross income differs somewhat from total compiled receipts, used as a criterion in Tables iii and iv. See below, p. 67, footnote 2.

various subsidiaries of a particular consolidated return had to be classified in a single industrial category, determined by the principal line of business of the complete system, we see that the privilege of filing consolidated returns resulted in an industrial classification of corporate statistical data which was un-

TABLE VI

PERCENTAGE RELATION OF CONSOLIDATED CORPORATIONS TO ALL CORPORATIONS, FOR EACH MANUFACTURING GROUP *

	In terms of gross income			In terms of total assets
	1931	1932	1933	1933
Foods	65.1	53.7	52.1	46.1
Liquors †	...	...	22.1	28.8
Tobacco	35.0	9.5	9.1	9.5
Textiles	23.4	16.0	15.6	21.0
Leather	44.1	24.0	21.0	27.5
Rubber	82.6	82.8	77.6	83.7
Forest products	29.8	26.2	27.4	39.6
Paper	36.0	33.9	31.8	53.3
Printing	34.6	28.3	28.1	46.8
Chemicals	79.2	76.6	70.6	78.8
Stone	45.5	31.8	31.1	32.0
Metals	65.7	57.9	57.4	62.6
Miscellaneous	38.2	36.7	33.0	44.2

* Calculated from data in *Statistics of Income* for 1931–33, for columns 1–3; same, issues for 1933–34, for column 4. Gross income is for all income tax returns, total assets for those with balance sheets.

† Included in foods, 1931–32.

avoidably imperfect. The data of a particular industrial class were augmented by the inclusion in that class of subsidiaries whose business properly belonged in other classes, and data for those other classes were correspondingly deficient.

We see further that the abandonment of the privilege in 1934 must have tended to purify the industrial classification, by bringing about the assignment of these subsidiaries to industrial classes in which they more properly belonged. Such a purification was by no means complete; for, as indicated above, if a subsidiary itself — though a single corporate legal entity — were engaged in several lines of business, all of its data must nevertheless be assigned to the single class reflecting its principal line of business. The purification was, however, undoubtedly substantial; and industrial-class data for 1934 and later years are probably more dependable than those of earlier years.[7] Moreover, the statistical data for a particular industrial class are not truly homogeneous over the 1931–36 period — the make-up of the class may have been extensively changed in 1934. (On this and related points, further comments are made below, Chapter XXVII.)

The foregoing points would be of slight significance if the consolidated returns had pertained to corporations of small or average size. But Tables v and vi emphatically show that the consolidated returns, since their number was very small, represented in the main very large enterprises. Hence, any reassignment of their subsidiaries among industrial classes could not fail to work very large changes in the industrial classification of the entire corporate system. Because the consolidated returns had been particularly numerous or important in certain lines of industry, these changes were especially significant in those lines (see below, page 374).

INDUSTRIAL DIFFERENCES IN RATE OF RETURN

The rate of return on equity, calculated by the method defined in Chapter II and illustrated in Table I, varies from industry to industry. Average rates of return for all corporations — without regard to size — are shown for each industrial divi-

[7] We may assume, however, that the abandonment of the consolidated-return privilege furnished an incentive toward actual merger into a single corporate entity of a group of subsidiaries formerly covered by a consolidated return. By such an operation, the tax advantage of offsetting losses against gains might still be enjoyed. To the extent that this operation has been used since 1934, the purification is nullified.

sion and manufacturing group in Table VII. In each year notable differences appear among the several divisions, and among the several manufacturing groups; and the course of variation from year to year differs among the divisions and groups. In 1932, the bottom year of the depression, the rate for public utilities was actually positive, while those for all the other divisions were negative and ranged to below −9 per cent (for service). In 1936, the most favorable year shown, the rate for service remained negative; but rates were positive for all other divisions, and ranged to nearly 8 per cent (for manufacturing). Rates for agriculture, construction, trade, and service dropped very low in the depression; but the timing of movement in depression and recovery differed greatly among these divisions. The 1932 drop was particularly severe for construction and service, whereas the agriculture and trade ratios had more nearly reached bottom in 1931. Recovery following 1932 was fairly prompt for trade, but was delayed for the other three divisions now under notice, and even 1936 did not restore a positive rate for service. Among the other divisions, manufacturing followed a course largely parallel to the aggregate, though one marked by more intense fluctuation; finance did not reach its low point until 1933, but thereafter followed the general pattern of recovery; mining showed a nearly steady rate 1931–33 and, after a sharp advance in 1934, a nearly steady rate also for 1934–35; and the rate for public utilities, after reaching its low point — which was still positive — in 1933, advanced slowly and was in 1936 only slightly higher than in 1931.

Diversity likewise appears among the group rates, shown in the lower section of the table. Even at the worst of the depression, rates remained positive for foods, chemicals, and tobacco; and for tobacco a remarkably sustained high rate, except for a sharp dip in 1933, appears throughout. Metals showed an exceptionally violent fluctuation, but its course was largely

TABLE VII

RATES OF RETURN FOR ALL CORPORATIONS,* EACH DIVISION, AND EACH MANUFACTURING GROUP

	1931	1932	1933	1934 **	1935	1936
Aggregate	−.60	−2.76	−.81	1.72	3.42	4.83
Divisions:						
Agriculture	−5.12	−5.61	−2.91	−3.21	.91	2.14
Mining	−2.78	−2.71	−2.39	.63	.73	2.03
Manufacturing .	−.96	−3.45	.68	3.01	5.68	7.94
Construction ...	−.86	−7.34	−5.18	−2.95	−.22	3.30
Public utilities ..	2.29	.67	.45	1.47	1.57	2.69
Trade	−4.19	−6.90	−.25	3.05	4.37	7.16
Service	−2.18	−9.44	−8.52	−5.52	−4.07	−.54
Finance	−1.10	−3.18	−3.32	1.41	3.68	3.98
Groups:						
Foods †	2.42	.26	3.84	6.13	7.35	7.52
Liquors †	...	...	9.35	11.46	12.26	16.57
Tobacco	13.65	13.29	5.87	10.50	12.15	12.83
Textiles ‡	−6.10	−7.64	2.80	.38	1.95	5.36
Leather	−3.32	−6.26	3.69	2.82	6.14	5.20
Rubber	−2.39	−4.08	.59	2.75	3.75	6.69
Forest products .	−7.94	−9.70	−3.77	−2.92	−.74	2.74
Paper	−.49	−3.32	.83	3.06	3.98	5.38
Printing	2.41	−.83	1.09	3.68	6.46	7.98
Chemicals §	1.08	.38	1.28	3.73	5.88	6.93
Stone	−1.92	−5.82	−1.40	1.64	4.01	7.62
Metals ¶	−1.97	−6.10	−.95	2.27	6.34	9.48
Miscellaneous manufacturing	−4.13	−7.85	−2.58	2.71	6.77	9.10

* The aggregate includes "nature not given," not shown separately here.
† Beverages included in foods in 1931–32, in liquors 1933–36.
‡ Includes clothing, which was separated in 1936.
§ Includes petroleum refining, which was separated in 1936.
¶ Includes motor vehicles, which was separated in 1936.
** See third footnote to Table IX.

parallel to that of the aggregate. Negative rates persisted for forest products until 1935, and even 1936 brought only a moderate positive figure for this group.

Other interesting diversities among the groups and divisions can be discovered in the table. Enough has been said to emphasize the differences in average rate among lines of industry, and therefore to suggest that the observed differences in rate among size classes, noted in Chapter II, may arise in part at least from partial concentration of particular industries in par-

CHART V

SIX-YEAR AVERAGES OF RATES OF RETURN, FOR ALL CORPORATE INDUSTRY AND SELECTED INDUSTRIAL DIVISIONS *

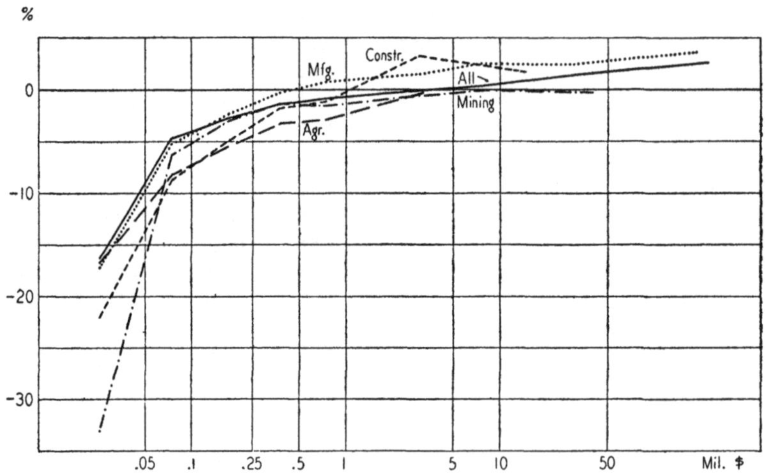

* Horizontal scale logarithmic. Data in Table B. See footnote to Chart I and third footnote to Table IX.

ticular size classes. Later chapters will give further attention to this point; but for the moment diverse levels of rate and diverse fluctuations in rate, as among lines of industry, can be accepted as established.[8]

Turning now to the record which makes distinctions accord-

[8] For further discussion of this diversity, with attention to a somewhat longer period of time and suggestion of a specialized measurement of the profit on capital actually devoted to selected lines of industry, see "Cyclical Changes in Corporate Profits," *Review of Economic Statistics*, May, 1939, pp. 49–61.

ing to size, we introduce first a six-year summary figure showing the rate of return on equity for each size class. This merely consists in averaging the six rates of return for 1931–36, for any particular size class (see above, page 29). Carrying this out for the aggregate of all corporations without regard to in-

CHART VI

SIX-YEAR AVERAGES OF RATES OF RETURN, FOR ALL CORPORATE INDUSTRY AND SELECTED INDUSTRIAL DIVISIONS *

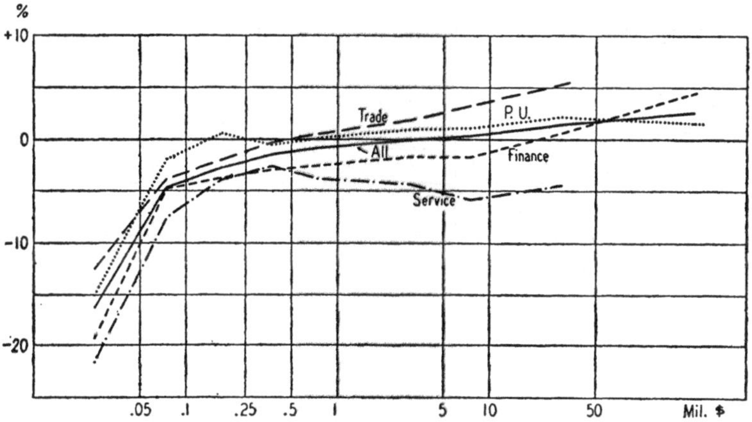

* Horizontal scale logarithmic. Data in Table B. See footnote to Chart I.

dustrial class, yields a kind of average of the six curves of Chart I, and the result is shown in the heavy curve of Chart V. This curve shows the average relation between size of enterprise and rate of return over the six-year period. (To some extent, the cyclical and other short-time variations have been averaged out.) Certain technical and theoretical limitations upon this summarization are discussed in some detail below (Chapter XXVIII), and are mentioned here merely by remarking that they probably do not seriously damage the significance of the resulting curve.

The other curves of Chart V were similarly obtained for the four divisions of industry engaged mainly in producing physical commodities. Chart VI makes similar comparisons for four divisions representing mainly the provision of services; Charts VII and VIII compare curves for selected manufacturing groups. Although following chapters will examine in detail the size-variation in rate of return for each year separately for the

CHART VII

SIX-YEAR AVERAGES OF RATES OF RETURN, FOR SELECTED MANUFACTURING GROUPS *

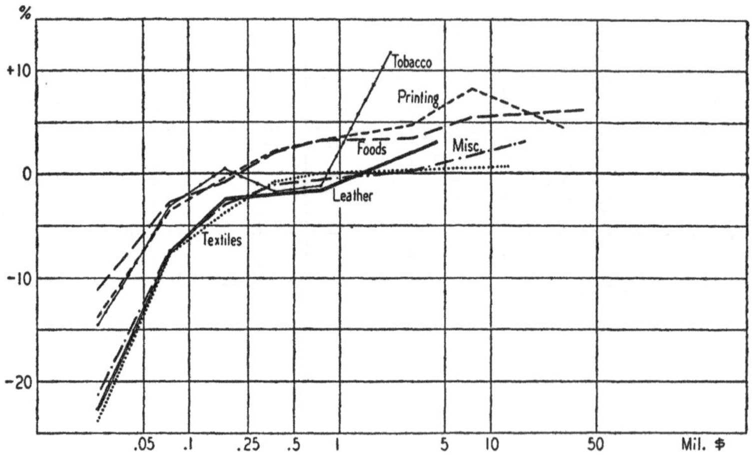

* Horizontal scale logarithmic. Data in Table B. See third footnote to Table IX.

various divisions and groups, these six-year summaries recorded in the four charts yield highly suggestive indications of the diversity among lines of industry as to the way in which rate of return varies with size of corporation. Although notable similarities exist among the curves, the diversities are sufficiently striking to leave no doubt that the change of earning power with size is non-uniform among industries.

The heavy curve of Chart V, which reproduces the "All" curve of Chart IV, shows the general relation between rate of return and size for all corporations without regard to line of industry. The main features have already been noted in the preceding chapter: a negative and very low rate for the smallest size class, a sharp advance in rate in the next higher classes, the appearance of positive rates in the middle of the size scale accompanied by a slackening in the rate of advance with in-

CHART VIII

SIX-YEAR AVERAGES OF RATES OF RETURN, FOR SELECTED MANUFACTURING GROUPS *

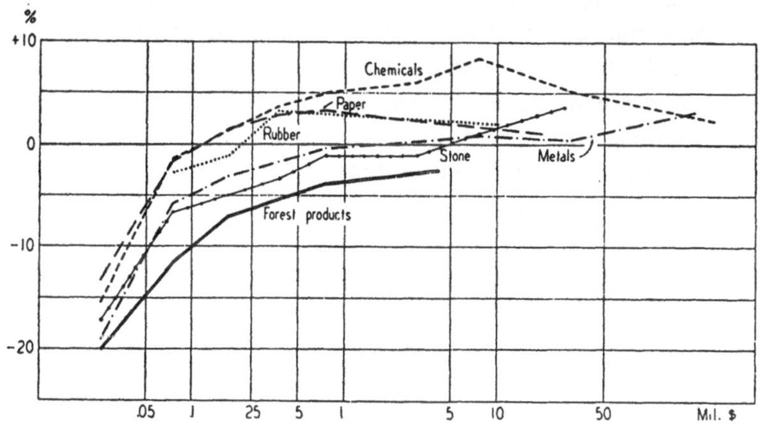

* Horizontal scale logarithmic. Data in Table B.

creasing size,[9] and a gradual but uninterrupted advance in the right portion of the curve.

Examination of Charts v and vi shows numerous differences among the divisions. A general point of difference between the two charts is that the curves of Chart v diverge at the left,

[9] The slackening in the pace of advance would appear even more prominently if the horizontal scales of the charts were natural, and not logarithmic. On a natural scale, the distance between pairs of plotted points would increase very greatly in passing to the right; and the line segments joining pairs of plotted points would be correspondingly flattened, and increasingly so toward the right end. We may say therefore that the rate of increase in rate of return per $1000 of assets is very slight indeed everywhere to the right of 100 or 250 thousand dollars.

while those of Chart VI diverge at the right. Several instances of downturns at the right appear among the divisions, and the most striking case is that of service.

Examination of Charts VII and VIII likewise reveals numerous differences, some of them striking, among the curves. We do not, however, propose to discuss the peculiarities of the curves of any of these four charts at this point. After the divisions are examined in detail in the following chapters, summary comparisons among the manufacturing groups will appear in Chapter XII, and among the divisions in Chapter XIX. For the present, Charts V–VIII indicate sufficient differences among divisions and among groups to suggest the possibility that differences among size classes, as to the dominant line of industry, may contribute to the relation between rate of return and size observed in Chapter II.

IV

MANUFACTURING DIVISION

AMONG THE NINE BROAD INDUSTRIAL DIVISIONS into which the corporation data of the Treasury are classified, the most important — in terms of a rough measure of gross operations — is manufacturing. Using total compiled receipts as a measure, the manufacturing division's percentage of the total for all corporations ranged between 40.0 and 43.9 in the years 1931–36 (Table III). If total assets were taken as a measure of importance, the public utilities and finance divisions would stand ahead of manufacturing; but as in each of these cases special reasons account for the very high assets figure, the total receipts figure appears to be more satisfactory as a measure of importance. On this basis we may say that manufacturing amounted to about two fifths of the entire corporate system in each recent year.

PRECISION OF CLASSIFICATION

The manufacturing division not only includes a wide range of manufacturing business, as indicated only in broad terms by the titles of its groups (stubs of Table IV). It also, because of integration of a particular manufacturing corporation — reaching backward to its supplies of materials and transportation and like services, or forward to its distribution outlets — and because of the practical limitations upon the classification of corporations by industry (already noted, page 34), affords in some sense a sample of a much broader range of business activities. This aspect of the case is probably much less significant since the abandonment of consolidated returns, but even an unconsolidated return of a single corporate entity *can* cover activities in a wide range of types of business. On the extent of this coverage of non-manufacturing business in the data for the manufacturing division, we have no adequate evidence; but we must bear in mind that the data for the division, though probably highly representative of actual manufacturing conditions, constitute a somewhat confused and imperfect sample.

Even in 1935, when the effects of the consolidated returns may be taken as completely eliminated from the data of all divisions except public utilities (which includes the carriers still permitted to file consolidated returns), the depletion charges for the manufacturing division were 127 million dollars whereas they were only 189 million dollars for the mining division and 6 million dollars for the agriculture division.[1] These results are clear indication that manufacturing corporations carried on well over half as much activity in the extractive industries as did those corporations actually classified in mining and agriculture (which covers also forestry). No similar data enable us to test with the same conclusiveness the coverage of the manufacturing data in other areas — for example, trade, construction, service, or finance.

The confusion due to integration no doubt works in both directions: some manufacturing activities are covered in other divisions and fail to enter into the figures as tabulated for the manufacturing division. We have no clear evidence of the extent of this inverse error, or as to which other divisions specifically cover manufacturing operations in their data. We may not even say with assurance that these inverse errors —coverage of manufacturing activities in other divisions — about offset the direct errors — coverage of other activities in the manufacturing division. That the manufacturing data as they stand

[1] These figures are for returns with balance sheets — pages 52–53 of *Statistics of Income for 1935, Part 2*. For all corporations, including also returns not accompanied by balance sheets, corresponding figures were 128 for manufacturing, 198 for mining and 6 for agriculture — *ibid.*, page 40.

cover the great bulk of manufacturing operations and only a moderate fraction of other activities can, however, be taken for granted. We may perhaps summarize by saying that the manufacturing data reflect jointly a dominant element, representing incomplete but very large coverage of manufacturing activities, and a subordinate element, representing a small and irregular sampling of all other corporate industry.

VARIATION OF RATE WITH SIZE

The calculated rates of return on equity for different size classes among manufacturing corporations are shown, for each of the years 1931–36, in Chart IX (similar in form to Chart I, for all corporations without regard to industrial type).[2] The same general features appear here as were observed in Chart I: the rates for small corporations are in most years very low (large negative numbers); the curves rise generally with increase in size, the rise being sharp for passage from smallest to moderate-sized classes; the six curves run generally parallel to each other; there is no intersection between any pair of curves, although 1931 and 1933 curves practically meet at their right ends. Certain broad differences appear, however: the spread among the curves is greater, particularly at the left, than in Chart I; the parallelism is not so nearly complete as in Chart I, particularly because here the 1933 curve has a longer range which is nearly horizontal; somewhat more numerous and considerable differences in direction among the curves, in their passage from size class to size class, appear here to the right of 500 thousand dollars. But the similarities to Chart I are more striking than the differences; and, although similarity may be partly due to the substantial fraction which manufacturing constitutes of the total, it would easily have been pos-

[2] In calculating the rate of return for this and other divisions, and for groups discussed later, taxes paid by size classes had to be estimated (see below, Chapter XXVI), before following out calculations such as in Table I.

sible for peculiarities in divisions other than manufacturing to render the total curves of Chart I notably different from the manufacturing curves of Chart IX. Pending examination of other divisions to ascertain whether they do in fact exhibit marked peculiarities, we can only regard the similarities as re-

CHART IX

RATE OF RETURN COMPARED WITH SIZE, FOR MANUFACTURING DIVISION *

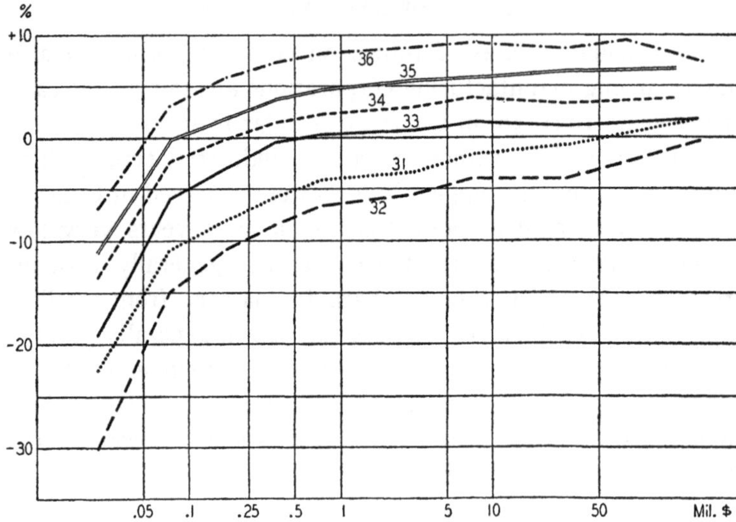

* Horizontal scale logarithmic. Data in Table IX.

markable. Manufacturing corporations have roughly the same relation between rate of return and size as all corporations.

Here again we observe that rates of return for the lowest size class remained negative even in 1936, the most prosperous year shown. But the rate for the highest class, although it remained positive in all other years, did fall below zero for 1932, the year of deepest depression. A striking feature of Chart IX is that only the curves for 1931, 1932, and 1936 show considerable variation to the right of 500 thousand dollars: for

1933–35, variation of rate of return with size is very narrow for all moderate and large size classes. The situation differs for 1931 and 1932: advance of rate continues, though somewhat irregularly, all the way up the size scale; and a particularly sharp advance appears in passing to the highest class. The obvious implication is that the largest manufacturing corporations had an exceptional capacity for resisting the depression's adverse influence on earnings. For 1936, advance in rate continues to the 5-million-dollar class, and a substantial drop occurs in the top class.

Some of these differences in rate, as among size classes, may reflect differing concentration of types of manufacturing in different size classes. Just as we suspected the apparent relation between rate of return and size in Chart I of being susceptible of partial explanation by observing that certain major lines of industry — certain industrial divisions — might make up disproportionate shares of certain size classes, so here we suspect that different kinds of manufacturing — having different typical rates of return — may be concentrated in different size classes. Until we have examined the evidence on specific groups (see specifications in Table IV), in succeeding chapters, this possibility can not be fully discussed. For the present, we merely make a general reservation: the apparent relation between rate of return and size as shown in Chart IX *may* reflect, not the effect of size on earning power, but largely the effect of typical differences in rate among lines of manufacturing activity.

TIME VARIATIONS

In order to bring out more clearly the year-to-year variations in rate of return, Chart X (similar in form to Chart II, for all corporations) shows the annual course of change in rate for all manufacturing corporations, for a small size class — 50–100 thousand dollars — and for a large size class — 10–50 million dollars. In all years except 1935 and 1936 the curve for the small class remained far below zero; even in the best year, 1936, these corporations as a group enjoyed only moderate profits. This does not imply, however, that many small manu-

CHART X

TIME VARIATIONS IN RATE OF RETURN, FOR MANUFACTURING DIVISION AND SELECTED SIZE CLASSES *

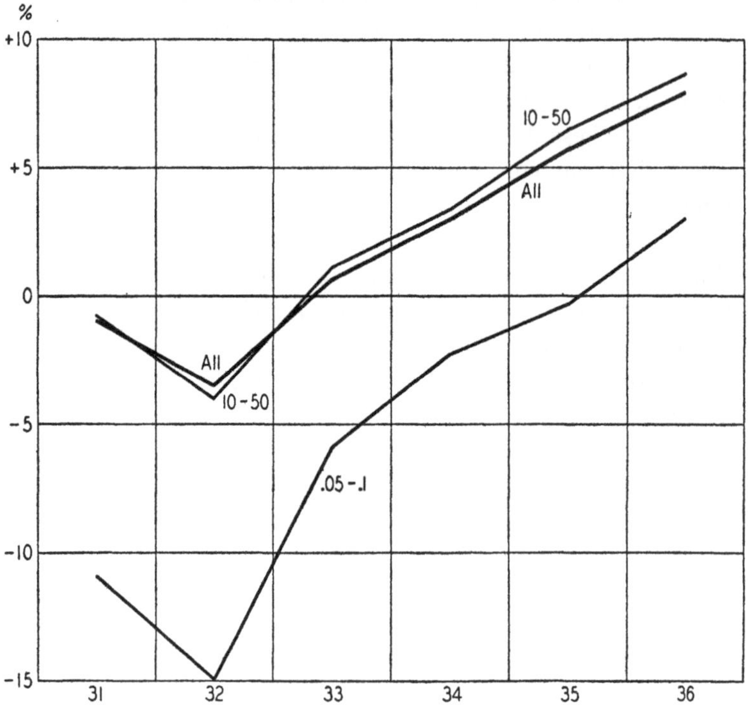

* Data in Table IX.

facturing corporations may not have had high positive net earnings in 1936 and that some such corporations may not have had profits even in so bad a year as 1932 (see below, Chapter XXV). We are dealing here with a composite figure for each size class; and, in so far as some corporations within the lowest class may have had positive earnings in any of the years 1931–34, others must have had even greater losses than those implied by the class rate figure.

Another notable feature of the curve for the small size class is that it fluctuates more widely than the other curves of the chart. The response of these small corporations to the business cycle is substantially greater than that of corporations in the larger size class, and cyclical intensity is even greater for the very lowest size class (not shown in the chart). The minimum cyclical response (not shown in the chart) is for the highest class; but examination of the record (Table IX) reveals that nearly all other classes have the narrower cyclical response shown for the one large size class in Chart X. The case for the very low size classes is, in other words, quite exceptional. There is again the possibility that this differential cyclical response according to size *may* result from concentration of certain types of manufacturing in particular size classes: those types peculiarly subject to the cycle *may* predominate in the lowest size classes.

The very wide fluctuation in rate of return for the lowest class should not be allowed to divert attention from the sharp cyclical responsiveness even of the highest class. For this class in the manufacturing division, the rate ranges from just under zero in the deep depression of 1932 to well over seven (nine, for the 50–100-million-dollar class) per cent in the recovery year — not a year of high general prosperity — 1936. This is a distinctly wider range than that shown for the highest class of all corporations (Table II). The profitability of even these largest manufacturing concerns, many of which may be highly integrated enterprises, is seriously affected by cyclical movements in general business conditions. We shall see in succeeding chapters that, within the manufacturing division, particular lines of manufacturing show various degrees of response to the cycle, and that these differences vary somewhat from size class to size class. The curves of Chart X are in a sense the average results of combining these diverse particular branches of manufacturing. To infer from these average results pertaining to the entire manufacturing division like results for a particular line of manufacturing is unwarranted.

PROFITABLE AND UNPROFITABLE CORPORATIONS

Using separate tabulations in *Statistics of Income* for corporations which do and those which do not have an income subject to tax — categories which we call income and deficit corporations, respectively — an interesting contrast between income and deficit corporations, as respects the relation between rate of return and size, can be worked out. Chart XI presents the size variation in rate of return in each of the six years for the income corporations alone (in the same form as Chart III, for all corporations). The most striking feature of the chart is that, despite irregularities in each curve and extensive lack of parallelism among the curves, these curves slope downward to the right. In general, for *income* corporations in the manufacturing division, rate of return diminishes as size increases. This finding is in accord with that of Chapter II (particularly pages 27–29) for all industrial divisions combined. The inescapable inference from a joint consideration of Charts IX and XI is that all of the upward-to-the-right sweep of the curves of Chart IX — and more — must be accounted for by the deficit corporations. In other words, corresponding curves for the deficit corporations must rise even more sharply with passage to the right than the curves of Chart IX.

The irregularities in the several curves of Chart XI are in sharp contrast with the general smoothness of the curves of Chart IX. The drift downward to the right, while unmistakable in Chart XI, is by no means steady; and the deviations from a steady course may reflect significant peculiarities in certain size classes, or mere statistical accidents.[8] Another feature of the

[8] That the deviations are purely accidental, however, is unlikely in view

chart is the nearly horizontal drift, except for the deviations of particular classes, in several of the curves between 100 thousand and 1 million dollars. This is followed, on the right, by

CHART XI

RATE OF RETURN COMPARED WITH SIZE, FOR INCOME CATEGORY OF MANUFACTURING DIVISION *

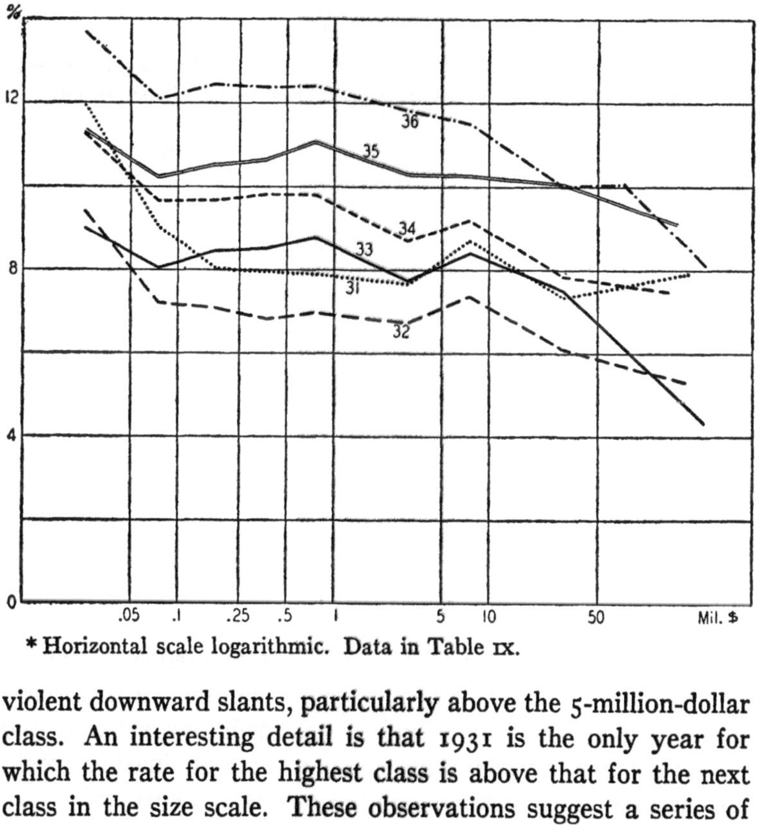

* Horizontal scale logarithmic. Data in Table IX.

violent downward slants, particularly above the 5-million-dollar class. An interesting detail is that 1931 is the only year for which the rate for the highest class is above that for the next class in the size scale. These observations suggest a series of

of the substantial number of corporations even in the larger size classes. Nevertheless, wide diversity in amount of net income (or loss) exists among the corporations in any one size class; and this implies that a single corporation, in a class which is not numerous, might dominate our rate figure.

questions concerning the degree of relationship between rate of return and size for the income corporations, but consideration of such questions must be postponed until detailed evidence is presented for the manufacturing groups — groups classified according to type of manufacturing activity.

The apparent greater spread among the curves, in Chart XI

TABLE VIII

ANNUAL PERCENTAGE RATIOS OF TOTAL ASSETS OF INCOME CATEGORY OF CORPORATIONS TO TOTAL ASSETS, IN EACH SIZE CLASS OF THE MANUFACTURING DIVISION *

Class †	1931	1932	1933	1934	1935	1936
0	33.3	15.3	25.9	33.9	37.3	44.1
50	35.2	19.0	35.5	45.5	50.1	59.8
100	36.1	20.7	41.0	49.1	55.6	67.4
250	35.4	24.0	45.4	52.9	59.9	72.2
500	36.1	25.0	47.5	55.0	62.3	75.8
1,000	35.4	24.0	49.7	57.6	66.6	80.5
5,000	36.1	27.3	47.4	58.7	67.6	83.3
10,000	41.2	27.0	49.7	59.1	68.7	87.4
50,000	39.7	30.7	54.8	53.3	67.9	92.0
100,000	...	...	...	...	...	86.7
Entire division	38.5	27.6	50.8	55.1	65.8	82.8

* Calculated from basic figures for total assets given in successive issues of *Statistics of Income* (for example, 1935 issue, Part 2, pp. 67–68).

† Lower limit of size class; unit, $1,000. Separate data for $100,000,000 class available only in 1936.

as compared with Chart IX, is due to the difference in scale of the two charts. If both charts were on the same vertical scale, the spread in Chart XI would appear definitely smaller, and the total range of variation in any one curve of Chart XI would appear very much smaller than the ranges of Chart IX.[4]

[4] It might be suggested that this could be partly explained by the tax charges themselves, which are borne by the income corporations and not by the deficit corporations. Changes in corporation tax rates were not considerable in the years 1931–36, although changes with respect to exempt income may account for the 1931 curve's being higher with respect to the

In considering time changes among the curves of Chart XI, the important fact that the make-up — of the income category of corporations — changes from year to year must not be overlooked. Particular corporations pass back and forth between

CHART XII

Six-year Average of Rates of Return Compared with Size, for Manufacturing Division and Income and Deficit Categories *

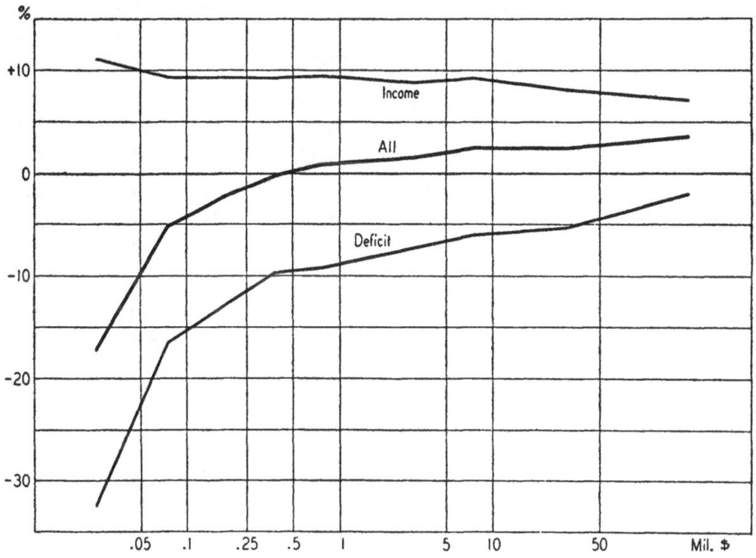

* Horizontal scale logarithmic. Data in Table B. See third footnote to Table IX.

income and deficit categories as time brings now profitable operation, now loss. The share which belongs to income corporations, of all assets in any one size class, may vary widely

other curves, at least in some small size classes, than would otherwise be the case. A fixed tax rate in all years would tend to make the spread among the income curves less wide than among the "combined income and deficit" curves. This, however, is probably not the chief explanation, because skewness of the distributions within each class is a controlling factor in some cases.

TABLE IX

RATES OF RETURN FOR MANUFACTURING DIVISION *

Class †	1931	1932	1933	1934 ‡	1935	1936
0	**−22.55**	**−30.07**	**−19.23**	**−13.48**	**−11.21**	**−6.90**
	11.95	9.43	9.00	11.25	11.35	13.68
	−41.38	*−37.79*	*−30.93*	*−30.63*	*−30.12*	*−29.90*
50	**−10.89**	**−14.95**	**−5.92**	**−2.27**	**−.33**	**3.07**
	9.05	7.21	8.05	9.67	10.23	12.10
	−22.55	*−20.46*	*−14.64*	*−14.12*	*−13.29*	*−14.11*
100	**−8.01**	**−10.84**	**−2.95**	**−.09**	**1.83**	**5.90**
	8.04	7.12	8.45	9.68	10.52	12.44
	−17.68	*−15.85*	*−11.50*	*−11.08*	*−11.28*	*−10.57*
250	**−5.75**	**−8.41**	**−.39**	**1.56**	**3.67**	**7.32**
	7.97	6.83	8.52	9.84	10.65	12.37
	−10.04	*−13.44*	*−8.35*	*−9.36*	*−8.45*	*−8.79*
500	**−4.08**	**−6.61**	**.33**	**2.31**	**4.67**	**8.18**
	7.91	6.99	8.79	9.83	11.08	12.40
	−11.30	*−11.32*	*−8.02*	*−8.15*	*−7.94*	*−8.79*
1,000	**−3.32**	**−5.48**	**.72**	**3.01**	**5.60**	**8.80**
	7.67	6.75	7.76	8.70	10.32	11.83
	−9.64	*−9.48*	*−6.73*	*−6.01*	*−5.34*	*−6.71*
5,000	**−1.52**	**−3.97**	**1.59**	**3.98**	**5.92**	**9.26**
	8.72	7.39	8.43	9.22	10.29	11.52
	−7.72	*−8.61*	*−5.41*	*−4.70*	*−5.12*	*−4.56*
10,000	**−.75**	**−4.00**	**1.11**	**3.37**	**6.48**	**8.63**
	7.35	6.11	7.53	7.86	10.08	10.02
	−6.95	*−7.87*	*−6.08*	*−3.96*	*−2.56*	*−4.57*
50,000	**1.71**	**−.23**	**1.72**	**3.84**	**6.68**	**9.53**
	7.92	5.33	4.33	7.50	9.12	10.06
	−2.47	*−2.92*	*−4.44*	*−.66*	*.02*	*−5.10*
100,000	...	...	...	...	...	**7.38**
	...	...	...	...	...	8.09
	...	...	...	...	...	*−1.25*
Entire division ..	**−.96**	**−3.45**	**.68**	**3.01**	**5.68**	**7.94**
	7.87	6.00	6.19	8.31	9.85	10.06
	−6.78	*−7.33*	*−5.35*	*−4.34*	*−4.18*	*−6.77*

* Expressed in per cent; ratio of profit (or loss) after taxes to estimated average equity, as explained in text, p. 18. Figures in boldface type are for

from year to year, as shown in Table VIII. And of course, even if the *share* did not change, the actual corporations in the income category might be very different — might, for example,

---

income and deficit categories of corporations combined, in ordinary type for the income category, in italics for the deficit category.

† Lower limit of class interval, in thousands of dollars of total assets. The 50,000-thousand-dollar class has no stated upper limit, 1931–35; the 100,000-thousand-dollar class has no stated upper limit, 1936.

‡ The figures here shown for the deficit category and for both categories combined in the 5-million-dollar class in 1934 are in error. Figures shown for the corresponding class and categories in 1934 for the agriculture division were so exceptional that query concerning them was sent to the Bureau of Internal Revenue, and reply indicated that the distortion in agriculture was due to the erroneous classification in that division of a deficit company which was classified in the foods group of manufacturing in 1933 and 1935 and presumably should have been in that group in 1934. This error affects various results for the agriculture and manufacturing divisions and the foods group as shown in this book, and the principal instances of error of this sort (corrections pertaining to figures other than rates of return on equity have not been noted) are indicated by footnotes referring back to this footnote.

The figures as shown in the tables and charts of the book have, however, not been corrected, and stand on the basis of data as actually published in *Statistics of Income for 1934, Part 2*. If the error had been corrected, the principal changes in rate-of-return figures actually used in the book would have been as follows:

	Deficit category		Both categories combined	
	As published	Corrected	As published	Corrected
Manufacturing division				
Entire division	−4.34	−4.52	3.01	2.93
5-million-dollar class	−4.70	−7.17	3.98	3.00
Six-year average, entire division	−5.79	−5.82	2.15	2.12
Six-year average, 5-million-dollar class	−6.02	−6.43	2.54	2.38
Foods group				
Entire group	−6.01	−9.86	6.13	5.37
5-million-dollar class	−2.31	−30.69	8.21	−.84
Six-year average, entire group	−7.00	−7.64	4.59	4.46
Six-year average, 5-million-dollar class	−5.76	−10.49	5.48	3.98
Agriculture division				
Entire division	−8.80	−5.31	−3.21	−1.11
5-million-dollar class	−31.71	−2.45	−16.99	1.01
Six-year average, entire division	−7.01	−6.43	−2.30	−1.95
Six-year average, classes grouped	−4.69	−3.67	−.30	.27

belong predominantly to a different line of manufacturing activity — in one year than in another.

To bring out the opposite relation between rate of return and size for income and for deficit corporations, Chart XII (like Chart IV) presents the six-year average rates of return. The curve for income and deficit corporations combined necessarily lies between the other curves. The striking feature, however, is that the deficit curve rises more sharply toward the right than does the combined curve, whereas the income curve declines toward the right. As already noted, the positive correlation between rate and size for the combined case is fully accounted for, and more, by the deficit case. Similar detailed comparisons are not presented graphically for specific years, but Table IX (similar to Table II) shows the corresponding record for selected size classes in each of the six years. These tabulated results support the findings from Chart XII: among the income corporations, rate of return declines moderately with increasing size; among the deficit corporations, rate of return rises (rate of loss declines) very sharply with increasing size.

SUMMARY

The examination of the manufacturing division has led to findings mainly in accord with those for all industries combined as reported in Chapter II. Rate of return rises as size increases, when income and deficit categories are combined; but separate study of these two categories shows rate of return declining with increasing size for income corporations, and hence the deficit corporations more than account for the apparent positive correlation for the combined case. Cyclical variations in rate are sharp, even for the highest size class; and they are violent for the lowest class. The similarity between the findings for the manufacturing division and those for the inclusive case of all corporations must not, however, lead us to conclude that this division is in truth merely a rough sample of all corporate in-

facts for thirteen sub-groups within the metals group; but these sub-group data — except in the case of motor vehicles in 1936 — are not available at all for the balance-sheet category of returns, and can not therefore be used for the present type of

TABLE X

Comparative Importance of Sub-groups of the Metals Manufacturing Group in 1935 *

	Number of corporations	Total gross income	Gross income per corporation
Sub-group			
Iron and steel	2,194	2,548	1,161
Railroad equipment	196	163	832
Motor vehicles	873	4,213	4,825
Factory machinery	1,528	485	317
Agricultural machinery	502	412	820
Electrical equipment	692	771	1,114
Miscellaneous machinery	2,415	860	356
Household equipment	1,281	474	370
Office equipment	400	284	711
Building material	2,195	601	274
Hardware and tools	2,745	880	320
Precious metal products	859	302	352
Other metal manufacturing	3,976	1,562	393
Entire metals group	19,856	13,555	683

* Compiled and computed from *Statistics of Income for 1935, Part 2*, pp. 36–37. Units: $1,000,000, for column 2; $1,000, for column 3.

analysis (see below, page 78). Moreover these sub-group data afford at best a very meagre summary of the income account; but they present a limited descriptive picture of the degree of diversity, as to line of activity, within the metals group.

Table x shows in its stubs the designations of these thirteen sub-groups, and significant data as to their comparative importance in 1935.[2] Manifestly, two sub-groups — motor vehicles,

[2] The item "gross income," as given in the table, differs slightly from "total compiled receipts," which we have heretofore cited as a measure of

and iron and steel (including only such fabrication as is implied in rolling or casting) — make up nearly half of the group total, in terms of gross income. The largest of the eleven other sub-groups is a poor third after these two. Gross income for each of seven sub-groups is less than 5 per cent of the group total. Of course, varying impact of business-cycle changes might result in a somewhat altered picture of relative importance of the sub-groups, if data for some year other than 1935 were examined; but no striking change involving the position of the leaders would be found in any recent year. We might fairly conclude that motor vehicles and iron and steel dominate the metals group; but for an analysis of the type we are making in this book this conclusion must be qualified. Some of the smaller sub-groups might be so concentrated in one or more size (assets-size) classes of the metals group that our calculated rates of profit for such size class or classes would in fact be dominated by a sub-group which, in general for all size classes combined, is comparatively unimportant. On the peculiarities of the motor vehicles sub-group, as revealed by 1936 data, see below (page 78).

No direct evidence on this point is available. As already noted, the sub-group tabulations include no balance-sheet items and, of course, no size classification according to amount of assets. Therefore we can not say, for example, how many of the 692 corporations of the electrical machinery sub-group are in each of our nine standard size classes. Or, in other terms, we can not say what portion of any one size class — say 500 thousand to 1 million dollars — for the metals group as a whole is made up of electrical machinery concerns. Very uncertain indirect evidence, however, appears in the third column of

---

importance. The difference results from the exclusion of tax-exempt interest, generally a small amount, from gross income. The published tabulations for the sub-groups state the gross income, but not the total receipts. See *Statistics of Income for 1935, Part 2*, pp. 36–37.

Table x. Those figures indicate an emphatic diversity among the sub-groups, as to average gross income in 1935. Again waiving any peculiarities due to citation of data for the single year 1935, and bearing in mind that gross income is not necessarily correlated closely with total assets, we observe certain striking facts. Average gross income per corporation is more than four times as great for motor vehicles as for the next two sub-groups, iron and steel, and electrical machinery; and it is more than ten times as great for motor vehicles as for seven of the sub-groups. After all reservations which may properly be applied to these comparisons, an unmistakable indication remains that there is a somewhat greater chance for one of the 873 motor-vehicles corporations to fall in one of the larger of the nine standard size classes than is the case for one of the 2745 hardware-and-tools corporations.[3] This conclusion is, of course, in accord with general knowledge as to the organization of these industries. All that can be said is that the available indirect evidence gives some indication that corporations of certain sub-groups are more likely to fall in certain size classes

[3] One of the reservations to be borne in mind in this connection is that the arithmetic average — the figure cited in the third column of Table x — is a poor statistical summary in a case of this sort: it is not a highly typical figure. The point at issue is that the frequency distribution upon which the average rests is almost certainly of the extremely skew type — while we have no direct evidence as to the form of the frequency distribution of gross income for these sub-groups (or for any of the Treasury groupings), much indirect evidence points unmistakably toward this inference as to extreme skewness. In such a very skew distribution, a mere handful of very large corporations — for example, three or four dominating automobile companies — might pull the average up, while the numerous bulk of remaining companies in the sub-group remained widely distributed among the various lower size groups. The essential facts of the statistical distribution are unknown, and the above conclusion in the text must be greatly tempered because of the possibilities involved in this skewness and its bearing upon the comparative size of arithmetic averages. Fortunately, the 1936 tabulations give us conclusive evidence in the case of automobiles — this 1936 group, formerly a sub-group of the metals group, is examined below, (p. 78).

than is the case for other sub-groups. To that extent, the rate-of-return figure for a particular size class may be dominated by the peculiar profit experience of a particular sub-group within the metals group.

A somewhat related question concerns the degree of integration, already remarked upon as affecting an interpretation of data for particular types of industry (see above, page 51). Little satisfactory evidence is available on this point. We can infer that in 1935 corporations of the metals group in the aggregate had no considerable activity in mining and other extractive industries; for depletion charges for the metals group were only 6.6 million dollars, whereas they were 128.3 for the manufacturing division as a whole, and 204.2 for the mining and agriculture divisions combined. No doubt by 1935 some of the "integration" formerly concealed in the figures had been removed by the abandonment of consolidated returns following the Act of 1934; but even as late as 1933, depletion charges for the metals group were only 12.1 million dollars, against 109.5 for the entire manufacturing division and 117.8 for the mining and agriculture divisions combined.[4] As respects integration, of metal manufacturing companies, reaching into other groups within the manufacturing division or into non-manufacturing divisions other than those dominated by extractive industries, even less evidence is available; although general information suggests that such integration may be extensive, and may well result in the coverage into the data of the metals group of substantial amounts which truly belong in other groups or divisions. Here also, however, we proceed on the assumption that the data of the metals group fairly represent that type of manufacturing.

[4] Figures cited are for all returns — those with and those without balance sheets — but figures for balance-sheet returns alone would be only slightly different. See *Statistics of Income for 1933*, pp. 142 and 145; and for 1935, Part 2, pp. 40 and 43.

SIZE VARIATION IN RATE

Chart XIII shows the relation between size and rate of return on equity, for the metals group, in each year 1931–36. The curves show the same general upward-to-the-right course observed previously in corresponding charts for the manufactur-

CHART XIII

RATE OF RETURN COMPARED WITH SIZE, FOR METALS GROUP *

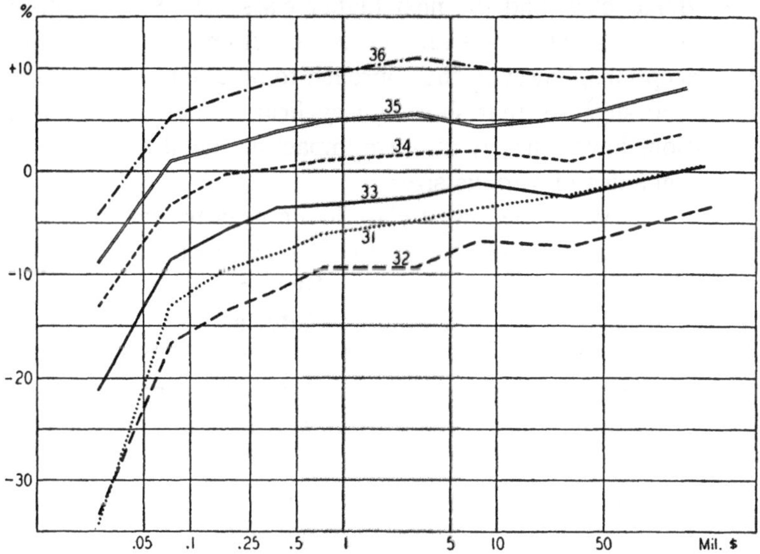

* Horizontal scale logarithmic. Data in Table XI. On old basis for 1936.

ing division and for all divisions combined: rate of return increases with size. The curves rise rapidly at the left, taper off to a nearly horizontal course or fluctuate narrowly between 500 thousand dollars and 50 million dollars; and then another unmistakable advance appears for the highest size class, in every year except 1936. Moreover, evidences of parallelism are somewhat more pronounced here than in the earlier charts examined; a truly surprising degree of similarity in direction of movement appears among the six curves. The most notable exceptions are in the drop from the 1-million-dollar to 5-million-dollar class in 1935 and 1936, and the rise from the 5-million-dollar class to the 10-million-dollar class in 1931 and 1935. Only two intersections appear in the entire chart. Less notable departures from parallelism appear in the very slight advance of the 1936 curve at the extreme right, and the nearly horizontal movement of the 1932 curve between the 500-thousand-dollar class and the next higher class. Here, as in other similar charts, the curves fan out at the left end. In spite of all the exceptions, however, the approach to parallelism is remarkable, and suggests that short-run cyclical changes in business conditions have a nearly uniform impact on metal manufacturing companies of various sizes.

In all six years the lowest class had a negative rate: even in the best year covered, 1936, these small metals companies showed a substantial average loss. By 1934, all but the three lowest size classes enjoyed a positive rate; and by 1935, all but the very lowest class. In 1931 and 1933, only the highest class had a positive rate; indeed, only in 1932 did that class have a negative rate. For metal manufacturing, then, the lowest size class had an unprofitable record in all six years, even the most favorable; and the highest size class failed to earn a profit only in the single year of deepest depression, 1932.

TIME VARIATIONS IN RATE

The annual record of the rate of return (Chart XIV) gives another and supporting view of the relationships observed above. The year-to-year changes in rate, for the entire metals group and the two selected size classes, are remarkably regular. The single dip from 1931 to 1932 is followed by four successive advances which, though not all of equal magnitude, are strikingly similar for all the curves. For all curves shown, emphatic

CHART XIV

TIME VARIATIONS IN RATE OF RETURN, FOR METALS GROUP AND SELECTED SIZE CLASSES *

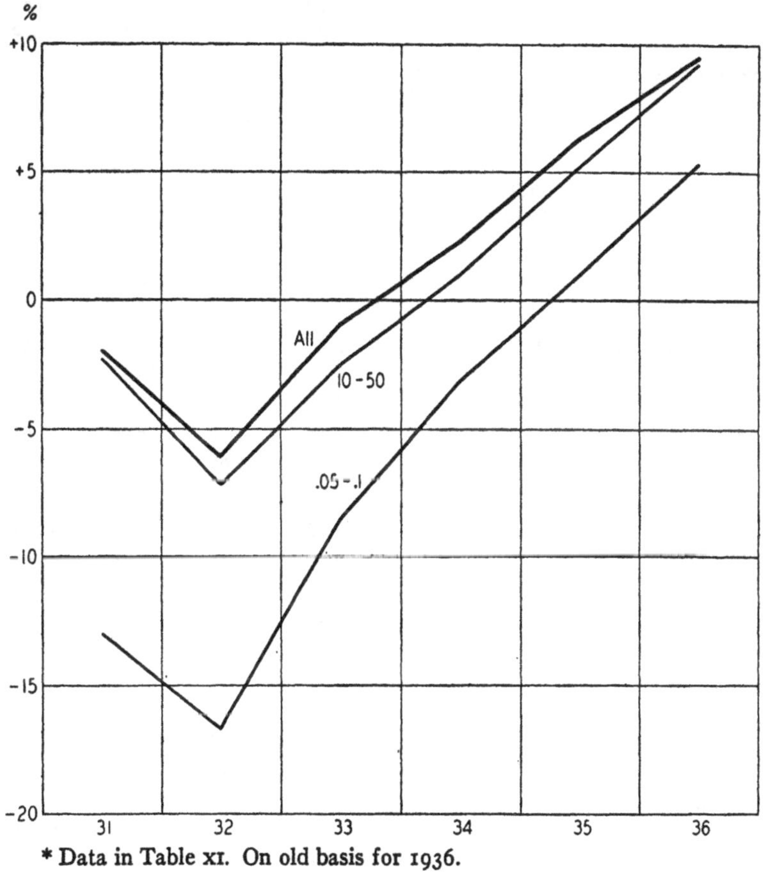

* Data in Table XI. On old basis for 1936.

recovery began in 1933; and the subsequent movement carried the curves far above their respective 1931 levels. If curves were shown for the other size classes, we should find them all — except that for the very lowest class — roughly parallel to the curve shown for the entire group. For the highest size

TABLE XI

Rates of Return for Metals Group *

Class †	1931	1932	1933	1934	1935	1936 ‡
0	−34.32	−33.35	−21.15	−13.08	−8.87	−4.23
	10.82	8.52	7.70	10.64	11.56	13.89
	−58.75	−37.90	−30.22	−27.39	−25.82	−25.72
50	−13.01	−16.69	−8.54	−3.17	.98	5.33
	8.82	6.96	7.07	9.48	10.56	13.34
	−20.83	−19.87	−15.18	−14.27	−11.41	−13.52
100	−9.47	−13.45	−5.71	−.26	2.45	7.30
	6.58	5.80	6.89	9.33	10.70	13.22
	−15.54	−16.05	−11.66	−9.20	−10.46	−9.53
250	−7.96	−11.56	−3.46	.31	3.89	8.89
	7.00	5.28	7.03	8.67	10.28	13.35
	−13.72	−14.51	−9.10	−8.60	−7.44	−9.52
500	−6.07	−9.27	−3.25	1.01	4.91	9.44
	7.30	5.01	6.56	8.47	11.33	13.27
	−10.61	−11.50	−8.32	−7.12	−6.72	−7.04
1,000	−4.77	−9.26	−2.52	1.70	5.60	11.08
	6.30	5.03	5.72	7.66	9.99	14.32
	−8.65	−10.94	−6.96	−5.83	−4.79	−7.66
5,000	−3.56	−6.68	−1.15	2.06	4.41	10.26
	6.70	6.04	6.70	7.16	9.07	12.41
	−7.38	−8.37	−5.38	−5.12	−7.47	−5.04
10,000	−2.31	−7.21	−2.54	1.01	5.23	9.18
	7.10	7.56	5.48	6.57	9.08	10.18
	−7.14	−8.70	−5.75	−4.20	−2.59	−6.36
50,000	.48	−3.43	.56	3.72	8.12	...
	8.23	4.63	5.80	7.29	11.16	9.05
	−2.77	−4.02	−1.89	−1.45	−.99	...
100,000	...	...	...	...	...	...
	...	...	...	...	...	10.86
	...	...	...	...	...	...
Classes grouped §	...	...	...	...	...	9.54
	...	...	...	...	...	...
	...	...	...	...	...	−1.03
Entire group	−1.97	−6.10	−.95	2.27	6.34	9.48
	7.60	5.52	5.91	7.39	10.44	11.33
	−5.96	−7.21	−4.24	−4.07	−3.69	−5.52

classes the intensity of the cyclical variation would appear definitely less than for the other curves. And only in case of the lowest size class does the cyclical intensity greatly exceed that of the group as a whole. Again a broad inference is suggested: cyclical changes in business have approximately uniform impact on nearly all the various sizes of metal companies.

The intensity of cyclical variation is very great, even when the lowest size class is ignored. For the highest size class, the rate ranges from below −3 per cent in 1932 to above 9 per cent in 1936. This range of 12 points is greater than the corresponding range, of under 10 points, for the entire manufacturing division (Table IX). A somewhat similar contrast appears when the group curve — without regard to size class — of Chart XIV is compared with the division curve of Chart X. The contrast in range for the lowest size class is not so emphatic — 30 points in Table XI against 23 points in Table IX — but the peculiar imperfections of the calculations for the lowest class justify some reservation in this case (see below, page 382).

That the cyclical variation in the metals group, as a whole and for its several size classes, should be exceptionally wide is entirely to be expected. A glance at the stubs of Table X discloses that the bulk of the metals group represents producers of durable capital goods. The large motor-vehicles sub-group, to be sure, manufactures products mainly for con-

---

* Expressed in per cent; ratio of profit (or loss) after taxes to estimated average equity, as explained in text, p. 18. Figures in boldface type are for income and deficit categories of corporations combined, in ordinary type for the income category, in italics for the deficit category.

† Lower limit of class interval, in thousands of dollars of total assets. The 50,000-thousand-dollar class has no stated upper limit, 1931–35; the 100,000-thousand-dollar class has no stated upper limit, 1936.

‡ 1936 figures on old basis: combining two new groups — metals and motor vehicles — of 1936 (see page 79).

§ High size classes combined, to conceal a single corporation. As such combination applies to only deficit category, other category is shown separately in the specific classes, but joint figure for both categories is shown only in "grouped" row.

sumers; but these products are durable, and are known to be highly responsive to cyclical conditions. For the metals group as a whole, practically all of the output is durable, and much of it is destined for use as capital equipment — on both counts, these enterprises are exceptionally influenced by the cycle. The surprising finding does not consist in this cyclical responsiveness; it consists rather in the nearly uniform way in which this cyclical responsiveness appears for the various size classes, regardless of the possibility noted above that a particular metals sub-group — perhaps more or less responsive to the cycle than is the metals group as a whole — may dominate some particular size class.

PROFITABLE AND UNPROFITABLE CORPORATIONS

The separate record of rate of return in relation to size for the income corporations — corporations having a taxable net income — of the metals group is not shown graphically but can be inferred from Table XI. Here again the general drift shows that rate of return tends to decrease as size increases. The total reduction between the lowest size class and the highest is, however, not large. Moreover, the approach to parallelism of changes from size class to size class is not marked for the income corporations. Most years show freakish peaks in one or more size classes; and in 1932, 1935, and 1936 these freakish movements largely conceal the general downward drift. For all years except 1932, the highest size class has a rate definitely above that of the next lowest class. No readily available explanation of the freakish peaks can be drawn from the published data, and even the fairly general upturn for the top class does not admit of ready explanation.

The general tendency for rate in the income category to decline as size increases, however, unmistakably indicates that the upward course of the curves of Chart XIII, covering both income and deficit categories, must be caused entirely by the deficit companies. This condition is brought out more clearly in Chart xv, which compares the income and deficit categories with each other, and with the combined curve, on the basis of six-year averages of rates. The upward-to-the-right course of

CHART XV

SIX-YEAR AVERAGE OF RATES OF RETURN COMPARED WITH SIZE, FOR METALS GROUP AND INCOME AND DEFICIT CATEGORIES *

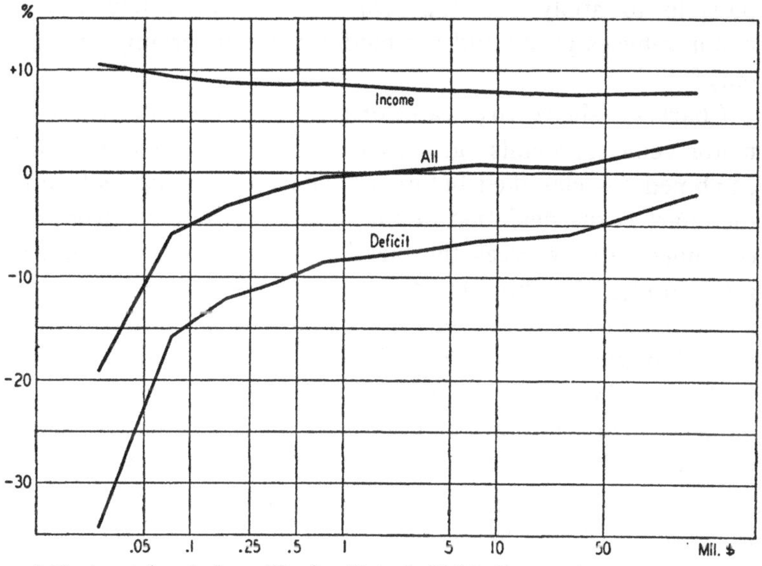

* Horizontal scale logarithmic. Data in Table B.

the deficit curve is somewhat steeper than that of the combined curve, whereas the income curve declines very gradually as size increases. Instead of similar charts for specific years, corresponding data for all size classes are presented in Table xi. The same finding is supported: broadly speaking the increase in rate of return with size for the two categories combined is accounted for, and more, by the deficit category, in each year of the record. In this respect, the experience for the metals group is similar to that already observed for the manufacturing division and for all divisions combined.

MOTOR VEHICLES IN 1936

Separate data, of the sort herein subject to analysis, were published for motor vehicles in 1936; and the other twelve sub-groups of the former metals group (see above, page 67) then remained in a new metals group. It therefore becomes possible to apply the standard analysis separately to the motor-vehicles group and the modified metals group, for 1936 only.[5]

Chart XVI shows 1936 rates of return for each size class for motor vehicles, metals (group as classified in 1936), and both combined (as classified before 1936). The striking feature of the chart is the deviation of the motor-vehicles rate from the combined rate, whereas the metals rate follows the combined rate closely. All three curves turn down for sizes somewhat above 1 million dollars, but the motor vehicles curve reaches new high levels above 50 millions. The intermediate decline begins at a lower level of size for motor vehicles, and is much more striking, than for the other curves. A moderate resumption of the upward course appears in the combined curve at the very right end, but the peak nevertheless remains somewhere left of 5 million dollars.

Another notable point in the chart is the low level of the motor vehicles rate for the lowest size class. The advance to the next size class is violent, and only less violent is that from the 250-thousand-dollar class to the next class above. In gen-

[5] The motor-vehicles group is much smaller, in terms of total assets, than the newly constituted metals group: 3.1 billion dollars, against 15.3. Concentration in highest size classes, however, differs notably between the two: about 72 per cent of assets above 50 million dollars per corporation for motor vehicles, as against about 44 per cent for metals. Hence, motor vehicles has a much heavier weight in top size classes than is indicated by the 3.1 to 15.3 ratio.

eral, the motor-vehicles curve is one of the least regular we have studied or are about to study (for cases of income and deficit corporations combined).[6] Unfortunately, the data are available only for 1936; and we can not know whether similar irregulari-

CHART XVI

RATE OF RETURN COMPARED WITH SIZE, FOR METALS GROUP AND ITS TWO SECTIONS, IN 1936 *

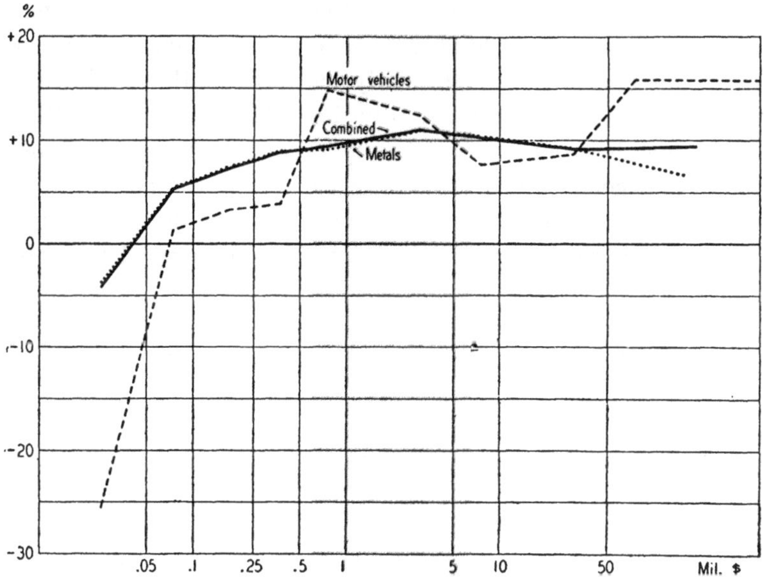

* Horizontal scale logarithmic. Data in Tables XI and C.

ties might have appeared in other years. In any case, Chart XVI suggests the possibility that more refined classification of manufacturing into specific lines might yield various cases in which relation between rate of return and size is irregular, and perhaps even cases in which the characteristic upward-to-the-right tendency of the curves might be significantly altered.

[6] Specific data for income and deficit categories of the motor vehicles and metals groups in 1936 are given below, p. 409.

VI

MANUFACTURED FOODS

THE SECOND LARGEST OF THE MANUFACTURING GROUPS, in terms of gross receipts, comprises foods and related products.[1] The group was considerably less important than metals in 1935, but had nevertheless nearly one fifth of the total gross receipts of the manufacturing division. This case, unlike that of the metals group, covers mainly producers of consumption goods, and goods which are almost entirely in the non-durable category.[2] These considerations should prepare us for findings differing in various important respects from those for the metals group.

[1] In 1931 and 1932, and earlier years, the group included beverages as one of its smaller sub-groups. With the repeal of prohibition and the reestablishment of the liquor industry, Treasury statistics — beginning in 1933 — carried an additional manufacturing group for liquors and beverages. Included in this new group were the corporations formerly carried in the beverage sub-group of the foods group, as well as the newer liquor companies. No complete homogeneity for the six-year period 1931–36 can be realized. If data for the foods group as actually tabulated in *Statistics of Income* are used, soft drinks and similar beverages are included in 1931 and 1932 but are excluded from foods (and included in a separate group) in 1933–36. If, on the other hand, the liquors and foods groups are added to form a single group in the years 1933–36, no true homogeneity is realized; for the rapid growth of the new liquor industry introduced many companies, some of them important, which were not covered in 1931–32. After consideration, the first of these alternatives seems the less objectionable; and we therefore analyse the foods group on the basis as published for all six years, and analyse the liquors group separately (see Chapter XI) for the four-year period for which data are given.

[2] This does not mean, of course, that many of these products can not be preserved, and thus held over a period. We are using *durable* in its narrow sense, implying capacity for continuous consumption over a protracted period.

FOODS SUB-GROUPS

The foods group is classified into a much less numerous list of sub-groups than is the metals group, in certain Treasury tabulations. The stubs for these sub-groups (Table XII) indicate considerable diversity as to the nature of products and processes; and extensive diversity also pertains within some, and perhaps all, of the sub-groups. The most important sub-

TABLE XII

COMPARATIVE IMPORTANCE OF SUB-GROUPS OF THE FOODS MANUFACTURING GROUP IN 1935 *

	Number of corporations	Total gross income	Gross income per corporation
Sub-group			
Bakery and confectionery ..	4,030	1,352	336
Canning	1,959	833	425
Milling	1,339	1,082	808
Packing house	975	3,692	3,787
Sugar	166	613	3,693
Other food manufacturing ..	4,906	1,756	358
Entire foods group	13,375	9,328	698

* Compiled and computed from *Statistics of Income for 1935, Part 2*, pp. 34–35. Units: $1,000,000, for column 2; $1,000, for column 3.

group is packing-house products, from the point of view of gross income in 1935.[3] This single sub-group accounted in 1935 for more than one third of the total gross income of the foods group (Table XII); and the heterogeneous miscellaneous sub-group, other food products, was a poor second.

The average size — in terms of 1935 gross income — per corporation varied widely among the sub-groups. The average was about equally large for two sub-groups, sugar and packing-house products; and for each it was more than ten times as great as for the bakery and other-food-products sub-groups.

[3] See footnote 2, page 66.

With the reservations already mentioned (see above, page 69), these disparities suggest that certain of the sub-groups may have disproportionate concentration in particular size (assets-size) classes, and thereby influence our findings as to variations in rate of return among the various size classes of the foods group. Here again, no unmistakable evidence is available, and we merely note the possibility that this factor may contribute to our results.

SIZE VARIATION IN RATE

Rate of return for the foods group shows a general tendency to increase as size increases (Chart XVII), but the degree of advance in rate between the lowest size class and the highest is markedly less than for the metals group. And this chart has several other features not observed in corresponding charts heretofore examined: the steepness of the curves at the left end, while greater than elsewhere in this chart, is not so marked as in the other charts; the differences in level among the curves are comparatively small; the approach to parallelism is by no means striking; a significant number of size classes have positive rates in 1931 or 1933, although only the highest class has a positive rate in 1932.[4]

The lack of extreme steepness at the left end of the curves suggests that the profit disadvantage of the very small companies is less serious in the foods group than in the manufacturing division as a whole. And this fact, coupled with the failure of any of the rates to rise to a level greatly above zero, emphasizes the greater approach to uniformity of rate

[4] Separate data for the highest class of our standard size scale are missing in 1933, 1935, and 1936, but the rate for the highest class shown is positive in each case. Strictly, this class is a combination of the 10-million-dollar class and the 50-million-dollar class: Treasury publications group two classes together in all cases in which separate publication might reveal information about a single corporation. This explains the "classes grouped" figures in Table XIII and various similar tables.

among size classes in the foods group than in the entire manufacturing division. The small differences in level among the curves, and also the persistence of positive rates for several size classes even in such a depressed year as 1931 and the smallness of several negative rates in a year of severe depression like 1933, indicate that the foods group does not yield as sharply to

CHART XVII

RATE OF RETURN COMPARED WITH SIZE, FOR FOODS GROUP *

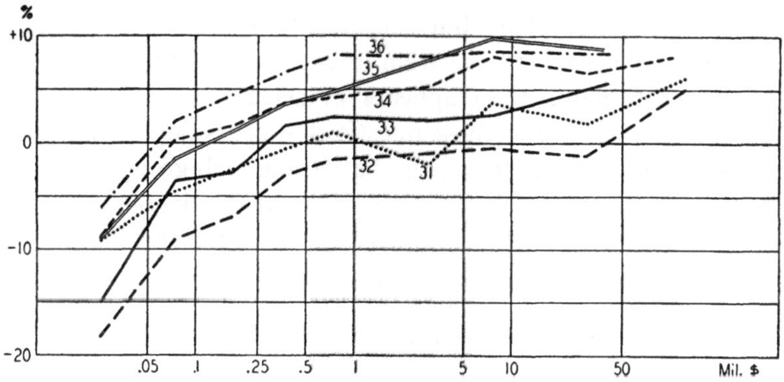

* Horizontal scale logarithmic. Data in Table XIII. See third footnote to Table IX.

cyclical changes in business as does the metals group. On the other hand, the considerable departures from parallelism — emphasized by several intersections among the curves — suggest that cyclical influences have an impact which is by no means uniform among the several size classes.

The narrower differentiation in rate of return with variation in size for the foods group, as compared with the metals group and the manufacturing division as a whole, is perhaps the most significant feature of Chart XVII (see also Charts IX and XIII). The explanation of this finding is not obvious, but a tentative inference is that mere size has distinctly less bearing upon profitability in the foods industries than in certain other lines.

We could easily believe that, for many foods industries, mere size of operating unit — because of the comparative simplicity of the processes, the presumptive absence of complicated and elaborate installations of capital equipment, and the relatively small utilization of an intricate technical and supervisory control — plays less part than in many other lines of manufacturing. Yet these considerations are not obviously applicable to the packing-house enterprises, which form so large a fraction of the group. Moreover these considerations relate to a single operating unit or plant, but conceivably also the foods industries derive less advantage from integration or horizontal combination of plants than appears in certain other industries. Satisfactory testing of these questions appears impossible until we know the extent to which the various sub-groups tend to concentrate in particular size classes, and the degree in which organizational and other peculiarities affect the specific profitability of the various sub-groups.

TIME VARIATIONS IN RATE

The comparatively narrow differences in level of the curves of Chart XVII have already been noted as reflecting a limited response of the food industries to cyclical changes in business. This point is further supported by the record of annual changes, for two selected size classes and for the entire group, as given in Chart XVIII. The decline from 1931 to 1932 was not very severe, and suggests that the effects of the great depression had largely been felt in these industries before the final year of severe general contraction. A sharp advance occurred in 1933 in all three curves, to a level above that of 1931 for two of the curves. Broadly speaking, the recovery was sharpest and most uniform in 1933. In 1935 and in 1936, advances appeared in two curves, and a decline in the third (the low size class in 1935, the high size class in 1936). One obvious interpretation of this record emphasizes the fact that the foods group is made up almost entirely of producers of non-durable consumption goods. The recent recovery came fairly early for these goods, and was seriously delayed for durable capital goods. A further element in a possible interpretation relates to

CHART XVIII

TIME VARIATIONS IN RATE OF RETURN, FOR FOODS GROUP AND SELECTED SIZE CLASSES *

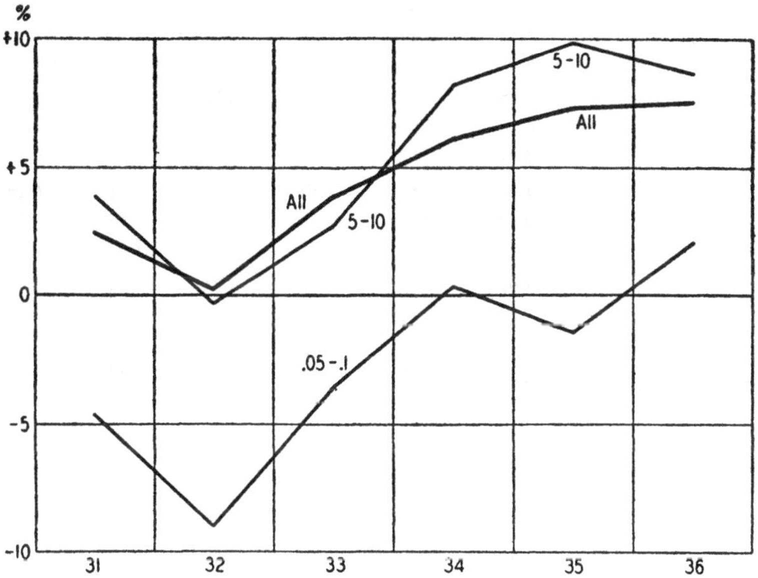

* Data in Table XIII. See third footnote to Table IX.

the effect of inventories on reported profits: many of these foods industries necessarily have heavy and changing commitments in inventories, and the bearing of inventories upon profits was augmented by sharp changes of prices in 1933.

The annual experience for the lowest size class differs notably from that outlined above (Table XIII). The 1931–32 decline was very severe, recovery in 1933 was only moderate, a sharp advance occurred in 1934, an actual though slight decline ap-

TABLE XIII

Rates of Return for Foods Group *

Class †	1931	1932	1933	1934 §	1935	1936
0	**−9.24**	**−18.28**	**−15.08**	**−8.78**	**−8.98**	**−6.11**
	13.76	10.27	7.84	10.94	9.82	11.31
	−32.10	*−28.58*	*−27.72*	*−24.27*	*−23.86*	*−25.93*
50	**−4.62**	**−9.00**	**−3.59**	**.35**	**−1.46**	**2.05**
	10.42	7.75	7.18	9.69	8.76	10.15
	−21.37	*−16.58*	*−11.76*	*−10.73*	*−11.86*	*−12.33*
100	**−2.44**	**−6.88**	**−2.73**	**1.60**	**1.11**	**4.58**
	9.72	6.86	7.22	9.45	9.44	10.43
	−15.42	*−13.69*	*−12.46*	*−11.06*	*−10.62*	*−9.62*
250	**−.48**	**−2.98**	**1.65**	**3.86**	**3.70**	**6.72**
	9.50	7.54	7.96	9.53	9.53	11.12
	−13.29	*−10.17*	*−7.10*	*−7.19*	*−7.48*	*−8.37*
500	**1.04**	**−1.50**	**2.48**	**4.34**	**4.79**	**8.16**
	9.47	9.05	8.47	9.40	9.91	10.86
	−10.87	*−8.87*	*−6.14*	*−8.37*	*−8.58*	*−5.20*
1,000	**−1.97**	**−.85**	**2.23**	**5.34**	**7.77**	**8.10**
	7.59	6.46	7.65	9.77	12.44	11.04
	−14.58	*−7.03*	*−7.33*	*−6.07*	*−5.01*	*−5.28*
5,000	**3.85**	**−.36**	**2.69**	**8.21**	**9.86**	**8.65**
	11.35	6.91	8.46	12.11	13.13	10.40
	−6.07	*−8.92*	*−6.01*	*−2.31*	*−6.17*	*−5.08*
10,000	**1.93**	**−1.11**	...	**6.60**	...	...
	8.42	6.97	7.51	8.09	10.44	9.30
	−7.06	*−9.04*	...	*.07*	...	...
50,000	**6.12**	**5.04**	...	**8.08**	...	...
	10.72	6.32	7.33	8.08	9.27	13.88
	−4.82	*.29*	...	...	...	...
100,000	...	...	...	...	...	...
	...	...	...	...	...	6.81
	...	...	...	...	...	...
Classes grouped ‡	...	...	**5.68**	...	**8.85**	**8.42**
	...	...	...	...	...	...
	...	...	*−2.11*	...	*2.21*	*−3.02*
Entire group ...	**2.42**	**.26**	**3.84**	**6.13**	**7.35**	**7.52**
	9.72	6.74	7.54	8.84	10.46	9.68
	−9.43	*−8.30*	*−6.23*	*−6.01*	*−4.94*	*−7.08*

peared in 1935, and the 1934–35 rates were scarcely above that of 1931. A mild further advance appeared in 1936, but the rate remained far below zero. This disparate cyclical experience admits of no ready explanation, unless we may assume — as seems not unlikely — that this lowest size class (and the same may be true of the next class, which is shown in Chart XVIII) is dominated by particular types of food enterprises having notably different response to the cycle from the enterprises which make up the bulk of other size classes.

Another striking fact is that the range of variation for the lowest size class is only moderately greater than for the other size classes shown — this also is contrary to the condition observed in the metals group and in the entire manufacturing division. Moreover, the range of variation even for the lowest class amounts to just over 12 points, against 30 points for the metals group (see above, page 75). This point again brings out the comparatively mild effect of cyclical variations in general business upon the foods industries.

PROFITABLE AND UNPROFITABLE CORPORATIONS

The separate record of rate of return for income corporations in the foods group can be traced in Table XIII, and is again not in line with the corresponding record for the metals group and the manufacturing division. To be sure, the comparatively

---

* Expressed in per cent; ratio of profit (or loss) after taxes to estimated average equity, as explained in text, p. 18. Figures in boldface type are for income and deficit categories of corporations combined, in ordinary type for the income category, in italics for the deficit category. This group includes beverages in 1931–32, but that subgroup is in the liquors group in 1933–36.

† Lower limit of class interval, in thousands of dollars of total assets. The 50,000-thousand-dollar class has no stated upper limit, 1931–35; the 100,000-thousand-dollar class has no stated upper limit, 1936.

‡ High size classes combined, to conceal a single corporation. As such combination applies to only deficit category, other category is shown separately in the specific classes, but joint figure for both categories is shown only in "grouped" row.

§ See third footnote to Table IX.

high rates for the lowest size class give some impression of a decline of rate with increasing size. But, if the lowest class is ignored, the impression disappears; rather, the movement appears as a highly irregular fluctuation about a nearly horizontal general level. For the income corporations of the foods

CHART XIX

SIX-YEAR AVERAGE OF RATES OF RETURN COMPARED WITH SIZE, FOR FOODS GROUP AND INCOME AND DEFICIT CATEGORIES *

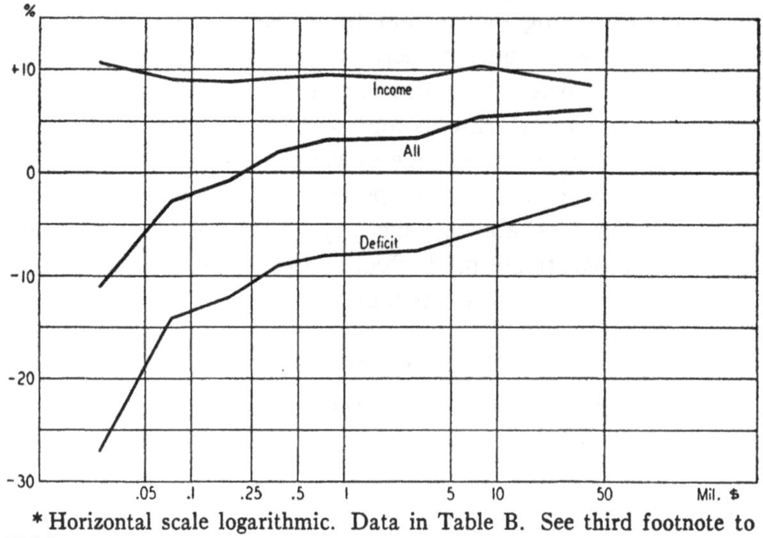

* Horizontal scale logarithmic. Data in Table B. See third footnote to Table IX.

group, then, no clear evidence exists of an association between rate of return and size. Still ignoring the lowest size class, we might even infer that a slight upward drift of rate with increasing size exists for some of the years; and this implies that *not* all of the upward course of the curves of Chart XVII can be accounted for by the deficit corporations.

Chart XIX compares the income and deficit categories, and those categories combined, on the basis of six-year averages of the various class rates. There is a slight downward drift at the left of the income curve, followed by a less regular upward drift, and a final drop at the right end. Correspondingly, the deficit curve has a slightly steeper upward course at the left and a less steep course at the right, than the combined curve. Similar data, for every size class, are given for all six years in Table XIII; but, because of the irregularities so frequently appearing in particular size classes of the foods group, these figures do not afford any conclusive indication of the role of the deficit corporations in determining the rates of return recorded in Chart XVII, for separate years.

The dominant fact about the record for the foods group is comparative stability — a stability over time and a stability as among size classes. Cyclical variation indeed is present; but its intensity is much less than in the metals group, it is more severe for the small size classes than for the entire group without being strikingly severe even for the smallest class, and it failed to bring a negative rate for the entire group even in 1932. Variation in rate from size class to size class is substantial, but is notably smaller than in metals or in manufacturing as a whole. Finally, failure of the rate for the income category to reveal a pronounced tendency to decline with increasing size suggests that no such wide dispersion in earning power among the corporations in the lower size classes exists here as in general manufacture (see below, Chapter XXV, for discussion of this concept of dispersion). The foods group reveals then a general approach to stability — by no means close, of course — which can tentatively be accounted for by the nature of the products and the form of organization. Industries engaged almost entirely in producing goods for consumers, and having comparatively simple plant and personnel structures and other organizational characteristics, are perhaps likely to show exceptional tendencies toward uniformity and stability.

VII

CHEMICAL INDUSTRIES

THE CHEMICALS GROUP, third in importance among the thirteen groups (as specified in 1935) of the manufacturing division, consists partly of producers of goods for use in further production, many of which are not highly durable; but it includes also, particularly in the petroleum refining and drug areas, many and some great producers of consumption goods. Moreover, various branches of chemical industry enjoy a growth impetus, characteristic of a rapidly developing technology, no longer notably effective in certain of the metal industries. The leading sub-group is oil refining, and this accounted for more than half the group total gross income in 1935 (Table XIV). In 1936 this sub-group was set apart as a new group, for which the full accounting detail published for other groups became available; and the remainder of the old chemicals group became a new chemicals group. Separate analyses for these 1936 groups appear below (page 99), but the main analysis, 1931–36, treats the chemicals group as one whole on the former basis. A poor second among the sub-groups is allied chemical substances, which includes drugs and soaps and similar products; and this sub-group, though less than half as important as oil refining, is more important than the three remaining sub-groups combined.[1]

The average gross income per corporation for the oil-refining sub-group is more than four times as great as that for chemicals proper, and more than ten times as great as that for the three remaining sub-groups. Petroleum therefore not only

[1] These comparisons, based on gross income, would probably not be seriously altered by using total receipts as a basis.

constitutes a very large share of the entire group, but some reason exists for believing that the petroleum companies are more likely than other chemical companies to fall in the high size classes (see below, page 99, for further evidence on this point). The peculiar cyclical and other conditions affecting the

TABLE XIV

COMPARATIVE IMPORTANCE OF SUB-GROUPS OF THE CHEMICALS MANUFACTURING GROUP IN 1935 *

	Number of corporations	Total gross income	Gross income per corporation
Sub-group			
Petroleum	853	4,177	4,897
Chemicals proper	631	695	1,101
Paints, etc.	1,098	391	356
Allied chemical substances	4,986	1,992	400
Fertilizers	401	173	431
Entire chemicals group	7,969	7,428	932

* Compiled and computed from *Statistics of Income for 1935, Part 2*, p. 36. Units: $1,000,000, for column 2; $1,000, for column 3.

petroleum industry are thus likely to distort our results, particularly for the higher size classes, in this group.

As might be expected, emphatic evidence exists of integration, at least backward toward raw material supplies, for this group; and, although this may apply predominantly in the petroleum industries, numerous other chemical companies are undoubtedly involved. Depletion charges for the group were 93 million dollars in 1935, against 128 millions for the manufacturing division as a whole and 204 millions for the mining and agriculture divisions.[2] Corresponding evidence as to integration forward, to the distributive area, is not available, although we may be sure that many of the petroleum and drug companies are to some extent thus integrated. Likewise, there is in the Treasury tax data no evidence as to the degree

[2] *Statistics of Income for 1935, Part 2*, pp. 40–42.

of horizontal combination. The integration which undoubtedly exists, plus further integration of which we have no evidence and whatever horizontal combination exists, impairs somewhat the precise significance of the group results which we shall examine: these results are not narrowly appropriate measures of strict manufacturing experience in the chemical field.

SIZE VARIATIONS IN RATE

A notably different relation between rate of return and size appears for the chemicals group than for other groups and divisions already studied (Chart xx). Although the characteristic tendency for rate to rise as size increases appears in the left portion of the chart, all of the curves decline in the right portion, and all but that for 1932 decline heavily. Other more or less striking peculiarities of the present chart include a comparatively sharp advance in rate from the lowest size class to the next, with a persisting advance at a slackening pace in the next larger classes up to the 1-million-dollar class (up to the class below this in 1935), and then a sharper advance (except for 1932) into the next higher class. A heavy drop appears in the 10-million-dollar class for most years. The total range in rate, among the various size classes in any one year, is generally less than for the metals group but more than for the foods group. The spread between the curves is distinctly less than for metals, but — except at the ends — greater than for foods. Numerous serious departures from parallelism appear, including several intersections among the curves. But the dominant feature of the chart is the general decline of the curves at the right — the existence of maximum points not far from 5 million dollars on the size scale.

The lack of parallelism is the next most significant feature of the chart, especially as it covers notable differences in general shape of the curves — outstanding instances of contrast involving the convergence of all curves at the right and the diverse courses of the 1934 and 1935 curves near the left, and of the 1931 and 1932 curves near the right. There can be little doubt that the chemicals group illustrates the possibility of far-from-uniform impact of the business cycle upon the various

CHART XX

RATE OF RETURN COMPARED WITH SIZE, FOR CHEMICALS GROUP *

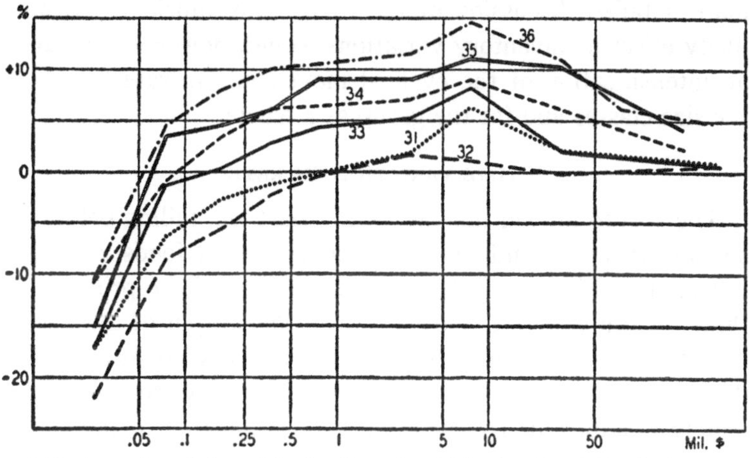

* Horizontal scale logarithmic. Data in Table xv. On old basis for 1936.

size classes. Once again the query is suggested whether the dominant position of certain sub-groups, having peculiar cyclical experience, may determine the rate-of-return results for particular size classes. Possibly the confused movements of the curves to the right of 10 million dollars may be due largely to the dominant position of the petroleum companies in those size classes (see below, page 99). No satisfactory evidence can be brought forward to test this hypothesis in each year, but an explanation which does not imply that mere size of a chemical company causes such strange shifts in rate of return is perhaps inevitable.

The role of inventories and price changes in the profit reckoning of the chemicals companies should not be overlooked, although inventories do not bulk extraordinarily large in this group, as compared with other manufacturing groups. That differences with respect to inventories may affect the apparent rates of return in various size classes differently, particularly if different types of chemical industry dominate different size classes, is not to be doubted (see below, Chapter XXII for more detailed discussion of the role of inventories). A more likely effect of inventory variations would, however, appear in an intensification of the cyclical movements in rate for all of the size classes and for the group as a whole.

TIME VARIATION IN RATE

The spread among the curves of Chart xx, falling below the spread for metals and generally above that for foods, probably reflects the different cyclical responsiveness of the products of these several groups of corporations. The output of the metals industries comprises mainly durable producers' goods and some durable consumption goods, that of the foods group includes mainly non-durable consumption goods, and that of the chemicals group is an uncertain mixture — durable and non-durable, producers' and consumption, goods. That the cyclical response in chemicals should be less than in metals, but more than in foods, is not at all surprising.

The annual changes in rate of return for selected size classes of the chemicals group show less uniformity between classes than has been observed in some earlier similar charts (Chart xxi). Only for 1931–32, 1934–35, and 1935–36 do the curves for both selected classes move by about equal amounts. Examination of other classes (Table xv) shows other and greater diversities. The curve for the entire group remains above zero in all years, and fluctuates very moderately. The forms of the curves, considering all six years together, differ significantly;

CHART XXI

TIME VARIATIONS IN RATE OF RETURN, FOR CHEMICALS GROUP AND SELECTED SIZE CLASSES *

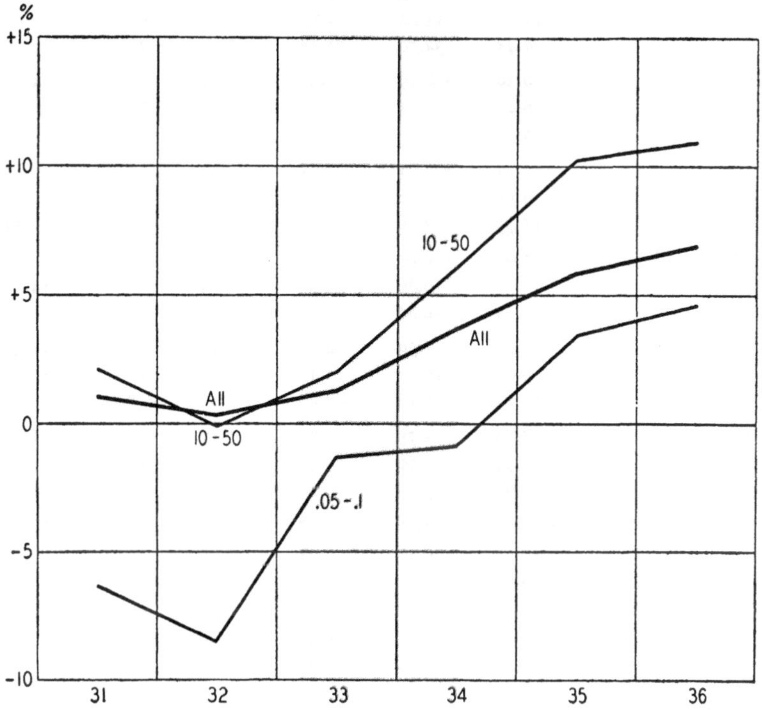

* Data in Table xv. On old basis for 1936.

and a similar statement holds for the size classes not shown in the chart. Again we infer that wide differences exist among the size classes, as to their responsiveness to the cycle.

PROFITABLE AND UNPROFITABLE CORPORATIONS

The divergence, from the experience of the two groups already studied and of the entire manufacturing division, which has thus far been noted in our analysis of the chemicals group, appears again in the relation between size and rate of return

TABLE XV

Rates of Return for Chemicals Group *

Class †	1931	1932	1933	1934	1935	1936 ‡
0	**−17.19**	**−22.05**	**−17.11**	**−10.81**	**−15.19**	**−10.50**
	13.77	13.24	12.22	19.67	16.28	17.24
	−40.44	*−32.39*	*−31.25*	*−36.20*	*−41.58*	*−38.15*
50	**−6.30**	**−8.49**	**−1.30**	**−.84**	**3.48**	**4.59**
	8.40	8.12	10.65	12.44	12.86	14.05
	−16.98	*−14.92*	*−10.16*	*−14.35*	*−12.12*	*−11.69*
100	**−2.73**	**−5.64**	**.37**	**3.52**	**4.55**	**8.14**
	9.33	9.64	10.11	12.15	12.35	14.83
	−15.43	*−12.79*	*−9.51*	*−10.24*	*−8.64*	*−9.86*
250	**−1.09**	**−2.19**	**2.92**	**6.19**	**6.15**	**10.11**
	9.72	9.86	10.40	14.24	13.33	14.11
	−11.15	*−9.86*	*−7.19*	*−10.84*	*−9.62*	*−6.48*
500	**−.11**	**−.39**	**4.38**	**6.46**	**9.09**	**10.59**
	9.69	10.32	11.32	13.28	17.32	15.80
	−10.15	*−7.58*	*−7.29*	*−7.64*	*−8.52*	*−9.95*
1,000	**1.89**	**1.75**	**5.31**	**7.17**	**9.12**	**11.56**
	10.95	10.50	9.48	11.05	12.44	13.74
	−10.05	*−7.13*	*−6.10*	*−7.62*	*−4.13*	*−8.09*
5,000	**6.36**	**1.18**	**8.32**	**9.02**	**11.15**	**14.71**
	14.11	10.40	13.85	12.65	14.83	18.29
	−5.21	*−8.42*	*−5.04*	*−9.01*	*−1.62*	*−2.02*
10,000	**2.06**	**−.11**	**2.01**	**6.07**	**10.29**	**10.98**
	9.07	5.82	9.93	11.17	13.42	12.14
	−7.51	*−6.93*	*−17.08*	*−4.43*	*−.05*	*−7.76*
50,000	**.92**	**.62**	**.60**	**2.26**	**4.17**	**6.17**
	5.08	3.63	2.38	6.33	6.27	7.41
	−1.88	*−1.37*	*−3.20*	*.06*	*.55*	*−1.11*
100,000	. . .	. . .	. . .	. . .	. . .	**4.89**
	. . .	. . .	. . .	. . .	. . .	5.32
	. . .	. . .	. . .	. . .	. . .	*−2.19*
Entire group . . .	**1.08**	**.38**	**1.28**	**3.73**	**5.88**	**6.93**
	6.60	4.88	4.38	9.22	9.00	8.00
	−3.24	*−2.87*	*−5.34*	*−1.37*	*−5.99*	*−4.87*

* Expressed in per cent; ratio of profit (or loss) after taxes to estimated average equity, as explained in text, p. 18. Figures in boldface type are for income and deficit categories of corporations combined, in ordinary type for the income category, in italics for the deficit category.

† Lower limit of class interval, in thousands of dollars of total assets. The 50,000-thousand-dollar class has no stated upper limit, 1931–35; the 100,000-thousand-dollar class has no stated upper limit, 1936.

‡ 1936 figures on old basis: combining the two new groups — petroleum and chemicals — of 1936 (see page 99).

for the income corporations (see Table xv). To be sure, a tendency for rate to decline with increasing size exists; but no careful examination of the table is needed to discover distinctions from groups previously studied. After the initial decline in the lower size classes, nearly all years show a slight upward general tendency as far up the size scale as the 5-million-dollar class, and then a severe decline follows for the highest class. Even more than Chart xx, this record suggests that strikingly different profit conditions prevail in different sections of the income scale, and raises once more the question whether the predominant type of chemical industry may change as we pass along the size scale. The freakish peaks and other sharp irregularities are another notable feature of the record of rates for income corporations. Whatever more complicated relationships may exist, data for the income category give no evidence of some simple relation between size and rate of return, or of any relation tolerably invariant under changing cyclical conditions.

The customary graphic comparison, based on six-year averages, between the income and deficit categories and both combined, appears in Chart xxii. The considerable irregularity of the income curve renders a somewhat irregular relation between the deficit curve and the combined curve inevitable. The movements of the income curve at its two ends also account for two aspects of the comparison between the deficit and combined curves: the deficit curve rises more steeply at the left end than the combined curve, and rises at the right end where the combined curve is declining. The closeness of the three curves at the right end is very striking, and suggests small dispersion in earning power among big chemicals companies (see below, page 330).

The corresponding tabular presentation, for each size class in all six years, yields little helpful guidance because of the striking irregularities in the particular classes (Table xv). We are left with the one sure conclusion that in the chemicals group the relation between size and rate of return, whatever its nature, is peculiarly subject to cyclical changes which — though not of great intensity — affect various size classes differently. But

CHART XXII

SIX-YEAR AVERAGE OF RATES OF RETURN COMPARED WITH SIZE, FOR CHEMICALS GROUP AND INCOME AND DEFICIT CATEGORIES *

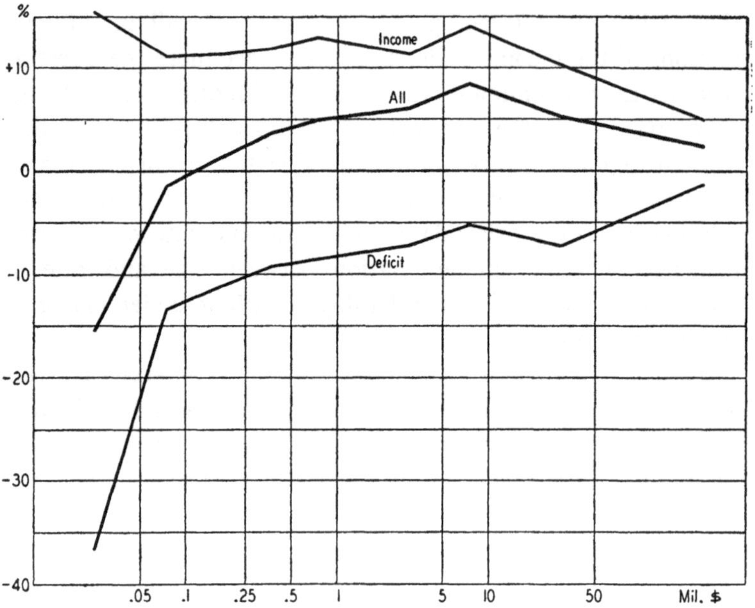

* Horizontal scale logarithmic. Data in Table B.

the comparisons of Chart XXII and similar comparisons from Table XV suggest further that — for both categories combined — the advance in rate of return with increasing size for the smaller size classes is accounted for by the deficit category, whereas the decline in rate of return with increasing size for the larger size classes is accounted for by the income category.[3]

[3] Even this contrast may be partly a reflection of dispersion, when the

PETROLEUM AND OTHER CHEMICALS, IN 1936

The chemicals group was split into two new groups, petroleum and chemicals, in 1936. The foregoing discussion for 1931–36 has treated the chemicals group, even for 1936, on the former basis; but we now compare the two new groups for the single year 1936.[4] The very great importance of petroleum, which was formerly a sub-group in chemicals, and the peculiarities of its rate-of-return record can not fail to cast some doubt upon the significance of the foregoing findings for the combined chemicals group.

Chart XXIII compares rate of return with size for the two new groups as classified in 1936, and as combined on the former basis. Remarkable relationships catch the eye. The new chemicals group — excluding petroleum — shows the steady advance of rate with increasing size, up to the very top of the size scale, noted generally in the metals and foods groups, the manufacturing division, and all divisions combined. But the petroleum curve, after violent advances in the second and third size classes, followed by a nearly flat course up to the 1-million-dollar class, and a further sharp advance to the next size class, drops violently in the 10-million-dollar class. Slight advances in the two top classes leave the rate lower than for any class except the two bottom size classes. It is petroleum,

latter is considered along with the rate for the combined categories. See below, Chapter XXV.

[4] The division here is much more nearly even than that observed in the case of the separation of motor vehicles from metals (see above, page 78). Here total assets for petroleum ran to above 1½ times total assets for the new chemicals group, in 1936. But striking differences appear in the specific size classes. Assets were greatly larger for chemicals in each size class up to 10-to-50-million dollars than for petroleum; but in the top classes petroleum exceeds chemicals — very greatly exceeds in the top class. Here then is an emphatic instance of "concentration in particular size classes" of a line of industry which was (until 1935) a sub-group of a manufacturing group.

then, which accounts for the downturn at the right observed in Chart xx. It is petroleum which yields the maximum points in the intermediate size classes of Chart xx. The chemicals industries as a group, after exclusion of petroleum, have no such characteristics.

CHART XXIII

RATE OF RETURN COMPARED WITH SIZE, FOR CHEMICALS GROUP AND ITS TWO SECTIONS, IN 1936 *

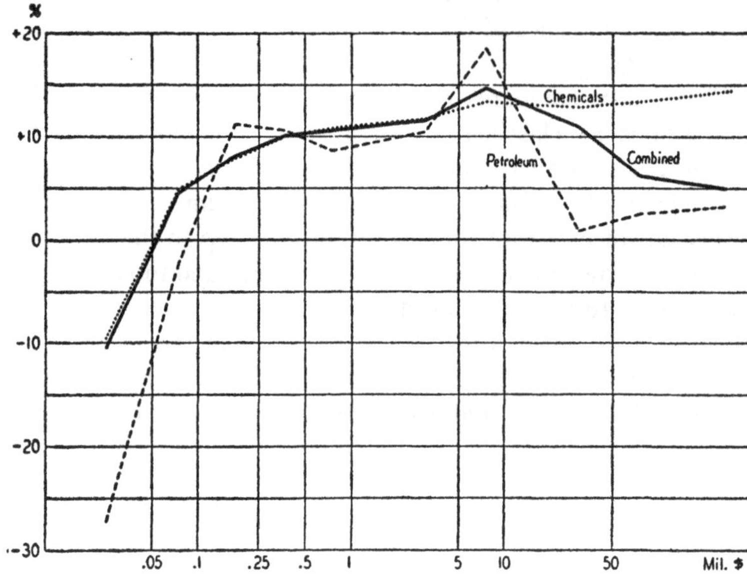

* Horizontal scale logarithmic. Data in Tables xv and C.

Minor diversities appear at various points in the chart. In general, the chemicals curve on the new basis is close to that on the old basis in the left portion of the chart — where the importance of petroleum is slight (see footnote 4, page 99). The much lower level reached by the petroleum curve than by the others in the smallest size classes may indicate the inability of non-integrated firms to earn a return in this industry; but the comparatively low positive rates in the top classes, where integration is probably extensive, implies a contradictory suggestion. We can at least conclude that petroleum stands apart as an industry in which the simple relationship between earning power and size, which we have observed in several charts, does not prevail. As these data are available only for 1936, no record of time variations can be presented; and the question of cyclical stability can not be explored.[5]

[5] Separate data for the income and deficit categories can indeed be calculated. They, with the rates for both categories combined, appear on page 409.

VIII

TEXTILES

THE TEXTILES GROUP — as constituted before 1936 — is the fourth in order of importance among the groups of the manufacturing division; and it is definitely smaller in business volume than the three groups already studied, having much less than one half the gross receipts of the metals group and only about two thirds the gross receipts of the chemicals group (Table IV). On the other hand, all of the remaining manufacturing groups run much smaller than textiles, the largest of them having considerably less than half the gross receipts of the textiles group; and the four groups — metals, foods, chemicals, and textiles — thus stand apart definitely as leaders in the manufacturing division. Together these four make up about three quarters of the division, in terms of gross receipts; and no one of the remaining groups accounts for as much as 5 per cent of the division's total gross receipts. In 1936, the textiles group was split into two new groups — textile fabrics (which we shall call textiles) and clothing — and these are discussed separately below (page 111). In the first sections of this chapter, however, 1936 data are treated on the former basis by combining the two new groups.

The manufacturing activities of the textiles group range over various stages of the fabricating process, from production of yarn and fabrics to making of clothing and other finished textile products ready for consumption. In this respect, the situation does not differ from that already noted in the metals and chemicals groups: in each we found producers of goods for further use in production and of goods for direct consumption. Most of the goods produced in the textiles group, whether for human consumption or industrial use, are of the sort generally considered as moderately durable. The textiles group differs, however, from the metals and chemicals groups in that here general knowledge tells us that integration of the various stages of production is much less common: makers of clothing, for

TABLE XVI

COMPARATIVE IMPORTANCE OF SUB-GROUPS OF THE TEXTILES MANUFACTURING GROUP IN 1935 *

	Number of corporations	Total gross income	Gross income per corporation
Sub-group			
Cotton goods	937	913	974
Woolen and worsted goods	566	552	976
Silk and rayon goods	879	518	589
Carpets	176	168	957
Other textiles	3,770	1,222	324
Clothing	8,010	1,939	242
Knit goods	1,318	594	451
Entire textiles group	15,656	5,907	377

* Compiled and computed from *Statistics of Income for 1935, Part 2*, p. 35. Units: $1,000,000, for column 2; $1,000, for column 3.

example, are generally unlikely to be engaged also in making yarn or cloth. The various sub-groups in the textiles group are therefore presumably much more homogeneous than certain of those in metals and chemicals — an outstanding contrast in this respect is between the clothing sub-group here and the motor-vehicles sub-group in metals or the oil-refining sub-group in chemicals.

Descriptions of the sub-groups appear in the stubs of Table XVI. Three clearly include producers of finished textile products, mainly for direct consumption: carpets and floor coverings, clothing, and knit goods. Three are clearly made up of producers of intermediate products: cotton, wool, and silk and rayon. The miscellaneous ("not elsewhere specified") sub-group includes a considerable range of enterprises of both sorts. As to importance (Column 2 of Table XVI), clothing leads; and its gross income in 1935 fell only slightly short of the combined gross income of the three sub-groups producing fabrics and other materials.

There is no such wide range in average size of corporation among these sub-groups as we found in groups studied earlier. The average is smallest for clothing; but the highest average, that for wool, is only about four times as great (Column 3 of Table XVI). There is no emphatic evidence here of any likelihood that a particular sub-group will dominate any particular size class in the entire textiles group. Our study below of the rates of return for various size classes need not therefore be qualified by the probability that certain size classes have a seriously different dominant type of textile activity than do other size classes (but see page 111).

SIZE VARIATION IN RATE

The two most striking characteristics of the comparison between size and rate of return for the textiles group (Chart XXIV) are the remarkable gap between the pair of curves for 1931 and 1932 and the sheaf of curves for 1933–36, and the very considerable approach to parallelism particularly within the two sets of curves. That the 1931 curve runs so closely at the same level as the 1932 curve throughout its course is emphatic indication that the full effect of the great depression had already been realized by 1931 in this industry. This may reflect largely the necessity of taking severe inventory losses, in an industry peculiarly exposed to price fluctuations, early in the depression; it may also reflect, but probably to a much smaller degree, the tendency for recovery to begin somewhat earlier in 1932 for the textiles industries, the end products of which are mainly consumption goods. That the 1933 curve should be mainly at a higher level than those of 1934 and 1935 may again be due largely to inventory and price conditions — the extraordinary advance in commodity prices in the early summer of 1933 coupled with a rapid accumulation of inventory may well have been a dominating factor in the year's profit record. On the other hand, we might think of the 1934 curve

CHART XXIV

RATE OF RETURN COMPARED WITH SIZE, FOR TEXTILES GROUP *

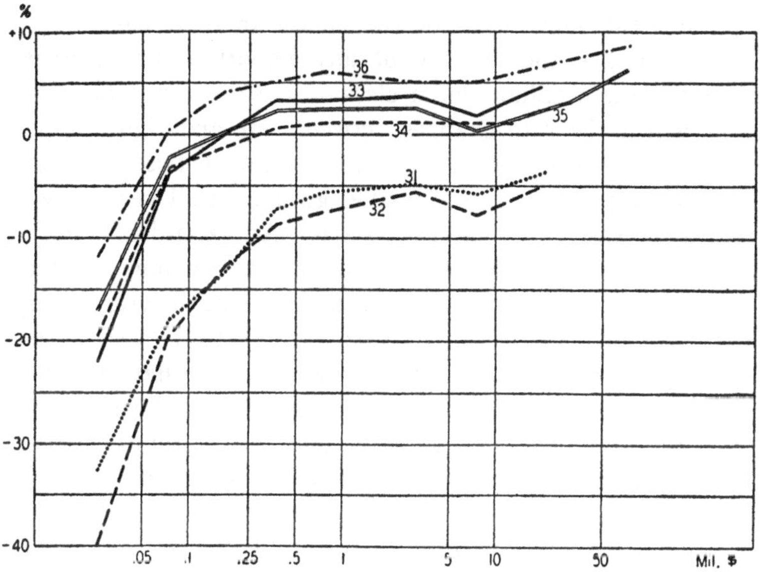

* Horizontal scale logarithmic. Data in Table XVII. On old basis for 1936.

as probably depressed below the 1933 curve because of the textile strikes of 1934, but this reasoning could not be advanced in explaining why the 1935 curve runs moderately below that of 1933.

The approach to parellelism between the 1931 and 1932 curves, and among the 1933–36 curves, is remarkable. Although there are some actual intersections among the curves, the points for any one size class — in the two groups of curves,

1931–32 and 1933–36 — are so closely clustered that the appearance of parallelism is impressive. When all six curves are considered together, the evidence of parallelism is less striking: the spread between the depression curves 1931–32 and the recovery curves 1933–36 becomes narrower toward the right of the chart. This is a clear indication that cyclical depression brought a heavier burden to the lower size classes than to the higher.

The great smoothness of the curves in their course from left to right — the absence of any important irregularities, except in the 5-million-dollar class — and the very large range over which the rate changes between left and right support strongly the view that a persistent relation between size and rate of return exists in the textiles group. In all years rate of return increases with increasing size. An exception appears: at or near 5 million dollars most of the curves show a general decline; but this is reversed at once, and (for all years except 1934) the increase of rate with size extends to the very largest textile corporations.[1] The tendency toward a flat or nearly horizontal movement in the middle range of size, which has been observed in similar charts for certain other groups, appears also for the textiles group particularly in the years 1933–36. But here the range of size covered by the flat movement is rather narrow, and the advance in rate at the left end of the curves continues fairly far along the size scale for most of the curves.

TIME VARIATION IN RATE

As already noted, the time variations in rate of return for this group are somewhat peculiar. They are recorded, for the entire group and two selected size classes, in Chart xxv.[2] The

[1] Unfortunately, necessary combinations of certain of the highest size classes for certain years, in the Treasury tabulations, damage the completeness of the picture at the right in this chart.

[2] Because of the incomplete data for the highest size classes, a somewhat

CHART XXV

TIME VARIATIONS IN RATE OF RETURN, FOR TEXTILES GROUP AND SELECTED SIZE CLASSES *

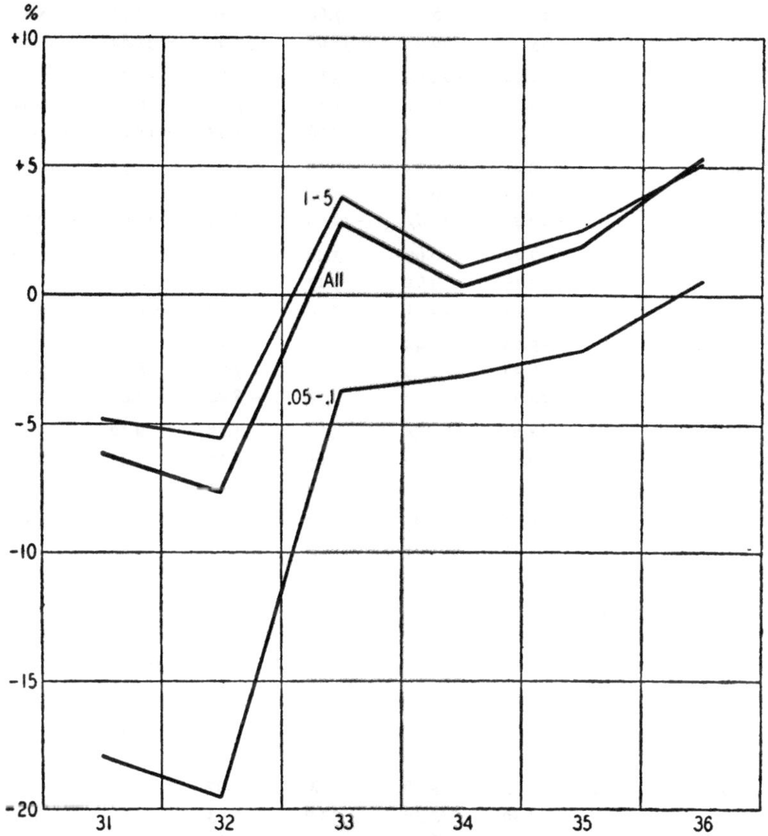

* Data in Table XVII. On old basis for 1936.

1931–32 decline in each curve is mild, probably for reasons already suggested. In all three curves, the 1932–33 advance is remarkably sharp, and the subsequent movement is either

different selection of the "large" size class is used here from that followed in previous similar charts.

TABLE XVII

Rates of Return for Textiles Group *

Class †	1931	1932	1933	1934	1935	1936 ‡
0	**−32.60**	**−40.08**	**−22.01**	**−19.58**	**−17.03**	**−11.86**
	11.93	6.37	7.64	6.86	7.72	8.80
	−55.55	*−49.68*	*−38.98*	*−37.45*	*−37.84*	*−31.83*
50	**−17.90**	**−19.54**	**−3.68**	**−3.13**	**−2.17**	**.56**
	8.70	6.92	7.82	7.37	8.12	9.09
	−32.33	*−26.14*	*−17.06*	*−15.53*	*−15.94*	*−15.77*
100	**−13.25**	**−12.62**	**.18**	**−1.22**	**.31**	**4.21**
	7.18	6.44	8.97	8.32	8.52	10.44
	−26.48	*−18.67*	*−12.63*	*−12.33*	*−12.63*	*−10.85*
250	**−7.22**	**−8.69**	**3.40**	**.69**	**2.36**	**5.09**
	7.35	6.61	9.17	8.64	8.86	9.82
	−15.12	*−14.31*	*−7.42*	*−9.86*	*−9.17*	*−9.31*
500	**−5.64**	**−7.45**	**3.38**	**1.10**	**2.49**	**6.18**
	6.38	5.19	8.62	7.64	8.32	9.76
	−12.63	*−12.30*	*−6.79*	*−8.42*	*−7.83*	*−7.48*
1,000	**−4.81**	**−5.54**	**3.80**	**1.15**	**2.52**	**5.13**
	6.39	4.70	7.65	6.71	7.40	8.16
	−9.76	*−8.92*	*−5.14*	*−5.92*	*−5.43*	*−6.15*
5,000	**−5.78**	**−7.87**	**1.80**	...	**.41**	**5.13**
	3.91	3.64	7.22	...	5.54	8.21
	−9.26	*−10.25*	*−6.85*	*−5.47*	*−6.02*	*−5.92*
10,000	...	...	...	...	**3.20**	**7.36**
	...	...	...	5.64	7.13	8.37
	...	...	*−4.11*	...	*−5.16*	*−2.45*
50,000	...	...	...	...	**6.35**	**8.65**
	...	...	...	...	6.35	8.65
	...	...	...	...	...	...
Classes grouped §	**−3.73**	**−5.16**	**4.59**	**1.07**	...	...
	3.58	3.39	7.66	5.93	...	...
	−7.90	*−8.15*	...	*−5.62*	...	...
Entire group ...	**−6.10**	**−7.64**	**2.80**	**.38**	**1.95**	**5.36**
	5.46	4.54	7.86	6.64	7.34	8.65
	−11.92	*−11.71*	*−7.94*	*−7.91*	*−7.74*	*−8.55*

* Expressed in per cent; ratio of profit (or loss) after taxes to estimated average equity, as explained in text, p. 18. Figures in boldface type are for income and deficit categories of corporations combined, in ordinary type for the income category, in italics for the deficit category.

† Lower limit of class interval, in thousands of dollars of total assets. The

very slowly upward or irregular. Both the group curve and that for the large class show actual declines in 1934. For the textiles group, as a whole and in nearly all of its size classes (see Table XVII, for other classes), the worst of the depression and also the bulk of the recovery came earlier than in most other branches of industry.

The intensity of fluctuation here is not greatly different from that for the metals group. The group curve here ranges over 13 points, and the curve of the lowest size class (Table XVII) ranges over 28 points. Despite the fact that many of the textile companies produce consumption goods, the industry is about as responsive — in its profits aspect — to the business cycle as is the most general example of a group composed of capital-goods industries. Again, the suggested explanation runs in terms of price and the vital role of commodity inventories. Many of these enterprises are engaged not only in a manufacturing operation, but also unavoidably in a speculative carrying of commodities dangerously subject to violent price fluctuations. That these commodities were exposed to extraordinarily adverse world-market conditions during the depression, and that they were especially influenced by domestic official recovery policies particularly in 1933, are well-known facts.

PROFITABLE AND UNPROFITABLE CORPORATIONS

The relation of size to rate of return for the income corporations of the textiles group (Table XVII) again admits of con-

---

50,000-thousand-dollar class has no stated upper limit, 1931–35; the 100,000-thousand-dollar class has no items, but defines the upper limit of the 50,000-thousand-dollar class in 1936.

‡ 1936 figures on old basis: combining the two new groups — textiles and clothing — of 1936 (see page 111).

§ High size classes combined, to conceal a single corporation. Where such combination applies to only income or deficit category, other category is shown separately in the specific classes, but joint figure for both categories is shown only in "grouped" row.

sideration in two time intervals, 1931–32 and 1933–36. The two depression years show an unmistakable tendency for the rate to decrease as size increases, although rates for the lower size classes ran much higher in 1931 than in 1932. In 1933–36,

CHART XXVI

SIX-YEAR AVERAGE OF RATES OF RETURN COMPARED WITH SIZE, FOR TEXTILES GROUP AND INCOME AND DEFICIT CATEGORIES *

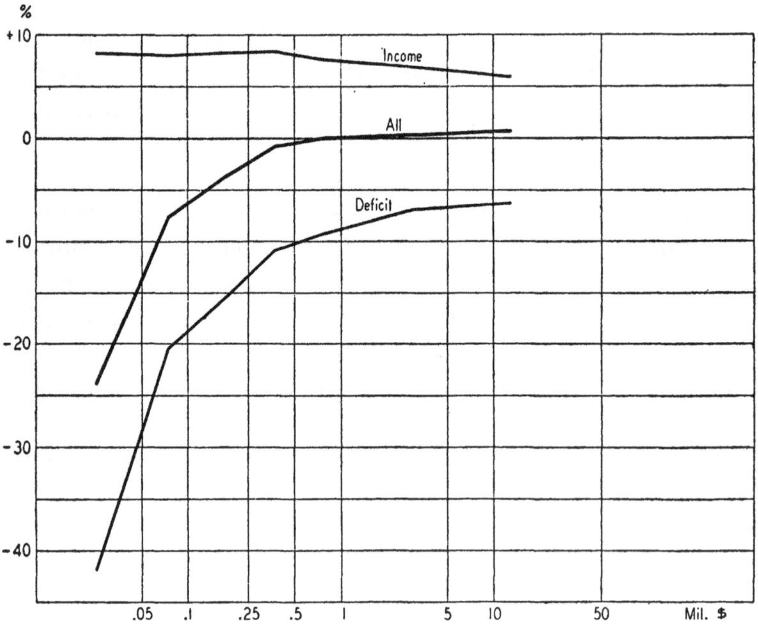

* Horizontal scale logarithmic. Data in Table B.

however, rates rise to a maximum in intermediate size classes and are irregularly lower for the high size classes. For these years, rate of return was maximum for intermediate size classes, and distinctly lower for the smaller corporations and for the larger corporations. Coupled with the moderate decline at the right ends of several of the curves of Chart XXIV, this suggests that the most profitable size for textile enterprises lies in the middle portion of the size scale. Although this evidence is by no means strong enough to be conclusive, it suggests that failure of extensive integration and large-scale organization to appear widely in the textiles industry may imply a recognition that too great size brings a reduction in earnings.

The relation between the income and deficit categories, and both combined, is presented on the basis of six-year averages in Chart XXVI. The slight curvature of the income curve accounts for the greater approach to rectilinearity in the middle size range of the deficit curve than in the combined curve. Rate of return increases more steadily with size for the deficit category than for both categories combined. It is not to be expected that these findings will be borne out in each separate year, because of the difference between 1931–32 and 1933–36 noted above with respect to the income category. Graphic comparisons for separate years are not presented, but the tabulated rates for all size classes shown in Table XVII bring out the moderate diversity among the years in the relation between the deficit category and the combined categories.

CLOTHING AND FABRICS IN 1936

Separate tabulation of two new groups — textile mill products (herein called textiles), and clothing and apparel — in 1936 supplies the basis of a helpful breakdown of the results discussed above.[3] The relation of rate of return to size for each group and for both combined is recorded in Chart XXVII. The curve for textile mill products is closely similar — in shape and

[3] The comparative importance of the two new groups, based on total assets in 1936, is: textiles, 3.77 billion dollars; clothing, .96. In terms of gross receipts, it is: textiles, 4.41 billion dollars; clothing, 2.24. A striking difference appears with respect to concentration in large companies: 2.19 billion dollars of total assets are held by companies having over 10 million dollars of assets each in the textiles group, against only 67 million dollars in the clothing group. The clothing group is strikingly one of small enterprise.

level — to that for the two groups combined — that is, on the basis discussed above. But the curve for clothing runs higher throughout its range (it is not available for top size classes — see footnote 3, page 111), and very considerably higher in the central range of the size scale. Moreover, the final movement

CHART XXVII

Rate of Return Compared with Size, for Textiles Group and its Two Sections, in 1936 *

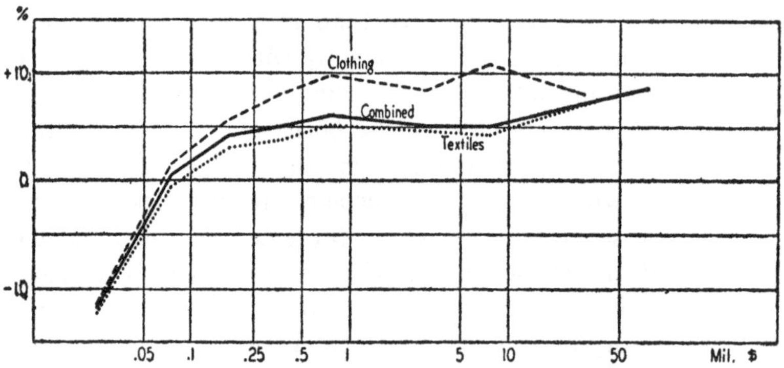

* Horizontal scale logarithmic. Data in Tables XVII and C.

of the clothing curve is definitely downward, whereas that of the textiles curve is as clearly upward. That the departure of the clothing curve from the combined curve is greater than that of the textiles curve from the combined curve, except at or near the left end, is a technical result of the comparatively greater concentration in the textiles group — its weight in the combined group rises as size increases.[4]

We are at a loss to know whether the disparity between clothing and textiles, as revealed in Chart XXVII, is characteristic or is merely peculiar to 1936. It is at least possible that, in industries for which inventory and price changes may be

[4] The detailed schedule of rates for income and deficit categories and both combined for the two 1936 groups is given on page 409.

highly important, the developments of such a year as 1936 might have led to an extraordinary difference in profit rate as between clothing and textile fabrics. The lack of concentration in the clothing group further suggests that, because a relatively small portion of the industry falls in the size classes above 500 thousand dollars, rates for the higher size classes may rest upon a large chance element in the clothing group. On the other hand, the high size classes in textiles include an important share of the industry, and such rates are correspondingly more dependable. In any case, until similar data for other years are available, great significance can not be attached to the indicated differences between clothing and textiles.

IX

PRINTING AND PAPER GROUPS

As NOTED IN THE PREVIOUS CHAPTER, all of the remaining groups in the manufacturing division are small in comparison with the four leading groups already discussed. Discussion of these remaining groups, although likely to bring out significant peculiarities and differences, will therefore be on a more restricted plan; and treatment of each in full detail and in a separate chapter does not appear necessary.

The present chapter treats together the two groups printing and publishing, and paper and pulp. No unmistakable logical necessity leads to joint consideration of these two groups. The logical reason might appear in the fact that one group provides the principal basic material of the other, but an equally strong argument might be adduced for treating paper and pulp along with the forest-products group, on the basis of like origin of principal raw materials. Suffice it to say that the selection of groups for joint treatment in this chapter, and likewise in the next two chapters, does not carry any decisive implications as to comparability of such groups.

The Treasury tabulations afford no basis for breaking either group — printing and publishing, or pulp and paper — into subgroups. Only the broad over-all tabulations are available for each group. We are aware from general knowledge that printing and publishing must cover a considerable range of somewhat diverse activities, principally newspaper publishing, periodical publishing, book manufacturing, job printing, and possible combinations among these. But no classifications of data are available in *Statistics of Income* to indicate the relative importance of these within the group, or to indicate the average size of corporation in each sub-group. Likewise for the other group, paper and pulp, we are aware that paper manufacture is somewhat specialized into newsprint, book paper, writing paper, wrapping paper, and paperboard, and other lines of paper, with various combinations in the case of particular

CHART XXVIII

RATE OF RETURN COMPARED WITH SIZE, FOR PRINTING GROUP *

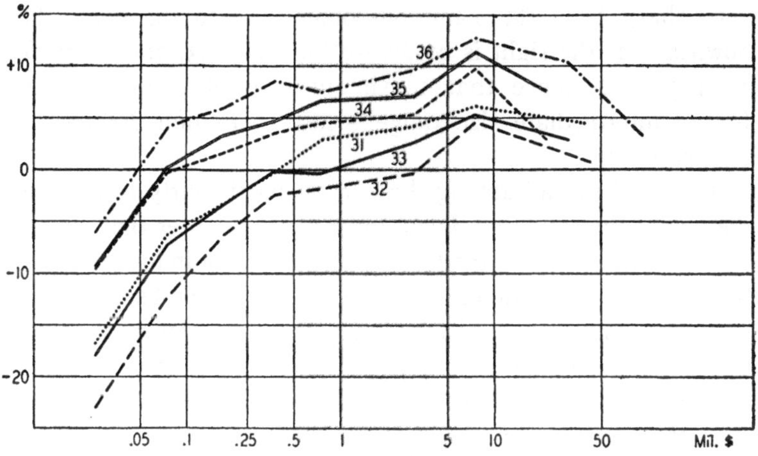

* Horizontal scale logarithmic. Data in Table XVIII.

corporations. But again we have no detailed data, and our analysis of the group figures must proceed without reference to the make-up of the group.

PRINTING AND PUBLISHING

For the printing and publishing group (herein called printing), rate of return increases as size increases up to a size range somewhat below the top, in all years and with only negligible irregularity (Chart XXVIII). Although there are few intersections among the curves, the somewhat exceptional course of the 1933 and 1936 curves at the left, and the 1934 curve at the right, detracts from an appearance of parallelism. With exceptions in 1933 and 1936, all years show a progressive advance toward the right, until the 5-million-dollar class is reached. These curves have no such horizontal drift in the middle size range as we have found in certain other groups, but they do show an emphatic downturn at the right end. The advance of rate with size, while less steep in the middle than at the left end, continues to about 10 million dollars; and is very sharp from the 1-million-dollar class to the next. The downturn at the right is moderate for 1931–33, and sharp for 1934–36. Evidence that maximum rate of return appears for an intermediate size range — near 5 million dollars — is unmistakable.

The total spread among the curves, particularly in the middle and at the right end, is not great; and we infer that cyclical responsiveness is only moderate in the printing industries. This is borne out by the annual record for the group and selected size classes (Chart XXIX); although, for the lower size class shown, the maximum range of variation is about 17 points. We have here a more stable industry than any heretofore examined; even the foods group showed a somewhat greater responsiveness to the cycle.

In all years, even in the deep depression of 1932, the high size class shown in the chart recorded an average profit; and even in 1932 the 1-million-dollar class (Table XVIII) barely failed to yield a profit. Although much of the output in these industries is in the form of consumption goods, a substantial fraction — particularly in the job-printing branch and in the advertising section of the newspaper and periodical branches — is without doubt made up of goods for use in further productive operations. That an industry with these characteristics should show so little effect of the business cycle is therefore somewhat surprising.

No separate graphic record is presented of the relation be-

CHART XXIX

TIME VARIATIONS IN RATE OF RETURN, FOR PRINTING GROUP AND SELECTED SIZE CLASSES *

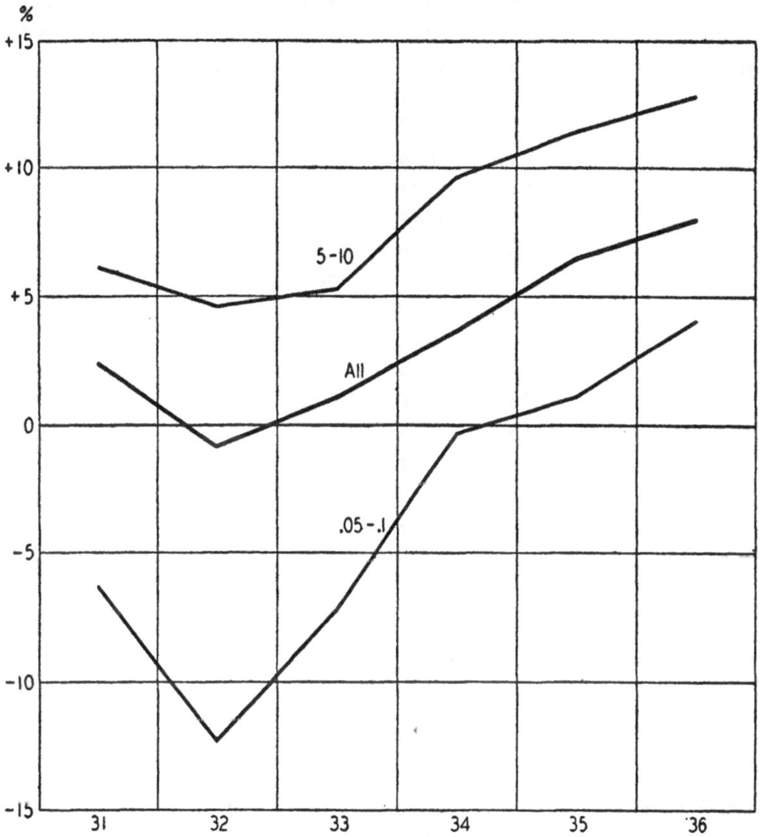

* Data in Table xviii.

tween size and rate of return for the income corporations of the group. Except for some decline from the lowest size class to the next class, and for some irregularities in particular classes, the upward-to-the-right tendency would be unmistakable if such a chart were shown (see Table xviii). This again

TABLE XVIII

Rates of Return for Printing Group *

Class †	1931	1932	1933	1934	1935	1936
0	**−16.81**	**−23.05**	**−18.01**	**−9.62**	**−9.50**	**−6.10**
	10.66	9.80	7.75	10.35	10.48	12.92
	−35.60	*−29.43*	*−25.86*	*−24.55*	*−28.90*	*−26.68*
50	**−6.30**	**−12.31**	**−7.26**	**−.30**	**1.13**	**4.11**
	8.03	6.33	6.42	8.85	9.59	10.84
	−19.13	*−17.57*	*−13.80*	*−12.20*	*−13.49*	*−11.10*
100	**−3.31**	**−6.26**	**−3.37**	**1.62**	**3.32**	**5.99**
	8.49	7.34	6.88	9.39	10.69	11.49
	−15.29	*−12.99*	*−10.52*	*−11.33*	*−12.27*	*−12.56*
250	**−.20**	**−2.40**	**−.07**	**3.59**	**4.66**	**8.61**
	9.23	7.23	7.19	9.34	10.72	13.70
	−14.15	*−9.43*	*−8.38*	*−10.36*	*−12.59*	*−15.65*
500	**2.87**	**−1.84**	**−.32**	**4.48**	**6.64**	**7.51**
	10.04	8.70	7.09	9.39	10.34	11.70
	−10.51	*−11.19*	*−11.54*	*−16.97*	*−16.17*	*−41.15*
1,000	**4.22**	**−.33**	**2.64**	**5.30**	**7.13**	**9.65**
	9.54	7.45	7.70	9.03	10.58	11.27
	−4.93	*−6.60*	*−5.02*	*−10.06*	*−11.39*	*−14.03*
5,000	**6.17**	**4.62**	**5.30**	**9.67**	**11.41**	**12.82**
	11.33	9.53	9.06	11.33	13.18	13.73
	−12.49	*−4.94*	*−4.50*	*−5.39*	*−14.59*	*−3.89*
10,000	. . .	. . .	. . .	. . .	. . .	**10.37**
	. . .	. . .	. . .	. . .	. . .	11.04
	. . .	*−6.60*	*−.29*	. . .	. . .	*−2.95*
Classes grouped ‡	**4.54**	**.77**	**2.86**	**2.89**	**7.62**	**3.35**
	11.28	2.58	3.46	9.45	10.84	3.35
	−.13	. . .	. . .	*−9.86*	*.60*	. . .
Entire group . . .	**2.41**	**−.83**	**1.09**	**3.68**	**6.46**	**7.98**
	10.30	4.98	5.46	9.62	11.05	10.55
	−6.61	*−10.56*	*−8.06*	*−11.72*	*−8.34*	*−16.08*

* Expressed in per cent; ratio of profit (or loss) after taxes to estimated average equity, as explained in text, p. 18. Figures in boldface type are for income and deficit categories of corporations combined, in ordinary type for the income category, in italics for the deficit category.

† Lower limit of class interval, in thousands of dollars of total assets. The 50,000-thousand-dollar class has no stated upper limit, 1931–35; the 100,000-thousand-dollar class has no stated upper limit, 1936; items of both these classes are covered in "Classes grouped."

‡ High size classes combined, to conceal a single corporation. Where such combination applies to only income category, other category is shown separately in the specific classes, but joint figure for both categories is shown only in "grouped" row.

distinguishes the printing group from several groups previously studied; here, even for the income corporations alone, rate of return increases as size increases. Detailed comparisons between the income and deficit categories and both combined are facilitated by Table XVIII (see also below, footnote 1, page 121).

PAPER AND PULP

The sheaf of curves representing the relation between size and rate of return for the paper and pulp group shows considerable lack of uniformity in the relation between rate of

CHART XXX

RATE OF RETURN COMPARED WITH SIZE, FOR PAPER GROUP *

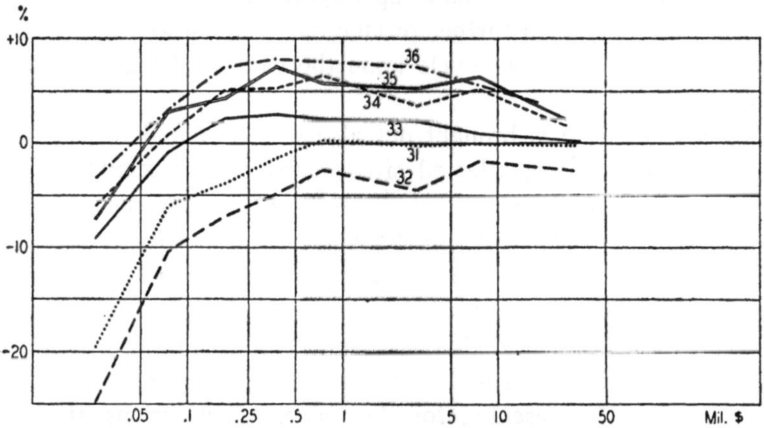

* Horizontal scale logarithmic. Data in Table XIX.

return and size (Chart XXX). That a tendency for rate of return to increase with size exists is manifest at and near the left end of the curves. Except for 1931–32, however, the tendency does not persist above fairly low size classes. The general drift of the 1933–36 curves to the right of 250 or 500 thousand dollars is slightly downward. Even for 1932, there is little net advance to the right of 1 million dollars. Moreover, the total range of variation in rate for any one of the four years 1933–36, even if we do not ignore the lowest size class, is smaller than in the case of any manufacturing group heretofore studied.

The case is somewhat different for the two depression years, 1931 and 1932. Curves for these two years not only advance to a point much farther to the right, but the total range of variation in rate is much wider, than for the 1933–36 curves. This disparity, along with the considerable irregularities in and numerous intersections between the 1934 and 1935 curves, robs the chart of any close approach to parallelism among the curves. The inescapable conclusion is that, though the cyclical responsiveness of the entire paper and pulp group — despite the fact that the group is made up largely of producers of basic materials for use in further production — is not great, the differential effects of the cycle upon the various size classes are notable.

This situation is brought out also in the annual record for the group and two selected size classes (Chart XXXI). The range of variation over time differs notably among the curves; and the curves also differ in shape, particularly with respect to comparative intensity of movement for 1931–32, 1932–33, and 1935–36. For 1935–36, the lower class shown in the chart records an almost negligible change. Maximum range of variation runs somewhat smaller than in the printing group.

No chart is presented for the income corporations of this group; but these data, along with similar data for the deficit category and both categories combined, appear in Table XIX. If the income curves were plotted, they would show, despite remarkable irregularities for particular size classes, a moderate downward-to-the-right tendency in most years. In this sense, the paper and pulp group does not differ from most other groups already studied: for the income corporations, rate of return declines gradually as size increases. For several years,

CHART XXXI

TIME VARIATIONS IN RATE OF RETURN, FOR PAPER GROUP AND SELECTED SIZE CLASSES *

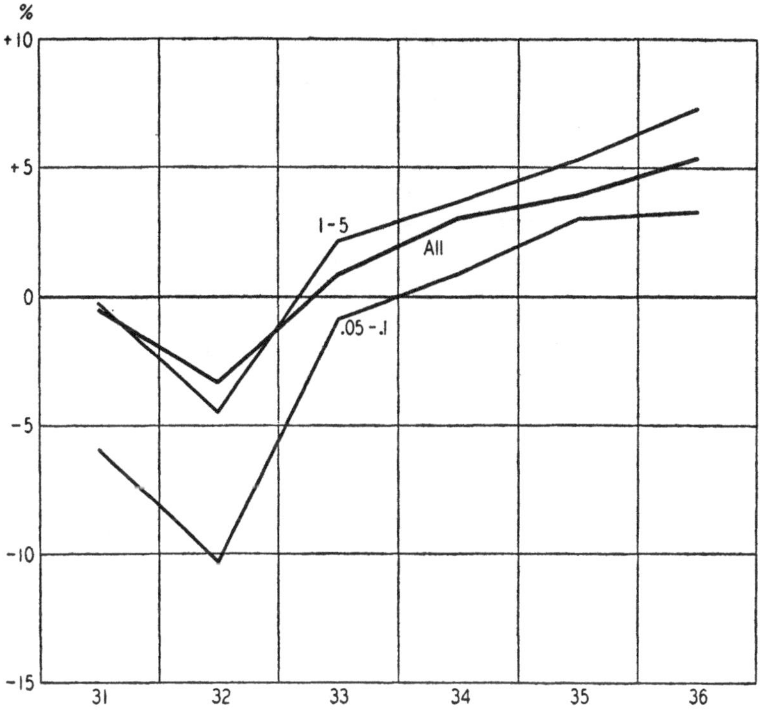

* Data in Table XIX.

however, the advance in rate from the lowest to moderate size classes — for the income category — is so systematic that it can not be called an irregularity.[1]

These two groups — printing and paper — reveal unmistakable evidence that rate of return reaches a maximum in some

[1] For this group, as well as for printing, the combinations of high size classes in certain years limits the size-range of the six-year averages of rates by the necessary combination of high size classes. These rates appear in Appendix, Table B.

TABLE XIX

Rates of Return for Paper Group *

Class †	1931	1932	1933	1934	1935	1936
0	**−19.57**	**−24.85**	**−9.17**	**−5.96**	**−7.21**	**−3.28**
	10.32	6.53	8.54	8.45	10.14	11.72
	−44.22	*−29.52*	*−23.50*	*−21.47*	*−30.13*	*−31.84*
50	**−5.95**	**−10.29**	**−.85**	**.88**	**3.05**	**3.30**
	7.10	6.18	7.54	10.49	10.29	10.66
	−14.09	*−16.37*	*−10.88*	*−16.23*	*−12.37*	*−14.24*
100	**−3.84**	**−6.98**	**2.42**	**5.24**	**4.36**	**7.28**
	7.88	6.79	10.19	12.07	12.96	12.54
	−15.44	*−11.84*	*−9.03*	*−9.69*	*−16.39*	*−11.57*
250	**−1.41**	**−4.83**	**2.80**	**5.32**	**7.34**	**8.08**
	8.59	6.15	9.86	11.28	12.29	11.16
	−9.49	*−10.51*	*−8.80*	*−9.09*	*−6.77*	*−4.95*
500	**.30**	**−2.56**	**2.30**	**6.53**	**5.76**	**7.84**
	8.87	6.15	8.26	12.31	11.19	12.55
	−8.48	*−7.86*	*−7.33*	*−7.93*	*−11.87*	*−9.23*
1,000	**−.21**	**−4.47**	**2.17**	**3.67**	**5.34**	**7.32**
	7.37	5.41	7.63	8.96	9.31	9.89
	−7.12	*−8.78*	*−5.74*	*−6.74*	*−5.51*	*−6.52*
5,000	**−.03**	**−1.74**	**.99**	**5.25**	**6.40**	...
	5.35	4.68	6.83	8.89	8.77	8.94
	−5.86	*−5.44*	*−5.53*	*−2.79*	*−3.54*	...
10,000	...	...	...	...	...	**5.18**
	...	...	...	...	...	7.01
	−4.20	*−4.26*	*−2.10*	*−2.86*	*−4.07*	*−5.37*
50,000	...	...	...	...	...	...
	...	...	...	...	...	...
	−.77	*−2.65*	*−1.65*	*−1.01*	*−1.95*	...
Classes grouped ‡	**−.33**	**−2.72**	**.10**	**1.67**	**2.31**	**3.96**
	3.50	2.09	4.95	5.71	6.58	2.34
	...	...	...	...	...	*−1.66*
Entire group ...	**−.49**	**−3.32**	**.83**	**3.06**	**3.98**	**5.38**
	4.90	4.34	6.76	8.11	8.53	8.11
	−4.25	*−5.28*	*−3.35*	*−3.53*	*−4.40*	*−4.65*

* Expressed in per cent; ratio of profit (or loss) after taxes to estimated average equity, as explained in text, p. 18. Figures in boldface type are for income and deficit categories of corporations combined, in ordinary type for the income category, in italics for the deficit category.

† Lower limit of class interval, in thousands of dollars of total assets. The

intermediate section of the size scale, and then declines with further increase in size. Fragmentary evidence of this sort has appeared in study of certain other groups, but printing and paper seem to afford the most clearly systematic cases so far examined. That these two groups represent mainly very different types of operation and organization only renders the finding more striking. The further observation that cyclical variations, while irregularly affecting the rate of return in various size classes of both groups, are comparatively mild also takes on special significance when the nature of the two industries and their products are considered.

50,000-thousand-dollar class has no stated upper limit, 1931–35; the 100,000-thousand-dollar class has no stated upper limit, 1936, and items of this class are covered in "Classes grouped."

‡ High size classes combined, to conceal a single corporation. Where such combination applies to only income or deficit category, other category is shown separately in the specific classes, but joint figure for both categories is shown only in "grouped" row.

X

FOREST PRODUCTS; STONE, CLAY, AND GLASS PRODUCTS

THE TWO GROUPS treated in this chapter — forest products; and stone, clay, and glass products (herein called stone) — are related in that their output is destined mainly for the construction industry. Except for the portion of these products used in residential building — generally regarded as consumption — and perhaps some portion going into certain forms of public construction, the output is largely destined for use by producers. Both groups are made up in important degree, then, of manufacturers of durable producers' goods.

The published tabulations give limited statistical summaries for two sub-groups within the forest products group, but no such details for the very heterogeneous stone group.[1] The two sub-groups in the forest products group are of nearly equal importance, and the average size per corporation does not differ widely between the sub-groups. We have therefore no reason for supposing that either sub-group will dominate any particular size class in the entire group. The unavailability of sub-group data prevents the making of even this rough test for the stone group; but general knowledge suggests that some types of activity presumably included in this group — for example, cement manufacture — may be dominated by very large

[1] In 1935, the sub-group data of the forest products group show:

	Number of corporations	Gross income: Total	Gross income: Average per corporation
Sawmills and planing mills	3,072	619	202
Other forest products	3,771	699	185

From *Statistics of Income for 1935, Part 2*, p. 35. Total in millions of dollars; average in thousands of dollars.

companies, whereas others — for example, brick manufacture — may be represented generally by small or moderate-sized companies. But this evidence is not sufficiently precise to warrant any sure inference that certain size classes of the entire group are specialized with respect to specific lines of activity.

FOREST PRODUCTS

This industry might fairly be described as resistant to recovery: only two curves of Chart XXXII pass above the zero

CHART XXXII

RATE OF RETURN COMPARED WITH SIZE, FOR FOREST PRODUCTS GROUP *

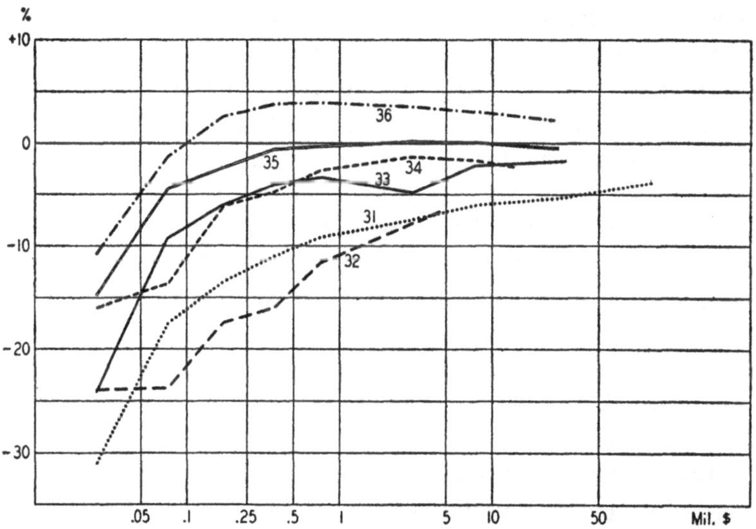

* Horizontal scale logarithmic. Data in Table XX.

line; and even one of those, that for 1935, runs only slightly above zero for the two size classes just below the highest shown. All rates 1931–34 fall below zero, some of them very far below zero. The lumber industry, in addition to long-standing unfavorable conditions within the industry, has suffered during the years since 1932 from the lagging recovery in the construction industry; and even in 1936 it enjoyed only moderate average rates of return.

In addition to the generally low level of the curves of Chart XXXII, the wide spread among the curves is notable, except near the right end; it reflects the severe effects of the cyclical situation in building and in general business. For all classes to the left of one million dollars, the spread is great; and even for the one-million-dollar class, the spread is wider than that observed in similar charts for several other manufacturing groups. To the right of five million dollars, absence of the 1932 curve precludes satisfactory comparisons. The approach to parallelism among the curves — even ignoring the peculiar flat movement at the left end of the 1932 curve and some irregularities in the 1934 curve — is only slight: the convergence near the right end is very remarkable. The exhibit suggests that the cyclical impact is far from uniform upon the various size classes, with a much greater intensity at the left than at the right. The drift of the curves, even if the lowest size class is ignored, is moderately upward-to-the-right; although 1934–36 curves show a clear decline following a maximum at some intermediate size. In the 1931 curve, advance in rate is well sustained to the right end of the curve. Rate of return in this group generally increases as size increases; but the relationship is not persistent over time, and is not clearly manifest for large size classes.

The annual record, shown in Chart XXXIII, brings out the intensity of cyclical variation. Except for the low size class shown, the range of fluctuation is large in comparison with corresponding curves for most groups already studied. Even for this low size class, the range is very wide; and a striking fact is the secondary drop in 1934. For the lowest size class (Table XX), the range is somewhat less wide than for the lowest class of the metals group; and the odd fact that the 1931 rate is much below the 1932 rate emphasizes a peculiar timing,

CHART XXXIII

TIME VARIATIONS IN RATE OF RETURN, FOR FOREST PRODUCTS GROUP AND SELECTED SIZE CLASSES *

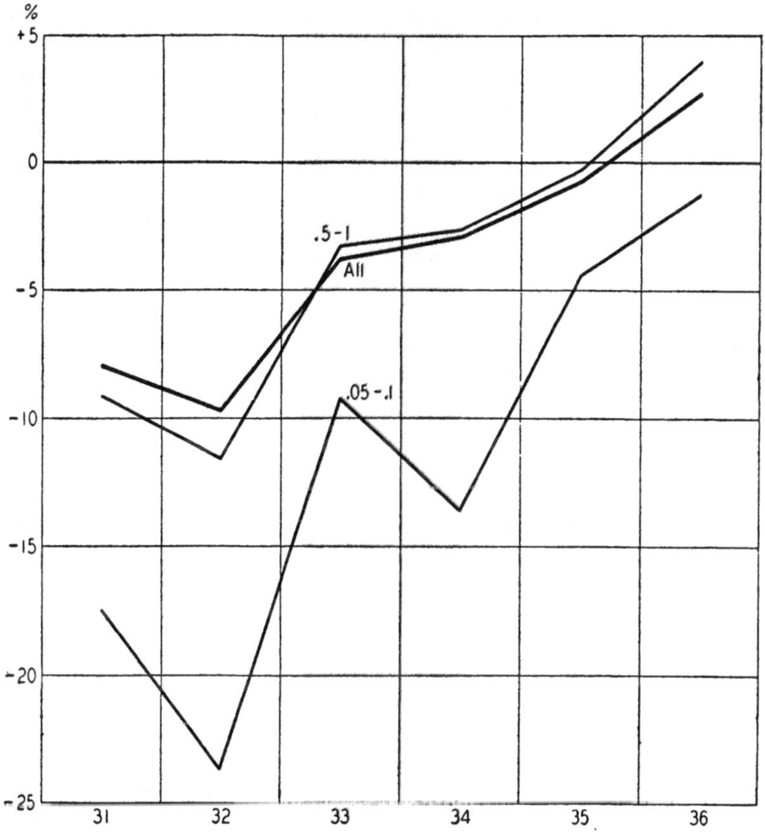

* Data in Table xx.

as well as the severe intensity of movement, of the cycle in this class. The "high" size class curve shown in the chart actually pertains to a fairly low point on the size scale — missing data in certain years prevented use of a higher class in the chart.

TABLE XX

Rates of Return for Forest Products Group *

Class †	1931	1932	1933	1934	1935	1936
0	**−30.99**	**−23.93**	**−24.01**	**−15.96**	**−14.84**	**−10.76**
	9.71	5.65	7.78	7.79	9.67	11.50
	−45.89	*−25.71*	*−35.86*	*−28.52*	*−33.57*	*−36.48*
50	**−17.47**	**−23.67**	**−9.23**	**−13.59**	**−4.41**	**−1.28**
	7.48	6.70	7.44	6.14	7.17	9.31
	−26.10	*−26.73*	*−17.26*	*−16.93*	*−15.58*	*−18.26*
100	**−13.46**	**−17.32**	**−6.12**	**−6.17**	**−2.38**	**2.60**
	6.14	5.74	6.11	6.13	7.61	10.07
	−19.64	*−19.37*	*−12.43*	*−13.91*	*−12.41*	*−10.77*
250	**−11.09**	**−15.85**	**−3.96**	**−4.73**	**−.60**	**3.82**
	4.62	4.13	5.12	6.80	7.09	8.90
	−14.98	*−17.75*	*−8.32*	*−11.66*	*−8.25*	*−7.64*
500	**−9.17**	**−11.59**	**−3.27**	**−2.63**	**−.30**	**3.96**
	4.58	3.56	5.97	5.70	6.70	8.75
	−13.03	*−13.40*	*−7.17*	*−6.62*	*−6.38*	*−7.05*
1,000	**−7.53**	. . .	**−4.87**	**−1.37**	**.11**	**3.59**
	4.97	. . .	4.05	5.39	5.34	7.11
	−10.07	*−9.32*	*−8.48*	*−5.20*	*−4.53*	*−6.02*
5,000	**−6.12**	. . .	**−2.23**	**−1.66**	**.07**	**3.06**
	2.85	. . .	2.15	2.73	3.25	7.86
	−7.55	*−7.28*	*−4.23*	*−4.08*	*−2.81*	*−3.73*
10,000	**−5.23**	. . .	. . .	. . .	. . .	. . .
	1.41	. . .	. . .	. . .	. . .	. . .
	−6.10	*−6.78*	. . .	. . .	*−3.69*	*−2.16*
50,000	**−3.85**	. . .	. . .	. . .	. . .	. . .
	. . .	. . .	. . .	. . .	. . .	. . .
	−3.85	*−3.26*	. . .	. . .	. . .	. . .
Classes grouped ‡	. . .	**−6.67**	**−1.72**	**−2.27**	**−.49**	**2.19**
	. . .	6.00	5.10	3.09	2.52	4.08
	. . .	. . .	*−2.53*	*−3.24*	. . .	. . .
Entire group . . .	**−7.94**	**−9.70**	**−3.77**	**−2.92**	**−.74**	**2.74**
	4.51	5.18	4.57	5.00	4.85	6.95
	−10.16	*−10.50*	*−6.46*	*−6.32*	*−6.07*	*−6.27*

* Expressed in per cent; ratio of profit (or loss) after taxes to estimated average equity, as explained in text, p. 18. Figures in boldface type are for income and deficit categories of corporations combined, in ordinary type for the income category, in italics for the deficit category.

† Lower limit of class interval, in thousands of dollars of total assets. The

cyclical impact upon this industry is much smaller than that observed in other manufacturing groups. The peculiar inversion of the rates for the lowest class, with 1934–36 rates falling below those of 1931 and 1933, can not be explained without knowledge as to the make-up of the lowest size class and as to the costs and other factors influencing profits of those companies.

LEATHER AND PRODUCTS

Except for the violent advance of all curves at their left ends and for 1931–32 at their right ends, the advance of rate of return with increase in size is only moderate and fairly irregular for the leather group (Chart XXXVIII). Again, fully detailed examination of the relationship is obstructed by incompleteness of data for the higher size classes: separate rates for the five-million-dollar class are available for only two years. That some advance of rate with size exists, even with the lowest class ignored, is apparent; but the irregular and gradual upward course of the curves in the middle of the size scale suggests that size has only moderate effect upon rate of return for an important fraction of this industry.

The fact that the group contains both producers of final goods — chiefly boots and shoes — and producers of basic materials renders significance of the group figures uncertain. Though we have no clear evidence (see above, page 135) that one of these types of activity tends to dominate particular size classes, this possibility must be recognized; and it is perhaps

† Lower limit of class interval, in thousands of dollars of total assets. The 50,000-thousand-dollar class has no stated upper limit, 1931–35; the 100,000-thousand-dollar class has no stated upper limit, 1936, and items of this class are covered in "Classes grouped."

‡ High size classes combined, to conceal a single corporation. Where such combination applies to only deficit category, other category is shown separately in the specific classes, but joint figure for both categories is shown only in "grouped" row.

more important because we know in general that integration between shoe production and leather production is rare.

The general spread among the curves is very wide, and severe cyclical effects on these industries are therefore indicated. As in the case of textiles (page 104), the curves of this

CHART XXXVIII

RATE OF RETURN COMPARED WITH SIZE, FOR LEATHER GROUP *

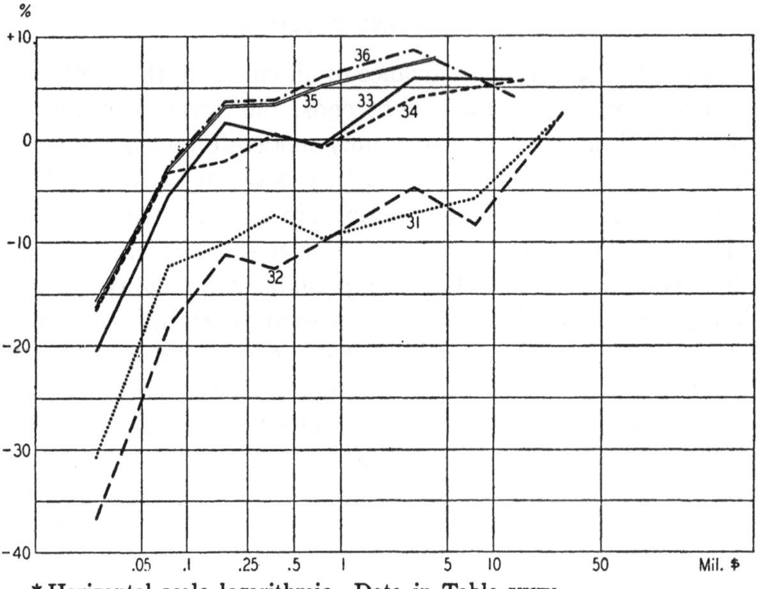

* Horizontal scale logarithmic. Data in Table XXIV.

chart run in two sets: 1931 and 1932 curves about equally low, and 1933–36 curves clustering together at a much higher level. The cyclical experience in leather products was in this respect similar to that in textiles, and probably for the same chief reasons. Examination of year-to-year fluctuations in rate (boldface data of Table XXIV, by rows, and Chart XLI) shows sharp variations for 1931–33, and generally moderate changes for 1933–36. We may remark that the tanning branch of the group

TABLE XXIV

Rates of Return for Leather Group *

Class †	1931	1932	1933	1934	1935	1936
0	**−30.79**	**−36.82**	**−20.48**	**−16.64**	**−15.80**	**−16.29**
	13.20	7.80	12.65	8.02	8.41	8.56
	−51.30	*−45.39*	*−38.99*	*−31.56*	*−32.87*	*−45.67*
50	**−12.28**	**−18.19**	**−5.57**	**−3.17**	**−2.85**	**−2.54**
	10.85	9.06	9.73	9.10	9.46	8.89
	−26.17	*−28.08*	*−19.84*	*−16.52*	*−16.95*	*−20.33*
100	**−10.09**	**−11.18**	**1.68**	**−2.00**	**3.22**	**3.73**
	9.26	7.21	11.02	8.49	10.56	10.50
	−19.95	*−18.82*	*−12.16*	*−13.60*	*−10.35*	*−10.63*
250	**−7.37**	**−12.44**	**.46**	**.64**	**3.53**	**3.84**
	7.77	7.10	8.93	8.26	9.07	9.03
	−14.80	*−18.32*	*−10.78*	*−10.84*	*−8.90*	*−9.80*
500	**−9.58**	**−10.03**	**−.45**	**−.77**	**5.24**	**6.15**
	4.97	5.84	9.24	9.76	10.36	10.65
	−14.40	*−14.30*	*−12.97*	*−10.42*	*−5.08*	*−6.78*
1,000	**−7.14**	**−4.68**	**5.97**	**4.16**	...	**8.74**
	8.96	8.24	10.78	8.09	9.68	10.18
	−14.22	*−11.83*	*−5.92*	*−9.81*	...	*−21.29*
5,000	**−5.79**	**−8.31**	...	...	...	...
	5.24	5.98	11.63	3.73	6.12	7.23
	−10.16	*−11.97*	...	...	...	...
10,000	...	...	...	...	...	...
	...	...	...	...	...	...
	−11.91	*−8.32*	...	...	...	...
Classes grouped ‡	**1.69**	**2.57**	**5.72**	**5.71**	**7.82**	**4.91**
	8.95	6.12	8.00	9.11	8.47	7.28
	...	...	*−8.24*	*−4.57*	*−.89*	*−24.09*
Entire group	**−3.32**	**−6.26**	**3.69**	**2.82**	**6.14**	**5.20**
	8.46	6.56	9.51	8.08	8.80	8.64
	−8.34	*−14.41*	*−10.90*	*−10.63*	*−8.11*	*−16.62*

* Expressed in per cent; ratio of profit (or loss) after taxes to estimated average equity, as explained in text, p. 18. Figures in boldface type are for income and deficit categories of corporations combined, in ordinary type for the income category, in italics for the deficit category.

† Lower limit of class interval, in thousands of dollars of total assets. The 50,000-thousand-dollar class has no stated upper limit, 1931–35; the 100,000-thousand-dollar class has no items, but defines the upper limit of the 50,000-thousand-dollar class in 1936. All items in the 50,000-thousand-dollar class are covered in "Classes grouped."

‡ High size classes combined, to conceal a single corporation. Where such combination applies to only income or deficit category, other category is shown separately in the specific classes, but joint figure for both categories is shown only in "grouped" row.

is especially subject to inventory fluctuations, and this factor may have influenced greatly the cyclical record for the group (see below, Chapter XXII).

The irregularities in the curves are fairly numerous, and there are several intersections. No close approach to parellelism

CHART XXXIX

RATE OF RETURN COMPARED WITH SIZE, FOR RUBBER GROUP *

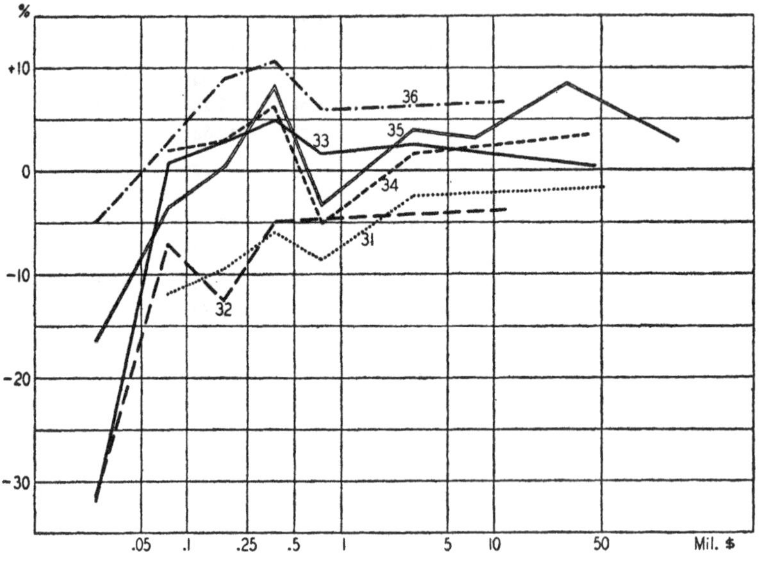

* Horizontal scale logarithmic. Data in Table xxv.

exists, and the cyclical impact upon the various size classes appears by no means uniform. Table xxiv also supports this.

RUBBER

Incompleteness of the size-class record here is so serious in all years except 1935 that few satisfactory inferences can be drawn from movements near the right ends of the curves (Chart xxxix). Not only are rates for several higher size-classes entirely missing, and some higher size classes grouped

TABLE XXV

Rates of Return for Rubber Group *

Class †	1931	1932	1933	1934	1935	1936
0	...	**−31.50**	**−32.00**	...	**−16.52**	**−4.98**
	20.91	16.67	7.98	25.42	14.27	15.05
	...	*−46.10*	*−105.09*	...	*−36.62*	*−24.69*
50	**−11.92**	**−7.04**	**.75**	**1.92**	**−3.58**	**2.77**
	8.28	12.89	15.46	12.93	10.93	13.45
	−33.64	*−13.49*	*−12.56*	*−17.11*	*−19.43*	*−14.95*
100	**−9.54**	**−12.49**	**2.83**	**2.95**	**.41**	**8.91**
	10.34	10.17	10.46	10.09	11.77	13.15
	−15.61	*−18.33*	*−7.48*	*−8.11*	*−16.04*	*−7.80*
250	**−5.95**	**−4.95**	**4.98**	**6.35**	**8.24**	**10.73**
	9.17	5.51	10.92	11.30	10.27	15.07
	−28.09	*−10.56*	*−7.58*	*−4.47*	*−3.29*	*−3.17*
500	**−8.59**	...	**1.56**	**−6.08**	**−3.28**	**5.96**
	7.00	...	10.29	5.61	9.08	11.94
	−8.40	*−10.71*	*−5.74*	*−16.87*	*−23.72*	*−11.96*
1,000	**−2.50**	**−2.40**	**2.50**	**1.67**	**3.84**	...
	7.30	4.28	6.92	5.95	9.31	12.55
	−9.66	*−5.36*	*−13.75*	*−6.51*	*−8.08*	...
5,000	...	...	...	...	**3.06**	...
	...	...	...	2.12	5.55	7.63
	−10.36	*−7.31*	*−2.44*	...	*−2.45*	...
10,000	...	...	...	...	**8.42**	...
	...	...	3.77	...	12.77	9.35
	...	*−11.88*	...	...	*−2.22*	...
50,000	...	...	...	...	**2.67**	...
	...	...	...	...	2.67	...
	...	*−3.33*	...	...	...	...
Classes grouped ‡	**−1.72**	**−3.85**	**.29**	**3.37**	...	...
	3.49	1.49	1.27	2.03	...	...
	−5.01	...	*−.85*	*4.62*	...	...
Entire group	**−2.39**	**−4.08**	**.59**	**2.75**	**3.75**	**6.69**
	4.13	1.85	3.13	3.22	5.58	7.35
	−6.78	*−5.52*	*−2.05*	*2.26*	*−6.62*	*−6.91*

* Expressed in per cent; ratio of profit (or loss) after taxes to estimated average equity, as explained in text, p. 18. Figures in boldface type are for income and deficit categories of corporations combined, in ordinary type for the income category, in italics for the deficit category. Equity for zero (lowest)

into broader classes; but two years, 1931 and 1934, can not be shown for the lowest size class. In those years, the equity had completely disappeared in this size class; and the negative value of the equity rendered the calculated "rate of return" meaningless. No doubt there were some rubber corporations in the lowest size class which had positive equity in 1931 and 1934, and therefore significant rates of return; but rate figures for the class as a whole are meaningless in both years. In both cases, of course, aggregate "profits" of the class were heavily negative.

Irregularities in the curves, so far as the curves can be shown, are numerous and sharp. A very slight tendency for rate of return to increase with size, even when the abbreviated record for the lowest class is ignored, can be inferred from the chart; but irregularities are so great that this tendency is too uncertain to be conclusive. One of the most consistent movements — appearing in every year, except for 1932 which has no separate data in the 500-thousand-dollar class — is the decline, generally sharp, from the 250-thousand-dollar class to the next higher class.

The cyclical variations are wide and non-uniform. The spread among the curves is large, and frequent intersections and differences of direction destroy all appearance of parallelism. Cyclical impact upon this group is severe, and is far from uniform among different size classes. Detailed evidence on this point, for the various size classes, appears in Table xxv.

---

class is negative in 1931 and 1934 in deficit category — hence, no rate figures. This also makes equity negative for combined categories, hence no rate figures.

† Lower limit of class interval, in thousands of dollars of total assets. The 50,000-thousand-dollar class has no stated upper limit, 1931–35; the 100,000-thousand-dollar class has no stated upper limit, 1936, and items of this class are covered in "Classes grouped."

‡ High size classes combined, to conceal a single corporation. Where such combination applies to only income or deficit category, other category is shown separately in the specific classes, but joint figure for both categories is shown only in "grouped" row.

MISCELLANEOUS MANUFACTURING

Rate of return increases with size, with remarkable consistency from class to class and with surprising uniformity among the different years, in the miscellaneous group (Chart XL). A slight flattening tendency appears in the middle range

CHART XL

Rate of Return Compared with Size, for Miscellaneous Manufacturing Group *

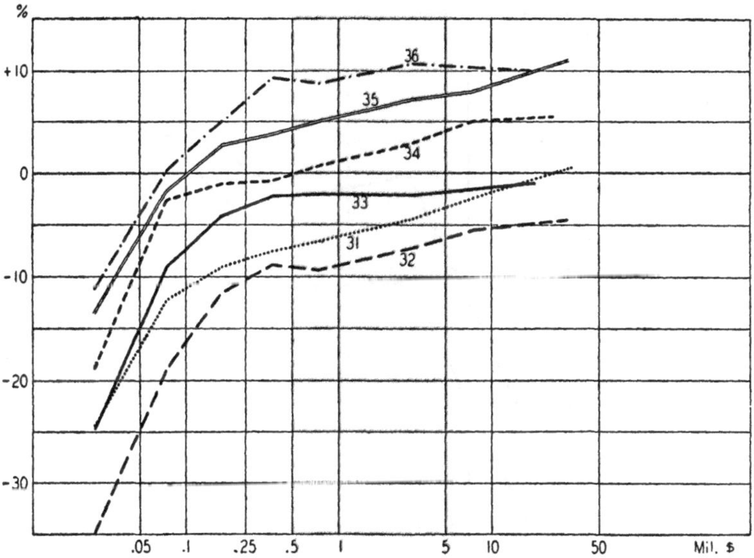

* Horizontal scale logarithmic. Data in Table XXVI.

of the size scale for three years, but the range over which it develops is not broad: the advance in rate is fairly persistent throughout the course of all curves except that for 1936. These curves — in their general shape, their spacing with respect to each other, and their tolerable approach to parallelism — seem remarkably similar to those for the manufacturing division as a whole (Chart IX). This is the more surprising as the name, miscellaneous, of this group does not imply that the industries included are a scattered sampling from all branches of manufacturing — rather, the group comprises a limited number of fairly specialized lines.

CHART XLI

TIME VARIATIONS IN RATE OF RETURN, FOR LEATHER GROUP AND SELECTED SIZE CLASSES *

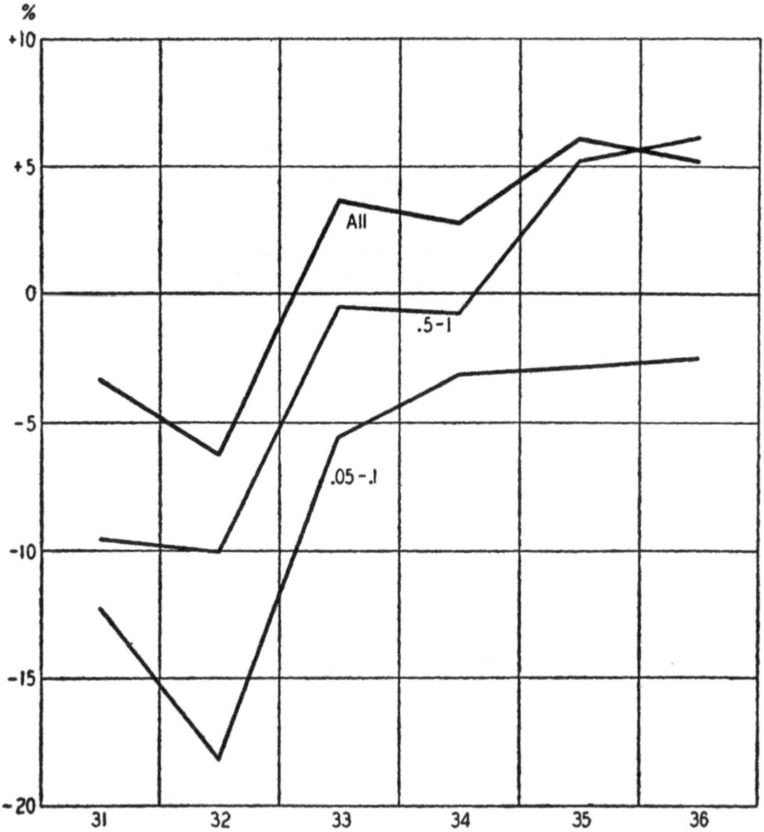

* Data in Table XXIV.

CHART XLII

TIME VARIATIONS IN RATE OF RETURN, FOR MISCELLANEOUS MANUFACTURING GROUP AND SELECTED SIZE CLASSES *

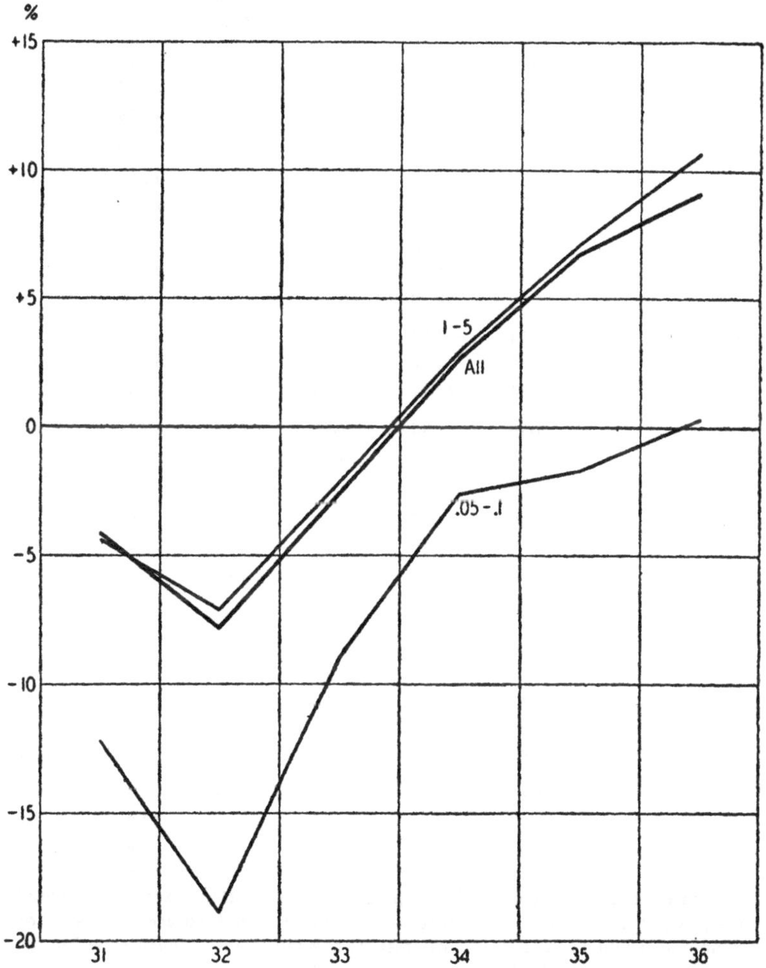

* Data in Table XXVI.

TABLE XXVI

Rates of Return for Miscellaneous Manufacturing Group *

Class †	1931	1932	1933	1934	1935	1936
0	**−24.49**	**−34.92**	**−24.77**	**−18.81**	**−13.52**	**−11.20**
	11.94	9.60	9.36	10.15	10.99	12.30
	−38.99	*−42.60*	*−34.85*	*−36.32*	*−32.72*	*−37.98*
50	**−12.20**	**−18.90**	**−9.00**	**−2.60**	**−1.69**	**.34**
	10.19	6.59	7.89	9.28	11.25	12.56
	−22.44	*−24.39*	*−18.68*	*−12.87*	*−12.69*	*−16.55*
100	**−9.01**	**−11.51**	**−4.11**	**−.97**	**2.74**	**5.04**
	7.49	7.38	8.70	9.52	11.44	12.17
	−18.10	*−16.22*	*−12.41*	*−11.60*	*−10.85*	*−13.38*
250	**−7.44**	**−8.82**	**−2.20**	**−.70**	**3.79**	**9.39**
	6.47	4.87	7.29	8.95	12.40	15.94
	−15.80	*−12.36*	*−8.11*	*−8.55*	*−9.54*	*−7.16*
500	**−6.54**	**−9.27**	**−2.08**	**.75**	**4.98**	**8.79**
	6.72	4.82	7.23	10.45	13.19	14.65
	−12.71	*−13.52*	*−9.54*	*−10.41*	*−8.42*	*−9.48*
1,000	**−4.39**	**−7.14**	**−2.16**	**2.95**	**7.12**	**10.67**
	8.16	7.88	6.64	8.38	12.54	14.14
	−11.88	*−11.13*	*−7.32*	*−3.90*	*−6.69*	*−6.74*
5,000	**−2.40**	**−5.41**	...	**5.05**	**7.92**	...
	16.16	6.56	11.17	13.73	13.25	9.99
	−10.34	*−11.03*	...	*−4.95*	*−2.69*	...
10,000	...	...	...	...	...	...
	...	...	...	...	...	...
	...	...	*−12.86*	*−6.10*	*−1.17*	...
Classes grouped ‡	**.54**	**−4.58**	**−1.05**	**5.44**	**10.97**	**10.01**
	14.95	4.64	8.80	10.84	14.68	12.17
	−10.68	*−10.32*	*−11.00*	...	...	*−2.65*
Entire group	**−4.13**	**−7.85**	**−2.58**	**2.71**	**6.77**	**9.10**
	11.21	5.74	8.30	10.67	13.24	12.80
	−13.44	*−13.06*	*−11.20*	*−7.77*	*−7.24*	*−8.59*

* Expressed in per cent; ratio of profit (or loss) after taxes to estimated average equity, as explained in text, p. 18. Figures in boldface type are for income and deficit categories of corporations combined, in ordinary type for the income category, in italics for the deficit category.

† Lower limit of class interval, in thousands of dollars of total assets. The 50,000-thousand-dollar class has no stated upper limit, 1931–35; the 100,000-thousand-dollar class has no stated upper limit, 1936; items of both these classes are covered in "Classes grouped."

‡ High size classes combined, to conceal a single corporation. Where such combination applies to only income or deficit category, other category is shown separately in the specific classes, but joint figure for both categories is shown only in "grouped" row.

The cyclical impact upon these industries is heavy, though not quite so severe as in some of the large capital-goods groups. The spread among the curves is very wide, and varies little through most of the size scale. The approach to parallelism is truly remarkable, few groups studied have presented any more nearly parallel movement in general and from class to class. The cyclical impact is highly uniform upon the various size classes of this group.

Details of the cyclical movement can be traced from Table XXVI. Chart XLII shows the historical record for the entire group and two selected size classes, and this should be compared with the corresponding record for the leather group (Chart XLI). The group curve of Chart XLII shows a severe cyclical fluctuation, with a sharp drop in 1932, and successive advances in the next four years. In the case of leather, the 1933–36 movement is irregular; and the net change from 1933 to 1936 is small. In the miscellaneous group, total range of fluctuation for the group as a whole amounts to nearly 17 points; and this is wide, though narrower than that of groups peculiarly responsive to the cycle. A somewhat similar movement, at about the same levels, appears for the middle-range size class (one million dollars) shown in the chart; and a not closely parallel movement, at much lower levels, appears for the low size class shown.

XII

SUMMARY OF FINDINGS FOR MANUFACTURING

FOLLOWING THE GENERAL TREATMENT of rates of return for the entire manufacturing division in Chapter IV, the various manufacturing groups have been examined separately in Chapters V–XI. This detailed study of the groups supplies at least a partial answer to an important question raised in Chapter IV — whether the findings for the entire manufacturing division may be illusory because the division is made up of different lines of manufacturing some of which may show very different relations between rate and size, or different cyclical variations. Before summarizing the evidence on the groups, certain additional points concerning the size classes in the division and the various groups should be examined.

DISTRIBUTION OF ASSETS

We have already presented evidence in Chapter III as to the distribution of the assets of the manufacturing division among its groups, and in Chapter IV as to the portion of the assets of each size class of the division which appears in the income category. Attention can now be turned to another distribution of assets, that among the size classes (both income and deficit categories combined). Table XXVII presents such a distribution for the entire division in each of the six years. The most striking fact is that nearly half the total is in the highest class in each of the first three years, and over two thirds in 1934–36 (combining classes above 50 million dollars in 1936). A second striking fact is that the distribution changes very little from year to year; a surprising stability marks the ratios, in spite of the wide cyclical changes of the period. The single important change over time is that already noted in the highest class; and it is explained largely by the abandonment of consolidated returns in 1934. The removal of the consolidated-return privilege shifted assets down the size scale; each formerly large consolidated corporation was replaced, in the

TABLE XXVII

PER CENT OF THE TOTAL ASSETS OF THE MANUFACTURING DIVISION FALLING IN EACH SIZE CLASS

Class *	1931	1932	1933	1934	1935	1936
0	1.2	1.3	1.4	1.5	1.6	1.5
50	1.5	1.5	1.5	1.7	1.7	1.6
100	3.5	3.5	3.5	4.0	4.0	3.9
250	3.9	3.9	3.9	4.5	4.5	4.4
500	4.9	4.7	4.8	5.8	5.8	5.6
1,000	13.7	13.7	13.9	16.8	16.7	16.1
5,000	6.7	6.9	7.0	8.1	8.0	8.0
10,000	18.2	18.1	18.1	20.3	20.0	19.4
50,000	46.5	46.2	45.8	37.3	37.8	7.6
100,000	...	...	...	...	...	32.0

* Lower limit of size class, in thousands of dollars. No upper limit for top class shown. Top class begins at 100 million dollars in 1936, 50 millions in 1931–35.

statistics, by its several subsidiaries each of which was presumably smaller than the parent (except for changes in accounting items — see Chapter XXVII).

Turning now to the separate groups, for which corresponding 1932 and 1936 figures are shown in Table XXVIII, we find much diversity among groups as to the degree of concentration of assets in high size classes. In several instances, necessary grouping of high size classes precludes detailed presentation of all nine percentages in 1932, or ten in 1936; but the main differences among groups are nevertheless discernible. Tobacco, rubber, chemicals, and metals have emphatically greater concentration in high size classes, and foods somewhat greater,

TABLE XXVIII

PER CENT OF THE TOTAL ASSETS OF EACH MANUFACTURING GROUP FALLING IN EACH SIZE CLASS *

Class †	1932	1936	1932	1936	1932	1936
	Foods		Tobacco		Textiles	
0	2.0	1.9	.2	.3	2.9	3.2
50	2.4	2.3	.3	.3	2.9	3.3
100	5.0	5.1	.8	.9	6.4	7.0
250	4.9	5.3	.7	1.1	7.7	8.0
500	5.2	6.0	.8	.9	10.1	10.3
1,000	13.9	16.7	6.6	96.6	29.9	29.9
5,000	7.5	7.1	90.5	...	11.8	12.0
10,000	24.4	55.7	...	...	28.3	21.3
50,000	34.8	...	...	...	...	4.9
100,000	...	...	...	...	...	...
	Leather		Rubber		Forest products	
0	2.6	2.5	.3	.4	1.9	2.3
50	3.0	2.8	.4	.5	2.8	3.2
100	7.6	8.2	1.2	1.5	7.6	8.6
250	8.7	9.0	1.6	2.4	8.2	10.4
500	9.8	11.7	96.6	3.3	10.0	11.1
1,000	25.1	25.0	...	91.9	69.6	24.9
5,000	15.2	40.7	...	...	...	13.2
10,000	28.0	...	...	...	...	26.3
50,000	...	...	...	...	...	...
100,000	...	...	...	...	...	...
	Paper		Printing		Chemicals	
0	.6	.7	4.3	5.5	.4	.5
50	.9	1.1	3.7	4.2	.5	.6
100	2.7	3.1	6.4	7.8	1.2	1.4
250	3.1	3.8	6.4	7.6	1.3	1.6
500	5.0	6.1	7.5	9.6	1.7	2.3
1,000	18.3	23.0	16.0	20.9	5.2	7.2
5,000	9.6	10.4	9.5	12.5	3.4	4.1
10,000	59.6	28.9	46.3	20.0	10.8	15.9
50,000	...	22.7	...	11.7	75.5	9.2
100,000	...	...	...	...	...	57.2
	Stone		Metals		Miscellaneous	
0	1.8	1.7	.8	.9	3.2	3.2
50	2.5	2.3	1.0	1.0	3.3	3.1
100	5.8	4.9	2.5	2.8	7.2	6.2
250	6.5	5.7	3.0	3.2	8.6	7.1
500	7.5	7.0	3.7	4.3	9.2	8.0
1,000	22.0	19.6	11.8	13.7	24.6	23.4
5,000	10.4	12.4	6.1	7.1	7.7	49.1
10,000	43.6	33.6	16.8	17.7	36.2	...
50,000	...	12.7	54.3	49.2	...	...
100,000	...	...	...	...	...	...

than the division as a whole. Textiles, leather, forest products, and printing have distinctly less concentration than the division as a whole. For the single year for which a segregation is available, 1936, notable disparities appear within groups: motor vehicles has greater concentration than other metals, petroleum greater concentration than other chemicals, and clothing less concentration than other textiles. Here, as in the more complete record of Table XXVII, we find only moderate variation between the two years shown; and we may fairly assume that the ratios are roughly stable from year to year. The change from deep depression of 1932 to considerable prosperity of 1936 brought only moderate changes in the percentage distributions.

The conclusion appears unmistakable that notable differences in concentration exist. Certain groups clearly have a larger portion of their assets in high size classes than other groups. The different size classes of the entire manufacturing division are not, therefore, made up of like proportions from the various groups. Accordingly, differences in typical rates of return among groups *may* contribute in some degree to differences in rate of return among the size classes of the entire division. If, in general, groups which have typically high rates of return tend to concentrate in high size classes, and *vice versa*, this fact alone would lead to some increase of rate with size for the division as a whole. This would be true even if, within a particular group, there were no variation of rate with size.

The last preceding seven chapters abundantly show, however, that increase of rate with size is characteristic of every group separately — such increase appearing in the lower portions of the size range for every group, and in the rest of the

* In each case, figure for highest class shown covers all classes above lower limit of that class. The 1936 data for textiles, chemicals, and metals are on old basis.

† Lower limit of class, in thousands of dollars.

TABLE XXIX

PER CENT OF THE TOTAL ASSETS OF EACH SIZE CLASS, OF THE GROUPS IN THE MANUFACTURING DIVISION, FALLING IN THE INCOME CATEGORY *

Class †	1932	1936	1932	1936	1932	1936
	Foods		Tobacco		Textiles	
0	22.5	45.3	18.0	24.6	17.2	43.3
50	27.6	59.1	33.8	34.5	20.6	62.1
100	30.4	66.3	46.0	61.3	23.0	69.7
250	38.2	73.6	41.8	66.6	27.8	73.8
500	39.0	79.7	45.5	70.0	27.6	78.1
1,000	42.9	78.3	63.0	98.3	24.6	79.5
5,000	47.8	84.4	94.5	...	21.2	77.1
10,000	46.0	91.7	...	...	27.2	90.2
50,000	74.2	...	...	...	...	100.0
100,000	...	...	...	...	...	...
	Leather		Rubber		Forest products	
0	16.9	46.2	19.5	41.7	9.2	42.5
50	28.1	58.2	22.0	57.4	8.8	54.2
100	30.0	67.2	20.4	75.3	8.0	60.0
250	24.2	69.6	31.4	73.3	8.6	64.6
500	21.6	72.1	14.7	68.2	9.3	66.0
1,000	22.2	83.3	...	93.6	3.0	65.8
5,000	24.0	90.4	...	...	...	56.4
10,000	72.6	...	...	...	...	63.0
50,000	...	...	...	...	...	...
100,000	...	...	...	...	...	...
	Paper		Printing		Chemicals	
0	13.8	53.5	14.8	42.4	20.1	40.3
50	26.2	64.4	19.3	61.8	26.1	57.2
100	26.5	74.0	29.2	69.2	30.2	69.8
250	32.5	79.4	38.3	75.7	36.5	78.4
500	35.6	72.5	43.5	79.1	39.5	77.1
1,000	27.7	78.8	41.9	86.4	48.7	85.6
5,000	34.0	100.0	63.4	92.4	45.2	82.3
10,000	10.8	79.9	80.7	92.4	51.5	89.4
50,000	...	43.3	...	100.0	37.4	81.5
100,000	...	...	...	...	...	90.3
	Stone		Metals		Miscellaneous	
0	8.9	39.7	9.7	45.8	13.7	41.3
50	11.6	51.5	11.7	63.4	18.2	53.9
100	11.2	56.2	11.5	69.8	19.6	65.8
250	8.8	59.3	14.3	74.6	18.6	70.2
500	18.7	70.6	13.0	77.6	21.6	72.5
1,000	14.7	74.2	10.4	83.2	19.5	80.3
5,000	15.3	86.7	11.1	83.5	31.0	88.1
10,000	22.0	84.2	9.4	91.1	32.9	...
50,000	...	100.0	6.3	84.2	...	...
100,000	...	...	...	...	...	...

range for most groups. We must hold therefore that, although differences in concentration among groups *may* have some bearing (particularly in high classes) upon the findings of Chapter IV, the principal and perhaps the entire cause of the basic relation there found between rate of return and size is that the same relation prevails, with only moderate lack of uniformity, in every group. A probably justifiable next step is to infer that the increase of rate with size for a particular group is unlikely to be caused by differences in concentration of assets among the sub-groups of that group. In other words, even if we had similar data — classified by size — for various sub-groups within each group, we should probably find in general the same basic relation: rate of return increases with size. Instances might become more numerous, in such a detailed study, for which the relation between rate and size had peculiarities distinguishing it more or less clearly from the relation for the entire division: instances of very slow upward movement of the rate, of flatness in the middle range, of downturn near the right end, and of irregularities from class to class might be more numerous. But that most of the curves would assume the typical form and direction now seems very likely.

Table XXIX presents 1932 and 1936 ratios showing the share of the total assets of each size class which fell in the income category. These figures correspond to those pertaining to the entire division, already presented for all six years, in Chapter IV. The purpose of this record is to bring out the great shift in assets between the categories, as a result of cyclical changes in business profits. For every size class in nearly every group the ratio rose very sharply from 1932 to 1936, as would be expected. The bearing of this upon comparisons of rate-of-

---

* In each case, figure for highest class shown covers all classes above lower limit of that class. The 1936 data for textiles, chemicals, and metals are on old basis.

† Lower limit, in thousands of dollars.

return curves for the income and deficit categories is obvious. In 1932 the deficit curve was the more important, and in 1936 the income curve.

RATE OF RETURN AND SIZE

The principal objective of the present investigation has been to examine the relation between rate of profit and size of corporations. A main purpose of the separate study of each manufacturing group was to ascertain whether the observed relation between rate of return and size for the entire manufacturing division might reflect differences among the groups rather than a significant basic correlation. Subordinate purposes included the determination of the relations between rate and size for the groups separately, as information significant on its own account, and the examination of cyclical and other differences among the groups.

The evidence presented in the last preceding seven chapters seems to remove any possibility that the findings of Chapter IV for the entire division can arise merely or largely from differences among the groups and in the way the groups combine into the division. That notable differences do exist among groups, and that these differences influence in detail the results for the entire division, can not be questioned. But the almost universal prevalence among the groups of a positive correlation between rate and size — a tendency for rate to increase as size increases — strengthens the conclusion that in manufacturing in general this correlation is characteristic and fundamental. Whatever be the causes of the increase of rate with size, they are not to be found in the accidental mingling of widely different types of industry in the manufacturing division.

Differences among the groups indeed abound, as the charts relating rate of return to size in previous chapters show. Many of these differences can be ignored as irregularities, limited to isolated size classes in isolated years, and possibly reflecting the smallness of the samples in those cases. Charts VII and VIII of Chapter III, which present six-year averages of rates for each group, largely eliminate these irregularities and also conceal or remove whatever cyclical variation may exist in the correlation between rate and size. It there appears that the increase of rate with size is most persistent and regular for miscellaneous manufacturing, textiles, leather, forest products, stone, metals, and foods; although the curves for stone and foods have one nearly horizontal segment, and that for metals has one small decline. The curve for printing declines sharply in the highest class; and those for chemicals, paper, and rubber decline in several high size classes. The tobacco curve, after an unmistakable dip in the middle size range, rises sharply at the top of the size scale. The liquor curve is not shown, because data do not exist for 1931–32. Several of these curves — such as those for textiles, forest products, stone, and rubber — give an incomplete picture of the relation between rate and size, particularly at the high end of the size scale. Whenever, in the basic source tabulations, two or more size classes are grouped for a particular year, corresponding groupings are necessary in other years when the six-year averages are computed. Hence, the right-hand points on several of the curves apply to a combination of several size classes, and such curves therefore fail to disclose the details of variation of rate with size.

Several of the curves show a much larger fraction of the total change of rate with size in the low ranges of the size scale than do other curves. An example of such a contrast is that between textiles and printing. In all curves, except that for tobacco, the bulk of the advance in rate occurs to the left of one million dollars. The maximum range of variation in rate, over the entire size scale, differs notably from group to group. It is much less for foods than for miscellaneous, for paper than for chemicals. But, except for the early downturn for paper and rubber and the intermediate dip for tobacco, all curves show an uninterrupted advance in rate as size increases up to about one million dollars. Beyond that point, differences among the curves become striking; and we may therefore infer that only in the size range above one million dollars can differences among the groups have a controlling influence upon the shape of the general curve for manufacturing (dotted curve of Chart v). The persistent advance of that curve from one million dollars up to the top size class may fairly be ascribed to the dominant place, in at least the high classes of the entire manufacturing division, of those groups which show persistent advance of rate in the high size classes. The possibility that something of this sort can happen is perhaps best illustrated by the special 1936 chart for chemicals (Chart xxiii), for it there appears that the sufficient explanation of the downturn of the chemicals (*including* petroleum) curve at the right end is the violent drop in the petroleum curve. The curve for chemicals with petroleum excluded shows, except for one nearly horizontal segment, a persistent advance.

A detailed study of the separate group charts in Chapters V to XI largely reinforces the inferences from Charts vii and viii. These group charts show curves for each of the six years, and in certain groups this annual separation presents a more detailed record at the right end — combinations of size classes, which somewhat spoil Charts vii and viii, are not likely to appear in every year for any one group. But, ignoring irregularities in particular size classes, each group chart gives a remarkable indication of stability in the form of the curve over the years. Indeed, a major basis of confidence in the findings of our analysis is that those findings are, with moderate reservations, pertinent to each of the six years — years of moderate prosperity as well as years of deep depression. The group charts of Chapters V to XI indicate, with few and generally unimportant qualifications, that the summary curves of Charts vii and viii are typical of their respective groups. That parallelism among the six curves of a particular group is not perfect has frequently been noted in previous chapters, and it has been observed that the approach to parellelism is much closer for some groups, such as metals and miscellaneous, than for others, such as forest products and rubber. In cases showing very poor approach to parallelism we must, of course, infer that the corresponding six-year summary curve is not highly typical. The worst cases of departure from parallelism appear in small groups (small in terms of importance or size), and the evidence of parallelism in groups which make up the bulk of the entire division is truly remarkable. Perhaps some reservation should be entered here, on the ground that breaking a very large group, which now shows close approach to parallelism, into two smaller sub-groups according to a narrower definition of type of business might yield for each such sub-group a set of six curves not closely parallel. No reason, however, appears for expecting this outcome rather than one which is more favorable to our argument of consistency; because some of the cases of close approach to parallelism actually found pertain to small groups.

CYCLICAL VARIATIONS

Much attention has been given along the way to cyclical changes in rate of return, for each group as a whole and for its several size classes. In general, cyclical variation has appeared more intense for groups chiefly made up of manufacturers of producers' goods and durable consumers' goods than for cases representing the manufacture of non-durable or semi-durable consumers' goods. And in general, cyclical variation is more intense for small size classes than for large.

Differences in timing appear among the groups and among the size classes. The arrival of the minimum rate of the depression occurs in different years for some groups than for others. But differences among size classes of a particular group, as to the date of the low point, seem less common. Differences among the groups, and also among the size classes of numerous particular groups, as to the relative levels in 1936 and 1931 are numerous: some groups or classes had realized by 1936 a much fuller recovery above 1931 levels, already severely depressed, than had others.

The evidence of the last seven chapters, as presented in the cyclical charts and the related tables and discussion, nevertheless strongly emphasizes one conclusion: the profit rate of every group and every size class felt the heavy pressure of the depression in its extreme stage, and shared in the remarkable revival from 1933 to 1936. The differences in timing and intensity have great moment for any detailed study of the cycle, but the central fact is that specialization as to line of industry or size does not afford a means of more than partial escape from cyclical instability.

XIII

MINING DIVISION

THE CORPORATE STATISTICAL DATA for this division must be recognized as much more imperfect, in representing the industrial activities presumably covered under the heading of the division, than is the case with most other broad divisions. Even after the abandonment of consolidated tax returns following the Act of 1934, integration of corporate activities was particularly effective in shifting into other divisions — chiefly manufacturing — business actually done in mineral extraction. Precisely how large a fraction of mineral industry, in a statistical sense, is thus transferred can not be known; but it is undoubtedly a large fraction, perhaps not much below half.

This effect of integration upon the statistics may fall with different weight upon the various lines of mineral activity — upon oil wells as compared with anthracite mining, for example. Integration may also have a greater bearing upon the mining statistics for corporations of one size than for those of another — the published record affords no clear light on this point. All of the foregoing considerations suggest a qualified acceptance of any findings resulting from our analysis of statistics for the mining division; those findings may well be indicative of conditions in the mineral industries, but they can not be accepted with the same confidence as corresponding findings in the manufacturing division.

STRUCTURE OF THE DIVISION

The statistics for the division, on the actual basis of classification, emphasize the smallness of the mineral industry in comparison with manufacturing, trade, and certain other divisions (Table III). Even if all mineral industry were classified in this division the resulting aggregates, though much larger than those now presented, would remain small in comparison with manufacturing and trade. But, despite its comparative smallness, the mining division is worthy of careful study because of the peculiar conditions influencing earning power in at least some of its branches. The basic nature of nearly all of its products, the slackening growth or possibly downward trend in utilization of certain minerals, the peculiar cost factors existing in some of these industries, the fact that mining is inevitably concerned with wasting assets, and the highly speculative character of many mining enterprises, all suggest that the type of analysis followed in these pages may yield exceptional results.

The limited statistics on the several groups within the division — statistics which do not include the essential equity and earnings data such as enabled us to study the manufacturing groups separately — are summarized in Table XXX, for the single year 1935. The range in importance, implied by total gross income, among five of the groups is not wide; and the one very small group is composed of miscellaneous enterprises. The three most important groups — oil and gas, bituminous coal, and metals — are probably very much understated because of the integration influence mentioned above. What the relative importance of these groups would be if that influence — which tends to cover mining statistics into other divisions, especially manufacturing — were absent can not be definitely known, but the very limited evidence from the depletion records (see above, pages 52 and 70) suggests that oil and gas might be even more emphatically the leading group. In any case, no single group in the actual statistics of the division is of commanding importance; and figures for the entire division are therefore unlikely to be dominated by any one group.

Differences among the groups as to average size of corporation — measured in terms of average gross income, despite its defects for this purpose — are notable. The average for anthracite runs more than ten times that for oil and gas, and even for metals the average is less than one third that for anthracite. Some of these disparities undoubtedly reflect differing degrees

TABLE XXX

Comparative Importance of Groups of the Mining Division in 1935 *

	Number of corporations	Total gross income	Gross income per corporation
Group			
Metal mining	908	533	587
Anthracite	123	232	1,886
Bituminous coal	2,012	768	382
Oil and gas	4,286	790	184
Other minerals	1,865	231	124
Other mining and quarrying	9,226	70	7.6
Entire mining division	18,420	2,625	142

* Compiled and computed from *Statistics of Income for 1935, Part 2*, p. 34. Units: $1,000,000, for column 2; $1,000, for column 3.

in which the integration influence discussed above bears upon these groups. But, for the data as they are actually tabulated, these differences in average size suggest the possibility of some specialization of various size classes in the mining division by type of mining activity. To that extent, the rates of return by size class for the entire division may be distorted because of differences in average rate of return among branches of mining industry.

SIZE VARIATION IN RATE

Except at the very left end of the curves, advance in rate of return with increasing size is very small for the mining division; and, for corporations above 500 thousand dollars in average size of total assets, the tendencies are so uncertain that little typical variation of rate with size can be inferred for most of the range in the size scale (Chart XLIII). But the inclination at the left end, for all curves except that of 1934 and possibly 1936, is exceptionally sharp: in no other division and in no manufacturing group do such remarkably low rates

CHART XLIII

RATE OF RETURN COMPARED WITH SIZE, FOR MINING DIVISION *

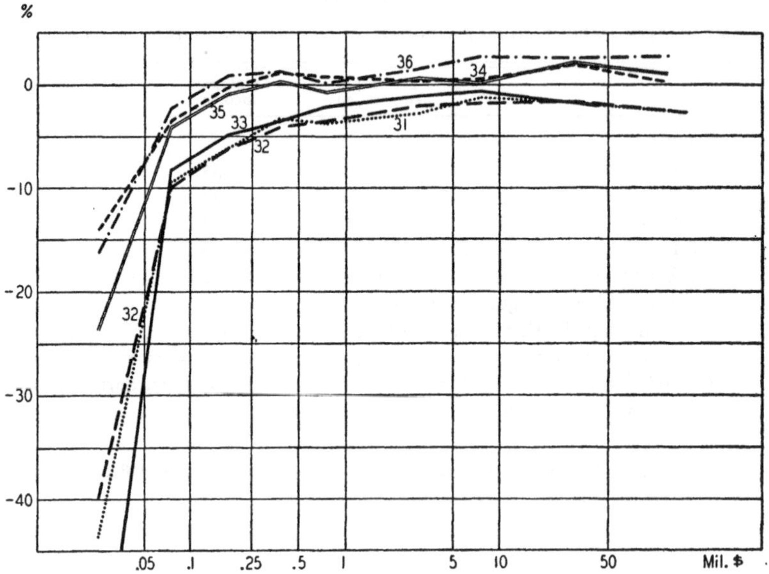

* Horizontal scale logarithmic. Data in Table XXXI. 1933 curve incomplete at left.

— high negative rates — appear for the lowest size class as in this division. This extraordinarily poor showing pertains, however, only to the lowest size class; rates for the 50-thousand-dollar class, while low, are not exceptionally low and are well clustered for the several years.

Further, but gradual, increase in rate of return with size continues systematically to the 250-thousand level. Beyond that, although some further advance occurs in some of the years, the movement is not uniform among the years; and the entire sheaf of curves gives the general impression of an irregular horizontal drift. One systematic tendency, of minor significance, is the definite dip at the right end of five of the curves; the very highest size class has in most years a moderately lower rate than the next-to-highest. The most emphatic impression from the chart, however, is that of a nearly horizontal movement above 250 thousand dollars: except for the lowest size classes, rate of return shows no systematic tendency to vary with size in this division.

Evidences of parallelism are not considerable. In some portions of the size range, to be sure, an approach to parallelism exists in pairs of curves — for example, the 1932 and 1933 curves, and those of 1934 and 1935, in substantial portions of their range. But the entire sheaf of six curves shows many intersections and no such broadly parallel movement as appeared in the manufacturing division and certain of its groups. And this holds, quite apart from the extreme diversity of inclination at the left ends of the curves.

TIME VARIATION IN RATE

As respects spread among the curves, the situation in this division is truly remarkable. Ignoring the lowest size class, we find a total spread strikingly narrow, much narrower than in most other divisions and in most manufacturing groups. In an industrial division largely concerned with production of basic materials, mainly for use in further production operations rather than in direct consumption, this evidence of very limited cyclical responsiveness is truly remarkable. A partial explanation may lie in the delayed recovery of the capital goods industries in 1934–35, which might account for the failure of the mining curves of those years to run at a distinctly higher level with reference to the 1931–33 curves; but this can not explain the scarcely higher rates for 1936. The lack of spread among the 1931–33 curves suggests, moreover, that this delayed recovery in capital goods can at best be only a partial explanation.

The narrow range of time variation is emphasized by Chart XLIV. The record for the lowest size class, which does experience extremely violent cyclical changes in rate, is not shown (see Table XXXI); curves for the division as a whole and the

CHART XLIV

TIME VARIATIONS IN RATE OF RETURN, FOR MINING DIVISION AND SELECTED SIZE CLASSES *

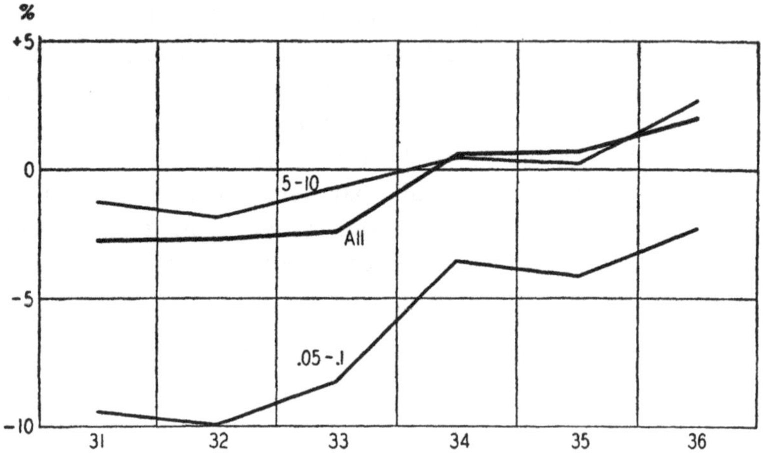

* Data in Table XXXI.

selected size classes show remarkably mild responsiveness to the cycle. The strikingly small variation of these curves, as they trace the course of earnings-rates in mining during severe fluctuations in general business, is quite contrary to the situation observed in the manufacturing division and most of its groups.

That this finding is out of accord with natural expectations, in view of the basic nature of the mineral industry, is obvious; and no ready explanation of the result appears. Conceivably, a partial explanation may be found in the charges for deple-

TABLE XXXI

Rates of Return for Mining Division *

Class †	1931	1932	1933	1934	1935	1936
0	**−43.70**	**−39.99**	**−60.46**	**−14.03**	**−23.67**	**−16.23**
	32.81	25.93	19.74	21.49	20.98	26.02
	−79.45	*−66.04*	*−94.15*	*−49.51*	*−75.28*	*−83.76*
50	**−9.41**	**−9.95**	**−8.22**	**−3.50**	**−4.11**	**−2.26**
	9.48	10.88	8.94	13.56	12.30	14.37
	−19.25	*−17.59*	*−15.17*	*−16.06*	*−16.42*	*−17.10*
100	**−6.18**	**−6.22**	**−4.95**	**−.28**	**−.96**	**.88**
	8.36	8.71	9.73	12.41	10.78	13.05
	−13.09	*−11.20*	*−11.78*	*−9.02*	*−10.54*	*−11.15*
250	**−3.34**	**−4.11**	**−3.60**	**1.15**	**.33**	**1.31**
	7.34	7.14	7.89	9.68	9.52	10.44
	−8.52	*−8.60*	*−8.90*	*−7.49*	*−9.07*	*−8.95*
500	**−3.73**	**−3.52**	**−2.15**	**.79**	**−.71**	**.20**
	5.83	6.61	6.49	8.53	8.31	8.57
	−8.04	*−7.11*	*−5.93*	*−4.73*	*−7.71*	*−8.25*
1,000	**−2.80**	**−2.03**	**−1.08**	**.35**	**.64**	**1.52**
	4.57	4.57	5.25	5.61	6.38	6.73
	−5.51	*−4.16*	*−3.29*	*−3.35*	*−3.51*	*−3.92*
5,000	**−1.24**	**−1.84**	**−.66**	**.49**	**.22**	**2.72**
	2.16	3.41	3.57	4.80	4.75	5.87
	−2.53	*−3.70*	*−2.90*	*−2.54*	*−3.66*	*−2.61*
10,000	**−1.78**	**−1.62**	...	**1.90**	**2.03**	**2.49**
	4.97	3.90	...	5.30	6.61	5.10
	−4.47	*−3.22*	*−2.99*	*−1.19*	*−1.85*	*−3.18*
50,000	**−2.74**	**−2.79**	...	**.22**	**.92**	...
	2.51	2.37	...	3.06	3.71	7.15
	−3.07	*−3.72*	*−3.05*	*−.67*	*−.18*	...
100,000	...	...	...	...	...	...
	...	...	...	...	...	3.03
	...	...	...	...	...	...
Classes grouped ‡	...	...	**−2.21**	...	...	**2.68**
	...	...	4.46	...	...	...
	...	...	...	...	...	*−3.58*
Entire division	**−2.78**	**−2.71**	**−2.39**	**.63**	**.73**	**2.03**
	4.78	4.28	5.29	5.62	6.18	5.65
	−4.68	*−4.57*	*−4.17*	*−2.36*	*−2.83*	*−5.15*

* Expressed in per cent; ratio of profit (or loss) after taxes to estimated average equity, as explained in text, p. 18. Figures in boldface type are for

tion, at least on the basis used in reckoning income for tax purposes; but necessarily detailed evidence is not available for testing this point. That extensive integration, to which we have referred above, may bring it about that the non-integrated (in the limited sense of non-integration with manufacture) mining concerns — those actually tabulated in the mining division — are less responsive to the cycle than is the mining industry as a whole is possible; but again essential evidence for testing the point can not be had. We are perhaps forced to rely chiefly upon the likelihood that many branches of mining had already by 1931 felt the full effects of depression and that the 1933–35 recovery did not appear promptly in these industries.

PROFITABLE AND UNPROFITABLE CORPORATIONS

We find that a distinctive situation for the mining division again appears in the record comparing rate of return with size for the income corporations as a separate category in the division (Table XXXI). The steep decline of rate with increasing size, even with the lowest size class ignored, is striking. Table XXXI shows a steeper generally downward course of rate of return for the income category, as size increases, than any other case thus far examined. We infer that there is an emphatic relationship: rate of return declines notably as size increases, for the income corporations of this division.

Ignoring several irregularities in all other portions of the size scale — and they are less numerous and less sharp than the irregularities found in most records of this (income cate-

---

income and deficit categories of corporations combined, in ordinary type for the income category, in italics for the deficit category.

† Lower limit of class interval, in thousands of dollars of total assets. The 50,000-thousand-dollar class has no stated upper limit, 1931–35; the 100,000-thousand-dollar class has no stated upper limit, 1936.

‡ High size classes combined, to conceal a single corporation. Where such combination applies to only income or deficit category, other category is shown separately in the specific classes, but joint figure for both categories is shown only in "grouped" row.

gory) sort — we observe an exceptional movement in the high size classes. The downward tendency is interrupted at about 10 million dollars, most of the annual series of rates advance from the 5-million-dollar class to the 10-million-dollar class, and then decline — generally by a greater amount — in passing to the highest size class. The peculiar, and fairly systematic, experience of the 10-million-dollar class is another point on which no satisfactory explanation can be given, with the factual record not more detailed than it is. The most obvious suggestion would be that this size class is dominated by some limited branch of the mineral industry, with a profit rate somewhat above average, or that the range of variation in rate of return among the corporations in this class is exceptionally great (see below, Chapter XXV).

Chart XLV compares curves for income and deficit categories, and for both combined, on a six-year average basis. We have already observed that the combined curve, except at its extreme left, is more nearly horizontal in this division than in most of the manufacturing groups. We noted also that the decline of rate with increasing size for the income category is steeper here than in most other cases studied. Accordingly, as Chart XLV confirms, the deficit curve should be very considerably steeper in its upward-to-the-right course than is the combined curve, and should approach in steepness some of the deficit-category curves heretofore studied (see Chart XXVI). For the deficit category of the mining division, rate of return unmistakably rises — rate of loss declines — with increasing size along most of the size scale. In the intermediate size classes, while rate varies little for the two categories combined, it rises steadily for the deficit category and as steadily declines for the income category. The figures for the separate categories (income, 24.50; deficit, −33.01) of the lowest class are not plotted, but evidently emphasize still further the widening spread at the left. As has already been suggested, in connection with other similar charts, the strikingly wide spread at the left suggests that the dispersion among the rates for specific corporations in any one size class is far greater for small than for large size classes (see below, Chapter XXV). These comparisons are based on six-year averages, but Table XXXI affords the data for similar comparisons in specific years.

CHART XLV

SIX-YEAR AVERAGE OF RATES OF RETURN, FOR MINING DIVISION AND INCOME AND DEFICIT CATEGORIES *

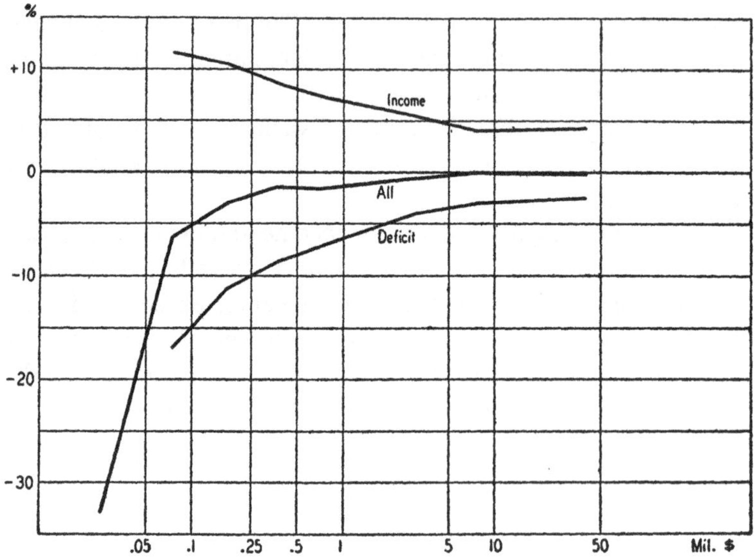

* Horizontal scale logarithmic. Data in Table B. Two points omitted in lowest class.

CONCLUSION

In several significant respects, the record of the mining division differs from that for manufacturing. Despite exceptionally low rates of return for the bottom size class, and a very sharp advance in rate to the next size class, curves relating rate of return to size presently flatten out and show no clear tendency away from horizontal in all the higher size classes. Cyclical intensity, for the division as a whole and for all size classes except the very lowest, is surprisingly small. This large division of industries, which is almost entirely engaged in furnishing basic materials to be used in further production and largely in capital-goods industries, shows an unexpected degree of uniformity from size class to size class and from year to year. That peculiarities of organization, operation, and accounting in these industries may afford a partial explanation is granted, but any full explanation seems hidden from analyses applicable to existing data.

XIV

AGRICULTURE, CONSTRUCTION

TREATMENT of the two smallest industrial divisions (see Table III), agriculture and construction, is combined in the present chapter; but this combination does not imply any logical connection between these two types of corporate industry. The agriculture division comprises mainly corporations engaged in farming and stock-raising and is therefore the second division, after mining, representing almost exclusively extractive industry. Construction includes, on the other hand, mainly producers of highly durable goods, partly for use in further productive operations and partly for direct human consumption. In view of the contract basis on which much construction work is done, one might urge that industries of this type should be treated along with the other service-rendering industries — those covered by the trade, public utilities, and service, and possibly finance, divisions. But, largely because of the tangible nature of the product and of the place of inventory and price in the cost-determining process, we have regarded construction as one of the commodity-producing divisions — along with manufacturing, mining, and agriculture.

The agriculture division, on the basis of corporate statistics, is a particularly imperfect sample of agricultural business as a whole. Hence, findings for corporate agriculture must not be regarded as indicative of general conditions in agriculture. Agriculture is the most deficient of the divisions in this sense; whereas, for such divisions as manufacturing and public utilities, corporate statistics cover very large fractions of total enterprise of the respective types. While incompleteness of coverage by the corporate data — implying existence of many enterprises of the non-corporate form — is especially marked in agriculture, it without doubt limits significantly the general applicability of the corporate data for such divisions as construction, trade, and service. In all of these, non-corporate enterprise bulks larger, in comparison with total enterprise of the specified type, than in manufacturing or especially in public utilities.

Group data, of the sort required for analysis of rate of return, are not available for agriculture or construction; and our analysis by size classes must therefore be restricted to the divisions as a whole. Limited tabulations of selected income-account items, of the sort examined in connection with the sub-groups within certain manufacturing groups (see page 67), are available; and these yield a rough picture of the make-up of these two divisions.

Agriculture is broken into two groups: farming, and related industries; and the latter includes such widely diverse enterprises as forestry and fishing. Farming is by far the larger group, and experience in this group may be expected to dominate calculated results for the entire agriculture division. As, however, the average size of corporation is about the same in the two groups, there is no reason to suppose that farming dominates certain size classes in the division and that related industries dominate other size classes.[1]

In construction there are three groups; two are of so nearly equal importance that neither dominates the division, and the

[1] In 1935, significant summary figures were:

	Number of corporations	Gross income: Total	Gross income: Average per corporation
Farming	8659	517	60
Related industries	1425	73	51

in million dollars for the total, and thousand dollars for the average.

third — shipbuilding, etc. — has much lower importance.[2] Average size runs much higher for shipbuilding than for the other two groups, and therefore some possibility exists that calculated results may be more heavily influenced by this group for the higher size classes than for the other size classes in the division.

AGRICULTURE

Curves relating rate of return to size of corporation, for the agriculture division, show a fairly sharp advance in rate from the lowest to the next size class in all years but 1931, and then a gradual but irregular upward course through the rest of the size scale (Chart XLVI). Absence or incompleteness of data in the highest size classes limits the lateral extent of several curves; but, so far as they do reach, all the curves show a substantial increase in rate from the 50-thousand-dollar class to the highest class shown. The evidence of parallelism, while considerable, is offset by irregularities — especially in the 1931 curve — and by lack of parallel tendencies at the ends, both left and right. The remarkable irregularity near the right of the 1934 curve reflects a tabulating error in the basic data, and this would have some effect also in Charts V and LXI.[3] The relation between rate of return and size, though persistent in all years, is not uniform from year to year.

The entire sheaf of curves stands low on the chart; very few of the plotted rates rise significantly above zero. In corporate agriculture, as in agriculture as a whole, prosperous conditions

[2] Pertinent data for 1935 run:

	Number of corporations	Gross income: Total	Gross income: Average per corporation
Construction above ground	11,169	576	52
Other construction under ground and on surface	6,303	795	126
Shipbuilding and repairing	215	121	565

in million dollars for the total, and thousand dollars for the average.

[3] See footnote to Table IX, Chapter IV, p. 63.

had not been restored by 1935; and no generally prosperous situation existed even in 1936. The total spread among the curves, though considerable, is moderate in comparison with that in manufacturing; but the vertical range for the lowest size

CHART XLVI

RATE OF RETURN COMPARED WITH SIZE, FOR AGRICULTURE DIVISION *

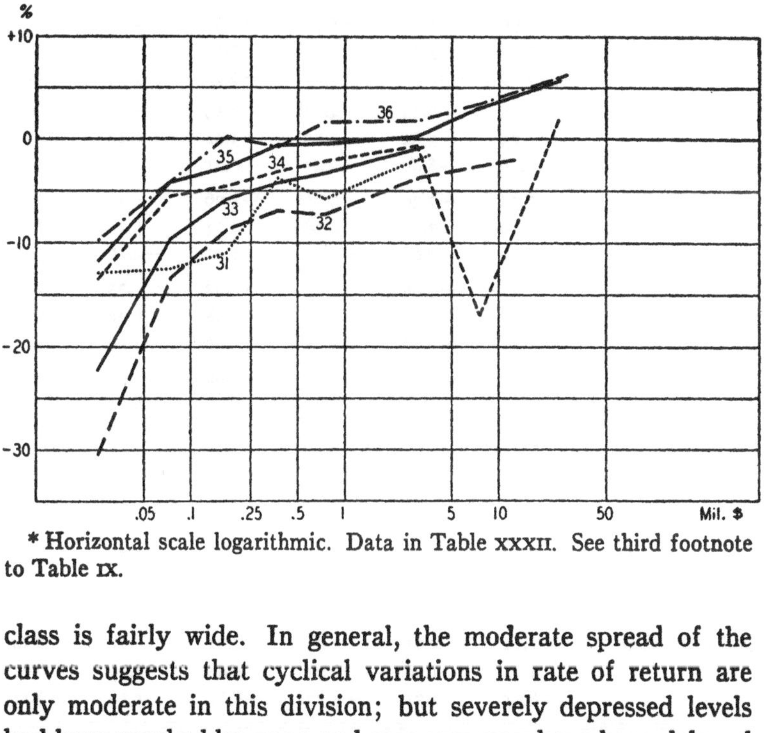

* Horizontal scale logarithmic. Data in Table XXXII. See third footnote to Table IX.

class is fairly wide. In general, the moderate spread of the curves suggests that cyclical variations in rate of return are only moderate in this division; but severely depressed levels had been reached by 1931 and recovery may have been delayed after 1933, and the spread might be considerably wider if a truly prosperous year were included.

Other graphic records, similar to those shown for manufacturing, are not presented for agriculture; but these comparisons can be followed out from Table XXXII. With many

TABLE XXXII

Rates of Return for Agriculture Division *

Class †	1931	1932	1933	1934 §	1935	1936
0	**−12.88**	**−30.51**	**−22.30**	**−13.47**	**−11.81**	**−9.79**
	10.35	6.54	8.09	8.06	11.46	11.79
	−36.32	*−37.24*	*−30.08*	*−23.63*	*−23.00*	*−27.77*
50	**−12.49**	**−13.38**	**−9.63**	**−5.51**	**−4.19**	**−4.15**
	5.30	4.68	5.12	6.73	7.15	10.70
	−18.79	*−16.36*	*−13.04*	*−9.89*	*−10.47*	*−16.38*
100	**−10.96**	**−8.75**	**−5.78**	**−4.56**	**−2.73**	**.24**
	2.27	3.25	4.87	7.14	5.99	8.08
	−16.59	*−10.97*	*−8.66*	*−9.97*	*−9.14*	*−8.89*
250	**−3.75**	**−6.94**	**−4.23**	**−3.14**	**−.55**	**−.69**
	4.13	3.84	3.79	5.02	6.26	6.05
	−10.16	*−8.69*	*−6.43*	*−6.75*	*−4.71*	*−7.51*
500	**−5.74**	**−7.30**	**−3.26**	**−2.06**	**−.41**	**1.68**
	3.40	3.14	4.18	4.74	5.25	6.05
	−8.49	*−9.08*	*−5.09*	*−4.91*	*−4.16*	*−4.49*
1,000	...	**−3.80**	...	**−.62**	**.33**	**1.78**
	...	2.71	...	4.38	6.44	5.61
	−5.78	*−4.86*	*−3.35*	*−2.86*	*−3.70*	*−3.32*
5,000	...	...	...	**−16.99**	**3.02**	**3.42**
	...	...	...	5.46	6.54	7.29
	−2.61	*−3.38*	*−1.94*	*−31.71*	*−.80*	*−3.41*
10,000	...	...	...	...	...	...
	...	...	...	...	...	...
	−4.49	*−4.39*	*−1.89*	*−4.71*	*−8.41*	*−3.36*
Classes grouped ‡	**−1.50**	**−1.99**	**−.68**	**1.88**	**5.71**	**6.37**
	2.11	.80	3.79	4.39	6.91	7.13
	...	...	...	...	...	...
Entire division ..	**−5.12**	**−5.61**	**−2.91**	**−3.21**	**.91**	**2.14**
	2.94	1.96	4.03	4.88	6.56	6.81
	−8.75	*−7.75*	*−5.57*	*−8.80*	*−5.10*	*−6.11*

* Expressed in per cent; ratio of profit (or loss) after taxes to estimated average equity, as explained in text, p. 18. Figures in boldface type are for income and deficit categories of corporations combined, in ordinary type for the income category, in italics for the deficit category.

† Lower limit of class interval, in thousands of dollars of total assets. The 50,000-thousand-dollar class has no stated upper limit, 1931–35; the 100,000-thousand-dollar class has no stated upper limit, 1936; items of both these classes are covered in "Classes grouped."

‡ High size classes combined, to conceal a single corporation. Where such combination applies to only income category, other category is shown separately in the specific classes, but joint figure for both categories is shown only in "grouped" row.

§ See third footnote to Table IX.

irregularities, the general course of rate of return in comparison with size is the same for the income category of this division as for manufacturing and most of its groups: rate declines with increasing size, and the decline is moderate except at the low end of the size scale. Data for the income category in the top size classes are available only for three years, but in these years an advance above somewhat lower size classes appears. The broad course of variation, however, would appear downward to the right if the curves were drawn.

CONSTRUCTION

The upward-to-the-right general course of curves relating rate of return to size is somewhat steeper for construction than for agriculture or for most manufacturing groups (Chart XLVII).

CHART XLVII

RATE OF RETURN COMPARED WITH SIZE, FOR CONSTRUCTION DIVISION *

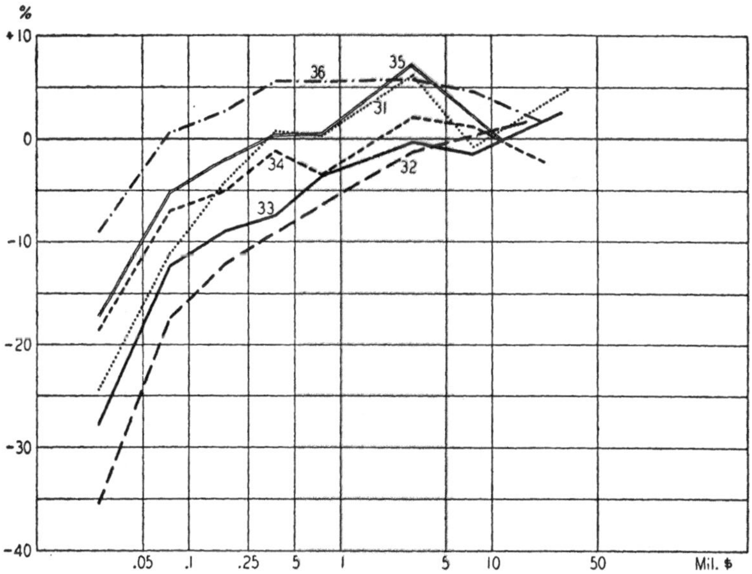

* Horizontal scale logarithmic. Data in Table XXXIII.

Moreover, although the curves are steepest at their left ends, the slackening in pace of advance to the right of 250 thousand dollars is not great, except in 1936; and a fairly rapid advance continues through all the middle section of the size range for 1931–35 curves. Declines appear in two curves to the right of 500 thousand dollars, and from the 1-million-dollar

CHART XLVIII

TIME VARIATIONS IN RATE OF RETURN, FOR CONSTRUCTION DIVISION AND SELECTED SIZE CLASSES *

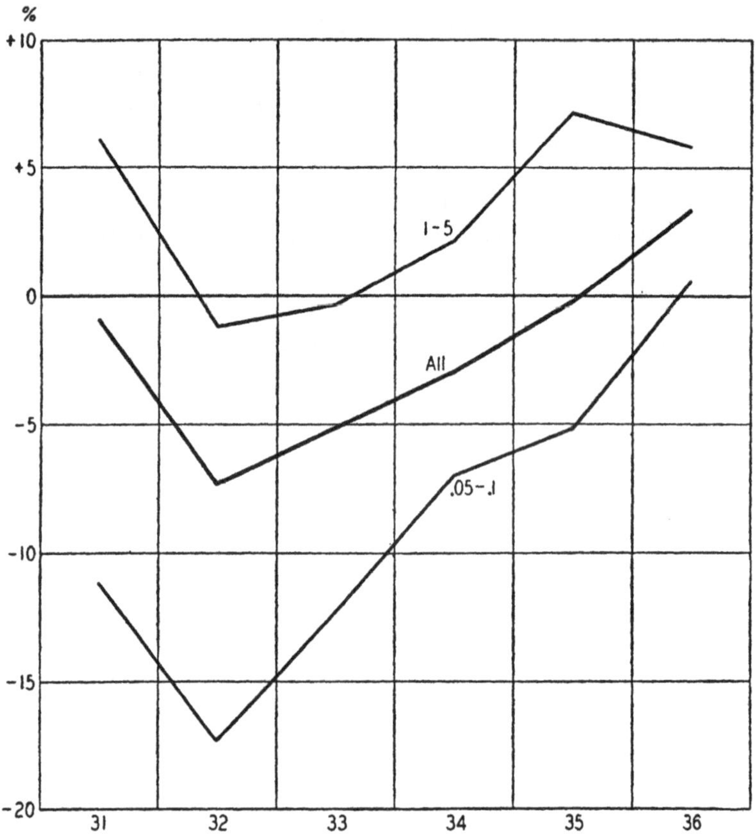

* Data in Table XXXIII.

TABLE XXXIII

Rates of Return for Construction Division *

Class †	1931	1932	1933	1934	1935	1936
0	**−24.52**	**−35.48**	**−27.80**	**−18.62**	**−17.26**	**−9.13**
	16.85	12.63	8.45	9.88	11.14	14.06
	−43.75	*−41.39*	*−33.88*	*−29.65*	*−34.09*	*−34.36*
50	**−11.15**	**−17.38**	**−12.30**	**−6.98**	**−5.20**	**.59**
	13.16	10.85	8.57	9.60	11.18	13.84
	−25.99	*−22.25*	*−16.50*	*−14.06*	*−16.71*	*−17.56*
100	**−4.17**	**−12.10**	**−8.94**	**−5.03**	**−1.96**	**2.70**
	13.75	10.85	8.44	9.32	10.76	11.91
	−17.80	*−16.79*	*−12.95*	*−11.13*	*−10.21*	*−11.50*
250	**.77**	**−8.99**	**−7.38**	**−1.20**	**.43**	**5.64**
	14.53	10.63	8.82	12.90	11.23	12.66
	−11.17	*−15.38*	*−11.50*	*−8.42*	*−6.02*	*−9.48*
500	**.28**	**−6.34**	**−3.58**	**−3.44**	**.45**	**5.59**
	14.63	8.10	7.21	9.07	11.14	12.65
	−13.19	*−11.93*	*−7.86*	*−8.87*	*−8.71*	*−8.12*
1,000	**6.04**	**−1.20**	**−.35**	**2.14**	**7.13**	**5.80**
	15.36	12.56	10.77	12.54	17.19	12.44
	−4.40	*−6.25*	*−4.68*	*−3.57*	*−4.19*	*−8.43*
5,000	**−.79**	...	**−1.47**	**1.24**	...	**4.61**
	10.32	...	4.72	3.90	...	6.94
	−5.79	*−5.30*	*−3.88*	*−10.15*	*−6.04*	*−2.77*
10,000	...	...	...	...	...	...
	...	...	12.10	4.57	...	11.99
	...	...	...	...	...	...
Classes grouped ‡	**4.89**	**1.63**	**2.44**	**−2.36**	**−.14**	**1.63**
	13.36	13.25	...	...	5.86	...
	1.51	*.13*	*.29*	*−5.94*	*−7.79*	*−5.08*
Entire division ..	**−.86**	**−7.34**	**−5.18**	**−2.95**	**−.22**	**3.30**
	14.34	11.54	9.19	8.56	11.25	11.89
	−11.50	*−12.43*	*−9.25*	*−9.82*	*−10.43*	*−11.25*

* Expressed in per cent; ratio of profit (or loss) after taxes to estimated average equity, as explained in text, p. 18. Figures in boldface type are for income and deficit categories of corporations combined, in ordinary type for the income category, in italics for the deficit category.

† Lower limit of class interval, in thousands of dollars of total assets. The 50,000-thousand-dollar class has no stated upper limit, 1931–35; the 100,000-thousand-dollar class has no items, but defines the upper limit of the 50,000-thousand-dollar class in 1936. All items in the 50,000-thousand-dollar class are covered in "Classes grouped."

‡ High size classes combined, to conceal a single corporation. Where such combination applies to only income or deficit category, other category is shown separately in the specific classes, but joint figure for both categories is shown only in "grouped" row.

class to the next class in all years for which both classes are shown (grouped classes at the top prevent this comparison for 1932 and 1935).

Parallelism is not a feature of the chart, and the relation between rate of return and size is by no means uniform from year to year. Numerous irregularities in particular curves, and a considerable convergence near the right ends, chiefly explain lack of parallelism. The total spread of the curves exceeds in general that found in the agriculture division, and cyclical variations therefore seem more severe than in agriculture. This is the more striking because construction supposedly suffered as much delay in recovery during 1934–35 as agriculture, if not more. Further evidence of the cyclical changes for construction appears in Chart XLVIII — the recovery following 1932 there appears substantial, despite the supposed lag in this industry.

Further detailed comparisons, particularly those involving the income and deficit categories of corporations, can be traced from Table XXXIII. It will be observed that extraordinary class-to-class iregularities appear in rates of return for the income category in most years; and there is very little clear evidence of a downward tendency as size increases, for these rates. Variation from year to year, in average level of rates for the income category, is much more striking than that found in similar comparisons for other divisions and groups. Taken together, the income-category data of this division give little impression of any systematic relationship among the rates for various classes; but this may be due in part to the smallness of sample in certain size classes.

XV

TRADE DIVISION

THE INDUSTRIAL DIVISIONS thus far discussed — manufacturing, mining, construction, and agriculture — represent corporate enterprises predominantly engaged in producing physical commodities. The four remaining divisions — finance, public utilities, service, and trade — represent predominantly the supplying of services.[1] Although finance and public utilities are emphatically more important than trade if importance is appraised in terms of total assets, the total receipts of the trade division greatly exceed those of the three other divisions of the service-producing type, and fall only moderately short of the total receipts of the leading division, manufacturing (see Table III). Hence, regarding trade as the most important of the four service-producing divisions, we discuss in the present chapter the relation between rate of return and size for trade.

SIZE VARIATION IN RATE

The rates of return on equity, calculated for all trade corporations classified by size, are shown for each year 1931–36 in Chart XLIX. Here again, the general features observed in the corresponding chart for all industries combined (Chart I)

[1] A ninth "division," listed separately in *Statistics of Income* tabulations, is styled "nature of business not given." Because of the obviously miscellaneous and unidentifiable economic nature of this division, and of the negligible magnitude of the statistical aggregates pertaining to it, no examination thereof is attempted in this book. The situation here is quite different from that of the "miscellaneous" group in manufacturing, which includes certain definitely specified lines of manufacturing production, and yields statistical figures of about the same magnitude as those of other small manufacturing groups.

appear: with only slight irregularities, all the curves sweep upward to the right, and thus reflect a tendency for rate of return to rise as size increases; the speed of the rise slackens as size increases; there is a rough parallelism among the six curves, throughout their courses; all rates for the lowest size class are

CHART XLIX

RATE OF RETURN COMPARED WITH SIZE, FOR TRADE DIVISION *

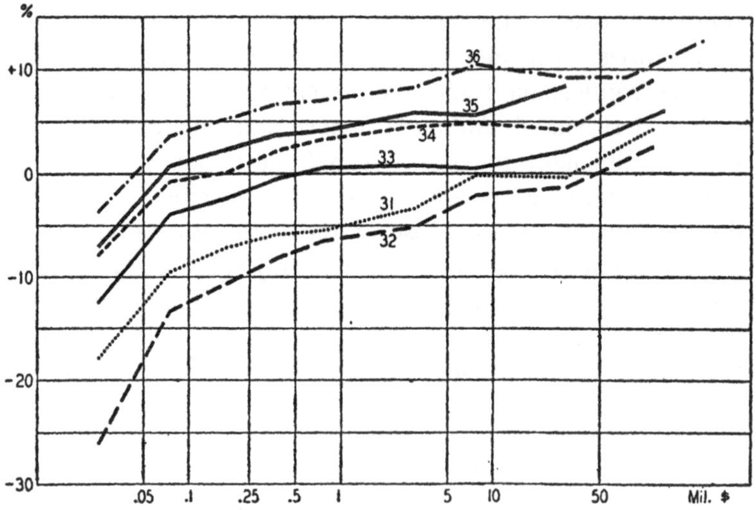

* Horizontal scale logarithmic. Data in Table xxxv.

negative, remaining below zero even in 1936, the best year shown; all rates for the highest class are positive, remaining above zero even in 1932, the poorest year shown.

The most remarkable approach to parallelism is in the case of the 1931 and 1932 curves; and the next nearest approach is for the 1934 and 1935 curves, when we exclude the final point of the 1935 curve which unfortunately must cover a combination of two size classes. But true parallelism in the chart as a whole is destroyed by numerous peculiarities of the specific curves. The spread among the curves is wider at the left than at the right, and convergence is notable near the extreme right; this suggests a somewhat greater cyclical responsiveness for small than for large trade corporations. Other but less striking departures from parallelism appear; for example, the 1933 curve is more nearly horizontal for a considerable range to the right of 500 thousand dollars of assets than are the other curves. This suggests that the cyclical recovery beginning in 1933 made itself felt for middle-sized and very large trade corporations more quickly than for small and moderately large corporations. Such a development suggests a question as to specialization by size: the question whether the moderately large corporations are predominantly engaged in a special line of trading activity such as large metropolitan department stores.

Another peculiarity of the chart which may suggest specialization by size is the general dip appearing in all curves except 1932 either in the 5-million-dollar class or the next higher size class. All curves show a sharp advance in rate for the highest class shown, and the final movements of the several curves are notably similar in inclination. Are we to infer that the fairly typical dip in rate near 10 million dollars indicates definitely that the mere fact of a size in that range brings somewhat lower profits in trade activities than a size somewhat smaller or considerably larger? Or may it be that certain special lines of trade activity or certain special types of operating organization — tending to have a somewhat lower earning power — predominate in the assets-range 5 to 50 million dollars, and thus bring down the average rate of return somewhere in that range? Unfortunately, the statistical record is less helpful here than in the case of the manufacturing division.

The foregoing specific questions about specialization are merely aspects of a more general question: may the entire picture given by Chart XLIX, of apparent correlation between rate of return and size, merely or largely reflect only the fact that particular types of trading activity, having particular typical rates of return, tend to predominate in particular size classes? This is the same question already raised many times above, in studying other divisions and the manufacturing groups. Unlike the case for the manufacturing division, for which available data permitted separate study of certain constituent groups, the trade division is not broken down into separate groups. As in the case of the sub-groups of a manufacturing group, *Statistics of Income* does, however, give a rough break-down of the trade division for a very limited list of income-account items — for example, page 38 of the 1935 issue, Part 2 — but without size classification. The stated groups are very broad; and, even if the complete tabulations were available for them, would not afford an analysis of significance comparable with that made for manufacturing in Chapters V to XII. For example, "retail" is too broad a category to enable us to answer the kind of questions raised above with respect to specialization. We may, however, observe some evidence in these figures of specialization by size — size measured not by total assets, but by "gross income" which not only is not necessarily correlated closely with total assets but also is an imperfect measure of total gross receipts. On this basis, the 1935 figures show the average gross income per corporation for the broad trade groups listed in Table XXXIV. Rough as this measure is for the purpose in hand (compare Table III), the differences among the figures are so wide as to leave little doubt of different size tendencies for different lines of trading activity: some specialization of type of activity by size almost surely exists.

The comparative importance of the five groups, in terms of total gross income in 1935, varies widely. The two major groups — wholesale, and retail — had gross incomes of about equal magnitude, and together accounted for about four fifths of the division. Wholesale and retail — enterprises combining both stages of distribution — had about one third the size of each of the two leading groups; and the two remaining groups were very small. In view of the large aggregate importance of the two leading groups, the most significant difference — from the point of view of possible specialization by size class — among the figures for average gross income per corporation is that between wholesale ($524,000) and retail ($178,000).

TABLE XXXIV

COMPARATIVE IMPORTANCE OF GROUPS OF THE TRADE DIVISION IN 1935 *

	Number of corporations	Total gross income	Gross income per corporation
Group			
Wholesale	29,072	15,220	524
Retail	86,270	15,355	178
Wholesale and retail	18,850	5,691	302
Commission	6,130	756	123
Other trade	9,104	508	56
Entire trade division	149,426	37,530	251

* Compiled and computed from *Statistics of Income for 1935, Part 2*, p. 38. Units: $1,000,000, for column 2; $1,000, for column 3.

We must bear in mind that differences in type of organization and method of operation may be quite as important — in thinking of specialization by size, and its implications with respect to rate of return — as line of trading activity. Thus, differences between the chain-store and independent-unit types of organization in the drug line may be quite as important as differences between the drug business and retailing of new automobiles. Either type of organization or line of business *may* be specialized by size; and various types of organization, as well as various lines of trading activity, *may* have various typical rates of return. It may fairly be suggested that the same question should be raised with respect to manufacturing: may it not be true that in manufacturing differences as to type of organization or method of operation have as much bearing upon the apparent correlation between rate of return and size as differences in commodity produced? No doubt such questions are important for manufacturing and the other commodity-producing divisions; and, with respect to all divisions, the data available give us no satisfactory means of answering or even tentatively answering these questions.

But for trade the situation is even worse than for manufacturing: in trade we are not even able to analyse separate data for particular lines. In trade we can make no detailed analysis, comparable to the analysis — at least for broad categories — carried out in Chapters V to XII for particular lines of manufacturing. We remain therefore completely uncertain as to the possible explanation of the apparent correlation between rate of return and size in the trade division, in terms of a size-specialization either by line of activity or by type of organization. With the data as they stand, we can merely conclude that the apparent indication of Chart XLIX — that rate of return rises with increasing size — *may* reflect a typical causal effect of size upon earning power in trade, but may on the other hand be wholly or partially explainable by considerations for which our evidence affords no test.

TIME VARIATION

Although Chart XLIX gives a fairly clear indication of time variations — mainly cyclical — in the rate of return and of the more or less uniform way, at least as to direction of change, in which the time variations affect the various size classes, we show in Chart L (similar to Chart II, for all corporations) the annual variations for two selected size classes and for all sizes combined. For trade, as for most divisions and groups already examined, the main outlines of the cyclical picture are clear and simple. The decline from 1931 to 1932 was followed by unmistakable advances in each succeeding year, though the pace of advance slackened somewhat in 1934 and greatly in 1935. The intensity of the cyclical fluctuation, particularly in

CHART L

TIME VARIATIONS IN RATE OF RETURN, FOR TRADE DIVISION AND SELECTED SIZE CLASSES *

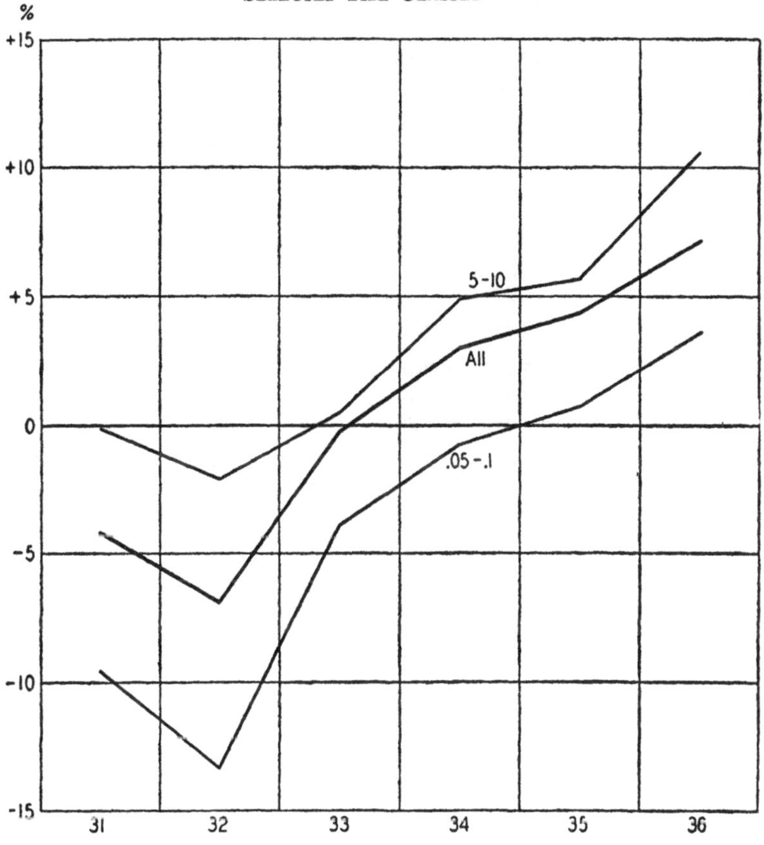

* Data in Table xxxv.

1931–33, was notably greater for the low size class than for the high class shown. Details for other size classes can be traced from Table xxxv.

How much of the 1931–32 decline and the 1932–33 advance may have been due to price changes, and the related matter of inventory valuation, we can not know from available data. We

TABLE XXXV

Rates of Return for Trade Division *

Class †	1931	1932	1933	1934	1935	1936
0	**−17.96**	**−26.02**	**−12.46**	**−7.90**	**−7.12**	**−3.71**
	10.75	7.06	7.37	9.09	8.97	10.54
	−34.73	*−33.15*	*−22.96*	*−21.79*	*−22.46*	*−23.30*
50	**−9.58**	**−13.31**	**−3.91**	**−.73**	**.75**	**3.61**
	7.18	5.19	6.20	7.65	8.43	9.71
	−19.77	*−17.77*	*−11.18*	*−10.81*	*−10.62*	*−10.22*
100	**−7.16**	**−10.62**	**−2.37**	**1.04**	**2.34**	**5.24**
	6.33	5.27	6.15	7.81	8.33	9.96
	−15.12	*−14.72*	*−9.40*	*−8.50*	*−8.60*	*−9.15*
250	**−5.84**	**−8.15**	**−.45**	**2.21**	**3.76**	**6.74**
	6.02	6.21	13.91	7.82	8.63	9.96
	−12.83	*−12.26*	*−7.58*	*−7.03*	*−7.23*	*−7.26*
500	**−5.43**	**−6.45**	**.60**	**3.37**	**4.12**	**7.08**
	6.05	6.49	7.31	8.55	9.05	10.11
	−11.62	*−10.56*	*−6.80*	*−7.20*	*−7.36*	*−8.68*
1,000	**−3.29**	**−5.09**	**.80**	**4.56**	**5.91**	**8.35**
	6.66	6.02	7.40	8.70	9.38	10.37
	−9.95	*−9.63*	*−7.42*	*−5.99*	*−7.35*	*−7.60*
5,000	**−.12**	**−2.09**	**.51**	**4.91**	**5.64**	**10.56**
	7.65	6.44	6.92	9.78	9.55	13.87
	−8.59	*−7.44*	*−7.52*	*−6.60*	*−5.15*	*−4.57*
10,000	**−.34**	**−1.25**	**2.22**	**4.30**	...	**9.27**
	7.70	8.02	7.86	8.44	9.94	11.14
	−7.29	*−5.84*	*−4.98*	*−5.88*	...	*−8.14*
50,000	**4.24**	**2.59**	**6.09**	**9.05**	...	**9.29**
	12.61	8.06	8.97	10.16	10.82	9.29
	−11.98	*−5.14*	*−2.62*	*2.87*	...	...
100,000	...	...	...	...	...	**12.73**
	...	...	...	...	...	12.73
	...	...	...	...	...	...
Classes grouped ‡	...	...	...	...	**8.38**	...
	...	...	...	...	...	...
	...	...	...	...	*−3.36*	...
Entire division ..	**−4.19**	**−6.90**	**−.25**	**3.05**	**4.37**	**7.16**
	8.32	6.86	7.49	8.77	9.44	10.70
	−13.91	*−12.90*	*−9.23*	*−8.60*	*−9.37*	*−11.13*

do know that inventory fluctuations can constitute an important fraction of profit or loss, as reckoned for tax purposes; and we may fairly suspect that numerous corporations in the trade division are especially susceptible to such influences. That 1931–33 was a period of widely varying prices, accompanied by much less wide fluctuations in the volume of transactions, is also known. Moreover, although cost changes theretofore may not have been marked, the N.R.A. brought substantial increases of cost in various branches of trade in 1933. Again in 1936, price changes became sharp; and may not have been attended by corresponding changes in cost. In view of these considerations, the sharpness of the cyclical changes in these curves points strongly to the hypothesis that price changes may be the major factor affecting earning power of trade corporations, whatever their size.

In studying Chart L, it is especially important to bear in mind the lack of exact comparability of data for 1934–36 with those of earlier years, because of the change in law concerning consolidated tax returns (see Chapter XXVII). This important change, deeply affecting the industrial classification of the tax-return statistics, was of especial importance in the trade division, for a particularly large number of trade corporations were formerly covered under consolidated returns falling in other industrial divisions (see page 374). In fact, the special tabulations of 1934 data show 4206, among the total of 127,457

---

* Expressed in per cent; ratio of profit (or loss) after taxes to estimated average equity, as explained in text, p. 18. Figures in boldface type are for income and deficit categories of corporations combined, in ordinary type for the income category, in italics for the deficit category.

† Lower limit of class interval, in thousands of dollars of total assets. The 50,000-thousand-dollar class has no stated upper limit, 1931–35; the 100,000-thousand-dollar class has no stated upper limit, 1936.

‡ High size classes combined, to conceal a single corporation. Where such combination applies to only deficit category, other category is shown separately in the specific classes, but joint figure for both categories is shown only in "grouped" row.

balance-sheet returns classified in trade in 1934, which had been covered by consolidated returns in 1933.[2] Total assets for these 4206 cases were $5,403,728,000 against $17,434,-130,000 for the entire trade division; hence these comparatively few corporations ran much larger on the average than the typical trade corporation. Now, obviously, not all of these 4206 trade returns of 1934, which were covered by consolidated returns in 1933, were classified elsewhere than in trade in 1933. Evidence exists, however, that less than half of them (by number) were covered by consolidated returns which had been classified in trade in 1933; and, of course, the remainder were therefore classified in other divisions than trade in 1933. Unfortunately this evidence pertains only to the number of corporations, and we can only guess what fraction of the above $5,403,728,000 was shifted from other divisions in 1933 to trade in 1934; but we may fairly assume it was a substantial fraction and included mainly corporations having large size. We remark that this argument has not been pursued here to the more or less offsetting cases wherein trade in 1933 lost assets to other divisions in 1934 (see page 376).

PROFITABLE AND UNPROFITABLE CORPORATIONS

Separate study of the income and deficit categories of the trade division, each classified by size, brings out a striking distinction from a similar analysis for all corporations without regard to industrial type (Chart III, and related textual discussion). The income category for trade does not show the progressive decline in rate of return as size increases, which was found for all divisions combined (rates for the income category appear in Table XXXV). Instead, if we ignore the lowest and the highest size classes, we should observe here a general tendency for rate of return to increase with increasing

[2] *Statistics of Income for 1934, Part 2*, pp. 71 and 168. See also pp. 25–26 in connection with concluding remarks herewith.

size, with some irregularities, in all six years. Hence, for profitable corporations in the trade division, rate of return tends to increase as size increases. These changes are really small, but the direction of movement is unmistakable. We may therefore not infer that the upward course of the curves of Chart XLIX,

CHART LI

SIX-YEAR AVERAGE OF RATES OF RETURN, FOR TRADE DIVISION AND INCOME AND DEFICIT CATEGORIES *

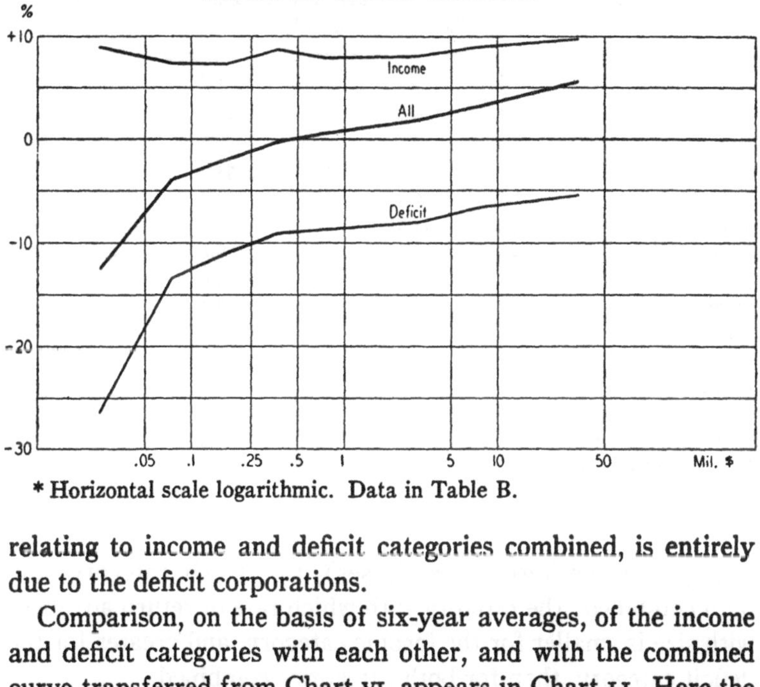

* Horizontal scale logarithmic. Data in Table B.

relating to income and deficit categories combined, is entirely due to the deficit corporations.

Comparison, on the basis of six-year averages, of the income and deficit categories with each other, and with the combined curve transferred from Chart VI, appears in Chart LI. Here the income and deficit curves do not move in generally opposite directions as size changes, as was the case in various other comparisons of this sort (see pages 30, 61, and 172). The income curve, except for one irregularity, has a generally concave upward shape, compared with the continuous advance of the deficit curve. For both curves the slope is upward to the right above 500 thousand dollars, and even above 100 thousand dollars if a single size class is excluded from the income curve.

Similar data for each year are given in Table XXXV. The same general conclusion follows: with some irregularities, rate of return increases with increasing size for the income category

TABLE XXXVI

ANNUAL PERCENTAGE RATIOS OF TOTAL ASSETS OF INCOME CATEGORY OF CORPORATIONS TO TOTAL ASSETS, IN EACH SIZE CLASS OF THE TRADE DIVISION *

Class †	1931	1932	1933	1934	1935	1936
0	34.6	16.1	31.1	39.8	42.3	49.7
50	36.7	18.7	39.4	50.8	55.6	64.7
100	36.0	19.9	43.2	55.2	61.7	72.3
250	36.1	22.0	47.9	59.5	65.2	78.0
500	34.4	24.5	50.8	62.1	67.1	79.7
1,000	39.2	29.3	53.8	66.1	73.0	84.8
5,000	46.1	38.6	57.4	65.9	72.6	81.8
10,000	46.2	36.0	54.6	67.0	85.2	88.8
50,000	64.9	49.3	72.8	85.5	...	100.0
100,000	...	...	...	...	...	100.0
Entire division	42.7	29.4	51.9	63.2	69.5	80.2

* Calculated from basic figures for total assets given in successive issues of *Statistics of Income* (for example, 1935 issue, Part 2, pp. 80–81).

† Lower limit of size class; unit, $1,000. Separate data for $100,000,000 class available only in 1936. Classes above $10,000,000 grouped in 1935.

(except for the lowest size classes), the deficit category, and both combined; the rapidity with which rate of return advances with size is smaller for the income category, and greater for the deficit category, than for both categories combined.

The remarkable shifts from the income category to the deficit category, and *vice versa*, are indicated by Table XXXVI. For each size class, and the entire division, the tabulated figures give the annual percentages of the total assets of the class which are held by the income corporations. For the division as a whole, the percentage drops sharply from 1931 to 1932, and then advances in each succeeding year — the total shift being from just under 30 per cent to just over 80. This course is followed, with some differences in intensity of change, for every size class: the 1932 figure is uniformly the minimum, and the 1936 figure is uniformly the maximum. Very large shifts of percentage occur in certain years for certain size classes. And we must remember these are based on net — or aggregate — figures; a shift of 3 per cent between two years, for a particular size class, merely reflects a change in the aggregate total assets of the income category as a portion of the total assets of both categories combined. Still greater shifts may actually have taken place and might appear, if we could trace the changes of specific corporations from (to) the income category to (from) the deficit category; but some of these shifts of specific corporations were probably cancelled out, and thus not reflected in our aggregate figures for total assets of the class as a whole. The bearing of this upon our analysis of profit rates is clear: the nature of the specific corporations — with respect to various elements bearing upon their equity and earning power — may be different for the corporations which become profitable from that for those which become unprofitable, in any one year.

SUMMARY

The economic implications of these findings for the trade division, and the possibility of their explanation on various assumptions as to specialization — according to line of trade activity or form of operating method or organization — can not be developed from the evidence as it stands. The lack of subclassification of the trade division data is a major obstacle to making even a start toward answering these questions. We are dealing here with data pertaining to a very broad and undoubtedly heterogeneous industrial division, and analysis of such data can only leave us with numerous important questions unanswered.

The broad fact that the major comparison of rate with size shows the same relationships for trade (Chart XLIX) as for manufacturing (Chart IX) and all divisions combined (Chart I) is the principal finding of this chapter. Our inability, with available evidence, to show in what degree these relationships reflect specialization within the trade division need not lead to a complete discounting of the finding. In manufacturing, where such a detailed examination of specific lines was possible, we found the main relationships persisting to a remarkable degree in most specific groups.

XVI

SERVICE DIVISION

THE SERVICE DIVISION, though distinctly less important than the leading divisions, occupies a fairly large place in the entire corporate system (Table III). But balance-sheet tabulations and classified data by size of corporation are available only for the division as a whole, and our size-class analysis of rate of return must therefore be limited to the entire division. Nevertheless, the division includes widely different branches of activity, as indicated by the stubs of Table XXXVII. Most of these groups provide services, but of widely different sorts, for direct consumption; but some provide mainly or partly services to other business enterprises and are accordingly in the producers' goods area.

The most important group, constituting nearly half of the total on the basis of gross income in 1935, is domestic service, which includes hotels and restaurants, laundries, office-building operation, and like enterprises. The next group in importance is business services, which includes mainly advertising and related enterprises; and this group runs to about one third the importance of the domestic service group. The four groups representing amusements should perhaps be considered together; in the aggregate they constitute nearly one quarter of the entire division. The most important of these four amusement groups is motion-picture theatre operation; and the least important, the smallest group of the entire division, is legitimate theatres — its gross income was only about 4 per cent of that of the motion-picture theatres. The professional service group, which constitutes about 7 per cent of the entire division, is perhaps the most heterogeneous of the groups. It includes a wide range of services — curative, educational, engineering, legal — some for direct consumption and some for use in other enterprises.

The average size of corporations varies only moderately among most of the groups; for nearly all of them the average

TABLE XXXVII

COMPARATIVE IMPORTANCE OF GROUPS OF THE SERVICE DIVISION IN 1935 *

	Number of corporations	Total gross income	Gross income per corporation
Group			
Domestic	24,311	1,847	76
Amusements			
Theatres, legitimate	543	18.3	34
Motion picture producers	259	214	825
Motion picture theatres	3,811	476	125
Other amusements	5,673	157	28
Total	10,286	865	84
Professional, etc.	7,344	254	35
Business services	7,087	564	80
Other services	5,532	179	32
Entire service division	54,560	3,708	68

* Compiled and computed from *Statistics of Income for 1935, Part 2*, pp. 38–39. Units: $1,000,000, for column 2; $1,000, for column 3.

gross income was below 100 thousand dollars in 1935. The outstanding exception is motion-picture producers: the 259 corporations in this group had an average gross income of over 800 thousand dollars, more than ten times the average for the entire division. Some reason exists, therefore, for anticipating that the rate-of-return figures for certain size classes in the service division may be dominated by conditions in one of the particular branches of activity covered by the division.

SIZE VARIATION IN RATE

A notable feature of the display of curves relating rate of return to size (Chart LII), in comparison with like curves for other divisions, is the unmistakable downward-to-the-right tendency for the class or classes immediately above 500 thousand dollars. With some irregularity, this downward tendency persists into the 5-million-dollar class for all years except 1931. On the other hand, an advance in rate appears in the top

CHART LII

RATE OF RETURN COMPARED WITH SIZE, FOR SERVICE DIVISION *

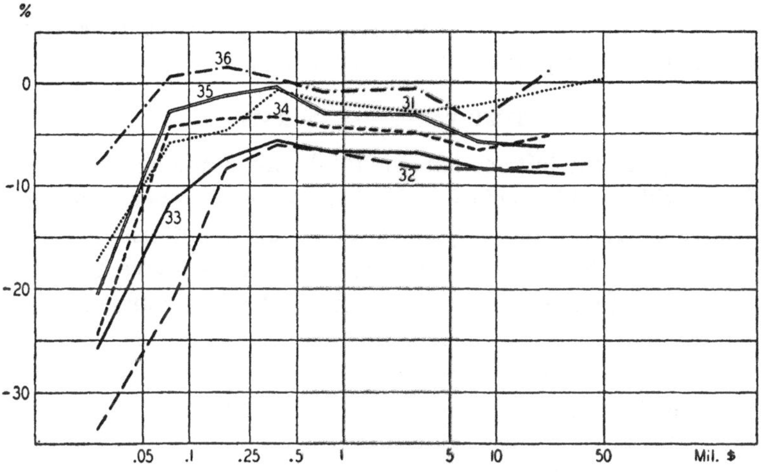

* Horizontal scale logarithmic. Data in Table XXXVIII.

size class for all years except 1933 and 1935. To the left of the 500-thousand-dollar boundary, most of the curves have a generally upward course; but, except for 1932, this advance in rate with increasing size is sharp only at the left ends of the curves. Ignoring the lowest size class — and in 1932 the next higher class — total variation in rate among the size classes is not large in any year; such variation as exists has a fairly clear maximum in the 250-thousand-dollar class, in all years except 1931 and 1936. For the service division, then, rate of return declines as size increases, above a fairly low size boundary.

Diverse class-to-class inclinations of the curves, and some intersections among the curves, preclude any significant appearance of parallelism. Such cyclical variations as appear in this division do not affect the various size classes uniformly. Lack of uniformity is strikingly manifest near the ends of the curves: the intersection of the 1931 curve with those for 1934 and 1935, and the persistence of a rapid advance in rate up to the third size class for the 1932 curve, emphasize the lack of parallelism to the left of 250 thousand dollars; intersections near the right are additional departures from parallelism.

TIME VARIATION IN RATE

Except in the left section, the total spread among the curves is not wide, and impact of cyclical variations in general business (particularly the recovery after 1933) on this division is thus not great. The fact that the 1931 curve runs above all other curves except that of 1936 through most of its course implies either that depression failed to have severe effects on these industries until 1932, or that the general revival had not reached extensively to these industries by 1935. The 1936 curve runs above all other curves except at one point, but absence of a record for some highly prosperous year precludes a comparison of the levels of the 1931–35 curves with a rate-of-return curve for service industries in most favorable cyclical conditions.

Further evidence of the peculiar cyclical response of this division appears in Chart LIII. The curve for the entire division shows 1931 higher than all other years except 1936, and the curve for the selected high size class shows 1931 above all later years. On the other hand, rate of return for the low size class shown in the chart had by 1934 recovered above the 1931 level. Moreover, except for the low size class shown the 1932–33 revival is smaller than we have observed in numerous groups of the manufacturing division. A progressive but moderate advance does appear for 1934–36; and in this respect the experi-

CHART LIII

Time Variations in Rate of Return, for Service Division and Selected Size Classes *

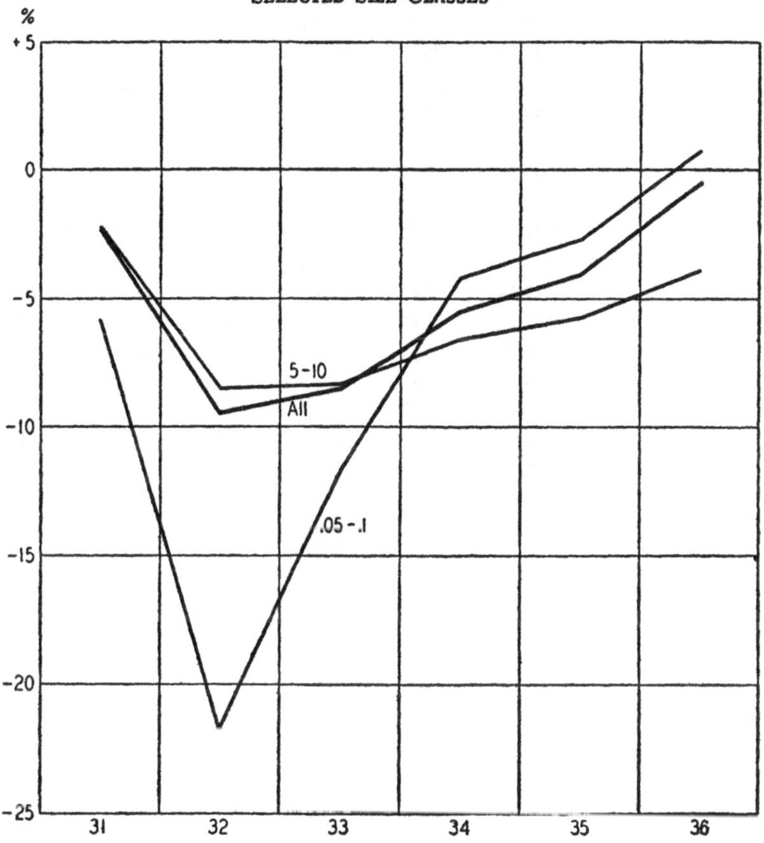

* Data in Table xxxviii.

ence of the service division is not peculiar. Further details, for other classes, are given in Table xxxviii.

PROFITABLE AND UNPROFITABLE CORPORATIONS

Rates of return for the income category of corporations in the service division show a general tendency to decline with

TABLE XXXVIII

Rates of Return for Service Division *

Class †	1931	1932	1933	1934	1935	1936
0	**−17.36**	**−33.58**	**−25.77**	**−24.53**	**−20.62**	**−7.91**
	15.92	13.81	13.50	18.83	20.50	23.88
	−48.30	*−45.86*	*−39.98*	*−62.08*	*−69.88*	*−50.47*
50	**−5.82**	**−21.80**	**−11.67**	**−4.22**	**−2.74**	**.73**
	10.53	8.96	10.43	11.48	13.49	14.62
	−20.73	*−31.91*	*−20.01*	*−14.79*	*−17.32*	*−18.36*
100	**−4.64**	**−8.35**	**−7.30**	**−3.41**	**−1.19**	**1.60**
	8.87	8.04	8.34	10.42	10.96	11.42
	−17.03	*−13.84*	*−13.00*	*−13.13*	*−12.66*	*−11.90*
250	**−.68**	**−6.00**	**−5.58**	**−3.32**	**−.37**	**.46**
	10.24	7.83	9.07	9.86	10.28	10.27
	−11.42	*−11.44*	*−11.17*	*−13.02*	*−6.78*	*−11.41*
500	**−1.83**	**−6.57**	**−6.56**	**−4.25**	**−2.91**	**−.81**
	9.34	6.76	6.15	7.74	8.44	9.10
	−11.58	*−11.97*	*−11.82*	*−12.54*	*−13.02*	*−10.67*
1,000	**−2.83**	**−8.21**	**−6.72**	**−4.82**	**−3.09**	**−.55**
	7.53	5.37	6.33	9.82	9.08	9.06
	−9.90	*−12.49*	*−10.48*	*−11.26*	*−10.36*	*−10.29*
5,000	**−2.12**	**−8.42**	**−8.31**	**−6.55**	**−5.73**	**−3.86**
	12.99	8.69	7.86	7.86	7.12	5.12
	−8.39	*−12.57*	*−12.48*	*−12.27*	*−12.17*	*−13.75*
10,000	...	...	...	...	...	...
	...	...	...	3.38	...	...
	−10.28	*−12.49*	*−13.22*	...	*−16.86*	*−13.57*
50,000	...	...	...	...	...	...
	...	...	...	4.69	...	...
	−.83	*−9.71*	*−13.39*	...	*−135.00*	...
Classes grouped ‡	**.28**	**−7.93**	**−8.90**	**−5.08**	**−6.22**	**1.04**
	4.46	6.83	5.46	...	4.96	11.64
	...	...	...	*−18.79*	...	...
Entire division	**−2.18**	**−9.44**	**−8.52**	**−5.52**	**−4.07**	**−.54**
	7.29	7.18	7.30	8.38	9.28	10.53
	−10.51	*−13.83*	*−13.66*	*−15.09*	*−14.96*	*−13.05*

* Expressed in per cent; ratio of profit (or loss) after taxes to estimated average equity, as explained in text, p. 18. Figures in boldface type are for income and deficit categories of corporations combined, in ordinary type for the income category, in italics for the deficit category.

† Lower limit of class interval, in thousands of dollars of total assets. The

increasing size (Table XXXVIII). In some years the rate for the income category rises sharply in the top size classes; nevertheless, the general downward tendency of rate with increasing size is unmistakable.

CHART LIV

SIX-YEAR AVERAGE OF RATES OF RETURN, FOR SERVICE DIVISION AND INCOME AND DEFICIT CATEGORIES *

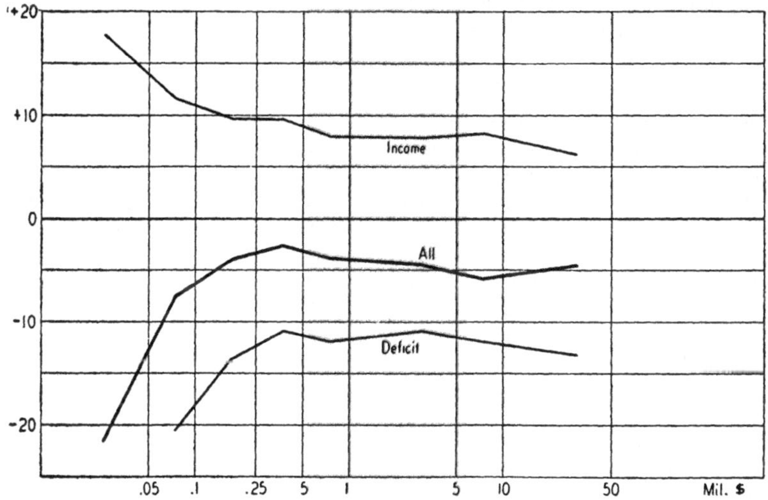

* Horizontal scale logarithmic. Data in Table B. One point omitted in lowest class.

In the service division, declining rate of return for the income category as size increases does not imply — as it does in numerous other divisions and most manufacturing groups — that the "deficit category accounts for all, and more, of the

50,000-thousand-dollar class has no stated upper limit, 1931–35; the 100,000-thousand-dollar class has no stated upper limit, 1936, and items of this class are covered in "Classes grouped."

‡ High size classes combined, to conceal a single corporation. Where such combination applies to only income or deficit category, other category is shown separately in the specific classes, but joint figure for both categories is shown only in "grouped" row.

advance of rate with size" for both categories combined. Here the deficit category, as well as the income category, shows an irregular but clear declining tendency above 5 million and perhaps 500 thousand dollars (see Chart LIV). To the left of 500 thousand dollars, to be sure, rate rises more rapidly with

TABLE XXXIX

ANNUAL PERCENTAGE RATIOS OF TOTAL ASSETS OF INCOME CATEGORY OF CORPORATIONS TO TOTAL ASSETS, IN EACH SIZE CLASS OF THE SERVICE DIVISION *

Class †	1931	1932	1933	1934	1935	1936
0	41.3	16.7	19.2	28.2	31.7	37.3
50	42.1	18.7	21.6	31.9	34.8	38.5
100	43.7	18.6	19.9	29.6	33.7	37.0
250	43.2	20.5	19.8	28.7	32.0	31.4
500	39.0	19.8	18.5	25.9	29.3	30.8
1,000	29.1	17.4	15.7	21.0	23.6	31.1
5,000	26.4	14.8	14.8	15.3	19.0	29.7
10,000	37.4	12.4	13.6	38.4	27.8	29.5
Entire division	36.3	16.2	16.4	26.8	27.0	31.8

* Calculated from basic figures for total assets given in successive issues of *Statistics of Income* (for example, 1935 issue, Part 2, p. 81).

† Lower limit of size class; unit, $1,000. Classes above $10,000,000 grouped in all years.

increasing size for the deficit category than for both categories combined. The downward inclination of the income curve largely explains the steeper advance of the deficit curve, as compared with the combined curve, in all the left section and the nearly horizontal drift of the deficit curve while the combined curve is declining in the middle section. Similar comparisons for particular years can be traced from Table XXXVIII.

The large net shifts in total assets from (to) the income category to (from) the deficit category — in passing from one year to the next — appear in Table XXXIX. In this division, the percentage of total assets held by the income category of corporations is not uniformly minimum in 1932 — several size classes have the minimum in 1933, and for the entire division the 1933 figure is only slightly above that for 1932. Another striking fact is that the 1931 percentage runs above that of 1936 (or any other year) in the entire division and in every size class except two. This is further confirmation of the moderate pace of the 1933–36 recovery in the service division.

XVII

PUBLIC UTILITIES

THE PUBLIC UTILITIES DIVISION, which includes transportation enterprises as well as other utilities, is one of the largest of the nine divisions (Table III). The division is made up of corporations providing services rather than commodities, having comparatively little occasion to carry inventories, and mainly operating in economic areas considerably affected with monopolistic or quasi-monopolistic characteristics and extensively subject to public regulation. It includes corporations ranging very widely in size, from small enterprises such as taxicab companies or local waterworks concerns to the giants of the railroad, telephone, and electric-power groups.

The data required for an analysis of rate of return by corporate size are available only for the division as a whole, although the division includes utility activities of widely different types. Gross income and certain related figures are available for several broad groups within the division, and these afford some indication of the comparative importance of these groups and of the average size of the corporations therein. Pertinent figures of this sort for 1935 are shown in Table XL. The stubs of this table emphasize the diversity of activities included in the division; the thirteen groups are separated into two broad sections, transportation and other utilities, of nearly equal importance. Within each section, and even to a greater extent within the entire division, the groups vary notably as to their importance — measured roughly in terms of total gross income in 1935 — and as to the average size (gross income) per corporation. Total gross income of the group ranges from 3.9 billion dollars for steam railroads to 45 million dollars for aerial transportation; average gross income per corporation ranges from 6.7 million dollars for steam railroads to 46 thousand dollars for water companies. The strikingly wide ranges in these figures suggest that profit conditions for certain of the more

TABLE XL

COMPARATIVE IMPORTANCE OF GROUPS OF THE PUBLIC UTILITIES DIVISION IN 1935 *

	Number of corporations	Total gross income	Gross income per corporation
Group			
Transportation			
Steam railroads	576	3,854	6,691
Electric railways	1,383	763	552
Water transportation	2,259	628	278
Aerial transportation	545	45	82
Bus, taxicab, etc.	2,821	271	96
Cartage and storage	10,261	812	79
Total	17,845	6,373	357
Other public utilities			
Electric power and light	1,621	2,495	1,539
Gas	1,007	630	626
Pipe lines	283	329	1,164
Telephone and telegraph	3,502	1,340	383
Radio broadcasting	505	97	192
Water companies	2,014	93	46
Terminals, etc.	1,660	228	137
Total	10,592	5,212	492
Entire public utilities division	28,437	11,585	407

* Compiled and computed from *Statistics of Income for 1935, Part 2*, pp. 37–38. Units: $1,000,000, for column 2; $1,000, for column 3.

important groups may dominate calculated figures for the entire division and most of its several size classes, and that certain particular groups — not necessarily the most important in all cases — may dominate the results for particular size classes. In this division, in greater degree than in most other divisions and most manufacturing groups studied, diversities among the branches of activity are likely to influence our calculations of rate of return for the division and its size classes. Irregularities in those results, and perhaps even the uniformities discovered, may be the consequences of peculiar conditions in particular branches of utility activity, and of the way these branches are matched together in the entire division and its size classes.

SIZE VARIATION IN RATE

The display of curves relating rate of return to size of corporation for the public utility division departs notably from

CHART LV

RATE OF RETURN COMPARED WITH SIZE, FOR PUBLIC UTILITIES DIVISION *

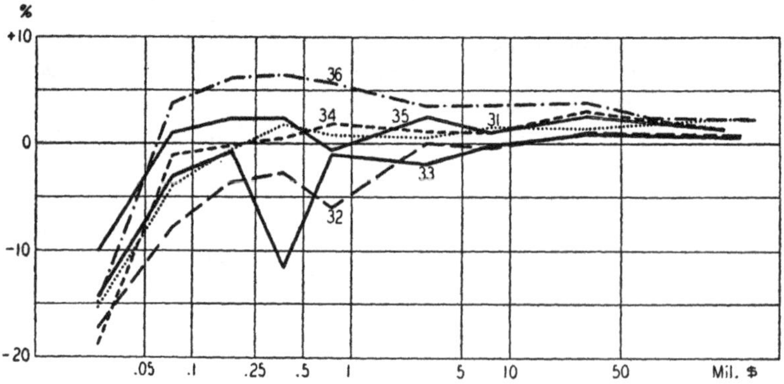

* Horizontal scale logarithmic. Data in Table XLI.

similar exhibits for most other divisions and most manufacturing groups (Chart LV).[1] The total range in variation of rate — omitting the lowest class — is comparatively small; and there is no such violent drop to extremely low levels even at the left ends of the curves as has been noted in numerous other cases. Except for the moderately sharp rise of the curves at the

[1] The remarkable irregularity near the left of the 1933 curve is not due to a tabulating error, as we learn from correspondence with the Bureau of Internal Revenue. It affects also Charts VI, LVII, and LXII.

very left, there is little evidence of a systematic advance in rate with increasing size: from the 50-thousand-dollar class to the right ends of the curves the movement is surprisingly horizontal, though the general tendency is very slightly upward in all years except 1932 and 1936. Ignoring the lowest size class, the total range of variation was just over 4 per cent in 1934, just over 3 per cent in 1935. For these industries, except among the very small corporations, little relation between rate of return and size is indicated. To what extent this condition reflects public regulation and other peculiarities of these industries can only be guessed, but the facts are emphatically clear. Another striking fact is that, except in 1932 and 1936, nearly all rates other than those for the lowest class fall fairly close to zero.

Remarkable irregularities appear in certain of the curves; the most notable of these is the severe drop in rate for the 500-thousand-dollar class of the 1932 curve. The true meaning of these irregularities can not be inferred from the available data; but the possibility, noted above, that particular branches of the utility industry may dominate particular size classes is a possible explanation. These irregularities are, however, not the only evidences of lack of parallelism among the curves. Numerous differences in direction at different size levels, and numerous actual intersections, appear among the curves. Moreover, there is a general convergence of the curves toward the right end: the total spread among the curves, nowhere large in comparison with that observed in several other divisions, narrows progressively as size increases above 500 thousand dollars.

TIME VARIATION IN RATE

The foregoing remarks suggest that, although the cyclical impact upon the industries of this division is not severe, it varies remarkably from size class to size class, and is generally greater for small sizes than for large. No such uniformity among most size classes, as respects cyclical response, appears here as was found in various other divisions and in most manufacturing groups. This peculiarity again is perhaps a consequence of tendencies for certain types of utility industry to concentrate in particular size classes, and may reflect in addition a more

CHART LVI

TIME VARIATIONS IN RATE OF RETURN, FOR PUBLIC UTILITIES DIVISION AND SELECTED SIZE CLASSES *

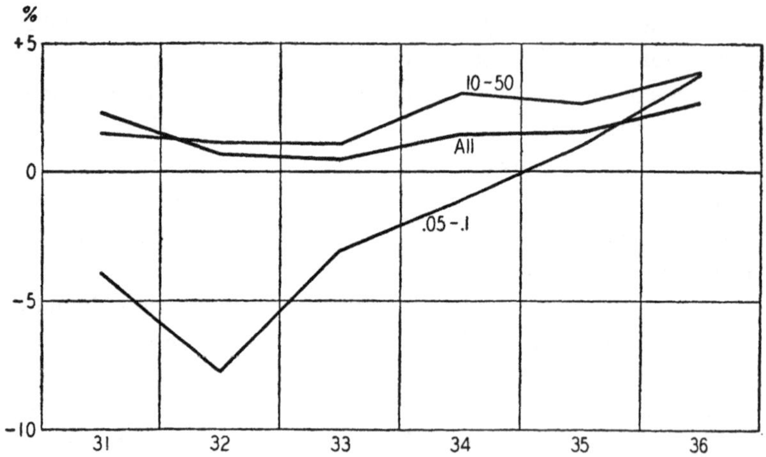

* Data in Table XLI.

nearly complete application of public regulation to the types of utility in the high size classes than to those in the low.

The observed diversity of cyclical response among size classes is brought out more sharply in Chart LVI. The curves for the division and the two selected size classes reveal not only a marked difference in intensity of time variation, but also extraordinary diversity in the course of variation. The most notable instance of this appears in the inverse movements of the curves for the two selected size classes in 1934–35. Other instances appear in the notable difference of inclination for these two curves in 1931–32 and 1932–33. Another striking

TABLE XLI

Rates of Return for Public Utilities Division *

Class †	1931	1932	1933	1934	1935	1936
0	**−15.04**	**−17.32**	**−14.31**	**−18.83**	**−10.08**	**−14.84**
	13.23	9.39	10.56	13.41	13.92	15.57
	−53.65	*−34.27*	*−36.83*	*−97.94*	*−68.00*	*−136.99*
50	**−3.95**	**−7.78**	**−3.08**	**−1.13**	**1.03**	**3.81**
	11.19	8.86	9.68	10.56	12.98	14.28
	−25.90	*−19.83*	*−15.87*	*−21.31*	*−25.27*	*−20.15*
100	**−.53**	**−3.62**	**−.69**	**−.07**	**2.39**	**6.13**
	8.37	8.11	7.29	9.24	11.25	14.08
	−15.42	*−15.66*	*−10.44*	*−16.96*	*−16.10*	*−15.77*
250	**1.83**	**−2.68**	**−11.61**	**.52**	**2.43**	**6.44**
	8.50	7.77	7.19	8.19	10.50	11.47
	−10.18	*−14.01*	*−37.73*	*−20.15*	*−22.83*	*−13.14*
500	**.80**	**−5.97**	**−.98**	**1.90**	**−.57**	**5.72**
	7.34	7.68	6.37	7.73	8.57	10.36
	−9.40	*−21.30*	*−12.33*	*−11.56*	*−24.45*	*−12.18*
1,000	**.62**	**.02**	**−1.91**	**1.17**	**2.53**	**3.58**
	6.36	6.30	6.08	7.05	7.52	7.94
	−8.48	*−9.18*	*−16.48*	*−10.42*	*−9.39*	*−10.60*
5,000	**1.63**	**−.39**	**−.17**	**1.06**	**1.06**	**3.63**
	6.93	5.09	5.10	5.44	5.11	6.48
	−6.73	*−7.95*	*−8.09*	*−7.52*	*−7.43*	*−5.96*
10,000	**1.49**	**1.11**	**1.09**	**3.11**	**2.66**	**3.89**
	6.36	5.60	5.29	5.84	6.08	6.74
	−7.52	*−5.54*	*−5.73*	*−5.36*	*−6.61*	*−5.91*
50,000	**2.53**	**.86**	**.62**	**1.40**	**1.39**	**2.50**
	5.89	4.65	4.22	4.63	4.29	4.65
	−1.05	*−2.00*	*−2.29*	*−2.19*	*−2.42*	*−5.71*
100,000	...	...	...	...	...	**2.29**
	...	...	...	...	...	4.32
	...	...	...	...	...	*−2.66*
Entire division	**2.29**	**.67**	**.45**	**1.47**	**1.57**	**2.69**
	6.03	4.90	4.52	5.13	5.00	5.18
	−2.04	*−2.85*	*−3.21*	*−3.30*	*−3.64*	*−4.16*

* Expressed in per cent; ratio of profit (or loss) after taxes to estimated average equity, as explained in text, p. 18. Figures in boldface type are for income and deficit categories of corporations combined, in ordinary type for the income category, in italics for the deficit category. Extreme figure in 250-thousand-dollar class for 1933 is not due to a tabulating error in the source.

† Lower limit of class interval, in thousands of dollars of total assets. The 50,000-thousand-dollar class has no stated upper limit, 1931–35; the 100,000-thousand-dollar class has no stated upper limit, 1936.

feature of the chart is the very slight total variation in the curve for the high size class shown, and this confirms the earlier observation that the curves of Chart LV converge toward the right. In all six years this curve, for the high class, lies between 1 and 4 per cent: its total fluctuation for 1932–36 is less than

CHART LVII

SIX-YEAR AVERAGE OF RATES OF RETURN, FOR PUBLIC UTILITIES DIVISION AND INCOME AND DEFICIT CATEGORIES *

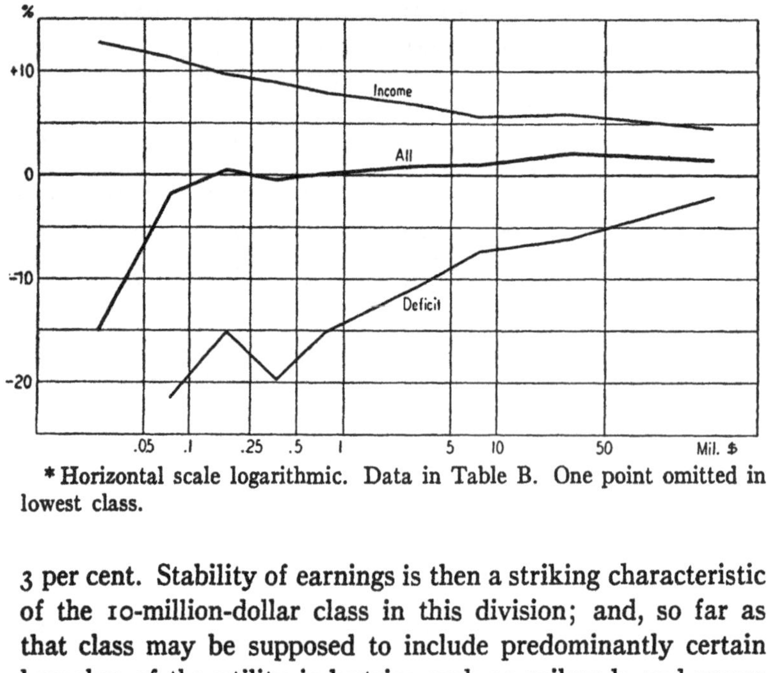

* Horizontal scale logarithmic. Data in Table B. One point omitted in lowest class.

3 per cent. Stability of earnings is then a striking characteristic of the 10-million-dollar class in this division; and, so far as that class may be supposed to include predominantly certain branches of the utility industries such as railroads and power companies, these results reflect a stable *average* rate of return for those branches. On the other hand, cyclical variation for the low size class shown is very wide, and the 1932–36 recovery is steady and sharp. Details for other classes appear in Table XLI.

PROFITABLE AND UNPROFITABLE CORPORATIONS

The income corporations of this division have rates of return which decline generally as size increases (Table XLI); although an interruption of the decline appears in the 10-million-dollar class in most years, and in the next lower class in 1931. Broadly

TABLE XLII

ANNUAL PERCENTAGE RATIOS OF TOTAL ASSETS OF INCOME CATEGORY OF CORPORATIONS TO TOTAL ASSETS, IN EACH SIZE CLASS OF THE PUBLIC UTILITIES DIVISION *

Class †	1931	1932	1933	1934	1935	1936
0	50.3	29.3	34.7	38.8	39.5	47.5
50	52.7	35.2	42.0	48.4	53.3	55.1
100	56.2	40.1	45.6	51.7	56.8	60.6
250	57.1	44.0	47.2	51.4	57.1	63.0
500	49.9	41.0	45.9	51.2	53.9	60.8
1,000	51.3	48.9	50.2	49.9	54.2	59.2
5,000	51.5	47.3	47.7	52.3	54.1	65.1
10,000	59.1	53.0	53.4	59.8	63.3	67.8
50,000	45.1	35.7	37.2	44.0	46.4	65.4
100,000	...	...	...	...	...	58.7
Entire division	46.8	37.9	39.4	47.0	49.6	61.0

* Calculated from basic figures for total assets given in successive issues of *Statistics of Income* (for example, 1935 issue, Part 2, pp. 79–80).

† Lower limit of size class; unit, $1,000. Separate data for $100,000,000 class available only in 1936.

speaking, this declining tendency is more systematic and at a steeper slope than we have found in other divisions. Irregularities are not numerous, and the most significant appear near the right ends of the curves.

Comparison of the income category with the deficit category and with both combined is shown in Chart LVII, on a six-year average basis, and can be traced for specific years from Table XLI. Although the combined curve — ignoring the lowest size class — rises only very gradually toward the right, the upward-to-the-right drift of the deficit curve is very considerable. This, of course, is inevitable because of the nearly steady downward-to-the-right course of the income curve. In this division, more markedly than in most others, inverse direction of movement of the income and deficit curves is the striking feature. The gap between the curves is very wide at the left, and becomes much narrower at the right. One suspects that this may reflect the heavy role of debt in these industries, and on this point a somewhat detailed inquiry appears below (Chapter XXIII).

Table XLII records the annual shifts in total assets between the income and deficit categories, for each size class. These changes are much less extensive than those found in other divisions — and this again is evidence of the remarkable cyclical stability of the public utilities division. Only for the two lowest size classes are the shifts truly wide, even during the years 1931–33; and a further striking fact is that, for the lowest size class, the tabulated percentage is lower in 1936 than in 1931.

XVIII

FINANCE DIVISION

THE LARGEST OF ALL DIVISIONS in the Treasury tabulations is finance (Table III), and this diverse but highly specialized collection of enterprises constitutes so large a segment of the total corporate system that we shall examine below figures for the system as a whole with finance excluded (page 242). The enterprises of this division have to some extent the same "service" characteristics as the three divisions last studied — trade, service, and public utilities. But the finance enterprises have in the main the peculiar characteristic of providing capital, in the form either of equity or of debt, or of serving as intermediaries in the provision of capital, for other divisions of corporate enterprise. In some degree enterprises outside the finance division provide these capital-supplying services, particularly in all cases where intercorporate indebtedness or equity holdings are notable; but the function is especially common and important among the finance enterprises.

Finance is another division for which analysis of rate of return by size of concern must be limited to the entire division. But within the division are groups of enterprises having widely different characteristics, and thus capable of impressing their peculiarities upon the calculated results for the division as a whole. The groups for which gross income and certain related data, though not balance-sheet figures or size classifications, are available are indicated by the stubs of Table XLIII. The largest of the nine groups, in terms of gross income in 1935, is investment trusts (including somewhat related enterprises); and insurance other than life, and real estate and realty holding companies are rather poor second and third. Then, in order, are four groups of nearly equal importance: life insurance, loan companies, national banks, and state and other banks. The eighth group in order, stock and bond brokers, amounts to only about 4 per cent of the division total; and the remaining group, joint-stock land banks, is exceedingly small.

TABLE XLIII

COMPARATIVE IMPORTANCE OF GROUPS OF THE FINANCE DIVISION IN 1935 *

	Number of corporations	Total gross income	Gross income per corporation
Group			
Banking and related companies			
National banks	6,549	717	110
State and private banks	13,487	656	49
Joint-stock land banks	44	4.5	103
Loan companies	23,329	756	32
Investment trusts, etc.	8,402	2,388	284
Stock and bond brokers, investment bankers	2,833	349	123
Real estate	86,985	1,201	14
Total	141,629	6,071	43
Insurance			
Life insurance	665	896	1,347
Other insurance	1,549	1,536	992
Total	2,214	2,432	1,099
Entire finance division	143,843	8,503	59

* Compiled and computed from *Statistics of Income for 1935, Part 2*, p. 39. Units: $1,000,000, for column 2; $1,000, for column 3.

Differences in average gross income per corporation appear mainly between the two insurance-company groups on the one hand and the seven groups in banking and related fields on the other. Roughly speaking, the insurance companies have on the average about twenty times the gross income per corporation as the companies of the seven other groups. Even among these seven groups, the range in average gross income is very wide: the average for investment trusts is more than twenty times that for realty companies. There can be little doubt, in view of this evidence, that particular size classes in the finance division may tend to be dominated by particular lines of financial activity.[1]

SIZE VARIATION IN RATE

The outstanding feature of the curves relating rate of return to size of corporation, for this division, is the unmistakable advance — for every year except 1936, for which the extra top size class spoils the comparison — in rate at the extreme right (Chart LVIII). Broadly, the curves have the shape of an elongated (and inverted) *S:* following the very sharp advance at the left, there is a long central range which shows an advance so gradual that the curves seem nearly horizontal, and then a striking advance develops for the top size classes in all years except 1936. This course of the curves is so systematic, appearing with little deviation in all years, that we must infer it is characteristic of the division.

For the finance division, rate of return rises generally as size increases, but the principal advances in rate occur for the very small sizes and for the very large sizes. This relation between size and rate seems largely independent of time, it is broadly characteristic of the curves for all years. Curves of this shape have not been found for any other division, or any manufacturing group except tobacco; although we have seen isolated instances of substantial advance in rate at the right end of a curve, we have found no other division and only one group in which a systematic advance of that sort appeared in all curves.

[1] Once more a warning must be sounded: the per-corporation figures of Table XLIII are *averages*, and they may conceal very wide ranges of variation within each group. For example, we know that certain particular banks are huge enterprises; and yet their inclusion in the first two groups does not prevent the per-corporation figures of those groups being very low.

Little doubt can exist that this peculiarity of the finance curves reflects a concentration in the top size classes of one or more groups within the division. If such a group had a higher average rate of return than the rest of the division, the rates for

CHART LVIII

Rate of Return Compared with Size, for Finance Division *

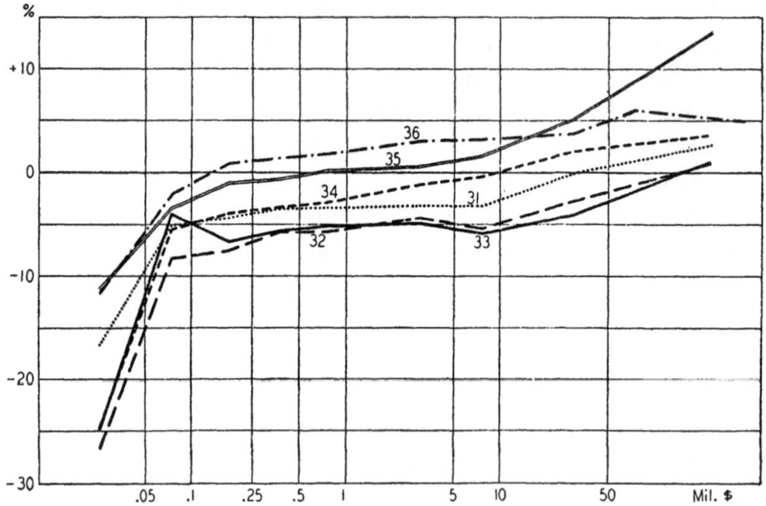

* Horizontal scale logarithmic. Data in Table XLIV.

the top size classes would be correspondingly elevated.[2] In any case, we must infer that mere increase in size of any financial concern whatever, until it moves up into one of the top size classes, would not imply an important increase in that concern's

[2] Presumably the life-insurance companies tend to fall in these top size classes. Because of peculiarities in the Revenue Act and the Regulations, with respect to calculation of income by life-insurance companies for tax purposes, the separate reckoning by our methods of profit for such companies might not yield results comparable with those for other finance enterprises. A somewhat different type of peculiarity may affect the profit figures for banks, and we have observed that certain huge banks must fall in these size classes.

rate of return on equity. In the finance division, more than in any other case studied, we must temper the indicated findings with reservations because of the probable specialization of particular size classes with respect to branch of financial activity.

TIME VARIATION IN RATE

Except for the peculiar course of the 1933 curve and that of the 1935 curve, and minor divergences among the other curves,

CHART LIX

TIME VARIATIONS IN RATE OF RETURN, FOR FINANCE DIVISION AND SELECTED SIZE CLASSES *

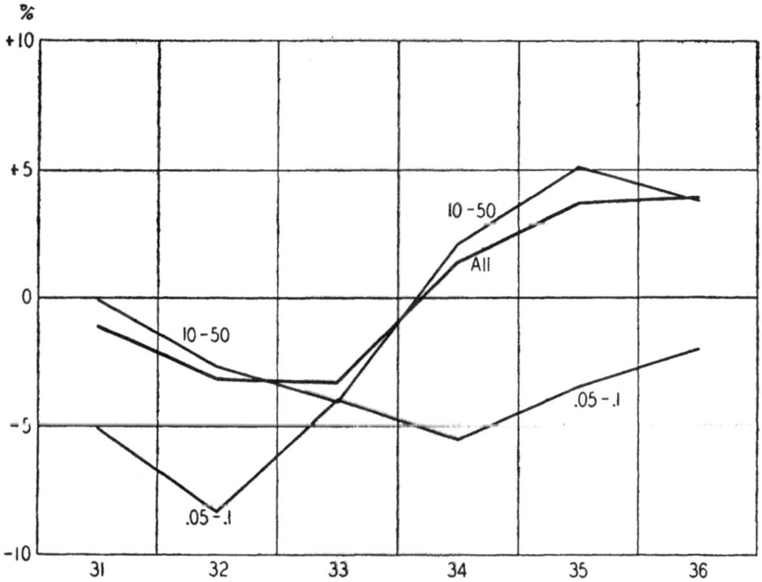

* Data in Table XLIV.

the approach to parallelism is fairly marked in Chart LVIII. Cyclical variations in general business have tolerably uniform impact upon all size classes. The total spread among the curves is only moderate: the cyclical impact during this period appears

TABLE XLIV

Rates of Return for Finance Division *

Class †	1931	1932	1933	1934	1935	1936
0	**−16.64**	**−26.77**	**−24.96**	**−24.90**	**−11.25**	**−11.72**
	10.31	7.56	8.79	8.41	7.24	14.74
	−48.49	*−40.73*	*−38.39*	*−47.97*	*−35.14*	*−38.09*
50	**−5.09**	**−8.30**	**−3.98**	**−5.49**	**−3.45**	**−2.00**
	6.54	5.04	5.79	7.72	4.24	7.90
	−18.17	*−13.99*	*−7.60*	*−11.35*	*−12.39*	*−10.22*
100	**−4.36**	**−7.50**	**−6.62**	**−3.92**	**−1.05**	**.92**
	5.74	4.69	5.58	6.53	4.82	10.30
	−14.12	*−12.40*	*−11.11*	*−9.00*	*−6.97*	*−9.23*
250	**−3.46**	**−5.73**	**−5.59**	**−3.27**	**−.62**	**1.42**
	5.24	4.37	4.88	5.76	4.79	7.75
	−10.69	*−9.68*	*−9.11*	*−7.16*	*−5.26*	*−7.44*
500	**−3.35**	**−5.68**	**−5.15**	**−2.83**	**.18**	**1.81**
	4.87	4.11	4.76	5.26	5.08	7.21
	−8.93	*−9.18*	*−8.53*	*−6.80*	*−3.25*	*−8.33*
1,000	**−3.16**	**−4.32**	**−4.85**	**−1.14**	**.62**	**3.07**
	5.21	4.09	4.85	5.09	6.41	7.14
	−7.67	*−7.02*	*−7.58*	*−4.07*	*−2.58*	*−6.80*
5,000	**−3.20**	**−5.38**	**−5.85**	**−.34**	**1.60**	**3.21**
	5.68	4.91	4.50	5.63	7.18	6.60
	−7.98	*−9.11*	*−9.56*	*−3.32*	*−1.48*	*−6.62*
10,000	**−.50**	**−2.66**	**−4.06**	**2.11**	**5.09**	**3.79**
	7.00	5.70	6.43	6.95	12.70	7.15
	−4.48	*−5.52*	*−8.02*	*−.27*	*.99*	*−7.54*
50,000	**2.72**	**.93**	**1.04**	**3.63**	**13.60**	**6.12**
	9.88	10.51	7.89	5.49	25.00	8.99
	.40	*−9.68*	*−.20*	*2.50*	*9.84*	*−3.37*
100,000	...	...	...	...	...	**.33**
	...	...	...	...	...	5.53
	...	...	...	...	...	*1.61*
Entire division	**−1.10**	**−3.18**	**−3.32**	**1.41**	**3.68**	**3.98**
	6.79	6.07	5.95	5.76	7.87	6.64
	−5.11	*−5.84*	*−5.97*	*−.94*	*1.37*	*−5.04*

* Expressed in per cent; ratio of profit (or loss) after taxes to estimated average equity, as explained in text, p. 18. Figures in boldface type are for income and deficit categories of corporations combined, in ordinary type for the income category, in italics for the deficit category.

† Lower limit of class interval, in thousands of dollars of total assets. The 50,000-thousand-dollar class has no stated upper limit, 1931–35; the 100,000-thousand-dollar class has no stated upper limit, 1936.

not to have been severe. This finding, in view of the experience with bank failures and other critical developments in financial institutions during the depression, is very striking.[8] We can perhaps explain the finding partly by remarking that recovery in these enterprises may have failed to develop vigorously by 1936. The abandonment of consolidated returns, following the Revenue Act of 1934, may have affected the structure of the finance division more than some other divisions and may render 1934–36 figures not comparable with those of 1931–33. Finally, the important place of insurance companies in the division, and the likelihood that their earning power is comparatively stable, must be noted as a partial explanation of the finding.

The time record for particular size classes (Chart LIX) must be read in the light of the foregoing remarks. Cyclical variation in rate is fairly narrow for the entire division, somewhat more sharp for the large size class shown, and mild and irregular for the low size class. This exhibit thus suggests that the indication of parallelism in Chart LVIII is to some extent illusory; the cycle does fall with significantly different impact upon different size classes. Details for other size classes appear in Table XLIV.

PROFITABLE AND UNPROFITABLE CORPORATIONS

We again find, in the record of rates for the income corporations of this division, a striking departure from conditions observed in most other cases studied (Table XLIV). Except for minor irregularities, curves for the income category, if charted, would have broadly a *U* shape: rate of return is high for the low size classes, low for the intermediate classes, and high for the top classes. This is in sharp contrast with the more or less sharp downward-to-the-right course generally found in the income curves of other divisions, and of manufacturing groups.

[8] Generally speaking, a corporation in liquidation is not covered in the tax data.

CHART LX

SIX-YEAR AVERAGE OF RATES OF RETURN, FOR FINANCE DIVISION AND INCOME AND DEFICIT CATEGORIES *

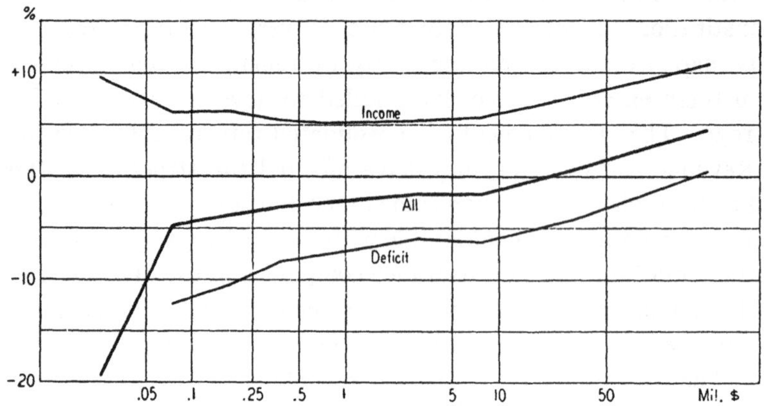

* Horizontal scale logarithmic. Data in Table B. One point omitted in lowest class.

TABLE XLV

ANNUAL PERCENTAGE RATIOS OF TOTAL ASSETS OF INCOME CATEGORY OF CORPORATIONS TO TOTAL ASSETS, IN EACH SIZE CLASS OF THE FINANCE DIVISION *

Class †	1931	1932	1933	1934	1935	1936
0	47.0	22.7	19.9	22.8	26.0	30.7
50	46.8	22.6	19.5	21.9	26.4	33.5
100	45.6	22.2	19.1	23.8	30.6	43.5
250	41.9	20.8	18.2	22.3	32.2	54.8
500	37.9	20.1	17.9	23.6	33.0	59.6
1,000	34.0	19.7	16.4	23.0	31.4	54.1
5,000	33.8	20.7	18.4	24.4	30.4	64.7
10,000	35.4	21.9	19.8	25.7	32.9	65.3
50,000	46.6	36.6	23.1	25.4	18.6	76.4
100,000	...	...	...	...	...	62.0
Entire division	41.1	28.4	20.6	24.8	24.5	63.0

* Calculated from basic figures for total assets given in successive issues of *Statistics of Income* (for example, 1935 issue, Part 2, p. 82).

† Lower limit of size class; unit, $1,000. Separate data for $100,000,000 class available only in 1936.

Coupled with the advance in the curves of Chart LVIII at their right ends, these high rates for the top classes of the income category suggest a general tendency for large financial corporations to yield a substantial rate of return. The condition can be tested further by examining also the deficit corporations, and Chart LX shows both categories on a six-year average basis. The *U* shape of the income-category curve is strikingly evident. But the total range of variation for that curve is just over 5 per cent, and correspondingly the shape of the deficit curve does not differ greatly from that for both categories combined.

The percentage of total assets held by the income category is given in Table XLV. In general, minimum figures appear in 1933 rather than 1932. In each class and for the entire division, all figures of 1932–35 remain below those of 1931; and even in 1936, the figures for the three lowest size classes are below those of 1931. Total variation from 1933 to 1936 is very large, and huge shifts of assets accordingly took place.

XIX

VARIATION OF RATE WITH SIZE

CHAPTERS IV and XIII to XVIII have examined variations in rate of return with size of corporation and over time for each of the eight industrial divisions. The present chapter summarizes, and discusses certain broad aspects of, the variations with size. Convenience dictates consideration of the divisions in two sets: those made up mainly of producers of commodities — manufacturing, mining, agriculture, and construction — and those made up mainly of providers of services — trade, service, public utilities, and finance. The summary comparisons for these two sets with the curve for all divisions combined, on the six-year average basis, are reproduced from Charts v and vi in Charts LXI and LXII.

PRODUCERS OF COMMODITIES

The curves of Chart LXI are tolerably consistent among themselves, except for the extremely low level for mining in the lowest size class and the notable irregularity for construction in the 1-million-dollar class. All curves, with a single slight interruption for mining, show advancing rate with increasing size until well above 1 million dollars. The advance thereafter continues, with interruption in one class, for manufacturing; but declines occur at the right for mining and construction. Examination of the charts, in previous chapters, which show annual curves for these four divisions discloses fairly good confirmation of the six-year summary curves for manufacturing and mining. For manufacturing, the shape of the six-year average curve — the persistent advance of rate with size — reappears with surprising approach to exactness in nearly every year. For mining, likewise, most of the annual curves confirm the indications of the average curve: the exceptionally low level in the lowest size class appears in three years, the minor dip in the 500-thousand-dollar class appears in four years, all six curves show rates above that of the 1-million-dollar class in

CHART LXI

SIX-YEAR AVERAGES OF RATES OF RETURN, FOR ALL CORPORATE INDUSTRY AND SELECTED INDUSTRIAL DIVISIONS *

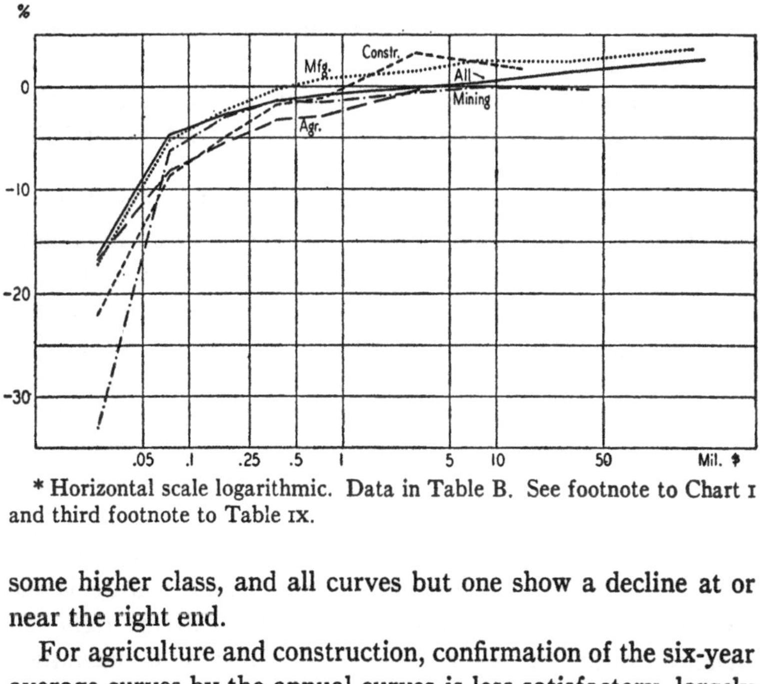

* Horizontal scale logarithmic. Data in Table B. See footnote to Chart I and third footnote to Table IX.

some higher class, and all curves but one show a decline at or near the right end.

For agriculture and construction, confirmation of the six-year average curves by the annual curves is less satisfactory, largely because the annual curves are marked by numerous single-class irregularities. These irregularities may reflect merely the accidental effects of the comparative smallness of these two divisions: neither division has the size to insure that data for specific classes, particularly high classes, rest upon adequate samples. Nevertheless, ignoring irregularities, even these two divisions have annual curves satisfactorily consistent with the curves of Chart LXI. Agriculture, even when the six years are studied separately, shows a persistent though somewhat irregular rise of rate with increasing size all along the size scale. Construction shows an advance in rate with size, continuing at a sharper pace than in other divisions in the intermediate classes (from 100 thousand dollars to 1 million dollars); and then all years but one confirm the downturn of the six-year average curve above 5 million dollars. For all four divisions, we may conclude that the separate annual curves confirm tolerably well the six-year average curves. The relation between rate and size, shown by the average curve, is a fairly stable relation persisting in various stages of the cycle.

Differences chiefly worthy of note among the four divisions can easily be summarized from the average curves. Maximum change of rate through the entire size scale is highest for mining, next highest for construction, next for manufacturing, and least for agriculture. Nearly all of the advance for mining appears at the left end of the curve, thereafter advance is slower, and a gradual decline appears at the right. In contrast, comparatively rapid advance of rate continues in construction up to the next-to-highest class, and then a sharp drop occurs in the top class. The advance in rate for agriculture, limited though it is, continues at a substantial pace along nearly all parts of the size scale. For manufacturing the striking feature is the scarcely interrupted advance in rate to the extreme right, an advance which, though gradual, is of substantial magnitude even above 1 million dollars in size.

But these remarks emphasize unduly the differences among these four curves. Real and significant as these differences are, they are less important than the broad consistency of the curves. All four divisions representing commodity producers have curves showing the relation between rate and size not notably different from the curve for all divisions combined. Strikingly different is the case for the four divisions representing producers of services, for here (Chart LXII) notable contrast exists among the curves.

CHART LXII

SIX-YEAR AVERAGES OF RATES OF RETURN, FOR ALL CORPORATE INDUSTRY AND SELECTED INDUSTRIAL DIVISIONS *

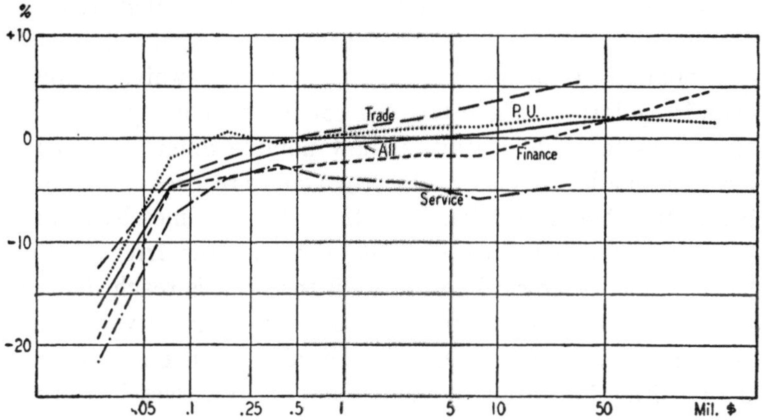

* Horizontal scale logarithmic. Data in Table B. See footnote to Chart I.

SUPPLIERS OF SERVICES

The six-year average curves for these divisions show closer consistency at the left end than appeared in Chart LXI: none of these divisions has the extremely low level recorded for mining in the lowest class. But, to the right of 500 thousand dollars, divergence becomes pronounced. The curve for public utilities roughly resembles that for mining; it has a somewhat irregular but slightly upward drift in its middle portion, and then declines at the extreme right. The curve for trade continues in a fairly rapid advance to the highest point of the size scale, and the pace of the advance is strikingly steady throughout the whole course except at the extreme left; no curve of Chart LXI has this shape. For finance, a long nearly horizontal stretch appears in the middle portion of the size scale, and this is followed by a renewed and brisk advance at the right. In the service curve, a clear maximum occurs below 500 thousand dollars — lower than in any curve of Chart LXI — and the decline above that size boundary is large, although a moderate upturn appears at the right end.

Examination of corresponding charts on an annual basis, as presented and discussed in previous chapters, again yields fair confirmation of the six-year average curves — waiving single-class irregularities where they appear in particular years. The six curves for public utilities show notable differences in the low and middle size classes: the 1936 curve reaches a maximum below 500 thousand dollars and thereafter declines by a large amount; whereas the 1932 curve, except for two irregularities, has a generally upward course until the peak is reached somewhat below 50 million dollars. The four other curves have a more nearly horizontal course in the middle range of size; and the resulting indication of the display of six curves is a broad scatter of rates in size classes around 250 thousand dollars, with a remarkable convergence of the curves at both ends of the size scale. At or near the ends of the scale, therefore, the average curve is typical of the annual curves; and its indication of difference in levels between low size classes and high is typical. But in the middle range of size the average curve is not typical, and gives no safe indication as to the existence of a maximum rate in some low size class. Consistency among the six annual curves, and hence between them and the six-year average curve, is emphatically clearer in each of the three other divisions. The unmistakable maximum appears in a low size class for service in every year, although the 1931 curve subsequently returns to a higher level at the extreme right. In finance, the nearly horizontal stretch in the middle range appears in every year; and in every year a sharp advance occurs to the right of

10 million dollars, although the 1936 curve shows a final decline at its extreme right. Consistency is even more remarkable among the six curves for trade; and it is damaged significantly only by the horizontal drift of the 1933 curve in the middle sizes, and by the sharp advance — probably due to grouping of the two top classes — in the 10-million-dollar class of the 1935 curve. This grouped class in the single year 1935 also forces similar grouping of the two top classes in the six-year average curve (see Chapter XXVIII), with the result that the final advance of rate in the 50-million-and-over class, which appears in all five years for which separate data are given, is concealed in the average curve. Otherwise, the trade curve of Chart LXII would show a still more striking continuation of its upward course at the right end.

Differences among the average curves for the four service supplying divisions — and these average curves are well confirmed by the annual curves in three cases and tolerably so in the fourth — are fairly striking. Though all show large advance of rate with size along some range of the size scale, the persistence of such advance in the different sections of the size scale varies from division to division. The extreme cases are trade and service: for the former, advance at the brisk pace persists to the right end of the curve; for the latter, an unmistakable maximum occurs in a moderately low size class. The advance in rate slackens above a moderately low size for both public utilities and finance; but for the former, a downturn occurs at the right, whereas a brisk advance reappears in the top size classes for finance.

GENERAL CONSISTENCY

Viewing all eight divisions together, we conclude that the advance in rate of return with increasing size is characteristic of all divisions in the low size classes, that it persists — though at a greatly slackened pace — in the middle size range for most divisions, and that it appears even in the top size classes for three divisions. The central finding of Chapter II, that rate of return advances with increasing size rapidly in the low size classes and persistently in the higher classes, is in large degree confirmed by separate study of the several divisions. Complete confirmation fails because of the clearly manifest differences among the divisions in the higher size classes. And even for the top size classes, three of the four largest divisions — manufacture, trade, and finance — show advancing rates; whereas public utilities shows a mild decline in rate above 50 million dollars.

We recall now that the summary, presented in Chapter XII, of the detailed study of the separate groups in the manufacturing division also brought out a general confirmation of the findings for the division as a whole, despite differences of some magnitude and considerable significance among the groups. If comparable data classified by groups were available for other divisions than manufacturing, and we could examine the relation between rate of return and size for these narrower industrial classes, differences — perhaps even more notable than those discovered among the manufacturing groups — would probably be found. But that such a detailed study would reveal any strong reason for abandoning or tempering the central finding of previous chapters seems highly unlikely. We may take it as strongly indicated though not fully established that, in all branches of industry large enough to show wide size distribution, (1) rate of return increases with size unmistakably in the low and moderately large size classes; (2) the advance in rate may continue in all size classes, or may disappear or even be replaced by a moderate reduction in the high size classes; (3) even in cases for which rate declines in the highest size classes, rates for those classes remain emphatically above those for the lowest class. And these conclusions appear valid in separate years, in any stage of the business cycle.

ECONOMIC IMPLICATIONS

It is no part of the purpose of the present book to examine carefully the numerous economic implications of the central findings of fact in the book, or even the more important of these implications. Such an examination would not only occupy much space; but it will require the attention of many specialists in accounting, finance, business policy, and economic theory.

I discuss briefly below (Chapters XXII–XXIV) certain important factors which may bear upon an interpretation of the findings, and show in all but one of the cases that the factor in question can not account in any significant degree for the findings. Thus, inventory profits, though of great importance in determining the level of rates of return and their cyclical course, can apparently account for no significant portion of the variation in rate with size. Likewise, the burden of debt, while such as to indicate notable differences between rate of earnings on the entire capital and rate of return on equity, has apparently no significant part in bringing about the advance of rate with increasing size. In the case of capital gains and losses, included in our figures for profits despite the theoretical objections to such inclusion, variations with size are to some extent in a direction to cause some of the observed advance in rate with size; but this effect of capital gains or losses is very small. The situation is more perplexing with respect to compensation of officers, which is sometimes assumed to conceal a substantial element of what is truly profit in the economic sense. The decision in this case rests upon doubtful assumptions as to the share of such compensation which can properly be regarded as profit, and I hold that any defensible assumption as to such share leaves the central finding of the book still unexplained. Quite possibly other factors than those examined, even briefly, in Chapters XXII–XXIV may have an important bearing upon the question.

Indeed, from the point of view of the economic theorist, the entire question of the appropriateness of the accounting definition of profits to the economic concept of profits must be examined in all its perplexing detail. And, in saying this, I waive all questions of the precision or lack thereof in the accounting definition itself, all questions as to the uniformity in applying such definition in the records of particular corporations even for tax purposes, and all questions as to the significance of tabulated Treasury data — in the form of aggregates for groups of corporations — as typical of specific corporations. The sole question in mind here is whether the generally and approximately enforced Treasury definition of accounting profit measures what is in the mind of the economist when he says profit.

One of the obstacles to answering this question is the known diversity of opinion among theorists as to what constitutes profit. Different theories of profit, and different classifications used in theoretical allocation of the product of industry among the factors or functions of production, lead to different views as to the content and identity of profit. Diverse opinions are held on the inclusion in profits, and the proportionate extent of such inclusion, of such elements as interest on the funds invested, reward (or insurance) for risk-taking, rent of conspicuous ability in leadership, compensation for performance in less conspicuous fashion of so-called entrepreneurial functions, mere chance or windfalls, and even compensation for fairly routine managerial activities. Clearly the factual findings of this book, highly significant though they are in some respects, have little or no direct bearing upon certain aspects of the theory of profits; although further study, and the accumulation of related facts, may bring out an important indirect bearing in some directions or upon some of these aspects of the profits theories.

On some aspects of the theoretical problem, the present evidence — as respects variation both over time and with size — is clearly helpful. Chief among these, perhaps, is the question whether profit, as defined for tax accounting purposes, contains any element over and above interest on the funds supplied — or left in the business — by the risk-taking owners. That such an excess exists on the average for large corporations in many lines of industry in most years is fairly clear, and that it does not exist for very small corporations on the average in nearly all lines of industry in any year is emphatically clear. Evidence examined in a limited way in Chapter XXV shows, however, that even among small corporations some earn very high rates of return: if we cease considering the question in terms of averages, we find a wide diversity of experience. This fact of diversity is of great importance not only to economic theory but also to public policy: it is relevant to the widely held opinion that, from the point of view of a reward which calls forth enterprising activity, the *chance* of securing a high profit rather than the assurance of securing a mere interest return is controlling. The enterpriser is by profession a risk taker, faces frankly the chance of loss, does not expend his efforts for winning a mere interest return on his capital, but hopes and strives to win the large reward.

I make no effort here to discuss this point at length, or to discuss various other theoretical points upon which I believe the book will give pertinent information and helpful guides to further study. Before closing this chapter, however, one consideration needs to be stressed. The corporate form of organization conceals and confuses, as many recent writings have emphasized, the factors or functions which economic theory formerly examined in studying the distribution of the product of industry. This confusion is probably most serious with respect to the functions, in any case somewhat vague, of the entrepreneur. We have not yet discovered the identity of the entrepreneur in the modern large corporation, though he appears readily enough as the active owner-manager of the small closely held corporation. In the large corporation the entrepreneurial functions appear to have been fractionalized and distributed, some being passed down the scale of employee organization to contract-wage officers whose main efforts go to routine managerial work, some being allocated to banking or other service agencies which are so essential to the corporation that they can and do share in the control of its basic policies, and some portion — perhaps ordinarily small, but latently or potentially of significant size — perhaps still remains to the owners who supply the risk-taking capital. Indeed, if we *define* entrepreneurial functions to include supplying the risk-taking capital, these owners still have an important share in entrepreneurial functions, though it may be the least desirable share. I see no way for accounting data, in the present state of our knowledge of accounts and of corporate organizational realities, to yield any conclusive evidence on the exercise of these entrepreneurial functions or on the reward for such exercise. That profit, as measured in this book, may contain a substantial element of reward (negative reward, on the average!) for entrepreneurship in the smaller companies is probable; but that it contains this element in any significant degree for larger companies is at best highly doubtful. I leave this question here, along with many other questions which arise insistently from an examination of the evidence presented in these chapters.

XX

CYCLICAL VARIATIONS IN RATE [1]

PREVIOUS CHAPTERS have shown graphic records of the time variations in rate for entire divisions and groups and selected size classes thereof, and included textual comments on these variations and their relations to each other. Although the main problem of the book concerns the relation between rate of return and corporate size, cyclical variation — and its differences among size classes and among lines of industry — is of very high importance on its own account.

THE ELEVEN-YEAR RECORD, ALL DIVISIONS

Marked instability of profits — in particular, profits on capital supplied by risk-taking owners rather than by creditors — is a characteristic manifestation of the trade cycle and can readily be regarded as caused by the cycle. That such instability may also be a contributing cause of the cycle, at least in some of its phases, is a challenging possibility which deserves continuing examination by the trade-cycle theorist. Violently changing profits may conceivably influence the cyclical course of economic conditions both directly and indirectly. The mechanism through which such influence may be transmitted is complex and sufficiently uncertain to require much further theoretical study.

Among the chiefly important direct elements in the mechanism are the effect of current and recent levels of profit upon the availability of funds for maintaining a particular rate of

[1] A portion of the text, with some alterations, and the three charts of this chapter are reproduced, by permission, from the *Review of Economic Statistics*, May, 1939. The separate study of rate of return on corporate investments, as there given, is not included here.

operations or meeting current claims from other units in the economic system, the relation between profit rates and price policies, and the effect of current and expected changes in the level of profit upon the disposition of the controlling agents to undertake further capital investment. Among the indirect elements of high importance are the transmission — however incomplete — of instability of profits into an instability of purchasing power in the hands of the owners, and the capacity of protracted negative profits to effect a transference of industrial control from risk-taking owners to creditors or from financially weak enterprise to strong enterprise.

My present purpose is not to pursue in theoretical terms these and other questions bearing upon the general problem of the effect of unstable profits upon the course of the trade cycle. I aim rather to present selected statistical measurements which are of interest in themselves as giving a partial historical account of an extraordinarily significant cyclical episode. But these measurements are especially intended to afford part of the factual background for a theoretical examination of the questions raised above. The statistical measurements here presented are the rates of return previously reported, and comparable data for earlier years: they are designed to bring out the profit experience of the equity owners of corporate business. Such owners, acting sometimes or in some cases directly but more generally through their acknowledged or unknown agents, have the power or necessity of making those decisions which perhaps transmit unstable profits into unstable economic activity.

Rates of return were obtained for the entire list — without regard to line of industry — of corporations filing tax returns (only those accompanied by balance sheets for 1931–36, as in previous chapters) for the years 1926–36. The course of the resulting percentages is shown in the heavy curve of Chart LXIII. The curve records a high rate of profit in 1926, a mild dip in 1927 when a brief but sharp contraction occurred in economic activity, renewed advance in the next two years to a secondary peak in 1929, severe decline but not to a negative level in 1930, further heavy declines in the next two years to a

CHART LXIII

TIME VARIATIONS IN RATE OF RETURN, FOR ALL DIVISIONS, FINANCE, AND ALL EXCEPT FINANCE *

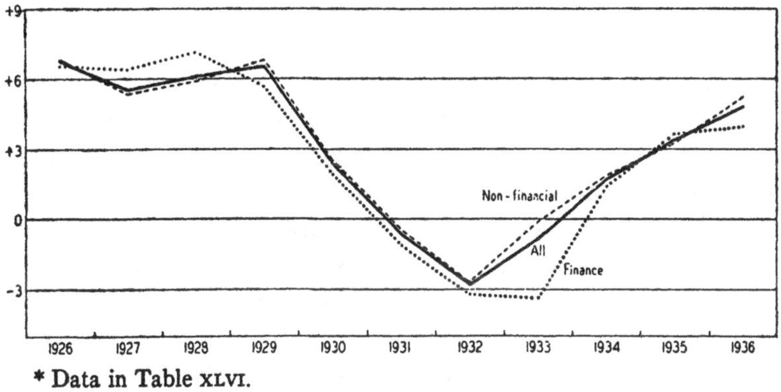

* Data in Table XLVI.

large negative rate in 1932, and sustained advance in the following four years.[2]

This course of fluctuation is broadly in accord with the general course of the trade cycle, as reflected in many important economic indices. That the movement of profits should thus,

[2] The specific figures shown in Chart LXIII differ moderately — for the nine years covered in both analyses — from those presented in an earlier study ("Corporate Earnings on Invested Capital," *Harvard Business Review*, XVI, 3, Spring, 1938, p. 346). The earlier study took as the equity at the beginning of the year the preceding year-end equity, as can appropriately and with no serious error be done for the entire list of corporations. The same procedure might have been used here for the general case of the entire list of corporations, but the need of comparability with the special cases of separate lines of industry — for which no such procedure is feasible — dictated the use of a denominator (for the rate of return) as defined above (Chapter II).

in its direction and timing, correspond to the movement of general economic conditions is not unexpected. The striking fact about the record is the violent intensity of the fluctuation in profits: the extreme range reaching from a peak of 6.78 to a bottom level of −2.76 per cent. That so wide a change, or even the narrower year-to-year changes, in the average earning power of corporate equity could occur without having momentous effects upon the policy decisions of corporate management and "control" is almost unthinkable.

This aspect of the situation is further emphasized when we remember that these figures are averages; they reflect the average rate of return when income data for nearly a half-million corporations are added together into a single set of totals. The wide variation in profit experience among corporations in any one year implies, for example, that many corporations in 1929 must have had rates below the average, some of them very much below and even negative. Correspondingly, many corporations must have had rates above the average, some of them very much above. Likewise in 1932, many corporations had rates above the severely low average figure, some of them very much above and even positive. Correspondingly, in that year many corporations had losses implying rates below the 1932 average, some of them far below. Within the corporate system, then, it is entirely likely that large numbers of corporations experience cyclical changes in the rate of return far more intense than the remarkably intense variation recorded in Chart LXIII. No satisfactory statistical basis for testing this conclusion for particular corporations is available, but we shall show below, and have seen from less full evidence in previous chapters, that some entire industrial groups within the corporate structure have much more severe cyclical variations in profits than those shown in Chart LXIII. For any such group, of course, average figures are used; and within the group, the particular corporations may have widely different intensities of profit fluctuation.

Before passing on to the analysis of separate lines of industry, two observations need be made concerning the comparability over time of the rates shown in Chart LXIII, and of similar rates for the separate industries. Two substantial breaks in homogeneity of the basic data affect the comparability over time, one in 1931 and one in 1934. Until 1930, *Statistics of Income* tabulations gave separate sets of figures, one set covering the income account for all corporate income-tax returns, the other set covering the assets and liabilities for those tax returns accompanied by balance sheets. Despite the requirement that balance sheets be filed with tax returns, a substantial number of tax returns include no balance sheets; and the two sets of data are therefore not precisely comparable. Since failure to submit balance sheets is more general among small than among large corporations, an attempt to bring the sets of figures into accord by an adjustment percentage based upon the number of returns — the ratio of the number of tax returns to the number of balance sheets — is not warranted.

The adjustment figure needs to rest upon some measure of the comparative economic importance of the two lists of corporations covered by the two sets of figures. A measure of this sort can be developed, from data for 1931 and later years, in terms of several items in the income account; and we have chosen "total compiled receipts," a rough measure of gross revenue, for this purpose. The corresponding adjustment ratio, calculated separately for each industrial class and the aggregate list of corporations, is the total compiled receipts for all returns — those with plus those without balance sheets — divided into the corresponding figure for returns with balance sheets, for the years 1931–33.[3]

[3] These ratios (per cent) are: aggregate, 97.5; agriculture, 95.5; mining, 98.4; manufacturing, 99.1; construction, 95.6; public utilities, 96.5; trade,

By applying this adjustment divisor to the tabulated balance-sheet figures for equity in the years 1926–30, those figures were stepped up to approximate comparability with the tabulated figures for profits after taxes in those years. The rate-of-return results for those years rest therefore upon an equity estimated from the sample of corporations — a very large sample — which did file balance sheets.[4] For 1931 and later years, *Statistics of Income* gives a tabulation, in the form studied in previous chapters, of income-account figures separately for the corporations which do file balance sheets. For these years, therefore, the rate-of-return results apply only to those corporations. But, as such corporations constitute an overwhelming fraction of all corporations, the results can scarcely be seriously in error when they are accepted as representative of the entire corporate list — including corporations which do, as well as those which do not, file balance sheets.

The second major break in homogeneity results from the change in law, in 1934, with respect to the privilege of filing consolidated tax returns; and frequent comments on this point appear in earlier chapters (see also Chapter XXVII). The changed practice went into effect mainly in 1934; but, for certain fiscal-year corporations, it did not occur until 1935.

97.3; service, 94.8; finance, 94.4; food, 99.1; textiles, 98.6; rubber, 99.8; forest products, 98.7; paper, 98.9; printing, 98.1; chemicals, 99.2; stone, 98.8; metals, 99.6; miscellaneous manufacturing, 98.4.

[4] These estimates are of course subject to a margin of error — ascribable to possible inappropriateness of the selection of total compiled receipts as the basis of adjustment, to the possibility that adjustment ratios based on 1931–33 may be somewhat in error for the earlier years and in varying degree for different years, and to the possibility that the actual relation between income and equity of corporations not filing balance sheets may differ substantially, and in varying degrees in different years, from that of those submitting balance sheets. In view of the smallness of the adjustment, however, it is highly improbable that any of these errors can have significant effects upon the results.

Between 1933 and later years, therefore, a break in homogeneity exists which may have substantial bearing upon the indicated course of rate of return. Comparisons of 1933 and earlier years with 1934 and later years are damaged. To a much smaller extent, comparisons of 1934 with later years are damaged.

For the aggregate list of corporations, without regard to industrial type, the legal change probably affects in large degree the denominator; separate coverage of each subsidiary into the tabulations presumably raised substantially the indicated equity. The effect upon the numerator of the rate-of-return ratio, though perhaps less important, was of uncertain direction. The very purpose of the change in law was to render taxable those profitable subsidiaries whose net income had formerly been offset against net losses of other subsidiaries, in the same consolidated system, before reckoning of taxes. Hence the tax element in our numerator was probably increased, and the numerator thereby reduced. The other element in the numerator, compiled net profits, is in all years a residual figure — after offsetting losses of some corporations against profits of others — for the aggregate list of all corporations; and this element might be supposed unaffected by the change in the law. But the likelihood that certain elements of income of a subsidiary — for example, the portion of dividends received from other subsidiaries — appears after the change of 1934 in the tabulated total of compiled net profits without any offsetting figure appearing in the tabulated total of compiled net losses (for the unprofitable corporations) implies that this element was probably raised in 1934 and later years. The net effect upon the numerator, of changes in its two elements, is uncertain both in direction and in magnitude, although the direction was probably toward an increase. In any case, the uncertain magnitude of change, both in the numerator and in the denominator, leaves us in doubt as to the probable direction of change in the rate-of-return ratio; we must merely note that a substantial change in indicated rate may have been caused by the abandonment of consolidated returns.[5]

ELEVEN-YEAR RECORD, PARTICULAR INDUSTRIES

The cyclical record, over the eleven-year period covering high prosperity and deep depression, as revealed for different lines of industry is of large significance. Unfortunately, questions of homogeneity are more serious here. The change in law of 1934 brought an improvement in the representativeness of the data for any one division or group, by taking each of numerous subsidiaries out of the division or group into which it had formerly been covered — because of inclusion in a single consolidated return — and assigning it to the division or group to which its principal business belongs. But the change also implies a serious break in homogeneity for certain divisions or groups: the sample of corporations upon which the rate of return is calculated may have been substantially changed in make-up in 1934 because of the reclassification of subsidiaries. The full extent of such changes in sample can not be appraised, but they may have affected substantially the indicated rates of return for various lines of industry. This danger is increased by the further fact that elements of income and deduction or of assets and liabilities, formerly offset within a single consolidated return, may appear in the tabulations after 1934, and one item may appear in one division (or group) whereas the formerly offsetting item may appear in another. We are forced to conclude that the 1934 break in homogeneity may

[5] The effects of the changed law upon the data for separate lines of industry were more complicated, as noted in previous chapters and in Chapter XXVII.

Other breaks in homogeneity besides the two already discussed — all of them minor, and mainly due to small changes in the law — are entirely ignored, for the aggregate and separate industries.

be considerably more serious for certain divisions or groups than for the aggregate list of all corporations.

The most important of the nine divisions, if importance is measured in terms of total assets, is finance, which includes banking institutions proper, insurance companies, and several other types of companies whose business is predominantly financial. This division constitutes a very important fraction of the corporate aggregate; it had total assets running between 39.3 and 47.8 per cent of the aggregate in the years 1931–36. Moreover, because the activities of these corporations are significantly different in nature from those of most corporations engaged in producing and distributing goods and services, and to a less extent because special provisions of the tax laws may affect in some degree the tabulated data for this division, the indicated profit experience of the finance division might be expected to show certain peculiarities. For this reason, and because of its great size, the finance division has been subtracted from the aggregate, to leave a non-financial aggregate; and this residual aggregate — including manufacturing, trade, and the other producing and distributing divisions — is in some respects a better standard of comparison than is the general aggregate, for the several divisions of non-financial business.

The rates of return for the finance division and for the non-financial aggregate (sum of the eight remaining divisions) are recorded, in the dotted curve and the short-dash curve, respectively, of Chart LXIII. Rates of return for the three divisions next in importance — public utilities (including transportation), manufacturing, and trade — appear in Chart LXIV and in the heavy solid curve of Chart LXV; and mining, though not next in importance, is also included in Chart LXIV because of the special significance of its fluctuations. The two remaining curves of Chart LXV present rates of return for two manufacturing groups, metals and chemicals, which are of interest because of the large size of these groups and of the cyclical significance of their profit experience. Data for three other divisions, omitting "nature not given," and for the nine remaining groups of the manufacturing division are given, along with the cases charted, in Table XLVI.

Referring to Chart LXIII, rate of return for the finance divi-

CHART LXIV

TIME VARIATIONS IN RATE OF RETURN, FOR SELECTED DIVISIONS *

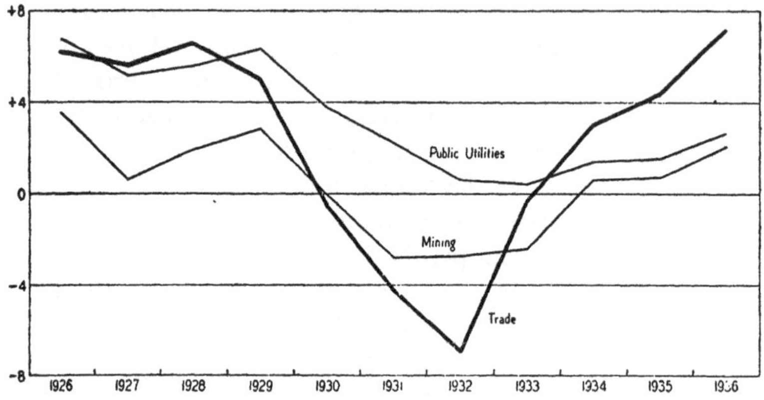

* Data in Table XLVI.

sion is observed to move differently from that for all corporations combined in several portions of the eleven-year period. The 1926–27 decline for finance was very slight, the figure was distinctly higher in 1928 than in 1926, the initial downturn of the great depression occurred in 1929 rather than in 1930, the low point of the depression was in 1933 instead of 1932, the 1933–34 advance was very sharp and brought the 1934 finance figure to about the level reached for all corporations combined after two years of revival, and the general 1935–36 advance did not appear except to a mild extent in finance.

Certain corresponding (and inverse) discrepancies appear between the non-financial aggregate and the general aggregate.

The peak for all non-financial divisions combined appeared in 1929, after a substantial 1926–27 decline and advances in 1928 and 1929; the 1929–30 decline was steeper for the non-financial aggregate than for finance; the rate for the non-financial aggregate rose sharply in 1933, while that for finance declined

CHART LXV

TIME VARIATIONS IN RATE OF RETURN, FOR ALL MANUFACTURING AND TWO MANUFACTURING GROUPS *

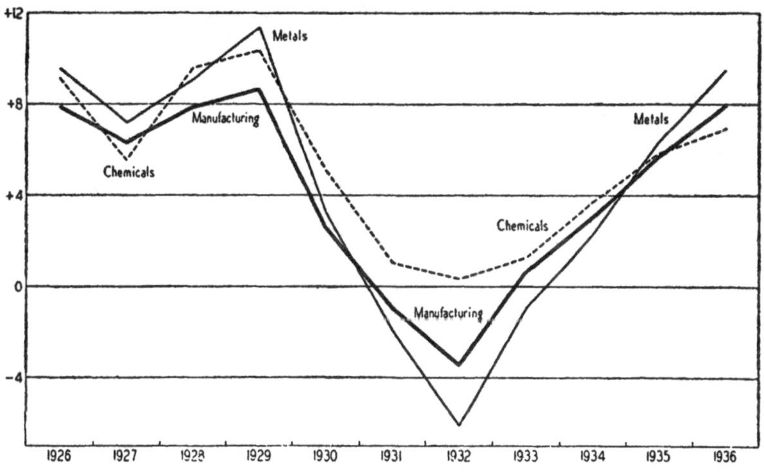

* Data in Table XLVI.

slightly; and the 1935–36 advance for the non-financial aggregate was about as sharp as that of 1932–33.

The cyclical variation in trade was much more intense than it was in mining or public utilities (Chart LXIV), and even more intense than that in manufacturing (Chart LXV). In trade, as in finance, the pre-depression peak occurred in 1928 and not in 1929; and a notable peculiarity is that the 1936 rate for trade was above the prosperity rates just before the great depression. Another striking feature of the trade curve is the violent 1932–33 advance, a sharper upward movement than in

TABLE XLVI

Rates of Return, in Per Cent, for the Industrial Divisions, Manufacturing Groups, All Divisions Combined, and All Except Finance Combined *

Division or group	1926	1927	1928	1929	1930	1931	1932	1933	1934	1935	1936
All divisions	6.78	5.58	6.15	6.56	2.40	−.60	−2.76	−.81	1.72	3.42	4.83
All, except finance	6.82	5.37	5.90	6.84	2.55	−.45	−2.64	−.09	1.88	3.29	5.24
Finance	6.58	6.42	7.16	5.70	1.98	−1.10	−3.18	−3.32	1.41	3.68	3.98
Agriculture	1.11	1.37	2.31	1.51	−2.89	−5.12	−5.61	−2.91	−3.21	.91	2.14
Mining	3.57	.66	1.96	2.86	−.03	−2.78	−2.71	−2.39	.63	.73	2.03
Construction	10.77	10.09	7.61	7.59	5.36	−.86	−7.34	−5.18	−2.95	−.22	3.30
Public utilities	6.80	5.16	5.54	6.32	3.80	2.29	.67	.45	1.47	1.57	2.69
Trade	6.20	5.62	6.59	5.01	−.52	−4.19	−6.90	−.25	3.05	4.37	7.16
Service	5.52	4.12	4.35	4.04	1.85	−2.18	−9.44	−8.52	−5.52	−4.07	−.54
Manufacturing	7.89	6.32	7.88	8.64	2.67	−.96	−3.45	.68	3.01	5.68	7.94
Foods	7.98	6.94	8.33	8.09	6.51	4.13	2.29	4.66	7.38	8.68	9.78
Textiles	2.20	5.45	3.54	2.92	−5.63	−6.10	−7.64	2.80	.38	1.95	5.36
Leather	4.51	7.55	4.82	3.86	−3.08	−3.32	−6.26	3.69	2.82	6.14	5.20
Rubber	5.20	5.26	.35	2.50	−4.28	−2.39	−4.08	.59	2.75	3.75	6.69
Forest products	3.44	1.02	2.46	2.43	−4.40	−7.94	−9.70	−3.77	−2.92	−.74	2.74
Paper	6.99	6.83	7.23	6.46	2.89	−.49	−3.32	.83	3.06	3.98	5.38
Printing	11.71	10.09	12.59	12.04	7.76	2.41	−.83	1.09	3.68	6.46	7.98
Chemicals	9.13	5.59	9.58	10.35	5.11	1.08	.38	1.28	3.73	5.88	6.93
Stone	6.62	6.35	6.71	6.25	1.77	−1.92	−5.82	−1.40	1.64	4.01	7.62
Metals	9.55	7.22	9.10	11.37	3.35	−1.97	−6.10	−.95	2.27	6.34	9.48
Miscellaneous manufacturing	7.41	6.20	7.72	5.80	−.73	−4.13	−7.85	−2.58	2.71	6.77	9.10

* The two sets of "All" figures include a ninth "division" — described as "nature of business not given" — which is not shown separately in this table. The textiles, chemicals, and metals groups are presented for 1936 on the former basis of classification, despite their separation into new groups in that year. The foods group includes tobacco and beverages in all years.

any of the other curves shown. The mining curve is distinguished by a particularly sharp drop in 1927, by a surprising approach to constancy during 1931–33, and by a further nearly horizontal drift in 1935. The notable features of the public-utilities curve include failure to drop below zero at any time during the depression, arrival of the low point in 1933 instead of 1932, and striking failure of the improvement up to 1936 to restore the profit rate even to the level of 1930.

For manufacturing (Chart LXV), the rate declined moderately in 1927, recovered to a new peak in 1929, declined steadily though with a slackening pace to 1932, and rose steadily — with a particularly sharp advance in 1933 — until the 1936 rate was only slightly below the 1929 peak. The manufacturing groups shown in Chart LXV are selected from the four most important — in terms of total assets or of gross business volume — among the eleven groups of the manufacturing division, the other two being foods and textiles.[6] The metals curve is chiefly of interest because of the violence of its cyclical movement: the ranges of variation here between 1929 and 1932, and between 1932 and 1936, were exceptionally large. For chemicals, on the other hand, not only is the intensity of fluctuation more moderate, but even at the minimum in 1932 the rate remained positive.

The diversities among these curves, and also among the tabulated records for the other divisions and groups (Table XLVI), are highly suggestive of the varying profit conditions of the several lines of industry. Many of these points of diversity admit of fairly simple economic interpretation, in the light of conditions peculiar to the particular industry or affecting industry in general, but such discussion is omitted.

[6] The 1936 figures for metals and chemicals are on the former basis: motor vehicles included in metals, petroleum included in chemicals.

COMPARATIVE LEVELS IN 1936 AND OTHER YEARS

With respect to all of the foregoing comparisons of rates at different times, and also like comparisons in earlier chapters, one important point deserves emphasis. These records of time variations relate to *rates* of return; and they do not therefore give trustworthy indications of the comparative levels, at different times, of the *amount* of corporate profits. Thus, the facts that the trade curve of Chart LXIV is higher in 1936 than in the boom of the 'twenties, and that all three curves of Chart LXV are nearly as high in 1936 as in 1929, do not indicate that the volume of profits had by 1936 recovered to about 1929 levels. The essential fact is that the equity — which is the denominator of the rate — declined over the period, chiefly because of accumulated losses in certain years after 1929, excess of dividend payments over earnings after taxes, and downward revisions of asset valuations. Some indication of the extent during the years 1931–36 of this reduction in equity appears in Chapter XXVIII. Direct examination of our average equity figures for all divisions combined shows a decline from 146.7 billion dollars in 1931 to 133.8 in 1936, and the decline from 1929 must have been much greater. And this decline occurred in spite of the large increase which automatically occurred in 1934 because of the effect of abandoning consolidated returns upon the accounts and statistics. To avoid this disturbing factor, we may compare 1933 with 1931 and 1936 with 1934; equity declined from 146.7 to 129.7 billion dollars from 1931 to 1933; from 142.8 to 133.8 from 1934 to 1936. So great a drop in the denominator of our rate-of-return ratio can not fail to influence heavily all comparisons of figures for later years with those of earlier years. These comparisons are significant for the *rates*, but they should not lead to inferences about *amounts*.

The same point bears to a smaller extent upon comparisons

among the lines of industry as to their relative declines into the depression, and recoveries into 1936. The contraction of equity undoubtedly influenced different divisions and groups of industry differently, and therefore caused different correlations between the rate and the amount. Here again the comparisons are valid for rates, but inferences concerning volumes must be avoided.

OTHER CYCLICAL COMPARISONS

This chapter will not review and summarize the detailed comparisons of earlier chapters with respect to cyclical variations in different lines of industry and different size classes. Two broad generalizations stand out, with few exceptions in the record as examined. The intensity of cyclical movement is generally greater for producers of durable goods, and especially capital goods, than for producers of non-durable goods. This finding is in line with the conclusions drawn from numerous other statistical studies of different types of industry, and also in line with theoretical expectations.

The second general conclusion is that intensity is greater for small corporations than for large. In some lines of industry this difference in cyclical intensity between small and large corporations is remarkably great. The broad truth seems to be that the burden of cyclical instability falls chiefly upon small enterprise, so far as that burden is revealed by effects upon profits.

XXI

INDUSTRIAL DIFFERENCES IN RATE

DISCUSSIONS IN FOREGOING CHAPTERS have included frequent mentions of differences among divisions or groups, as to the relation between rate of return and corporate size and as to cyclical variations in rate. Chief emphasis in the present chapter is upon differences among industrial divisions and manufacturing groups in the level of average rate, without regard to variations with size or over time.

For this purpose a preliminary view can be obtained from the six-year averages of the rates for entire divisions and groups, with all size classes and both income and deficit categories combined (Table XLVII). As already remarked, these six-year averages are not entirely satisfactory typical numbers, because of the considerable scatter among the six annual figures in any one case and of the avoidance of any scheme of weighting in calculating the averages (see also Chapter XXVIII). A further defect exists when the purpose is to make comparisons among lines of industry. Industries for which the recovery after the great depression occurred early or was particularly vigorous are likely for that reason alone to have higher six-year averages than industries which had the opposite experience. In other words, while these six-year averages cover a period in which business in general reached the bottom of depression and then recovered with moderate vigor, the average for a particular line of industry may be influenced by the fact that such industry had a greater or smaller number of deeply depressed years between 1931 and 1936 than did business in general. These "technical" effects of the timing of the cycle in particular industries are likely to be increased in cases for which the cyclical intensity is high. The averages would be more trustworthy if the period were much longer than six years. This defect in the averages, while undoubtedly contributing to some of the differences observed in Table XLVII, can at most contribute only in moderate degree.

TABLE XLVII

SIX-YEAR AVERAGES OF RATES OF RETURN FOR EACH DIVISION AND GROUP AND ALL DIVISIONS IN THE AGGREGATE *

Aggregate	.97	Groups (*continued*):	
Divisions:		Tobacco	11.38
Agriculture	−2.30	Textiles	−.54
Mining	−.75	Leather	1.38
Manufacturing	2.15	Rubber	1.22
Construction	−2.21	Forest products	−3.72
Public utilities	1.52	Paper	1.58
Trade	.54	Printing	3.46
Service	−5.04	Chemicals	3.21
Finance	.24	Stone	.69
Groups:		Metals	1.51
Foods	4.59	Miscellaneous	.67
Liquors	12.41 †		

* See third footnote to Table IX.
† Based on four years only, 1933–36.

The differences among rates in Table XLVII are far too great to be ascribed to any technical peculiarities in the data or in the period covered. They undoubtedly represent mainly true differences in earning power which actually existed among lines of industry in the period under study. Whether such differences existed also in other periods can not be known without a similar examination of corresponding data for such periods. The 1931–36 period surely had many peculiarities which may have influenced the comparative rates of profit as among industries; but even these peculiarities of the recent economic situation could scarcely have accounted for all, or indeed the main share, of the differences shown by Table XLVII. An important share, at least, of the differences must be accepted as reflecting diversity of earning power among lines of industry for time periods extending substantially beyond the specific period 1931–36.

Before commenting upon the indications of the table, be it noted again that all figures shown are averages — averages over the corporations in the specified division or group, and averages over the six years 1931–36. The figure for all divisions combined is just under 1 per cent: corporate industry as a whole enjoyed a positive rate of return, but the average annual return amounted to less than 1 per cent of the equity. Such an average rate, even for a period of which one third was in deep depression, is manifestly low, and we can well doubt that it would prove adequate for the maintenance of the private-capital system. We are left with the confidence that past periods, and the hope that future periods which contain a better balancing of depression and "prosperity" than 1931–36, must show a somewhat higher rate than .97.

DIFFERENCES AMONG LINES OF INDUSTRY

Turning now to figures for the eight industrial divisions, we find six of them below the general figure of .97; and four of these are actually negative. Each of these four divisions had an average loss during the six-year period; and one of them, service, had losses at a very heavy rate. The separate annual figures largely confirm this showing of negative earning power: four of the six annual rates were negative for agriculture, three for mining, five for construction, and all six for service. Three of the negative rates — all except that for mining — were higher numerically than the highest positive rate (2.15) shown.

Among the positive rates, those for trade and finance are very small; and the remarks made above concerning the .97 rate for all industry apply with greater force to these cases.

The rate for public utilities was only moderately higher than that for all industry; and even the manufacturing rate, the highest among the divisions, was not large. Again it may be noticed that all of these average rates are held down by the severe effects of the great depression; and failure of the ensuing recovery to develop briskly, as was true in public utilities (which includes railroads), may have depressed some of the averages. But industry has to live, or fail to live, through bad times as well as good; and the 1931–36 period included a sufficient stretch of recovery to warrant our attaching real significance to these low rates and not merely regarding them as statistical accidents caused by selection of the time period for averaging.

Figures for the thirteen manufacturing groups also show wide diversity. Eight of them are below the average for the entire division, and two of these are negative. Annual figures were negative for textiles in only two years, but these 1931 and 1932 losses were at such heavy rates that the subsequent recovery did not offset them. The very heavy average rate of loss in forest products is confirmed by the annual figures, five of which were negative. Two of the positive rates are very high, but one of these (liquors) covers only four years and misses the worst effects of the depression. But even the rate for foods is higher than the highest (numerically) negative rate; and both printing and chemicals show fairly high average rates. Among the manufacturing groups five show positive rates of return above 3 per cent, which may be regarded as moderately high for a period such as 1931–36.[1] Three of these represent almost entirely producers of non-durable consumers' goods, and even for printing and chemicals the major share of the product may be of this type.

[1] The rate for liquors applies to only four years; but, if it were based upon the full period, 1931–32 rates could scarcely have been low enough to reduce the average below 3 per cent.

IMPLICATIONS

I do not propose to discuss even briefly the economic implications contained in or suggested by these results, and related results in other portions of the book; for adequate discussion must touch upon an intricate body of collateral evidence and extend to great length. Something may be gained, however, by pointing — even before intensive and elaborate study is given to the matter — to some of the highly important questions raised by the facts in their simple form.

One such question has already been touched upon. Does such an average rate of profit as the .97 for all industry, or most of the moderate positive rates for divisions such as trade and public utilities or groups such as leather and metals, encourage the development or even insure the maintenance of the corporate system on a private-capital basis? Such a question must be considered, of course, after generous allowances for the fact that 1931–36 may have been too heavily weighted by depression. But even for the better years of this period, many divisions and groups showed only moderate rates. The question can not be brushed aside on mere technical grounds, but must be faced because the national economic system may be destined for years of experience with rates of profit — after heavy taxes — not greatly above those shown in the table.

A somewhat related question concerns the control of corporate industry. Do the low rates, and particularly the negative rates, imply an extensive passage of control from present owners to creditors, or to new owners who buy assets at bargain-counter prices? The contraction of equity, shown by our figures for the years 1931–36, is not wholly the result of downward revaluations of assets; it is in important degree due also to the eroding effects of losses. What happens to an entire industry when the equity disappears? That poor managerial and entrepreneurial leadership should be eliminated is recognized, and an effective system brings about such elimination. But that all leadership, good as well as bad, should be cast aside because an entire industry suffers cumulative loss seems scarcely in the general interest.

Question also arises as to the effect of these wide differences in profit rates upon the differential development of industries. Do the high-rate industries secure new capital at the expense of low-rate industries, and is capital actually being withdrawn from low-rate industries? Of course, such questions pertain not only to entire industries, but to size classes within an industry and to particular corporations within a size class. The abundant evidences of diversity which we have found suggest the difficulties: these questions can be answered only after painstaking study of particular cases and the peculiar factors at work.

Do the data suggest the existence of monopoly, or near-monopoly, in certain lines of industry? At best, these figures can yield mere suggestions on this point; but, if high rates seem to prevail in those lines in which monopoly is thought to exist, this fact alone may point the way to further investigation. But this question of monopoly, like the others I have mentioned and many which I have not mentioned, can only be examined in the light of a wide range of evidence touching many factors besides profits. Our findings can, with respect to all such questions, merely suggest possible points of attack and perhaps indicate lines of investigation.

XXII

INVENTORY PROFITS

THIS CHAPTER and the two immediately following examine certain important factors in the reckoning of profits which may have a large bearing upon the findings, as to both cyclical fluctuations and size variations in rate of return, reported in the foregoing chapters. The factors to be examined are by no means all that might be worth discussion, but are selected because they are among the most important and because the available data admit of at least approximate determination of their effects. The specific factors are studied only in part: some of the tests are made only for isolated industrial divisions or groups, and for isolated years in the six-year period covered in earlier chapters. The object is to indicate, by these isolated tests, methods of analysis which might prove useful in a more elaborate and comprehensive survey; and the analysis aims also, in the specific cases studied, to reveal the probable extent to which these factors can affect our findings. The first such factor, to be examined in this chapter, is inventory profits arising from price fluctuations.

An important step in the calculation of profits for the income-tax return, in the case of any corporation carrying inventory as an incident to its operations, involves determining the excess in the value of inventory at the beginning of the year over that at the end of the year, and counting this excess among those deductions from gross sales designated as cost of goods sold. If end-year inventory exceeds beginning-year inventory, the excess is of course negative and acts as a partial offset against other items in cost of goods sold. If the excess is positive, it lowers the residual figure for profits; if the "excess" is negative, it raises profits.

The suggestion is frequently made that, for an industry obliged to carry large inventories in order to operate and especially if the inventory comprises commodities subject to wide price changes, this form of reckoning results in an illusory showing of profit (or loss). In periods of rising prices, calculated profits are said to be raised by the appreciation of value — reflecting the year's advance in prices — locked up in the inventory; and corresponding reverse effects appear when prices are falling. The further suggestion is often made that this form of reckoning profit, particularly when the revenue act carries an inadequate or no loss-carry-forward provision, results in unfairly burdensome taxation upon companies exposed to severe inventory fluctuations. And, whatever the provisions with respect to loss-carry-forward, it is held that this form of reckoning means that a substantial portion of all corporate income taxes collected in a particular year may in fact fall upon "income" which is nothing more than a fictitious and presumably temporary appreciation in value. It is not the main purpose of this section to discuss the tax questions thus raised; but our present purpose is instead to examine whether these inventory profits differ among size classes of corporations in such manner as to explain, at least in significant part, the main findings of this book concerning the relation of rate of return to size.

Accordingly, emphasis will not be placed upon various alternative methods — such as the base-stock method, or the last-in-first-out basis of valuation — of reckoning inventory, which have been suggested for easing the differential tax burden of enterprises which carry large inventories of widely fluctuating value, and for other purposes. The emphasis will instead be upon a specially designed definition of inventory appreciation (which, of course, may be negative in some cases), which seems suited to our immediate purpose. This definition, although it has some defects from the points of view of accounting method and economic theory, comes close enough to the concept out of which the issues stated above arise to insure that our analysis will yield helpful information on these questions. The definition also takes a form which lends itself to the type of calculation which seems feasible for the actual experimental examination of existing data.

WORKING DEFINITION OF INVENTORY PROFIT

This special definition designates as inventory profit (plus, if there is appreciation in value; minus, if value is reduced) during a particular year the year's change in value of a fixed physical volume of inventory, such physical volume being that held at the beginning or end of the year, whichever is smaller. This amounts to saying that (1) all or part, depending on whether physical inventory declined or rose during the year, of the end-year physical inventory was actually held at the beginning of the year, and (2) the change in value of this physical volume between the beginning and the end of the year, reflecting only price change, is the inventory profit (or loss). Obviously, the year's operations of a particular corporation may, and in general probably do, bring it about that many or all of the identical commodities held at the beginning of the year are not held at the end of the year. Moreover, such operations may result in changes during the year in the proportions of types or categories of commodities held — for example, the proportion between raw materials and finished articles, or that between one type of raw material and another — regardless of the identity of certain specific commodities within the inventory. The definition ignores these realistic difficulties: it regards the end-year inventory (or an amount thereof equivalent to beginning-year inventory) as a replacement of, if not identical with, the same amount of physical inventory at the beginning of the year. Ignoring the first difficulty raises no theoretical or practical issues: it matters not whether during the year a ton of steel wire is replaced, in the inventory, by another ton of exactly similar steel wire.

Ignoring the second difficulty — changing proportions among types of commodities in the inventory — does raise a theoretical issue. Presumably, for those types of commodities which have been reduced during the year, sales have taken place in which price-appreciation profits — assuming a year of rising prices — have been "realized." And, for those types which have increased in the inventory, certain price-appreciation profits — not yet realized — are locked up in inventory at the end of the year. What the definition implicitly assumes is that the price-appreciation profits since the year's beginning realized from the sale of commodities of the first type are equivalent to inventory profits during the same period locked up in another type of commodity in the inventory at the end of the year — in this sense, the second type is regarded as "replacing" the first type. The basic theoretical issue is whether commodities of the second type did in fact enjoy the same appreciation, up to time of sale of commodities of the first type, as did the commodities thus sold. Abundant evidence indicates that different types of commodities do not ordinarily appreciate at the same rate.

As a practical matter, the application of our definition — involving use of a price index, as will be seen — assumes maintenance or "replacement" of the inventory in this unrealistic sense. To what extent this leads to a faulty appraisal of "inventory profits" can not be determined from theoretical considerations. Moreover, an empirical determination is utterly impossible with data on inventories as reported to the Treasury, or as ordinarily reported for other purposes by corporations: details as to the make-up of the inventory are either entirely absent or too meagre to admit of specific examination of each type of commodity.

A further remark, on what the definition does not include, is in order. The view is sometimes held that part of the profit realized in sales is an "inventory gain," although a more informing terminology would call it price appreciation (during the period of retention in inventory). Thus, if a raw material is purchased and entered into inventory where it remains for four months — during which manufacturing processes are applied to it — and is then sold, part of the profit realized in sale *may* reflect an advance in price of the raw material during the four months — particularly if price changes in the finished commodity are responsive to those in the raw material. Unless such material is replaced in the year's inventory, our definition does not regard this gain as inventory profit; although, in the uncommon case in which the period held included a full (accounting) year instead of four months, the year's portion of the total of such gain between date of purchase and date of sale would be covered by our definition. The point of view of the definition is more closely akin to, though not identical with, the base-stock scheme of inventory accounting. The definition regards a certain volume of inventory — but a volume which may differ from one year to another, and not a fixed normal or base volume — as essential to carrying on a business; and it regards changes in value of that volume, due to price fluctuations, as constituting inventory profit (or loss). This is a profit which is likely to be temporary and evanescent, a profit which may be illusory because it is not subsequently realized and is in fact likely to be offset by an inverse price movement.

A final point relates to the method of determining inventory valuation: in general the Treasury insists on determination by a first-in–first-out formula; and the Treasury permits valuation either on a cost basis or on the lower of cost or market, so long as a consistent policy is followed by a corporation (apparently, most corporations use the lower of cost or market basis). These provisions generally have an important bearing upon an estimate of inventory profits; but, in the experiment actually reported herein, the turnover of inventory seems to be so fast that the effects of these provisions on valuation — and changes in valuation over time — can be ignored. They are ignored in the estimates reported, except as noted in the details of the report below.

METHOD OF ESTIMATE

The test calculations — looking toward the application of this special definition of inventory profit to a specific case in order to show whether such profits account for a significant share of total profits — has been confined to one manufacturing group, food products, in the two years 1932 and 1936. No attempt was made to apply the test to all divisions or groups in which inventory is important, or to all of the six years under study. One reason for avoiding such general application is that the "correction" to reported profits, to allow for inventory profits, is sufficiently open to error — because of the form of the basic data and of the method of estimate — to suggest further research before a complete application of the method and a full reporting of results is undertaken. Another reason is that this discussion is not directed to making comparisons, of the profit effect of holding inventory, among industries. The investigation is directed rather to formulating in tentative terms a method of analysis, to testing such method by direct application in a single case wherein inventories are known to be important, and to pointing out certain tentative findings suggested by this specific test as to the bearing of inventory upon the indicated variations of profits over time and among size classes.

In the following paragraphs, the method will be described and illustrated for 1932, and results will then be presented for 1936 as well as 1932.[1] In all steps, the operations described for

[1] In any comparison between 1932 and 1936, for this group, the fact that the beverages sub-group was included in the foods group in 1931–32 but in the liquors group thereafter should be borne in mind. Moreover, largely because of industrial reclassification in 1934 resulting from the

1932 may be understood as having been carried out similarly for 1936. The inventory data used are given in *Statistics of Income* tabulations for separate industries classified by size of assets.[2] In many respects, these figures are not such as we should like for this analysis; but the method here applied is designed to use as effectively as possible the data as presented. It there appears that in 1932 inventories constituted about one eighth of total assets — 832 million dollars, out of 6817 — and this is about the same proportion as that for the entire manufacturing division. Some groups, such as leather, had a higher share of assets in inventories; and others, such as printing, a lower share. Because of its magnitude (one of the four leading groups in manufacturing), because its proportion of inventories to assets was typical of all manufacturing, and because of certain special factors favoring the study of this group by a method involving price index numbers, the foods group was selected for the test.

The inventory figures as published, like the other balance-sheet figures, pertain to the end of the year.[3] It becomes necessary, for the following analysis, to have corresponding figures for the beginning of the year. In other words, we need inventory at the beginning of the year 1932 for each size class of corporations, separately for income and deficit categories, as such class (and category) was constituted at the end of 1932. This final provision means that inventory figures, for a class (and category) similarly described, at the end of 1931 will not meet our needs: shifts of corporations from size class to size class and between the income and deficit categories must have occurred on a wide scale from 1931 to 1932. This is the same

abandonment of consolidated tax returns, the make-up of the group may have been very different in 1936 than in 1932.

[2] Issue of 1932, pages 168–169.

[3] Strictly, the end of its taxable year for each corporation. We ignore differences in dating of fiscal years, and here assume that all inventories are stated for the end of the calendar year: December 31.

difficulty which is encountered in another connection in this book (Chapter XXIII); and the method of estimating beginning-year figures there evolved and explained is, with one exception to be noted immediately below, used here.

The first requisite is a list, by size classes and separately for the two categories, of estimated net capital assets at the beginning of 1932. Such figures are available in the source tabulations for the end of 1932, and the beginning-year figures are obtained by applying a fixed ratio to the end-year figures. Here occurs a departure from the precise method used in the similar debt analysis (below, page 290): the ratio used here depends, not on the joint experience of the group itself and of all divisions combined, but on the experience of the foods group alone. Thus, the total net capital assets of the entire foods group — all classes and both categories combined — at the beginning of 1932 is *assumed* the same as that at the end of 1931. This, of course, ignores shifts in industrial classification between the two years, entrance of entirely new foods corporations and exit of old corporations during 1932. No means appears for estimating the magnitude of this error, but I see no reason for faith that it would be reduced by following the more complicated procedure — making the ratio depend on all divisions combined as well as on foods.[4]

It was next assumed, as in the debt analysis, that the ratio thus obtained could be applied to each size class, separately by income and deficit categories, to obtain estimates of net capital assets for the beginning of 1932. This operation is parallel to that used in the debt study, as are the further operations incident to estimating beginning-year inventories. These operations will not here be described in detail, nor is it essential to list again the assumptions made and the possible errors intro-

[4] The case for such a procedure is better in the debt analysis chiefly because that analysis is concerned with large divisions rather than a small group.

duced. In all respects, these points follow those developed in the debt study. The method is illustrated, for a single size class, in Table XLVIII. The result is a list of estimated beginning-year inventories (valued as at the end of 1931) as shown, along with the end-year (1932) figures, in Table XLIX.

TABLE XLVIII

SPECIMEN COMPUTATION OF ESTIMATED INVENTORY AT THE BEGINNING OF THE YEAR; 500-THOUSAND-DOLLAR CLASS OF FOODS GROUP IN 1932 *

	Income category (1)	Deficit category (2)	Both categories combined (3)
a. Net capital assets, end 1931	97,632	84,191	181,823
b. Inventory, end 1931	30,104	27,858	57,962
c. Ratio of *b* to *a*	.3083	.3309	.3188
d. Ratios pertinent to beginning 1932	.3136	.3248	...
e. Net capital assets, end 1932	62,008	109,267	171,275
f. Estimated net capital assets, beginning 1932	63,967	112,720	176,687
g. Estimated inventory, beginning 1932	20,060	36,615	56,675

* Money figures in thousands of dollars. Rows *a*, *b*, *e* transcribed from *Statistics of Income* for 1931, and 1932. The 1931 figures pertain to a class *described* similarly to that of 1932, but *not* made up of the same corporations entirely — see text.

Row *d*, column 1 is average of Row *c*, columns 1 and 3; Row *d*, column 2 is average of Row *c*, columns 2 and 3 — see text.

Row *f* is Row *e* multiplied by 1.0316, which is the ratio of end-year 1931 to end-year 1932 figures for the entire group, both categories combined.

Row *g* is Row *f* multiplied by Row *d*.

DETERMINATION OF INVENTORY PROFITS

From here on the analysis differs from that of the debt study, as it aims at an entirely different goal. As already indicated (page 258), we aim to determine the change in value during 1932 — due to price changes — of the physical volume of inventory at the beginning or at the end of 1932, whichever is smaller. The first task, then, is to determine — for each category in each size class — whether the beginning-year or end-year physical inventory is greater. Preliminary to answering this question is a determination of the price at which the inventory at the beginning of 1932 (end of 1931) was valued, and that at which inventory at the end of 1932 was valued. Here we encounter the difficulty of deciding between cost and the lower of cost or market, as the price basis. This difficulty was fortunately avoided in the foods-group test case because the average turnover of inventory is very rapid — in almost all the classes and both categories, at least six times a year.[5] Hence, if we ignore different rates of turnover for different sections of the inventory (despite the errors this undoubtedly introduces), the inventory — identical commodities — at the end of the year has not been in possession of the company — on a first-in-first-out basis — more than two months; and, if price changes were small during those two months, the difference between cost and market would be slight.[6]

The measure of price movement selected was a weighted average of wholesale indices published by the United States Bureau of Labor Statistics. The indices were those for the

[5] Only a rough estimate of turnover could be made: gross sales of the year was divided by inventory at the end of the year. Some improvement could have been effected by using average of beginning-year and end-year inventories as the divisor, but this would have been at best not a close estimate of the true average inventory for the year. The question of differences in the valuation basis of numerator and denominator — sales and inventory — could not be answered at all, though this is always significant in precise appraisals of turnover. Likewise no allowance could be made for different rates of turnover for different sections of the inventory. The rough rates found, however, were so high that I doubt if any of these refinements would have altered the practical decisions made.

[6] Actually, "cost" would tend to be an average for the two months; and "market" would pertain to December 31. In the cases under test, these alternatives were considered, and the differences in indicated price bases of inventory valuation — from the end of one year to the next — were so slight that I took round figures derived from averaging these differences, as stated in the text.

TABLE XLIX

ESTIMATES OF INVENTORY LOSSES, AND OF COMPILED PROFITS AND LOSSES EXCLUDING INVENTORY LOSSES, FOR FOODS GROUP IN 1932 *

Class †	Category	Inventory at: Beginning (1)	Inventory at: End (2)	Inventory loss (3)	Compiled net profit or loss (4)	Ratio of (3) to (4) (5)	Net profit or loss excluding inventory (6)
0	Income	3,756 L	3,288	675	2,600	.260	3,275
	Deficit	14,801 L	12,872	2,666	−16,979	.157	−14,313
	Both	...	...	3,341	−14,379	.232	−11,038
50	Income	5,570 L	4,829	1,004	2,869	.350	3,873
	Deficit	18,248	14,101 L	3,103	−12,089	.257	−8,986
	Both	...	...	4,107	−9,220	.445	−5,113
100	Income	13,565 L	11,823	2,441	6,008	.406	8,449
	Deficit	39,494	31,250 L	6,870	−21,412	.321	−14,542
	Both	...	...	9,311	−15,404	.604	−6,093
250	Income	16,461 L	16,828	2,963	8,531	.347	11,494
	Deficit	35,110	25,858 L	5,683	−14,894	.382	−9,211
	Both	...	...	8,646	−6,363	1.359	2,283
500	Income	20,060 L	20,120	3,608	11,309	.319	14,917
	Deficit	36,615 L	31,736	6,583	−14,015	.471	−7,432
	Both	...	...	10,191	−2,706	3.77	7,485

TABLE XLIX (*Continued*)

1,000	Income	51,539 *L*	60,537	9,262	24,281	.382	33,543
	Deficit	98,126	65,061 *L*	14,330	−27,650	.518	−13,320
	Both	...	...	23,592	−3,369	7.00	20,223
5,000	Income	30,044 *L*	31,782	5,402	16,272	.332	21,674
	Deficit	38,320	21,534 *L*	4,740	−15,758	.301	−11,018
	Both	...	...	10,142	514	19.74	10,656
10,000	Income	88,370 *L*	96,667	15,890	49,740	.319	65,630
	Deficit	113,940 *L*	102,201	20,500	−58,384	.351	−37,884
	Both	...	...	36,390	−8,644	4.21	27,746
50,000	Income	257,535	184,260 *L*	40,540	96,694	.419	137,234
	Deficit	78,317 *L*	97,625	14,090	1,043	13.51	15,133
	Both	...	...	54,630	97,737	.559	152,367
Entire group	Income	469,847 *L*	430,133	84,560	218,305	.387	302,865
	Deficit	496,020	402,239 *L*	88,430	−180,139	.491	−91,709
	Both	...	...	172,990	38,166	4.53	211,156

* Unit: $1,000, for columns 1, 2, 3, 4, 6; 1, for column 5. Column 2 compiled from *Statistics of Income for 1932*, pp. 168–69; column 1 estimated by method described in text; column 5 ignores signs; column 6 is column 4 plus column 3 (*minus* inventory losses).

† Lower limit of class, in thousands of dollars.

L Value representing the lower physical inventory.

foods group, and the grains and the livestock-and-poultry subgroups of the farm-products group of the U.S.B.L.S. index; and they were given weights of 20, 3, and 6, respectively. The object of combining these indices was to cover raw materials as well as manufactured food products. The food-products index covers some food raw materials, but not the grains and animals. The weights used were approximately as they stood in the U.S.B.L.S. general index in 1931. Though there is no good reason for assurance that these weights reflect the proportions in which the three sets of commodities enter the inventories of the companies under study — either as a whole or in the several size classes and categories — no reason appeared for some other choice. Use of these weights has whatever advantage consistency may give: each of the three indices is itself a weighted index, so that we are by implication assuming that the inventory is made up in the proportions indicated by the internal weights in each of the three indices. Manifestly, this may be seriously in error, particularly when we are studying the not very numerous corporations of a particular size class and of one category (income or deficit). I see no means of appraising the extent of this error, but doubt if it can significantly distort the findings reported below. Examination of December figures and the averages of November-December figures, of this special index, for 1931 and 1932 led to .82 as measuring the price basis of the end of 1932 with respect to the beginning of 1932 (end of 1931) as unity.[7]

It is now possible to determine, for each size class and each category, whether the end-year or beginning-year inventory is the smaller — in physical terms, assuming value related to physical volume by the special wholesale price measure chosen. Thus, for example, a class for which the 1932 end-year value is more than 18 per cent below the beginning-year value can be

[7] The corresponding figure for 1936 was 1.03: end-year price was found 3 per cent above beginning-year.

assumed to have a smaller physical inventory at the end of the year. In this manner, for each class and category of Table XLIX, a selection between the end-year and beginning-year inventories was made; and those selected as lower are labelled *L* in the table. An interesting fact — somewhat uncertainly explicable by the effect of prices on realization of net income — is that the *L* items are beginning-year figures for the income category and end-year figures for the deficit category, in five of the classes and the entire group: one category increased and the other decreased physical inventory, during 1932. I omit further discussion of this suggestive comparison.

These *L* items are taken to represent the inventory with respect to which what we have defined as inventory profit (or loss) accrued through price fluctuation during 1932. The *L* item is the value, at the year's end or beginning as the case may be, of that physical volume of inventory which was held both at the beginning and at the end of the year. Application to these *L* items of the percentage price change during the year yielded the estimated inventory profits (losses, in all cases for 1932) during the year.[8] These estimated losses are listed in the third column of Table XLIX, wherein the sum of the two categories for each size class is also shown.

It is well to remark again that the application of identical price-change percentages to all size classes and both categories may do violence to the facts. The corporations of one size class may in fact hold on the average inventory made up in such a way that its actual average rate of price change during 1932 differs from that implied by the general price measure used, and differs from that for certain other size classes. The issue involved is again the appropriateness of the weighting system

[8] The price index being .82, for end 1932 compared with end 1931, the percentage taken was 18 for cases in which *L* was at the beginning and 22 for cases in which *L* was at the end. For the 1936 test case, 3 per cent was taken for both sets of cases, as the index was 1.03 for that year.

of the price index to the make-up of the inventory of a given size class and category. That errors on this account, especially in comparisons between class and class and category and category, may be substantial can not be doubted; but that they are large enough to nullify or even seriously qualify the broad findings below seems to me improbable.

I remark also that we are dealing in the whole analysis with *class* figures, which afford no indication as to the experience of the particular corporations within the class. Thus, conceivably, 20 out of 50 corporations in a particular class might have an increase in physical inventory during the year, whereas the other 30 have a decrease. I do not see that this fact has any bearing upon our estimate of the year's aggregate inventory profits, and of the relation thereof to total accounting profits, *for the class.*[9]

Finally, it should be emphasized that the method of analysis does not include all of the year's change in value, through price changes, of the inventory. Thus, if the *L* figure is at the end of the year, *some* of the (larger) physical inventory held at the beginning of the year is assumed to have been sold during the year without being replaced; and that portion of inventory may have experienced a gain or loss in value, through price changes, between January 1 and date of sale. Likewise, if the *L* figure is at the beginning of the year, *some* of the (larger) end-year physical inventory is assumed to have been acquired during the year in excess of sales; and that portion may have experienced gain or loss in value between date of acquisition and December 31. Either of these elements might properly be called inventory profits in our sense; but they do not come within our narrow definition, which calculates inventory profits only for the *L* item. For this and other reasons, we may fairly say that — except for errors in the estimating process — our

[9] The point may, however, have a significant bearing upon considerations of tax policy with respect to inventories.

calculated inventory profits (or losses) are probably understated by substantial amounts.

RELATION OF INVENTORY TO TOTAL PROFITS

The fourth column of Table XLIX lists the compiled net profits (or losses) which, except for the tax correction, have been used in calculating rate of return on equity. These figures are taken directly from the same source tabulations as the other items — net capital assets, inventories at end of year, and gross sales — used at various stages of this test analysis. The fifth column of the table expresses the estimated inventory losses as ratios to the general profit (or loss) figures — before tax deduction — in Column 4. The final column of the table shows the results of deducting Column 3 items from those of Column 4, with due regard to signs: it gives estimates of profit and loss *not* due to changes in inventory valuation (in the narrow sense covered by our definition). Table L presents the 1936 test case in the same form.

The most significant results, for our purpose, appear in Column 5 of Table XLIX (and likewise of Table L). Fixing attention for the present upon 1932, the striking fact appears that for the foods group as a whole, each category being considered separately, inventory losses run to more than one third (almost one half, for deficit category) of the tabulated figures for compiled net profit or loss. In other words, excluding inventory profits (losses in 1932), as narrowly defined in this chapter, would increase the tabulated profits of the income corporations by about one third, and decrease the tabulated losses of the deficit corporations by nearly one half. The proportionate effect upon the entire group with both categories combined is far greater, because of the offset of profits against losses in general, whereas the inventory element is negative for both categories. Thus, in this case, the ratio of inventory loss to the combined figure (positive profits) of Column 4 is (as

TABLE L

ESTIMATES OF INVENTORY GAINS, AND OF COMPILED PROFITS AND LOSSES EXCLUDING INVENTORY GAINS, FOR THE FOODS GROUP IN 1936 *

Class †	Category	Inventory at: Beginning (1)	Inventory at: End (2)	Inventory gain (3)	Compiled net profit or loss (4)	Ratio of (3) to (4) (5)	Net profit or loss excluding inventory (6)
0	Income	7,320 L	8,095	220	3,875	.0568	3,655
	Deficit	8,565 L	8,970	257	−6,642	.0387	−6,899
	Both	...	...	477	−2,767	.1724	−3,244
50	Income	12,656 L	14,668	380	5,991	.0634	5,611
	Deficit	8,424	7,944 L	238	−3,517	.0676	−3,755
	Both	...	...	618	2,474	.2501	1,856
100	Income	33,154 L	39,897	995	15,730	.0633	14,735
	Deficit	17,164	15,900 L	477	−5,155	.0926	−5,632
	Both	...	...	1,472	10,575	.1392	9,103
250	Income	37,504 L	50,944	1,125	19,978	.0563	18,853
	Deficit	15,117	12,803 L	384	−3,711	.1035	−4,095
	Both	...	...	1,509	16,267	.0928	14,758
500	Income	55,724 L	64,791	1,672	24,656	.0678	22,984
	Deficit	12,798	12,514 L	375	−2,025	.1854	−2,400
	Both	...	...	2,047	22,631	.0904	20,584

TABLE L (*Continued*)

1,000	Income	133,727 L	183,862	4,012	66,803	.0600	62,791
	Deficit	41,949	37,204 L	1,116	−5,924	.1883	−7,040
	Both	...	...	5,128	60,879	.0842	55,751
5,000	Income	74,662 L	82,643	2,240	27,017	.0829	24,777
	Deficit	13,095	12,920 L	388	−1,420	.2736	−1,808
	Both	...	...	2,628	25,597	.1027	22,969
10,000	Income	517,375 L	574,715	15,521	234,095	.0664	218,574
	Deficit	18,536 L	30,650	556	−3,651	.1523	−4,207
	Both	...	...	16,077	230,444	.0698	214,367
Entire group	Income	901,012 L	1,019,615	27,030	398,145	.0679	371,115
	Deficit	118,212 L	138,906	3,546	−32,045	.1107	−35,591
	Both	...	...	30,576	366,100	.0834	335,524

* Unit: $1,000, for columns 1, 2, 3, 4, 6; 1, for column 5. Column 2 compiled from *Statistics of Income for 1936, Part 2*, pp. 101–102, Table 6 (top three classes of income category are combined to match the "classes grouped" of deficit category); column 1 estimated by method described in text; column 5 ignores signs; column 6 is column 4 minus column 3.

† Lower limit of class, in thousands of dollars.

L Value representing the lower physical inventory.

shown in Column 5) over 450 per cent: inventory losses run 4½ times the tabulated profit; and, if they were moderately larger, would convert that profit into a loss. Exclusion of inventory losses from total profits (Column 6) yields a greatly altered indication of the profit experience of the foods group in 1932, and the use of this revised profits figure (after tax adjustment) in the numerator of our rate-of-return ratio would correspondingly yield a greatly altered ratio for 1932.[10] Indicated profits for the income category are raised very sharply, indicated losses for the deficit category are greatly reduced, and indicated profits for the combined group are very greatly increased.

Similar examination of the 1936 results shows similar effects in the opposite direction: exclusion of inventory profits reduces substantially the general profits figure, and hence implies a reduction in the indicated rate of return for the foods group as a whole. The upward price movement of 1936 was much less sharp than the downward movement of 1932, and therefore the alterations in 1936 are less striking. If our test had been applied to a year of rapid price advance, there can be little doubt that exclusion of inventory profits would result in alterations in indicated profit and indicated rate of return of about the same order of magnitude as those found for 1932, but in the opposite direction. Clearly, in a year of declining prices, inventory losses decrease profits (or increase losses) as compiled; and, if the price decline is sharp, the effect is very large and may even change a profit into an indicated loss. Likewise, in a year of rising prices, inventory profits increase profits (or decrease losses) as compiled; and, if the price advance is sharp, the

[10] I assume here the tax adjustment unchanged, as implied in present laws. If the law were altered to lift the income tax from "inventory profits," on the ground that they are an illusory form of "income," the rate-of-return ratio would need corresponding further alteration. I waive the question whether some modification of the equity — denominator of the rate of return — is also implied if inventory profit is excluded from the numerator.

effect is very large and may even change a loss into an indicated profit.

The foods group is only a test case, and the results found in this case may differ substantially from like results which might be found by testing other lines of industry; but differences would be with respect to degree, not direction. Broadly speaking, we may expect the effects of inventory profits upon general profits to be large in cases for which inventory runs large in comparison with an appropriate measure of the magnitude of the industry and for which price fluctuations are of wide amplitude. The bearing of these findings upon the cyclical course of the rate of return on equity, as reported in previous chapters, is obvious. For a particular industrial division (excluding those which carry no inventory) or group, or a particular size class, the intensity of the cyclical movement is exaggerated by inventory profits and losses; and even the shape and timing of the cyclical movement may be distorted in some degree for the same reason. Furthermore, comparisons of cyclical movement among divisions or groups or among size classes in any one division or group may be somewhat distorted by the differential effects of the inventory element. Without carrying through the full inventory analysis, as outlined, for foods in other years and for other groups and the divisions in all years, these points can not be examined quantitatively. I forego such a comprehensive series of tests largely because the method used does not seem as yet sufficiently refined to warrant close comparisons of indicated differences among divisions and groups.

The bearing of these findings on tax policy is evident. If the revenue laws excluded from taxable corporate income inventory profits (or losses), as we have narrowly defined them, tax revenue would be increased in a year like 1932 and reduced in a year of rising prices.[11] The theoretical warrant for such

[11] The amount of the change in revenue would differ from industry to industry and from year to year. In the foods group in 1932 — neglecting

exclusion of inventory profits from the tax base is that such profits are not yet realized, and may in fact disappear before they can be realized. I remark that if the revenue laws provided for loss-carry-over on a liberal basis, the issue would largely disappear; and certain other changes in tax provisions might accomplish about the same result.

Of still greater significance, for purposes of this book, are the differences among size classes in the effect of inventories on indicated profits (or losses) and rates of return. Again considering first only the 1932 results (Table XLIX), the ratio of inventory profit (strictly, loss) to compiled net profit or loss is nowhere less than three tenths except in the lowest size class and in the deficit category of the next higher size class. Despite numerous erratic high ratios, particularly for the combined categories in all but one of the higher size classes and in the deficit category of the highest class, the ratios show remarkably small variation. That so many of them run close to three tenths is an astonishing outcome, and can scarcely be due entirely to accident.

When we pass to Column 6 of the table, giving tentative estimates of profit or loss after exclusion of the inventory losses, we find of course all the figures higher (with due regard to sign) than those of Column 4. We also find the shift of the size-class figures, for both categories combined, from minus to plus coming at a much lower point on the size scale — 250 thousand dollars, instead of 5,000, or more surely (after a secondary dip into the minus area) 50,000.

Still more helpful for our purpose is a computation of rate of return using this modified concept of profits in the numerator

actual or effective graduation in rates, shifts of corporations from the deficit to the income category, and the possibility that certain corporations might not be able to meet the increased tax liability without becoming insolvent — the increase in revenue would be over one third. In years of sharply rising prices, loss in revenue might run to about the same proportion of existing revenue.

(Table LI). The first column gives the figures for profit or loss excluding inventory losses (from Column 6 of Table XLIX) after deduction of estimated taxes.[12] Column 2 presents the estimated average equity for the year, and Column 3 the resulting rates of return — items of Column 1 divided by those of Column 2. The basic rates of return on equity, as given in Chapter VI, are shown for comparison in Column 4. Of course, each figure of Column 3 is higher than the corresponding figure of Column 4, because each class and category shows estimated inventory profits which were negative in 1932 — the price movement was downward.

The point of vital interest in this investigation, however, is the relation of the modified rate of return (Column 3) to size. Considering first the class figures for both categories combined, we observe rates increasing with increasing size in the five lowest size classes. From 1 to 50 million dollars, changes in rate are somewhat irregular but very narrow; and a sharp final increase appears in the highest size class. The general course of the rate is unmistakably upward with increasing size, though a considerable intermediate range in the size scale shows a nearly horizontal movement. This relationship is in all essential respects similar to that for the basic rates, as calculated in Chapter VI and shown in Column 4. Similarly, examination of the income and deficit categories separately shows a notable similarity between variations in the modified rates of Column 3 and the basic rates of Column 4.

We conclude that inventory profits (or losses), despite their heavy influence on compiled profits or losses, do *not* account in any appreciable degree for the relationship between rate of

[12] I use here the same tax estimates as in Chapter VI, ignoring a possibility that taxes *might* be changed on this basis of reckoning "profits." Likewise in Column 2, I use the equity figures of Chapter VI, ignoring possible appropriate changes consistent with the new definition of the year's accumulation of surplus.

TABLE LI

RATES OF RETURN ON EQUITY, WITH ESTIMATED INVENTORY LOSSES EXCLUDED FROM PROFITS OR LOSSES, FOR THE FOODS GROUP IN 1932 *

Class †	Category	Net profit or loss after taxes, excluding inventory loss (1)	Average equity for 1932 (2)	Rate of return: Excluding inventory (3)	Rate of return: From Chapter VI (4)
0	Income	3,007	20,694	14.53	10.27
	Deficit	−14,313	59,412	−24.07	−28.58
	Both	−11,306	80,106	−14.11	−18.28
50	Income	3,556	32,935	10.80	7.75
	Deficit	−8,986	72,958	−12.32	−16.58
	Both	−5,430	105,893	−5.13	−9.00
100	Income	7,756	77,504	10.00	6.86
	Deficit	−14,542	156,382	−9.30	−13.69
	Both	−6,786	233,886	−2.90	−6.88
250	Income	10,504	100,021	10.50	7.54
	Deficit	−9,211	146,494	−6.29	−10.17
	Both	1,293	246,515	.52	−2.98
500	Income	13,600	110,372	12.33	9.05
	Deficit	−7,432	158,046	−4.70	−8.87
	Both	6,168	268,418	2.30	−1.50
1,000.......	Income	30,717	331,830	9.26	6.46
	Deficit	−13,320	393,430	−3.38	−7.03
	Both	17,397	725,260	2.40	−.85
5,000.......	Income	19,760	207,978	9.50	6.91
	Deficit	−11,018	176,678	−6.24	−8.92
	Both	8,742	384,656	2.28	−.36
10,000......	Income	60,046	633,344	9.49	6.97
	Deficit	−37,884	646,253	−5.86	−9.04
	Both	22,162	1,279,597	1.73	−1.11
50,000......	Income	126,005	1,353,058	9.31	6.32
	Deficit	15,133	361,806	4.18	.29
	Both	141,138	1,714,864	8.23	5.04
Entire group	Income	277,727	2,867,738	9.68	6.74
	Deficit	−91,709	2,171,460	−4.23	−8.30
	Both	186,018	5,039,198	3.69	.26

* Unit: $1,000, for columns 1 and 2; 1 per cent, for columns 3 and 4. Items of column 1 derived from column 6 of Table XLIX by applying tax corrections from Table A of Appendix.

† Lower limit of class interval, in thousands of dollars.

and it must not be supposed that the results shown are better than tentative and roughly approximate even for these two cases.

These tests indicate emphatic negative answers to the basic questions posed at the head of this chapter. Perhaps application of the test to other divisions or to certain manufacturing groups might indicate the contrary, and perhaps application of a greatly refined set of tests even to these two divisions might reverse the findings. I think this unlikely, however, and feel safe in holding the opinion after these experiments — despite all their imperfections — that differences in interest burden do not account in any significant degree for the major relationship between rate of return and size as revealed in the central analyses of this book.

OBSTACLES TO ANALYSES

The desired approach, for testing the questions posed above, would consist in studying the rate of return not on owners' equity — as carried out in the foregoing chapters — but on the sum of creditors' and owners' capital. Thus, the denominator of our new rate of return would be equity plus debt, and the numerator would be profits after taxes plus interest paid. Unfortunately, the needed data are not available for carrying out such a calculation separately for each size class.

Lack of pertinence of data. So far as the general list of corporations — all divisions combined — is concerned, the interest-paid figure is available for each size class.[1] But the debt item is not adequately given by the tabulations. The balance sheets

[1] This is subject to the reservation that the *tabulated* figure for interest paid *may* not represent accurately total payments of interest. It is possible for interest, as for certain other deductions permitted by the Revenue Act, to be reported on the return — in part, at least — in such manner that its identity is concealed and it can not be tabulated separately as interest paid. On how many returns this occurs, and how serious the consequences may be as respects the tabulated interest item, can not be known.

as tabulated give two items of indebtedness: notes and accounts payable, and bonds and mortgages.[2]

The first of these mingles two elements of debt, only one of which, notes payable, ordinarily bears interest. And no entirely satisfactory basis exists for segregating the interest-bearing portion from the total. The method actually adopted for segregating notes payable — a method clearly subject to a serious margin of error — is described below (page 295). An economist might hold that he is in any case interested in total debt, and in an average rate on total debt, even though part of it actually pays no interest; but even this position seems open to objection, for the accounts payable are in practice likely to arise as a direct incident to making purchases rather than from a conscious intent to obtain working capital by borrowing, as is more likely to be the case in respect to notes payable.

For the specific divisions and groups, the situation is still less satisfactory. The tabulations by size classes for each division and group give no data on interest paid; this item must be estimated for each size class, presumably by an elaborate and somewhat dubious process, as we shall see. For each division and group the remarks made above about the debt figures also apply, so that calculation of rate of return on debt for the several size classes of any one division or group is liable to serious errors in both the numerator and the denominator.

We are nevertheless forced to direct attention to specific divisions or groups rather than to the general list. The reason is

[2] Here again, the items as tabulated *may* not tell the whole story. For certain returns, some elements of debt may be concealed in the catch-all item "other liabilities"; and there is no way of knowing how serious this defect is. It may be remarked here also that there is less incentive for careful checking of the balance sheet submitted with a return than of the income statement, by internal revenue officers; and this may imply that corporations do not develop a habit of reporting the balance sheet as carefully as the income account.

that the situation for the general list is likely to reflect unduly the circumstances of the finance division, which includes banks and similar institutions. This would introduce a special difficulty: the deposits of banks (whether they bear interest or not) are tabulated in "other liabilities" and can not be segregated therefrom, and thus a very large element of interest-bearing debt of the finance division can not be brought into the denominator of our rate. On the other hand, the interest which banks pay on such deposits presumably is tabulated in the "interest paid" item of *Statistics of Income*, and would find its way into the numerator of the rate. There can be no doubt that this would result in a serious distortion of the indicated rate on debt, not only for the finance division but also — because finance bulks so large in the total — for all divisions combined.

But even without this special difficulty, it would still be unwise to overlook the peculiarities of finance corporations — especially banks — with reference to debt and interest. There can be little doubt that questions concerning the relation of debt and interest to equity and profits have very different import for financial enterprises than for ordinary industrial concerns. For this reason also, as finance bulks so large in the total, an analysis of the general list which combines all divisions seems unlikely to yield findings having clear economic significance. We must therefore design our tests of the burden of interest for specific non-financial divisions, and work out a scheme of analysis applicable to such cases.

Time specification of data. A serious general difficulty arises from the fact that the balance-sheet figures pertain to the end of the year.[3] The interest-paid item, on the other hand, pertains to the whole year — except for a moderately small number of part-year returns. Analysis of rate of return on creditors' capi-

[3] Ordinarily the calendar year, but various other dates not more than six months from December 31 for fiscal-year companies.

tal therefore requires some passage from the end-year debt figures, as tabulated from balance sheets, to averages for the year. Because of rapid changes in outstanding debt — particularly short-term debt (notes and accounts payable) — in certain years under study, this correction is even more important for the debt-interest analysis than for the equity-profits analysis (see Chapter XXVIII). On the other hand, we have no obvious basis — unlike the case with respect to equity — for making at least a partial reconstruction of the debt figure for the beginning of the year.[4] In other words, no item in the income account can be regarded as obviously an addition to or subtraction from debt, during the year.

If we were not dealing with size classes, and separately for income and deficit categories, beginning-year figures might roughly be assumed identical with those for the end of the preceding year. Even this assumption would be hazardous, because of changes from year to year in industrial classification of specific corporations, or in the inclusion of new corporations or exclusion of old corporations. But the assumption is certainly unwarranted for the analysis as actually planned — by size classes and separately by income and deficit categories. Extensive shifts — in some years, very extensive shifts — occur which take many specific corporations from one size class to another, or from (to) the income category to (from) the deficit category. Under these circumstances the assumption that, for example, the debt tabulated at the end of 1931 for corporations *then* in the 100-thousand-dollar size class and in the income category thereof is the debt at the beginning of 1932

[4] We ignore the *course* of change during the year; although this, particularly for short-term debt, may have a serious effect on the average for the year. One of the many experiments tried in this analysis aimed at estimating and allowing for the month-to-month changes in short-term debt; but no dependable results were obtained. We shall be content therefore with an average of figures for the beginning and for the end of the year as rough estimates of the year's average.

for corporations which were in that class and that category *at the end of 1932* is obviously absurd. By accident the assumption might be approximately valid in some very rare case, but only by highly improbable accident.

We are therefore confronted with the need of some other device for estimating the debt at the beginning of the year, for the corporations which fall in a specified class and category at the end of that year. Such estimates are needed separately for short-term and long-term debt; although in most cases the year's change in long-term debt is less likely to be large, and could accordingly be estimated by somewhat cruder devices with safety.

The device actually adopted, after a considerable series of experiments most of which were fruitless, rests upon two assumptions each of which may involve moderate error. The first is that the net capital assets — book value of physical assets after reserves for depreciation and depletion — is so highly stable that the beginning-year figure for same can safely be inferred from the end-year figure, for a specified class and category. The second is that the ratio of debt to net capital assets, at the *end* of a particular year, for the corporations *then* in a specified class (and, to a smaller extent, in a specified category), can be taken as identical with the same ratio at the *beginning* of the following year for the corporations falling in that class (and category) at the end of such following year. The first of these assumptions enables us to project, for a given class and category of corporations, the year-end figure for net capital assets back to the beginning of that year. The second assumption enables us to calculate, from such assumed beginning-year figure for net capital assets, the desired beginning-year figures for short-term and long-term debt. The method is described in detail below (page 290), and further comments on its validity are there presented.

For the moment, two general comments will suffice. The first assumption is the choice of the least of several evils. Of all the items in the tabulated balance sheet, which might be taken as measures of aggregate importance of a group of corporations and used as a reference base for determining comparative importance of some other item, net capital assets is one of the most stable and perhaps the most stable.[5] Even this item is not entirely stable, particularly in years when discretionary revaluations are made. And in ordinary years, some instability results from depreciation and depletion — for which an estimated allowance might be made — and from replacements or new purchases or installations of equipment and plant, or sale or abandonment of old capital assets. As will appear, some gross allowance can be made for these causes of instability, and net capital assets remains the most dependable basis of reference for our purpose.[6]

The second assumption really involves sampling theory. It amounts to regarding a list of corporations classified in a par-

[5] The one absolutely "stable" item in the tabulations is number of corporations. The *number* of corporations in a specified class at the beginning of a year — ignoring part-year returns — is exactly the same as that at the end of the year. Why not, then, get the ratio of debt to number of corporations — the average debt per corporation — at the end of one year, and apply this ratio to the number of corporations in the specified class at the end of the next year to get the estimated debt at the beginning of that year? The reason is that both theory and experience show that such averages per corporation are highly untrustworthy because of the varying importance (or size) of corporations in the class and of the skewness of such variation. Some basis of reference which takes account — as mere number does not — of importance must therefore be used. Such a basis as total assets (or liabilities) might be suggested; but this is highly unstable, partly for the very reason that debt (a part of total liabilities) varies so considerably during the year. Instability will likewise be found to characterize nearly all the other balance-sheet items as tabulated in *Statistics of Income*, except net capital assets (and bonds and mortgages, which we seek to estimate), as well as nearly all of the income-account items.

[6] A further point in its favor is that, unlike many balance-sheet items, it does not include an "intercorporate element" which is likely to disappear when a merger or some similar corporate rearrangement takes place.

ticular way — for example, in a particular category and size class — at the end of one year as a good sample (so far as the ratio of debt to net capital assets is concerned) of the quite different list of corporations classified in the same way in the next year. This assumption seems tolerably safe, except in those rare cases in which the number of corporations is so small as to render the sample possibly unrepresentative because of the dominant effect of one or two particular companies on the ratio. This amounts to saying the assumption is less good for high size classes than low, because corporations generally are less numerous in the former than in the latter. Reason appears also for greater confidence in the assumption when applied to an entire size class than when applied to either the income or the deficit category separately, because of the numerous shifts between the two categories from one year to the next. This subordinate conclusion leads to a special step in the analysis, as we shall see (page 293).

The rate of interest. A further deep-reaching difficulty appears because we have no precise knowledge of the rate — or rates — of interest on outstanding debt. Such knowledge is needed because, as is evident from the foregoing, we must estimate interest paid — by size class, by industry — through the application of an interest rate to the estimated debt.

Published interest rates on short-term debt pertain almost exclusively to bank loans or closely-related types of borrowing, and reflect in most cases also the rates on new loans rather than average rates on outstanding loans. This second point is relatively unimportant for short-term debt; for the very shortness of the maturity generally implies that average rates on outstanding debt can not differ greatly from quoted rates on new loans, except in a period of very violently changing rates. Published rates on long-term debt have two similar defects: such rates are customarily quoted only for the obligations of prominent listed corporations and only for new borrowings.[7] Here the second objection is likely to be serious, for many long-term obligations may have been outstanding so long that their face rates — unless readjustments through refunding or other operations have occurred — are significantly out of line with rates on new long-term funds.[8]

It is fairly clear that we can not accept published rates as appropriate multipliers for estimating long-term interest paid upon the known (or estimated) long-term debt outstanding. Less strong objections stand against accepting quoted bank rates on short-term loans as appropriate for corporate short-term debt outstanding.[9] The method actually used does assume as the rate on outstanding notes payable a selected average of quoted rates on new bank loans. Just how large a share of the notes payable of industrial corporations is made up of bank loans, or how this share varies among industries or among

[7] Currently reported "yield" figures on outstanding (old) obligations are of no use for our purpose — the base of the yield is market value, not the amount of the obligation.

[8] Reference here to face rates suggests another disturbing factor in the situation. The average rate on outstanding debt, as a basis for calculating interest paid, should take account of defaulted interest. We may be sure that in some of the years under study defaults on interest were significantly large; and, although companies in actual liquidation ordinarily do not file returns covered in the tabulations (file "inactive" returns), companies in default but not in process of liquidation would presumably be tabulated: their figures for debt would enter the totals, but the face amount of their interest charges would not enter the interest-paid total. This point may explain partly the indicated low average rate on bonds in the trade division, though I think only in small part. (See below, page 299.)

[9] A long series of experiments, looking toward an independent determination of both the average rates — short-term and long-term — without use of quoted figures, led to disappointing results. I hope later to reexamine these experimental methods, which rested mainly on correlation operations; and, if they can be sufficiently improved, will report them in another place for the information of scholars who may be interested in the experiments as examples of statistical technique or for their economic implications. For the purpose of this book, however, the entire approach was abandoned; and the alternative treatment described in the text may be regarded as suggested by the earlier experiments and as a substitute for them.

size classes or between the income and deficit categories, can not be known. That the share is, for most classes or groups of corporations, more than half appears quite likely; that it is close to 100 per cent seems highly unlikely. In any case, the assumption amounts to taking the same rate for non-banking as for banking lenders. This may not be seriously wrong; for, as short-term loans are in question, it may well be doubted if *on the average* corporations would pay a significantly higher rate or could get a significantly lower rate on borrowings from non-banking lenders than on borrowings from banks.[10]

The assumption also ignores possible differences, even in bank rate, among industries; although good reason exists for believing such differences may be significant. Finally, this rate was assumed uniform for all size classes, and for both the income and deficit categories — again an assumption almost certainly at variance with the facts.

With the short-term rate thus taken, the interest paid on outstanding short-term debt for an entire division (or group) could be estimated. By deducting this from total interest paid, the residual element of interest on long-term debt could be found; and dividing this by the amount of such debt yielded estimated rate of long-term interest. Such estimates could be worked out separately for each industrial division or group, and for the incomc and deficit categories; but the rates so found had to be assumed uniform in all size classes of the given industry or category.

The entire method thus made some allowance — however imperfect — for differences in rate on outstanding long-term debt as among industries and as between categories, but none whatever for the short-term rate. No sure judgment can be formed, on *a priori* grounds, concerning the wisdom of this dis-

[10] Many serious qualifications need be made on this assertion when a particular corporation is considered, or even for some entire industries under certain circumstances.

tinction: we can not be sure whether differences in rate among industries and between the income and deficit categories are more likely to be significant for short-term or for long-term debt. Various arguments point in each direction, and none seems decisive. I lean toward an answer in favor of long-term debt, chiefly because of the bearing of defaults upon the question; but the case is far from clear, and I confess the entire method rests upon practical necessity rather than upon theoretical appropriateness.

METHOD OF ESTIMATE

The actual analysis, looking toward an estimate of the average rate of return on borrowed and owned capital, by size classes, was confined to two selected divisions, manufacturing and trade; and the illustrative computations in this chapter are for manufacturing only. The analysis was likewise confined — in its final stages — to two years, 1932 and 1936, in the six-year period under study; but certain operations had to be carried out for 1931 and 1935 also, because they are the respective preceding years. The foregoing section has outlined the assumptions and indicated the procedure of the analysis; and the present section, in explaining the detailed steps, will include further remarks on the validity of the assumptions.

Estimated rate on long-term debt. The first set of operations aims at estimating for an entire division or group (the manufacturing division, in the illustration), separately by income and deficit categories, the net capital assets at the beginning of the year (1932 in the illustration). The year-end figures for the entire division (both categories combined) are found as at the end of 1932 and of 1931 — rows *g* and *h* of Table LII. The net change over the year 1932, expressed as a ratio to the 1932 figure, is taken as one index of the adjustment to be applied to the year-end figure of 1932 in order to secure the figure for the beginning of that year. If it were taken as the sole index, the figure for the beginning of 1932 would be merely that for the end of 1931. The objections to this procedure rest upon possible differences in the make-up of the manufacturing division in 1932 and in 1931, mainly because of shifts in classification of specific corporations between the manufacturing and other

TABLE LII

ESTIMATE OF NET CAPITAL ASSETS AT THE BEGINNING OF 1932, FOR EACH CATEGORY OF THE MANUFACTURING DIVISION *

a. Net capital assets, end of 1932, income corps.	5,877,543
b. Adjustment	487,836
c. Estimated net capital assets, beginning of 1932	6,365,379
d. Net capital assets, end of 1932, deficit corps.	19,744,808
e. Adjustment	1,638,819
f. Estimated net capital assets, beginning of 1932	21,383,627
g. Net capital assets, end of 1932, both categories	25,622,351
h. Comparable figure for end of 1931	28,285,950
i. Difference: $h - g$	2,663,559
j. Relative difference: i/g (%)	10.39
k. Comparable figure for all divisions combined	6.22
l. Sum of *j* and *k*	16.61
m. Average of *j* and *k*: $l/2$	8.30

* Rows *a* and *d* are transcribed from the source; *g* is sum of *a* and *d*; *h* is calculated like *g*, but for 1931; *k* is calculated for 1932 like *j*, but applies to the entire list of corporations; *b* is $a \times m$, and *e* is $d \times m$; *c* is sum of *a* and *b*, and *f* is sum of *d* and *e*.

All money figures are in thousands of dollars.

divisions. Therefore a second index of adjustment is also considered: the corresponding ratio calculated in the same manner for all divisions combined.

This more general index avoids disturbances due to the changes in industrial classification and, except for dropping of old corporations or addition of new corporations in the 1932 tabulation of the complete corporation list, reflects the combined effects of the real causes of change in net capital assets:

depreciation and depletion during 1932, purchases and sales (involving non-corporate parties, when all divisions combined are being considered), installations and abandonments, and revaluations. The first index presumably reflects the same factors, as they acted particularly in the manufacturing division; but it is influenced also by the reclassification factor. Neither index satisfactorily measures what we seek — the actual change during 1932 in the book value of net capital assets for the corporations actually in the manufacturing division in 1932. The first index suffers from the reclassification factor, the second index is defective because the basic factors listed above may operate with different force in other divisions than in manufacturing. I see no basis for choosing between the two, or even for deciding which is the less accurate; and I therefore take the simple mean of the two indices (row *m* of Table LII) as the desired adjustment factor.[11] The lack of close consistency between the two indices suggests the existence of a considerable margin of error in the adjustment; but, as the level of the adjustment percentages is low, the relative effect of this margin of error on the estimated beginning-year figure is probably small. This is another way of saying that net capital assets is a highly stable figure from year to year — even in years of extensive revaluations — when entire groups of corporations are under consideration.

The adjustment percentage was then applied to the end-year figures for 1932, separately for the income and deficit categories, to yield the estimated beginning-year figures —

[11] The two indices clearly differ substantially for manufacturing in 1932: the second is about half the first. Such pairs of indices were calculated for manufacturing and for trade, annually 1931–36. (A special correction was needed in 1934, because the abandonment of consolidated returns caused an extraordinary set of reclassifications.) In most of these pairs, the discrepancy does not appear more serious than that shown in Table LII; and only one pair, that for manufacturing in 1936, showed the two indices with opposite signs.

rows *c* and *f* of Table LII. At this point another error may enter: that some of the basic factors, mentioned above as working changes in the value of capital assets, may operate with different force for income than for deficit corporations seems very likely. I see no clear basis for deciding which category will feel the effects with greater force, much less for appraising the magnitude of the error; but I suspect this error may be somewhat greater than the general error in the adjustment percentage, mentioned above.

The next set of operations aims at estimating the debt of the manufacturing division, separately for short-term and long-term debt and separately for the income and deficit categories, at the beginning of 1932. Preliminary computations apply to 1931 (upper section of Table LIII). For each category and for both combined, the ratio of debt (the illustration is worked out for short-term debt, and the work is exactly parallel for long-term debt) to net capital assets — both at the end of 1931 — is calculated. This ratio for the income category might be suggested as the appropriate multiplier, to be applied to the estimated net capital assets of that category for the beginning of 1932, for the purpose of estimating the short-term debt at the beginning of 1932. The objection to such procedure is that some of the income corporations in 1932 may have been deficit corporations in 1931, and *vice versa*. Hence the ratio for the deficit category of 1931 may have some appropriateness for making the beginning-year estimate of debt of the income category for 1932. More generally the 1931 ratio for the combined categories may have some appropriateness. We have no basis for ascertaining the shares of the income category in 1932 coming from the income and from the deficit categories in 1931.

The compromise actually used was to take, as the multiplier for estimating beginning-year debt from net capital assets in 1932 for the income category, the simple mean of the income and combined ratios at the end of 1931. This amounts roughly to weighting the 1931 income category twice as much as the 1931 deficit category, in making the estimate for the 1932 income category. As noted above (page 286), the entire question is one of sampling: we are using a list of corporations at

TABLE LIII

ESTIMATE OF AVERAGE SHORT-TERM DEBT IN 1932, FOR EACH CATEGORY OF THE MANUFACTURING DIVISION *

CALCULATION OF RATIOS FOR END OF 1931

Category	Net capital assets (a)	Notes and accounts payable (b)	Ratios (%) (c)
Income	8,759,363	2,013,802	22.99
Deficit	19,526,587	4,002,960	20.50
Both	28,285,950	6,016,762	21.27

ESTIMATE OF SHORT-TERM DEBT, BEGINNING OF 1932, AND 1932 AVERAGE

	Income corps.	Deficit corps.
a. Adjusted ratio (%)	22.13	20.88
b. Estimated net capital assets, beginning 1932	6,365,379	21,383,627
c. Estimated short-term debt, beginning 1932	1,408,658	4,464,901
d. Short-term debt, end of 1932	1,224,902	4,282,362
e. Estimated average, 1932	1,316,780	4,373,632

* In upper section, column *c* is *b/a*. Data are for end of 1931, and are transcribed from the source.

In lower section, Row *a* is average of first and third ratios of upper section for income corporations, and of second and third ratios for deficit corporations. Row *b* is taken from Table LII. Row *c* is *a* multiplied by *b*. Row *d* is transscribed from source. Row *e* is simple average of *c* and *d*.

All money figures are in thousands of dollars. "Short-term debt" is used as equivalent to "Notes and accounts payable."

the end of 1931 as a sample — so far as the ratio of debt to capital assets is concerned — of a somewhat different list in 1932. We know the 1932 list consists mainly of elements drawn from two portions (categories) of the 1931 list, but we do not know to what extent the 1932 list is made up from each portion in 1931. The rough scheme of weighting is adopted arbitrarily, and gives some recognition to the probability that income corporations in 1932 are somewhat more likely to have been income than deficit corporations in 1931.

In a similar manner, the deficit ratio and the combined ratio for the end of 1931 are averaged to obtain the ratio to be applied as a multiplier to net capital assets at the beginning of 1932 for the 1932 deficit category. Accordingly, estimated short-term debt figures for the beginning of 1932, for both categories separately, are obtained — row *c* of the lower section of Table LIII. The beginning-year figure is then averaged with the end-year figure, to yield an estimated average short-term debt for the year — row *e* of Table LIII.[12] An exactly similar set of calculations was worked out for long-term debt, to yield estimated long-term debt as an average for 1932, separately for income and deficit categories.

The next set of operations leads to the estimate of the average rate of interest paid on long-term debt in 1932, separately for income and deficit categories. With an estimate of the amount of long-term debt in 1932 worked out, we need only the interest paid on long-term debt in order to secure the desired rate through direct division of the second item by the first. *Statistics of Income* gives total interest paid, without regard to maturity of the debt.[13] In order to segregate the interest paid on long-term debt, we proceed by indirection: first calculate interest paid on short-term debt, and then deduct this from total interest.

Available already are the estimates of average notes and accounts payable for the year 1932, separately for income and deficit categories. An initial operation consists in estimating

[12] As already remarked, all attempt to allow for a non-linear *course* of debt during the year 1932 was abandoned.

[13] Actually, as already observed, the tabulated figure for interest paid may miss certain such payments; but we are forced to ignore this deficiency.

notes payable by applying a percentage to notes and accounts payable, it being assumed that accounts payable do not bear interest.[14] No entirely satisfactory evaluation of this percentage exists. *Statistics of Income* has not tabulated notes and accounts separately since 1927, and any survey of the current situation resting upon selected corporations — few of which separate the two items in their published accounts — would be unsatisfactory from a sampling point of view. After examination of the data, decision was reached to use the percentages as calculated from *Statistics of Income* tabulations of 1926 and 1927. The somewhat similar tabulations for 1924 and 1925 were not used because they did not separate income and deficit corporations. Thus the percentage chosen was the ratio of notes payable for 1926 plus notes payable for 1927 to the sum of notes and accounts payable for the two years (for the manufacturing division), computed separately for income and deficit categories. These ratios were 50 per cent for the income category, and 60 per cent for the deficit category. Manifestly, carrying these identical ratios over to a situation more than five years later (nine years for the 1936 computations) involves a very dubious assumption as to stability of the borrowing practices of industry. That the level of the ratios, and the disparity between the income and deficit ratios, should be the same in 1932 as in 1926–27 is certainly open to grave doubts, especially when we consider the intervening changes in banking policies and methods as well as in industrial purchasing methods. I have nevertheless decided to accept these ratios for the purpose in hand, and recognize that this may introduce one of the major errors in the estimate.

The remaining assumption in this set of operations concerns the interest rate on short-term debt. For this I have taken the average rate charged by member banks outside New York City

[14] The actual "interest cost" to the debtor, resulting from failure to enjoy discounts on certain accounts payable, is ignored.

on loans to customers.[15] No account is taken of the possibility — indeed probability — that the average rate may be different for the two categories of corporations, or of the fact that corporations may borrow at different rates from banking and non-banking lenders. The actual computations then follow readily, as outlined in Table LIV.

The resulting estimates of the rate on long-term debt — 6.82 per cent for income corporations in manufacturing, and 6.66 for deficit corporations — are surprising chiefly because the first exceeds the second, and even this may be explained on the assumption that defaults held down interest payments in the deficit category. The general level of the two rates does not appear seriously out of line with what might have been expected, though the truth is that we have no valid basis for forming any expectation. Similar pairs of rates were worked out for each year 1931–36, for trade as well as manufacturing, and appear in Table LV.[16] In general the rates for long-term debt in manufacturing are not surprising. Differences between the two categories are narrow in nearly all years; and the general level of the rates, with the steady decline in later years probably reflecting in part refunding at lower rates and other readjustments, does not seem improbable. The rather high income-category rate for 1931 is not readily explained, and may result from a joint impact of some of the errors discussed above. For trade, except in 1931, the rates seem lower than should be expected; and I see no ready explanation, except that the errors in the method may fall with greater force in this division

[15] Monthly figures are simple averages of the two outside-New York series — northern and eastern cities, southern and western cities — published in the *Annual Report of the Federal Reserve Board*, 1937, p. 101. The annual average figure was secured by weighting the monthly figures by the member-bank data for "all other" loans, outside New York.

[16] In order to carry out the calculations for 1931, certain special adaptations of data for the preceding year (1930) were necessary; because such data were in a different form. These special steps are not described herein.

than in manufacturing. Certainly, no important reason exists for believing that trade corporations ordinarily borrow on long term at definitely lower rates than manufacturing corporations. I conclude that all these estimates of long-term rates may be

TABLE LIV

ESTIMATE OF AVERAGE RATE OF INTEREST PAID ON LONG-TERM DEBT OUTSTANDING IN 1932, FOR EACH CATEGORY OF THE MANUFACTURING DIVISION *

	Income corps.	Deficit corps.
a. Estimated average short-term debt, 1932	1,316,780	4,373,632
b. Per cent taken as notes	50.	60.
c. Estimated interest-bearing portion of debt ...	658,390	2,624,179
d. Average assumed rate of interest (%)	5.34	5.34
e. Estimated short-term interest paid	35,158	140,131
f. Total interest paid	106,586	428,408
g. Residue, estimated as paid on long-term debt ..	71,428	288,277
h. Estimated average long-term debt, 1932	1,046,884	4,329,024
i. Estimated rate on long-term debt (%)	6.82	6.66

* Row *a* is from Table LIII; *b* is explained in text, page 296; *c* is *a* multiplied by *b*; *d* is explained in text, page 296; *e* is *c* multiplied by *d*; *f* is transcribed from the source; *g* is *f* minus *e*; *h* is from a table similar to Table LIII, but for long-term debt; *i* is *g* divided by *h*.

All money figures are in thousands of dollars.

substantially in error; and I urge that they are here presented, not as results significant in themselves, but as intermediate steps in an estimating process which includes a later allowance at least in part for such errors.

Estimate of debt by size classes. For each size class in the manufacturing division in 1932, separately for the income and deficit categories, steps parallel to those outlined above (pages 290–295) were followed in estimating the year's average of short-term and of long-term debt. The only major alteration in procedure was in the determination of the adjustment factor used in getting beginning-year capital assets from the corresponding end-year figure. This factor could not be worked out independently for each size class, because shifts in corporations from size class to size class are numerous in passing from one year to another. Hence, year-end figures for 1931 are not comparable with similar figures for 1932, for any one size class.

TABLE LV

ESTIMATED RATES ON LONG-TERM DEBT, FOR EACH CATEGORY, MANUFACTURING AND TRADE DIVISIONS *

	Manufacturing		Trade	
	Income	Deficit	Income	Deficit
1931	8.24	6.22	9.80	6.61
1932	6.82	6.66	3.14	4.15
1933	5.95	5.79	4.02	4.28
1934	4.79	5.09	3.91	3.42
1935	4.90	4.22	2.88	2.09
1936	4.37	4.04	3.21	2.54

* Stated in per cent.

Hence, the adjustment factor used for each size class was identical with that used for the entire manufacturing division. This of course may introduce significant errors, for the various elements tending to change the net capital assets may operate with different force in different size classes. With this reservation, the estimates of debt, on the basis of an average for the year, were worked out along lines traced for the entire division. The calculations for short-term debt for one size class in manufacturing in 1932 appear in Table LVI. The final step shown is the application of the same percentages (50 for income corporations, 60 for deficit) to notes and accounts in order to estimate notes. Here again an additional error may enter: however nearly correct those percentages may be for the entire division, they may be in error for a particular size class. Corporations in one size class may tend to have a larger share of short-term debt in the form of notes than those in another size class; but we have no basis for making an allowance on this account, and must allow the error to slip in.

These computations were followed through for the other size

classes. Similar operations — except the final step — were carried out for long-term debt. Corresponding computations were made for manufacturing in 1936, and for trade in 1932 and 1936. Thus, for each of the four test cases — manufacturing

TABLE LVI

ESTIMATE OF SHORT-TERM DEBT FOR THE 250-THOUSAND-DOLLAR CLASS OF THE MANUFACTURING DIVISION IN 1932 *

CALCULATION OF RATIOS FOR END OF 1931

Category	Net capital assets	Notes and accounts payable	Ratios (%)
Income	338,923	113,934	33.61
Deficit	696,869	338,146	48.52
Both	1,035,792	452,080	43.65

ESTIMATE OF SHORT-TERM DEBT

	Income corps.	Deficit corps.
a. Adjusted ratio (%)	38.63	46.08
b. Estimated net capital assets, beginning 1932	225,020	829,380
c. Estimated short-term debt, beginning 1932	86,925	382,178
d. Short-term debt, end of 1932	63,826	301,502
e. Estimated average, for 1932	75,376	341,840
f. Per cent assumed as Notes	50.	60.
g. Estimated Notes, average for 1932	37,688	205,104

* Notes describing operations are like those of Table LIII, except that estimated net capital assets is somewhat differently calculated in this case (see text, page 298).

All money figures are in thousands of dollars.

in 1932 and in 1936, and trade in the same years — final estimates of average-for-the-year debt, separately for short-term interest-bearing debt and long-term debt, were worked out for every size class. Such a set of figures — for the income category — appears in certain items of Column 1 of Table LVII.

Allocation of interest by size classes. We are now in a position to estimate the interest charges for each size class of the manufacturing division in 1932, separately for income and deficit categories. For this purpose, we have the estimated short-term and long-term debt figures just found, and the in-

TABLE LVII

Estimate of Interest Paid, by Size Classes, for Income Category of Manufacturing Division in 1932 *

Class †		Debt (1)	Preliminary estimate (2)	Final estimate (3)
0	a.	15,574	832	−4
	b.	4,409	301	...
	c.	19,983	1,133	1,129
50	a.	18,266	975	−5
	b.	7,966	543	...
	c.	26,232	1,518	1,513
100	a.	36,243	1,935	−11
	b.	19,685	1,343	...
	c.	55,928	3,278	3,267
250	a.	37,688	2,013	−12
	b.	26,186	1,786	...
	c.	63,874	3,799	3,787
500	a.	38,350	2,048	−13
	b.	29,795	2,032	...
	c.	68,145	4,080	4,067
1,000	a.	78,525	4,193	−33
	b.	88,335	6,024	...
	c.	166,860	10,217	10,184
5,000	a.	32,217	1,720	−21
	b.	68,810	4,693	...
	c.	101,027	6,413	6,392
10,000	a.	94,496	5,046	−52
	b.	164,060	11,189	...
	c.	258,556	16,235	16,183
50,000	a.	300,709	16,058	−193
	b.	648,078	44,199	...
	c.	948,787	60,257	60,064

* All money figures are in thousands of dollars.

† Lower limit of size class, in thousands of dollars.

For column 1, *a* is Notes payable, estimated as in row *g* of Table LVI; *b* is Bonds and mortgages, estimated by a similar process (down to row *e* of Table LVI); *c* is *a* plus *b*.

For column 2, *a* is 5.34 per cent of *a* of column 1; *b* is 6.82 per cent of *b* of column 1; *c* is *a* plus *b*.

For column 3, *a* is the adjustment — obtained by adding items *c* of column 2, to get 106,930, comparing this with "true" interest of 106,586 transcribed from source, and distributing error proportionately among classes; *c* is *c* of column 2 plus *a* of column 3.

terest rates developed in the previous section. These rates are applied uniformly to all size classes, despite the considerable probability that the actual rates vary from class to class — here another unavoidable error enters. Application of the rates to the debt figures yields a preliminary set of estimates for interest paid, as shown in Column 2 of Table LVII. The aggregate of these estimates should check with the figure for interest paid given for the entire division (income category alone) in *Statistics of Income*. The discrepancy, which turns out remarkably small, is distributed proportionately among the several size classes. We then have, in Column 3, the desired final estimates of interest paid by each size class, in the income category.

Similar calculations were worked out for the deficit category of manufacturing in 1932, for manufacturing in 1936, and for trade in both years. In all cases, the discrepancy to be distributed among the size classes proved small — running always under 1 per cent for manufacturing and between 1 and 4 per cent for trade. This does not necessarily imply that the allocations of interest among the size classes are correct or nearly so, although the failure of large discrepancies to appear is some indication that the various errors noted along the way in our long and intricate analysis have not cumulated heavily in one direction. It is still entirely possible, however, that our allocation of interest among size classes is seriously in error — that the interest apportioned to certain classes is much too high and offsets much-too-low allocations to other classes. I know of no satisfactory means of checking this possibility, and feel forced to leave the question open with a final warning that such errors may vitiate the tentative findings of the next section.

THE RESULTS AND THEIR IMPORT

With the final estimates of interest paid, by size classes, and the previous estimates of debt and also the figures developed earlier in the book for profits (after taxes) and equity, we can proceed to the final test of the importance of interest in the rate-of-return analysis. This test can be worked out for every division and group for each of the years 1931–36, but is presented here (Table LVIII) only for the manufacturing and trade divisions in 1932 and 1936. For each of these four cases, and separately for the income and deficit categories and for the two categories combined, the table gives by size classes three rates: (1) ratio of interest paid to total interest-bearing debt, (2) rate of return on equity (previously developed in Chapter IV or XV), and (3) combined rate of return on debt plus equity.

Comparison between (2) and (3), for the two categories combined, is of chief interest for our purpose. Broadly speaking, the combined rate of return on borrowed plus owned capital runs higher than the rate of return on equity. But the striking fact appears that, while the increase of the combined rate with size is somewhat less rapid than that of the return on equity, the relationship between rate and size emphatically persists. Even for the combined rate of return on debt plus equity, an increase of rate with increasing size is unmistakably present. This appears for both divisions in both years. Conceivably, if we had tested these divisions in other years, or other divisions or certain groups in these or other years, different findings *might* have appeared; but I regard such an outcome as highly improbable except in so few cases as to be regarded as nontypical. Conceivably also, the numerous possible errors noticed at various stages of our analysis *may* have caused the observed findings, but this also I regard as highly improbable. I remain of opinion that the evidence of Table LVIII is valid: the relationship between rate of return and size can not be accounted for by differences among size classes as to debt and interest burden.

TABLE LVIII

RATES ON INTEREST-BEARING DEBT, EQUITY, AND BOTH, FOR MANUFACTURING AND FOR TRADE, IN 1932 AND 1936 *

	Rate on debt		Rate on equity		Rate on both combined	
Class †	1932	1936	1932	1936	1932	1936
			Manufacturing			
0	**5.58**	**3.98**	**−30.07**	**−6.90**	**−19.16**	**−2.95**
	5.65	4.07	9.43	13.68	8.67	11.29
	5.57	*3.94*	*−37.79*	*−29.90*	*−23.77*	*−14.48*
50	**5.70**	**4.01**	**−14.95**	**3.07**	**−9.77**	**3.32**
	5.77	4.09	7.21	12.10	6.95	10.46
	5.68	*3.95*	*−20.46*	*−14.11*	*−13.45*	*−7.59*
100	**5.76**	**4.04**	**−10.84**	**5.90**	**−7.24**	**5.48**
	5.84	4.11	7.12	12.44	6.93	10.92
	5.74	*3.95*	*−15.85*	*−10.57*	*−10.78*	*−5.94*
250	**5.83**	**4.05**	**−8.41**	**7.32**	**−5.79**	**6.67**
	5.93	4.12	6.83	12.37	6.72	11.06
	5.81	*3.96*	*−13.44*	*−8.79*	*−9.58*	*−4.96*
500	**5.87**	**4.07**	**−6.61**	**8.18**	**−4.62**	**7.41**
	5.96	4.14	6.99	12.40	6.88	11.17
	5.85	*3.96*	*−11.32*	*−8.79*	*−8.30*	*−4.90*
1,000	**6.03**	**4.09**	**−5.48**	**8.80**	**−3.80**	**8.09**
	6.10	4.15	6.75	11.83	6.69	10.89
	6.01	*3.97*	*−9.48*	*−6.71*	*−6.96*	*−3.81*
5,000	**6.21**	**4.15**	**−3.97**	**9.26**	**−2.39**	**8.41**
	6.33	4.21	7.39	11.52	7.28	10.74
	6.18	*3.98*	*−8.61*	*−4.56*	*−5.99*	*−2.10*
10,000	**6.24**	**4.17**	**−4.00**	**8.63**	**−2.47**	**7.91**
	6.26	4.23	6.11	10.02	6.12	9.20
	6.23	*3.98*	*−7.87*	*−4.57*	*−5.51*	*−2.02*
50,000	**6.29**	**4.17**	**−.23**	**7.77**	**.80**	**7.18**
	6.33	4.24	5.33	8.46	5.46	7.91
	6.28	*3.97*	*−2.92*	*−1.60*	*−1.33*	*.87*

TABLE LVIII (*Continued*)

Class †	Rate on debt 1932	Rate on debt 1936	Rate on equity 1932	Rate on equity 1936	Rate on both combined 1932	Rate on both combined 1936
		Trade				
0	**5.30**	**3.90**	**−26.02**	**−3.71**	**−16.37**	**−1.09**
	5.11	3.97	7.06	10.54	6.66	8.85
	5.32	*3.86*	*−33.15*	*−23.30*	*−20.58*	*−11.51*
50	**5.15**	**3.79**	**−13.31**	**3.61**	**−8.48**	**3.66**
	4.84	3.93	5.19	9.71	5.13	8.36
	5.20	*3.65*	*−17.77*	*−10.22*	*−11.43*	*−4.81*
100	**5.09**	**3.70**	**−10.62**	**5.24**	**−6.68**	**4.90**
	4.81	3.82	5.27	9.96	5.18	8.95
	5.13	*3.57*	*−14.72*	*−9.15*	*−9.44*	*−4.55*
250	**5.04**	**3.77**	**−8.15**	**6.74**	**−5.17**	**6.02**
	4.80	3.90	6.21	9.96	5.98	8.70
	5.09	*3.52*	*−12.26*	*−7.26*	*−8.09*	*−3.28*
500	**4.99**	**3.79**	**−6.45**	**7.08**	**−3.98**	**6.24**
	4.78	3.90	6.49	10.11	6.20	8.78
	5.05	*3.55*	*−10.56*	*−8.68*	*−7.00*	*−3.76*
1,000	**4.88**	**3.78**	**−5.09**	**8.35**	**−3.06**	**7.13**
	4.59	3.88	6.02	10.37	5.79	8.81
	4.96	*3.47*	*−9.63*	*−7.60*	*−6.03*	*−2.82*
5,000	**4.81**	**3.81**	**−2.09**	**10.56**	**−.78**	**8.80**
	4.50	3.91	6.44	13.87	6.13	11.45
	4.93	*3.49*	*−7.44*	*−4.57*	*−4.90*	*−1.92*
10,000	**4.59**	**3.78**	**−1.25**	**9.27**	**−.19**	**7.79**
	4.28	3.80	8.02	11.14	7.06	9.16
	4.75	*3.53*	*−5.84*	*−8.14*	*−3.23*	*−4.98*
50,000	**4.80**	**3.92**	**2.59**	**11.29**	**3.22**	**9.72**
	4.68	3.92	8.06	11.29	7.50	9.72
	4.84	...	*−5.14*	...	*−1.10*	...

* Boldface type, both categories combined; ordinary type, income category; italics, deficit. Classes over 50 million dollars, combined in 1936.

† Lower limit, in thousands of dollars.

XXIV

VARIOUS INCOME-ACCOUNT ITEMS

THE TWO PRECEDING CHAPTERS have discussed possible effects upon the calculated rates of return of inventory fluctuations and interest payments. The present chapter gives similar attention to compensation of officers and to capital gains and losses, and comments briefly upon certain other items of the income account.

COMPENSATION OF OFFICERS

Various writers have suggested that a portion of profits, in the true economic sense, does not appear in the residual item called profits in the income account but is distributed in the form of executive salaries. The known facts concerning bonus and other incentive contracts — by which executives of certain large companies, and perhaps of smaller and less prominent companies, receive part of their compensation according to a formula related to net earnings — suggest this inference. Likewise, it is known that the officers are frequently the principal owners of small closely-held companies; and present tax laws, with corporation rates running sharply above individual rates in lower brackets, offer an incentive to such officer-owners to take their business profits in the form of salaries rather than dividends.[1] Both of these considerations sup-

[1] I ignore here the efforts, at best only moderately effective, of the Bureau of Internal Revenue to resist unreasonable use of this device for tax avoidance. Going behind the facts of corporate salary payments, to ascertain motives, is a difficult and often a futile task; and, with the best tax administration, large opportunity for discretion in the allocation of earnings between salaries and "profits" would remain. I ignore also the possibility that officer-owners have an incentive to take an advantage of minority owners.

port the view that some portion of executive salaries, in a group of corporations, represents profits in the strict economic sense.

That all of executive salaries of a particular corporation should, except in very rare cases, be reckoned as profits is very doubtful. In small companies, officers frequently perform some of the ordinary labor of the enterprise, labor which in truth contains no element of management, labor which might as well be done by hired hands probably having no administrative ability and certainly having none of the qualities which the economist ascribes to the entrepreneur. This is not to deny that the officer-owner of a small enterprise does devote some of his time and energy to managerial tasks and even to entrepreneurial activities. But the bulk of his work, particularly in the very small company, is typically identical with ordinary labor; and his business is often, more than anything else, a means of earning a wage. Even in large companies, though perhaps not always in the giant companies, the officers typically give part of their time and energy to managerial tasks for which trained employees could serve as well, and only a portion to those entrepreneurial tasks with which the economist sometimes associates the concept of profits. To call the compensation of an officer, so long as it is merely pay for performing managerial tasks, a distribution of profits implies an even greater confusion of the concept and theory of profits than the growth of corporate industry has unavoidably created. It must be admitted, however, that an officer who is a mere manager may get into such a strategic position in a company that his bargaining power secures for him compensation above the level appropriate for the duties he performs. But it is difficult to visualize his having a notable strategic advantage unless he does in fact bear or stand ready to bear responsibilities which are truly entrepreneurial. The fact is that we have as yet made but a beginning in the study of executive compensation, the methods of its determination, and its implications for economic theory and business practice.[2]

Our immediate purpose is to inquire whether executive compensation, if it is regarded as entirely or in substantial part a distribution of profits, can explain any of our findings with respect to rate of return, particularly the finding that rate of return increases with size of corporation. The suggested method of testing this question is obvious: executive compensation is one of the charges which has been deducted from gross income to arrive at the residual figure for profits, therefore executive compensation — or such fraction of it as we may determine — should be added to profits to yield a reconstructed figure more inclusive of profits in the economic sense. This test can not be carried out for the Treasury tabulations except for the entire divisions and groups, and for the size classes of all divisions combined. Data on executive compensation are tabulated in *Statistics of Income* only with these two breakdowns; and I have seen no way of estimating corresponding figures for the size classes of specific divisions and groups, along the lines used in estimating taxes (Chapter XXVI). Moreover, compensation of officers, as reported on tax returns, may not cover all of the officers — particularly in large companies — about whom the issues of the present chapter arise. For large companies, salaries of various important executives may be buried in entries in the tax return under "salaries and wages" in "cost of goods sold" or in "other deductions," and thus fail to be covered in the specific item tabulated. No basis exists for a quantitative appraisal of this concealed executive compensation, but it almost surely increases in magnitude with increase in corporate size.[3]

[2] See John C. Baker, *Executive Salaries and Bonus Plans*. New York: McGraw Hill, 1938.

[3] A further point is that such compensation is not tabulated for insurance companies filing Form 1120L, and most of these are large.

TABLE LIX

Compensation of Officers as Percentage of Equity, All Divisions Combined *

Class †	1931	1932	1933	1934	1935	1936
0	**24.20**	**21.98**	**23.73**	**29.51**	**32.75**	**38.02**
	21.90	19.82	24.40	27.87	31.25	33.63
	25.78	*22.54*	*23.43*	*30.78*	*34.05*	*43.98*
50	**12.28**	**9.91**	**8.18**	**11.69**	**12.53**	**15.59**
	12.70	10.92	13.16	14.65	15.93	17.48
	11.98	*9.61*	*6.18*	*9.17*	*9.23*	*11.41*
100	**7.06**	**6.21**	**6.21**	**6.82**	**7.64**	**9.45**
	6.89	7.28	8.24	8.80	9.62	11.20
	7.20	*5.88*	*4.99*	*5.04*	*5.32*	*6.10*
250	**4.95**	**3.97**	**3.99**	**4.20**	**4.63**	**5.56**
	5.58	4.76	5.42	5.36	5.86	6.53
	4.52	*3.69*	*3.09*	*3.09*	*3.11*	*3.36*
500	**3.24**	**2.67**	**2.62**	**2.74**	**3.10**	**3.88**
	3.71	3.22	3.51	3.48	3.92	4.33
	2.94	*2.47*	*2.03*	*2.02*	*2.06*	*2.15*
1,000	**1.74**	**1.46**	**1.43**	**1.40**	**1.53**	**1.85**
	2.01	1.59	1.78	1.66	1.87	2.07
	1.57	*1.41*	*1.22*	*1.14*	*1.11*	*1.19*
5,000	**1.03**	**.85**	**.84**	**.74**	**.80**	**.96**
	1.15	.88	.97	.83	.96	1.03
	.96	*.83*	*.74*	*.65*	*.60*	*.70*
10,000	**.72**	**.59**	**.56**	**.45**	**.48**	**.56**
	.77	.55	.55	.47	.52	.58
	.67	*.61*	*.56*	*.43*	*.42*	*.49*
50,000	**.23**	**.20**	**.18**	**.16**	**.17**	**.35**
	.25	.17	.16	.14	.14	.37
	.22	*.22*	*.20*	*.17*	*.20*	*.24*
100,000	. . .	. . .	. . .	. . .	. . .	**.15**
	. . .	. . .	. . .	. . .	. . .	.16
	. . .	. . .	. . .	. . .	. . .	*.13*
Entire list combined	**1.75**	**1.50**	**1.49**	**1.47**	**1.62**	**1.94**
	1.83	1.28	1.58	1.62	1.80	1.80
	1.70	*1.60*	*1.42*	*1.33*	*1.42*	*2.48*

* Boldface type, both categories combined; ordinary type, income category; italics, deficit.

† Lower limit, in thousands of dollars.

Taking the data on compensation of officers as they stand in the *Statistics of Income* classification of all industrial divisions combined by size classes, the ratio of such compensation to equity — the denominator of our rate of return — can be calculated. These ratios are shown in Table LIX, and are in a form for direct comparison with the corresponding rates of return. But first certain characteristics of the size distribution of these ratios, separately by income and deficit categories and for the two categories combined, are worthy of notice. For every year, for each category and both combined, and without a single exception along the size scale, these ratios decline with increasing size. Here is a most nearly perfect relationship between ratio and size. This systematic decline with increasing size occurs at a sharp pace; and, except for the income category of 1931, the ratio in the lowest size class is more than 100 times that in the highest class. Without doubt this reflects in part the point noted above: not all officers of large companies are actually covered in the tabulated item. It also reflects the fact that even a very small company generally has several "officers" because of legal requirements upon corporations, even though some or perhaps all of these officers are in effect merely working for wages most of the time.

For the very lowest size class, the ratio of the deficit category is distinctly above that of the income category in every year except 1933. With few exceptions (three of which are strikingly in the highest class), the reverse holds for all other size classes. The situation in this respect for the lowest size class may reflect chiefly the effect of net profits and losses on the average equity as calculated in this book (see below, Chapter XXVIII). If the level of compensation of officers is customarily determined by reference to some inclusive measure of the size of the enterprise, as an index of executive responsibility, such a figure as total assets might be a more appropriate base for the ratios than a residual figure like equity. Such a change in computing the ratio might largely remove the disparity between the categories for the lowest size class, without appreciably altering the corresponding situation shown in the table for other classes.

Time variations are not of heavy intensity, and may not be wholly a reflection of the business cycle. For the combined results, ignoring size classes, the low point is in 1934 for the deficit category and both combined, but in 1932 for the income category. Figures for the size classes, both categories combined, show the low point in 1932 for the lowest size class, 1933 for three of the next four classes, and 1934 for the four top classes. This clearly suggests either that the reduction of salaries, incident to the depression, continued longer in the typical large corporation than in the small, or that resumption of salary increases occurred sooner after the coming of improvement for the typical small corporation than for large. When it is remembered that small companies typically remained in the red longer than large, this differential in timing of the minimum in salaries is emphasized; although one may adopt the simple explanation that the early resumption of salaries kept the small companies from showing profits until well after the upturn of 1933. For nearly all classes the minimum occurred earlier for the income than for the deficit category; again, because of the mere magnitude of the salaries, a possible explanation is that numerous companies remained in the deficit category because of persistent heavy deductions for salary payments. The only year of striking advance in all the figures is 1936, and we may suspect that the undistributed-profits tax "forced" a distribution of corporate earnings to officers quite as effectively as to stockholders.

One qualification should be in view when examining time variations in these data, particularly if an attempt is made to draw inferences from these percentages concerning the amount of executive compensation. The denominator of these ratios is equity, and the reduction of equity because of net losses, or dividend distribution in excess of earnings, or downward revaluations in assets, may have been large in certain years (see below, page 383). Consequently, the denominator runs at lower levels in later than in earlier portions of the six-year period; and this differential is likely to be greater for the deficit than for the income category. This bears upon comparison of 1936 with 1931: actual salary payments by typical corporations may have run lower in 1936 than in 1931, although the computed ratios suggest the contrary.

COMPENSATION AND RATES OF RETURN

The sharp decline, with increasing size of corporation, of all the ratios of executive compensation to equity indicates at once that, if we make the flat assumption that such compensation should be counted in full as a distribution of profits, our previous findings as to the relation between rate of return (profits) and size will be almost completely destroyed. Thus, Table LX shows the result of a direct combination of executive compensation with profit (or loss) after taxes: the ratios of Table LIX have merely been added to those of Table II. The evidence of a decline of rate (without regard to sign) with size persists if the categories are considered separately. For the income category, the indicated decline is definitely more pronounced and regular than that indicated in Chart III; and this would be expected from the results shown in Table LIX. For the deficit category, rate of return still rises (becomes a smaller negative number) as size increases in most years and most parts of the size scale; but striking irregularities appear, especially in the lowest size class for 1935 and 1936, in the second size class for 1933, and in the shape of movement for 1934. When we turn to the rates for both categories combined, only 1932 is found to have the type of movement noted in Chapter II; and even here the rise of rate with size is greatly reduced from that of Chart I. In all the other years the general course of the rate is

TABLE LX

Composite Rate of Return, Counting Full Compensation of Officers as Profits, All Divisions Combined *

Class †	1931	1932	1933	1934	1935	1936
0	**4.89**	**−6.11**	**4.79**	**15.47**	**21.98**	**31.13**
	33.88	28.70	33.21	38.56	42.73	46.53
	−15.18	*−14.99*	*−8.15*	*−2.48*	*4.07*	*10.20*
50	**3.70**	**−3.06**	**3.81**	**8.86**	**11.29**	**17.21**
	20.74	17.29	20.26	23.45	25.51	28.29
	−8.61	*−9.12*	*−2.68*	*−3.58*	*−2.46*	*−1.45*
100	**1.32**	**−3.15**	**1.96**	**5.60**	**8.34**	**13.24**
	12.74	13.40	15.13	17.37	18.98	22.31
	−8.57	*−8.43*	*−5.97*	*−4.99*	*−4.18*	*−4.07*
250	**.47**	**−3.06**	**1.00**	**3.98**	**6.44**	**10.08**
	12.49	10.86	12.69	13.77	15.18	16.85
	−7.81	*−8.00*	*−6.30*	*−5.28*	*−4.38*	*−5.13*
500	**−.50**	**−3.41**	**.55**	**2.98**	**5.17**	**8.64**
	10.35	9.21	10.74	11.71	13.21	14.38
	−7.35	*−8.02*	*−6.10*	*−5.51*	*−4.93*	*−6.61*
1,000	**−1.17**	**−3.13**	**−.43**	**2.37**	**4.40**	**7.09**
	8.53	7.19	8.60	9.20	10.75	11.50
	−6.82	*−6.83*	*−6.00*	*−4.22*	*−3.54*	*−5.83*
5,000	**−.71**	**−3.03**	**−.82**	**1.95**	**3.70**	**6.44**
	8.22	6.79	7.53	8.21	9.07	9.81
	−6.28	*−7.42*	*−6.65*	*−4.35*	*−2.87*	*−5.16*
10,000	**.26**	**−2.00**	**−.17**	**2.95**	**4.77**	**6.22**
	7.75	6.46	7.32	7.42	9.02	8.98
	−5.35	*−5.93*	*−6.05*	*−2.03*	*−1.17*	*−5.83*
50,000	**2.36**	**.50**	**1.06**	**3.19**	**4.50**	**6.34**
	7.28	5.51	4.81	5.90	7.05	8.55
	−1.28	*−2.15*	*−1.75*	*.25*	*1.74*	*−4.31*
100,000	...	...	...	...	...	**4.77**
	...	...	...	...	...	6.12
	...	...	...	...	...	*−1.21*
Entire list combined	**1.15**	**−1.26**	**.68**	**3.19**	**5.04**	**6.77**
	8.86	6.84	7.35	8.37	9.74	9.61
	−4.24	*−4.97*	*−4.06*	*−1.80*	*−.48*	*−3.51*

* Boldface type, both categories combined; ordinary type, income category; italics, deficit.

† Lower limit, in thousands of dollars.

downward with increasing size, with some evidence of upturn at or near the top of the size scale. The entire display emphatically contradicts the finding of Chapter II.

Data of this sort are not available for the size classes of separate divisions and groups; but little doubt can exist that corresponding revisions of the rates would be found, with only moderate irregularities and non-uniformities among the divisions and groups. In most, if not all cases, we should find the relation between rate of return and size as observed in Chapters IV to XVIII greatly altered and perhaps inverted. Regarding *all* executive compensation as profits therefore takes away the force of our main inference from the analysis reported in this book.

I hold, of course, that not all of executive compensation should be regarded as profits. This seems a sound position to take even in considering large companies, but especially so with reference to small companies. In large companies, as already remarked, most executives do some work of the routine managerial sort, compensation for which is a fair cost against the gross income of the company and should not be considered as a distribution of profit. In small companies, the typical officer does a much larger share of work of this sort; and in very small companies his work is likely to be almost entirely in the form of ordinary labor. That more than a very slight fraction of the salary of such an officer should be considered as anything but one of the wage costs of the business seems to me a view bordering upon absurdity. The average total compensation of officers per company, in the lowest size class, was less than $3000 in 1935; and this salary total covers generally more than one officer, as the number of officers reported on the tax return is likely to run at least as high as three or four. But suppose that each company had only two officers, and that half of $3000 was the salary of each. Can we suppose that any considerable fraction of this $1500 is anything but a wage for doing the ordinary tasks of the business? To imagine that it is made up of profits in any considerable degree is to visualize the officer in his capacity as workman exploiting himself in his capacity as owner.[4]

An experimental computation, which treats half of executive compensation as concealed profits, may be informing; and a similar record of results on this basis appears in Table LXI. Here, until 1935–36, the advance of rate with increasing size persists, for both categories combined. The income category again shows a steady decrease of rate with size in all years, and the deficit category shows a steady advance of rate (decline of negative rate) with size in all years. With some reservations, then, this set of results bears out qualitatively the central finding of previous chapters; though quantitatively the change of rate with size is much smaller, for the combined categories, here than in Table II. This experimental computation is shown, not because I regard half of executive compensation as truly a concealed profit, but to demonstrate that treating even so much as half as profit leaves the main finding of previous chapters essentially sustained. In fact, one half strikes me as too large a fraction to regard as profits, far too large for small companies, and probably somewhat large for large companies. I rest my case on the conviction that most of the salaries of officers of small companies must be merely wages, and that a

[4] Nevertheless, on grounds of economic theory, the case may be stronger than I put it above. Suppose the company with two 1500-dollar officers is operating at a "loss." The economist may hold that the loss results from an excess payment of wages to these two men, that the excess ought to be counted as an offset against the loss in any study of business competition. My position is that the company probably could not hire outsiders to perform the ordinary labor done by the officers at wages averaging much below $1500. The fact seems to me to be as follows: the $1500 is roughly a competitive wage, the "loss" shown in the company account is a largely truthful showing of the company's inability to compete successfully. Again I remark that *some* part of the $1500 may not be wage; but insist that most of it is.

TABLE LXI

Composite Rate of Return, Counting Half of Compensation of Officers as Profits, All Divisions Combined *

Class †	1931	1932	1933	1934	1935	1936
0	**−7.21**	**−17.10**	**−7.08**	**.71**	**5.60**	**12.12**
	22.93	18.79	21.01	24.63	27.11	29.71
	−28.07	*−26.26*	*−19.87*	*−17.87*	*−12.96*	*−11.79*
50	**−2.44**	**−8.01**	**−.28**	**3.02**	**5.02**	**9.41**
	14.39	11.83	13.68	16.12	17.55	19.55
	−14.60	*−13.92*	*−5.77*	*−8.17*	*−7.15*	*−7.16*
100	**−2.21**	**−6.26**	**−1.15**	**2.19**	**4.52**	**8.52**
	9.30	9.76	11.01	12.97	14.17	16.71
	−12.17	*−11.37*	*−8.47*	*−7.51*	*−6.84*	*−7.12*
250	**−2.00**	**−5.05**	**−.99**	**1.88**	**4.12**	**7.30**
	9.70	8.48	9.98	11.09	12.25	13.59
	−10.07	*−9.84*	*−7.84*	*−6.82*	*−5.93*	*−6.81*
500	**−2.12**	**−4.74**	**−.76**	**1.61**	**3.62**	**6.70**
	8.49	7.60	8.99	9.97	11.25	12.22
	−8.82	*−9.26*	*−7.12*	*−6.52*	*−5.96*	*−7.68*
1,000	**−2.04**	**−3.86**	**−1.14**	**1.67**	**3.64**	**6.17**
	7.53	6.39	7.71	8.37	9.81	10.46
	−7.60	*−7.53*	*−6.61*	*−4.79*	*−4.09*	*−6.42*
5,000	**−1.22**	**−3.46**	**−1.24**	**1.58**	**3.30**	**5.96**
	7.64	6.35	7.04	7.80	8.59	9.29
	−6.76	*−7.84*	*−7.02*	*−4.67*	*−3.17*	*−5.51*
10,000	**−.10**	**−2.29**	**−.45**	**2.73**	**4.53**	**5.94**
	7.37	6.18	7.05	7.19	8.76	8.69
	−5.69	*−6.23*	*−6.33*	*−2.25*	*−1.38*	*−6.08*
50,000	**2.25**	**.40**	**.97**	**3.11**	**4.42**	**6.16**
	7.16	5.43	4.73	5.83	6.98	8.37
	−1.39	*−2.26*	*−1.85*	*.16*	*1.64*	*−4.43*
100,000	...	...	...	...	...	**4.69**
	...	...	...	...	...	6.04
	...	...	...	...	...	*−1.28*
Entire list combined	**.28**	**−2.01**	**−.07**	**2.45**	**4.23**	**5.80**
	7.94	6.20	6.56	7.56	8.84	8.71
	−5.09	*−5.77*	*−4.77*	*−2.46*	*−1.19*	*−4.75*

* Boldface type, both categories combined; ordinary type, income category; italics, deficit.

† Lower limit, in thousands of dollars.

TABLE LXIII

Rates of Return, Adjusted for Capital Net Gain or Loss, All Divisions Combined *

Class †	1931	1932	1933	1934	1935	1936
0	**−16.56**	**−25.04**	**−15.67**	**−13.04**	**−10.64**	**−7.07**
	11.34	8.20	8.22	10.10	10.44	12.00
	−35.74	*−33.52*	*−26.54*	*−31.04*	*−28.84*	*−32.97*
50	**−7.82**	**−11.31**	**−3.58**	**−2.62**	**−1.56**	**1.34**
	7.67	6.09	6.80	8.59	8.61	10.22
	−19.01	*−16.49*	*−7.64*	*−12.18*	*−11.47*	*−12.66*
100	**−4.89**	**−8.19**	**−4.33**	**−1.20**	**.35**	**3.31**
	5.56	5.90	6.59	8.28	8.46	10.34
	−13.94	*−12.70*	*−9.30*	*−9.74*	*−9.21*	*−10.10*
250	**−3.49**	**−5.86**	**−2.06**	**−.09**	**1.38**	**3.93**
	6.80	6.05	7.11	8.15	8.46	9.49
	−10.59	*−10.09*	*−7.77*	*−7.87*	*−7.39*	*−8.53*
500	**−2.78**	**−4.68**	**−1.14**	**.31**	**1.68**	**4.35**
	6.54	6.03	7.13	8.00	8.58	9.32
	−8.67	*−8.60*	*−6.52*	*−7.16*	*−6.98*	*−8.34*
1,000	**−1.58**	**−3.17**	**−.39**	**1.11**	**2.60**	**4.71**
	6.52	5.72	6.81	7.37	8.34	8.69
	−6.29	*−6.36*	*−4.84*	*−4.93*	*−4.58*	*−6.92*
5,000	**−.15**	**−1.87**	**.48**	**1.40**	**2.64**	**5.04**
	7.25	6.05	6.77	7.14	7.57	8.22
	−4.76	*−5.41*	*−3.91*	*−4.38*	*−3.39*	*−5.90*
10,000	**.69**	**−1.03**	**.97**	**2.48**	**4.16**	**5.31**
	7.14	6.31	7.19	6.89	8.20	7.99
	−4.13	*−4.44*	*−3.89*	*−2.43*	*−1.48*	*−6.41*
50,000	**2.58**	**.75**	**1.22**	**2.95**	**4.18**	**5.53**
	7.04	5.48	4.75	5.72	6.76	7.68
	−.73	*−1.76*	*−1.44*	*−.03*	*1.40*	*−4.78*
100,000	...	...	...	...	...	**4.48**
	...	...	...	...	...	5.80
	...	...	...	...	...	*−1.39*
Entire list combined	**.26**	**−1.74**	**.14**	**1.74**	**3.22**	**4.51**
	7.03	5.70	5.87	6.64	7.58	7.40
	−4.49	*−5.15*	*−3.94*	*−2.99*	*−1.90*	*−5.97*

* Boldface type, both categories combined; ordinary type, income category; italics, deficit.

† Lower limit, in thousands of dollars.

bined. In general, the effect is to reduce very moderately the amount of change of rate of return with size, as found in Chapter II. But the reduction is so small that the basic finding — that rate of return increases with size in all years — is not altered. Although capital gains (or losses) presumably have somewhat greater importance in some lines of industry than in others, little doubt can exist that the elimination of capital gain (or loss) from profits for separate divisions and groups — if size-class data were available for making such elimination — would yield consistent findings. Probably in every case we should find the amount of change in rate with size somewhat reduced, but the fact of an increase of rate with size undisturbed. The conclusion seems entirely safe that the main findings of earlier chapters would be altered in no essential way if capital gains and losses were excluded from the income account.

DEPRECIATION AND DEPLETION

Among the other items of the income account which are sometimes regarded as concealing profit (or loss) are rent paid, charges for bad debts (if made on a reserve basis), charges for depreciation and for depletion. That rent may contain an element of profit, particularly if owners of property rented to a corporation exercise control over the corporation, is entirely possible; but I see no means of making estimates of this factor by size classes or indeed for entire divisions or groups, and regard it as unlikely to have significant magnitude. That a reserve for bad debts in a particular year may run too high or too low because of faulty judgment can not be doubted, and this fact may distort the reported profit slightly. The influence on profits is certainly slight in most types of industry, and probably does not vary greatly from size class to size class. In any case, no means exist for estimating the magnitude of this factor, and I ignore it.

The charge for depreciation is, in most lines of industry, a more significant element in the profit reckoning; and possibility exists that variations in this element may have a substantial bearing upon our results. If we could know that small companies generally depreciate property at faster rates than large, we should have to temper somewhat our findings as to the amount of change in rate of return with size, although it seems scarcely possible that the fact of an increase of rate of return with size could be upset or seriously threatened. I doubt, however, that the suggested differential in speed of depreciation between small and large companies exists; and no evidence appears readily available for testing the question.

The possibility that depreciation may have an effect upon the cyclical movement of rate of return is perhaps more serious. If companies followed in any considerable degree the practice of adapting depreciation charges to the indicated current level of earnings, instead of using a rigid formula, this effect would be unmistakably present: variations in depreciation charges would tend to reduce the intensity of cyclical fluctuation in rate of return, and the record of rate of return would understate the cyclical variation in true profits. That some companies do follow such practices for corporate accounting purposes is entirely possible, and some evidence exists that the practice is not uncommon. But the case is different in accounting for tax purposes: the tax laws and regulations definitely discourage such a practice. It is contrary to the interest of the government to permit the charging of higher depreciation in prosperity, and it is probably contrary to the interest of companies — even with no loss-carry-over privilege — to reduce charges (as reported in tax returns) in depression. The figures for profits which we use, therefore, are probably not seriously damaged by this factor. One important reservation must be made: the numerous and large downward revaluations of physical assets during and immediately following the depression were undoubtedly designed in part to reduce subsequent depreciation charges and hence raise indicated profits in corporate accounts. Whether these effects were extensively reflected in accounts for tax purposes, in view of the Treasury restrictions upon depreciation reckoning, is uncertain; but we can assume that such effects are by no means fully present in the tabulations used in this book.

The case with respect to depletion is more complicated. Not only do tax provisions permit reckoning of depletion, at least in some lines of industry, in a manner which renders the depletion charge somewhat responsive to the cycle; but the importance of the charge varies greatly from industry to industry, and is indeed zero in many lines. If the industries for which depletion is important tend to concentrate in certain size classes, possibility exists that the amount of the charge may influence the indicated correlation between rate of return and size. I have seen no way to examine this question quantitatively without much more detailed and pertinent data than any which now exist, and must leave the matter open with the remark that it is probably of little importance — from the point of view of our problem — except in a limited list of industries such as mining, lumber, and petroleum.

XXV

RATE VARIATIONS WITHIN EACH SIZE CLASS

THE ENTIRE ANALYSIS thus far has been concerned with *average* rates of return: for each size class the rate of return has been calculated from aggregate figures for all corporations in that class. The single break-down thus far examined is that between the income category and the deficit category of each size class. Operations of this sort have been carried out for each industrial division and all combined, and for each manufacturing group. But each such operation yields only an *average* rate of return for the class, either as a whole or separately by categories, under study. This average is a weighted average: it is as though we knew the rate of return for each corporation in the class, weighted that rate by the equity of that corporation, added all these weighted rates, and then divided by the total equity of the class. The discussion of the results as presented has contained frequent references to the possibility — indeed, the certainty — that the individual rates for some specific corporations in a particular class differ widely from the average rate of the class as a whole. The very fact that the reported rate for the income category of a particular class is positive, whereas that for the deficit category is negative, emphasizes the existence of different rates among the specific corporations of the class when the class is considered as a whole (both categories combined). Thus, the rate for the class as a whole is a weighted average of two rates — the positive rate for the income category and the (often large) negative rate for the deficit category. The observed greater spread between the rates for the two categories in low size classes than in high classes — as in Chart IV — has been noted as evidence that variation in rate among the specific corporations of a class may tend to be greater for low classes than for high.

Nevertheless, no detailed evidence has thus far been presented as to the range of variation in rate among the specific corporations in a particular size class. Such evidence would have an important bearing upon the interpretation of our results, heretofore presented in the form of mere averages. For example, may it not be possible that, despite the large negative rate — as an average — generally found even in years of moderate prosperity for the lowest size class, some corporations in that class enjoyed handsome positive rates? And may it not be possible that, despite a substantial positive rate — on the average — generally found even in years of mild if not severe depression for the highest size class, some corporations in that class suffered losses at a high rate? Completely satisfactory answers to these questions might perhaps require analysis of specific figures for each separate corporation, or at least a tabulation of the corporations in a particular size class in subclasses according to the level of their rates of return (both positive and negative).

NEW DATA FOR 1936

Until 1936, no such data were available, but *Statistics of Income for 1936, Part 2* (pages 167–183) presents tabulations which go very far toward meeting this requirement. We are therefore in a position for the first time to give partial but broadly definitive answers to the foregoing questions and similar questions concerning the variability of rate of return among corporations in any size class. No attempt is made here to exploit in full this rich store of new information, chiefly because the forms of statistical distribution among the tabulated items are so exceptional that an elaborate and intricate statistical analysis will be needed to bring out adequately even the main implications of the data. But enough will be done here with these new data to show conclusively that variability among the rates of return of the specific corporations making up each size class is very great, and somewhat less surely whether such variability runs definitely higher for small corporations than for large. In other words, it will be shown that, whatever be the average rate of return for an entire size class, many corporations within that class have specific rates differing very widely, both positively and negatively, from that average. And it will be shown, somewhat less surely, that this range of variation among the specific rates runs relatively greater for low size classes than for high. Thus, the average class rates heretofore under examination, though having undoubted significance in examining differences among classes, can not be accepted as highly typical of the rates realized by specific corporations. This has large bearing upon the questions of "mortality" of corporations, growth of small corporations into large, cyclical stability, and related questions noted in Chapter I.

The new data include, separately for each size class (measured, as heretofore, in terms of total assets) and for each division and group of industry, a classification of corporations according to the amount of net income or loss.[1] This body of data is illustrated for two size classes of the manufacturing division in Table LXIV, and we now proceed to an analysis directed to securing tentative answers to the questions posed above.[2] If we here reproduced the data as published for every

[1] This is the net income (or loss) as defined for reckoning excess-profits tax. It therefore differs from the compiled net profits, heretofore used in our analysis, only by the exclusion of the portion of interest on Government securities which is not subject to excess-profits tax. Unfortunately, it is *not* the figure after deduction of Federal taxes — normal income, etc. — and I see no satisfactory means of estimating this deduction. In this sense, therefore, the figure differs significantly from the numerator of our rate of return.

[2] I omit from examination in this book two other, somewhat related, new bodies of data appearing for the first time in *Statistics of Income for 1936, Part 2*. These are a classification of each size class (in terms of total

TABLE LXIV

NUMBER OF CORPORATIONS, IN TWO SELECTED ASSETS-SIZE CLASSES OF THE MANUFACTURING DIVISION IN 1936, HAVING NET INCOME OR LOSS IN STATED AMOUNTS *

Amount of net income or loss †	Assets between 50 and 100 thousand dollars		Assets between 1 and 5 million dollars	
	Income corporations	Deficit corporations	Income corporations	Deficit corporations
0	1,708	1,802	18	41
1	1,062	741	21	39
2	809	496	16	18
3	572	349	17	18
4	504	294	12	25
5	1,391	735	65	78
10	613	296	82	56
15	301	138	67	49
20	156	71	85	36
25	238	100	328	172
50	39	32	549	150
100	10	9	1,120	124
250	...	...	670	38
500	...	...	246	10
1,000	...	...	59	6
Total	7,403	5,063	3,355	860
Total, class	...	12,466	...	4,215

* Data from *Statistics of Income for 1936, Part 2*, p. 168.

† Lower limit (without regard to sign) of class interval, in thousands of dollars. Upper limit of highest class is $5,000,000; no corporations in these lists with net income or loss exceeding that limit.

assets-size class in the manufacturing division, the result would take the form designated by statisticians as a correlation table — indicating correlation between size of assets and amount of net income or loss. This might at once suggest an analysis by the special techniques applied by statisticians to correla-

assets) according to amount of "total compiled receipts" (pages 139–149 of the source), and a classification of each size class — size here measured in total compiled receipts — according to amount of net income or loss (pages 150–166).

tion problems, and the results of such analysis — properly conducted and properly interpreted — would without doubt be of high significance. But these results, except in limited aspects, would not bear upon the questions we raise. Moreover, the distribution of cases (corporations) in these correlation tables has such important peculiarities — partly because of inherent peculiarities in the variation among the cases, and partly because of wide differences in width of the class intervals both for assets and for net income or loss — that application of correlation methods is difficult. Such analysis, particularly as it is not essential for our immediate purpose, is therefore postponed and forms no part of this book.

VARIABILITY WITHIN ASSETS-CLASSES

It is at once obvious from Table LXIV that great variation exists, among corporations in either assets-class, with respect to the *amount* of net income or loss. Considering only the smaller of the two assets-size classes, we find ten corporations with more than $100,000 in net income, nine with more than $100,000 in net loss; and although the great majority of corporations have very small net incomes or losses, an important number have incomes or losses ranging between $5,000 and $100,000. The fact that any corporations with assets *not* over $100,000 can have a net income, or even a net loss, *exceeding* $100,000 is indeed surprising. But the general fact that wide variation exists in the amount of net income or loss, among these 12,466 corporations, should not surprise us: common knowledge should lead us to expect high variability, even among the corporations of a single assets-size class. That we should have expected so great variability, ignoring cases over $100,000 (of income or loss), is less clear. It is a further surprising fact that about two fifths of the manufacturing corporations in this assets-size class — not the lowest, but next to the lowest, size class studied in this book — had net losses in so favorable a year as 1936. On the other hand, only about one fifth of the corporations in the larger assets-size class shown — not the top class, but well toward the top, among those we have been studying — had losses in 1936. These facts together tend to confirm a point already noted: the great proving ground of corporate success is in the small-company area, there the test of profitability applies severely, and there the danger of a rapid march toward insolvency is great.

Data such as those in the two pairs of columns of Table LXIV do not lend themselves well to interpretation of their variability in precise terms, chiefly because of the varying width of the class interval (for net income and loss). Each pair of columns is a frequency series, giving number of corporations in each class interval, the intervals ranging widely from negative (loss) figures to positive (income) figures. A graphic presentation of these data, such as ordinarily used in studying frequency series, is difficult and not very helpful. It is difficult because the frequency runs very large in the low class intervals, and yet there is some frequency far out on the positive and negative ends of the size (of net income or loss) scale. The tabular presentation can, however, be improved by a simple device which, though only approximate, eliminates the visual effects of the varying width of the class interval. This device consists in calculating, for each class interval, the average number of corporations per interval of fixed width. Thus, if there are 238 corporations in the $25,000 to $50,000 class interval, the average number of corporations in that class per interval $5,000 wide is 238/5 or 47.6. This amounts to breaking the given interval, which is $25,000 wide, into five sub-intervals, each $5,000 wide, and allocating one fifth of the 238 corporations to each sub-interval.[3] After the five lowest class intervals, each only $1,000 wide, were combined into a single class $5,000 wide, the adjust-

[3] This undoubtedly involves some error, for the 238 corporations are almost certainly not distributed equally among the sub-intervals 25–30,

ment described above was applied to the data of Table LXIV to yield Table LXV.

An approach to statistical regularity now appears, especially for the smaller of the two assets-classes. A clear mode (maximum frequency) appears for the 0 to $5,000 class of net income, and from that point the frequencies drop off with fair regularity and very rapidly in both positive and negative directions. The larger of the two assets-classes shows less regularity. There the mode stands in the 0 to $5,000 class of net loss; but, although frequencies on the negative side drop off with fair regularity, frequencies on the positive side vary irregularly in

TABLE LXV

AVERAGE NUMBER OF CORPORATIONS PER $5,000 RANGE OF NET INCOME OR LOSS IN THE VARIOUS NET INCOME AND LOSS CLASSES OF THE MANUFACTURING SERIES SHOWN IN TABLE LXIV *

Amount of net income or loss †	Assets between 50 and 100 thousand dollars		Assets between 1 and 5 million dollars	
	Income corporations	Deficit corporations	Income corporations	Deficit corporations
0	4,655	3,682	84	141
5	1,391	735	65	78
10	613	296	82	56
15	301	138	67	49
20	156	71	85	36
25	47.6	20	65.6	34.4
50	3.9	3.2	54.9	15.0
100	.33	.30	37.33	4.13
250	...	...	13.40	.76
500	...	...	2.46	.10
1,000	...	...	.07	.01

* Data of lowest five classes therein combined into a single class $5,000 wide. Number of corporations in each net income or loss class (above $25,000) of Table LXIV then divided by width of that class in units of $5,000.

† Lower limit of class interval, in thousands of dollars.

30–35, 35–40, 40–45, and 45–50 (thousand dollars). For present purposes, the error can be ignored.

the five lowest class intervals and do not begin a systematic decline until $25,000 of net income is reached.

The presentation of Table LXV helps to an understanding of the form of variation among the frequencies according to amount of net income and loss. This variation, while not nearly of the simple form called normal in statistical theory, nevertheless possesses enough regularity and a sufficiently clear indication of concentration at a mode to warrant study by some of the ordinary statistical techniques. Among other inferences which may be drawn from this evidence is the conclusion that an average for such a series — particularly for that belonging to the lower assets-class, but sufficiently for the other — is tolerably typical. In other words, these series are not of the extremely irregular or non-normal type for which an average stands widely isolated from the point where high, if not maximum, frequency is concentrated. The implications of this finding, for the work of the foregoing chapters, are notable: we may now be confident that, in general and probably with the few exceptions limited to very high assets-classes in small groups or divisions, the average rates of return found for various size classes are tolerably good typical numbers — measuring what statisticians call central tendencies.

VARIABILITY IN TERMS OF RATE

The data of Table LXIV are classified by *amount* of net income or loss. We are interested, instead, in the *rate* of return. As already indicated, the amount of net income or loss is not identical with the numerator of our rate-of-return ratio — it excludes the small amount of income from interest on Government securities not subject to excess-profits tax and it does not exclude Federal taxes. Ignoring these defects, which can not be remedied by satisfactory estimates based upon the data as published, we shall compute a "rate of return" in which the amount of net income or loss is taken as numerator. This rate will therefore not be directly comparable with the rates heretofore studied, but it will be satisfactory for the present study of variability.

For the denominator of the rate we must make an assumption: that the average per corporation of the total equity pertinent to the assets-size class under study — the average-for-the-year equity of the assets-class, as used in Chapter IV, divided by the number of corporations in that class — is the same as the average total equity per corporation of the corporations in *each* net income (or loss) class in that assets-class. The assumption and the calculation are applied separately to income and deficit categories. This assumption may involve a considerable error, particularly in the high assets-classes; but it seems improbable that the equity per corporation varies widely among the corporations of any of the narrower assets-classes — for example, 50 to 100 thousand dollars — especially if the income and deficit categories are considered separately. As we pass to wider assets-classes — for example 50 to 100 million dollars — the assumption is manifestly less safe, particularly when we deal with a net income (or loss) class having a small frequency.

Neglecting the errors involved in the assumption, which may damage the numerical precision but do not destroy the qualitative implications of our results, we calculate the rate of return associated with each boundary between two net income (or loss) classes. Thus, the rate for the boundary $5,000 — between the $4,000 to $5,000 and the $5,000 to $10,000 classes — is $5,000 divided by the average equity per corporation.[4] By this process, the stubs of Table LXIV are replaced by those of Tables LXVI and LXVII; and the new stubs differ

[4] For the cases in manufacturing under examination, we have

Assets-class	Category	Total equity	Number of corporations	Average equity
50–100	Income	335,262	7,403	45.2
	Deficit	176,007	5,063	34.8
1,000–5,000	Income	5,236,986	3,355	1,561
	Deficit	1,022,183	860	1,189

(All money figures in thousands of dollars.)

not only between the two assets-classes but also between the two categories in each assets-class.

The result is a restatement of the data of Table LXIV, on the basis of *rate* of net income or loss. In the $50,000 to $100,000

TABLE LXVI

NUMBER OF CORPORATIONS, IN THE $50,000 TO $100,000 ASSETS-CLASS OF THE MANUFACTURING DIVISION IN 1936, HAVING SPECIFIED RATES OF RETURN

Income corporations			Deficit corporations		
Rate of net income *	Number of corporations Actual	Cumulative	Rate of net loss *	Number of corporations Actual	Cumulative
00.0	1,708	7,403	00.0	1,802	5,063
2.2	1,062	5,695	2.9	741	3,261
4.4	809	4,633	5.7	496	2,520
6.6	572	3,824	8.6	349	2,024
8.8	504	3,252	11.5	294	1,675
11.1	1,391	2,748	14.4	735	1,381
22.1	613	1,357	28.8	296	646
33.2	301	744	43.1	138	350
44.2	156	443	57.4	71	212
55.3	238	287	71.8	100	141
110.6	39	49	143.7	32	41
221.3	10	10	287.6	9	9
553.	...	...	718.	...	...

* Amount of net income or loss divided by average equity per corporation. Data in per cent. Lower limit of class specified. No corporation had a rate of net income above 553 per cent, none a rate of net loss greater than 718 per cent.

assets-class, 49 companies had positive rates above 110 per cent, and 41 negative rates below (larger negatively than) 143 per cent. In the $1,000,000 to $5,000,000 assets-class, no means is available for determining whether *any* of the 59 most profitable companies earned at a rate above 110 per cent, although we know their rates exceeded 64 per cent and did not exceed 321 per cent. That some of them earned above 110 per cent is entirely likely, but it is also likely that some of the 49 most profitable companies of the lower assets-class earned at rates much above 110 per cent. In the higher assets-class, only 6 companies had losses at rates greater than 84 per cent; and

TABLE LXVII

NUMBER OF CORPORATIONS, IN THE $1,000,000 TO $5,000,000 ASSETS-CLASS OF THE MANUFACTURING DIVISION IN 1936, HAVING SPECIFIED RATES OF RETURN

Income corporations			Deficit corporations		
Rate of net income *	Number of corporations Actual	Cumulative	Rate of net loss *	Number of corporations Actual	Cumulative
0.000	18	3,355	0.000	41	860
.064	21	3,337	.084	39	819
.128	16	3,316	.168	18	780
.192	17	3,300	.252	18	762
.257	12	3,283	.337	25	744
.321	65	3,271	.421	78	719
.641	82	3,206	.841	56	641
.961	67	3,124	1.261	49	585
1.283	85	3,057	1.681	36	536
1.604	328	2,972	2.10	172	500
3.21	549	2,644	4.21	150	328
6.41	1,120	2,095	8.41	124	178
16.04	670	975	21.0	38	54
32.1	246	305	42.1	10	16
64.1	59	59	84.1	6	6
321.	...	...	421.	...	...

* Amount of net income or loss divided by average equity per corporation. Data in per cent. Lower limit of class specified. No corporation had a rate of net income above 321 per cent, none a rate of net loss greater than 421 per cent.

few if any of these are likely to have had negative rates as great as 143 per cent.

A mere study of extreme cases in the two frequency series of Tables LXVI and LXVII gives, however, no satisfactory appraisal of the variability within those series. Indeed, because of the considerable departure of the shape of these series —

particularly that for the higher assets-size class — from the nearly normal form to which customary measures of variability are most appropriately applied, no highly precise and readily interpreted measure of variability (or dispersion) can be applied to these series. The least objectionable of the simple measures, for series such as those here under examination, is the quartile index of variability. One formula for calculation of this index requires the determination of the upper and lower quartiles, computation of half the range between them, and division of this result by the median of the series.[5]

The indices found are 4.3 for the smaller assets-size class, and 1.2 for the larger assets-size class. This emphatically indicates that variability, on a relative basis, is distinctly greater for the low size class than for the high: variability in rate of return runs greater among small corporations than among large. Whether the index of variability would in fact decrease progressively as size increases, for the manufacturing division, and whether a similar relation would be found for other divisions and for the manufacturing groups, are questions not determined by specific tests, although isolated tests for particular cases tend to bear out the finding of the case here shown. We may conclude that, with some but probably not numerous exceptions, a decrease of relative variability in rate of return with increasing size is characteristic of corporate experience in 1936; and

[5] The needed figures here are:

	50–100-thousand-dollar class	1–5-million-dollar class
a. Upper quartile	9.4	15.4
b. Lower quartile	−3.4	.8
c. Difference (*a–b*)	12.8	14.6
d. Half of difference	6.4	7.3
e. Median	1.5	6.3
f. Index (*d*/*e*)	4.3	1.2

Figures for *a*, *b*, and *d* are rates of return (%). Actual determination of the median and quartiles rests upon approximations, but the errors involved can not possibly account for any large share of the difference between the two resulting indices.

no reason appears for doubting that a similar conclusion holds for other recent years. We infer tentatively that in general, regardless of the year or the line of industry, small corporations experience greater relative variability in their rates of return than large corporations.

XXVI

TAX ESTIMATE

THE PRESENT AND SECOND FOLLOWING CHAPTER describe and discuss certain statistical adjustments and analytical methods used in the main portions of the foregoing account.[1] This chapter and Chapter XXVIII also comment on the bearing of these methods upon the interpretation and significance of the results obtained. In addition, several peculiarities in the basic data, which govern the analytical results in some degree, are discussed briefly.

EXCLUSION OF TAXES FROM PROFITS

The entire study regards profits as the surplus income accruing to owners' equity, after all charges including Federal taxes. The theoretical validity of deducting Federal taxes, in order to arrive at our profits figure, appears clear, because we are here thinking of profits as the share of income "available" for the stockholders. The point of view of the entire investigation is that of the risk-taking suppliers of capital: profits are considered as the return on such capital. Accordingly, all portions of income — and the Federal tax is such a portion — against which these suppliers of capital have no claim, must be excluded in reckoning profits.

For certain other purposes, different definitions of "profits" might be defended. In a study of taxation, strong reasons might be advanced for designating net income before taxes, rather than after taxes, as profits. And even for more general economic studies — for example, a study of differential profit rates among

[1] Several specific matters of method, pertaining to limited portions of the work, have been explained at the points to which they pertain.

industries as factors in the allocation of new capital investment — a particular theory as to the incidence of a Federal tax on corporate income might indicate that net income before taxes is an appropriate definition of profits. Again, as we have shown in Chapter XXIII, the rate of return on corporate capital may be calculated in terms of risk capital plus borrowed capital; but the most appropriate numerator in this case — although it would be a specially defined net income figure — would scarcely be called "profits," and Federal taxes might or might not be excluded. Another type of analysis might define "profits" in terms of the excess of gross sales revenue over cost of goods sold; but here the determination of elements to be included in "cost of goods" is perplexing, and the pertinence of such a measure to any analysis of the return on *capital* is limited and perhaps non-existent. Even from the point of view adopted in this book — with profits regarded as the return on risk-taking capital — some uncertainty as to accounting definition exists: we have already discussed (Chapter XXIV) the possibility that compensation of officers includes an element of "profit" in the sense of this book. Nevertheless, for the main analyses we have, with no hesitation or doubt, excluded Federal taxes from profits; and, with somewhat less confidence, the "compiled net profits" figure of *Statistics of Income* has been accepted as a measure of net earnings before taxes.

This decision, to exclude Federal taxes from profits, unfortunately necessitated the making of one of the principal sets of adjustments (and estimates) involved in the investigation. Data for Federal taxes paid — actually, for the Federal tax liability as calculated in the tax return — are tabulated in *Statistics of Income* for each industrial division and manufacturing group as a whole, and for the various size classes in the general list of all divisions combined.[2] But they are not

[2] For example, Rows 41–43 of pages 52–59 and pages 60–63 and Row 41 of pages 64–65 of *Statistics of Income for 1935, Part 2.*

tabulated for the separate size classes of each industrial division and each manufacturing group.[3] Hence, in order to carry out our analysis of rate of return by size classes for each separate line of industry (or of manufacturing), the tax figure for each size class had to be estimated.

OBSTACLES TO TAX ESTIMATE, 1931–35

If the tax payable in any one year were, under the law, calculated at a flat rate on the statutory net income of that year, the estimate would involve no difficulty because the figures for statutory net income are given by size classes for each division and group.[4] These conditions are, however, not met exactly in any of the six years under study. For 1931–35, imperfect realization of the conditions is so limited and of such a nature as to suggest the scheme of estimating to be described in the next sub-section. For 1936, the graduation of normal tax rates and the undistributed-profits tax introduced further difficulties, and this case will be discussed separately in the second following sub-section. The simple conditions described above are not met — in some or all of the years 1931–35 — for the following reasons:

(1) For 1933 and later years an excess-profits tax applied to certain portions of corporate income; and this tax, unlike the capital-stock tax with which it is associated, is reported on the income-tax return and tabulated in *Statistics of Income.* Separate figures are published for this tax in reference to each entire division and group, and to the size classes of the general list of all divisions combined; but no formula was discovered for estimating this tax separately for the size classes of each division and group. Neither an empirical formula nor an *a priori* formula appeared feasible. The limited data on excess-

[3] *Ibid.*, pages 66–83.

[4] For example, next to right column of Table 6, pages 66–83, *Statistics of Income for 1935, Part 2.*

profits taxes actually published showed no such statistical regularity as to suggest an empirical formula, and no theoretical reasons appear for expecting any regular correlation of the excess-profits tax with size of corporation. (Further analysis of the special tabulations of 1936, described in Chapter XXV, may suggest such correlation.) An *a priori* formula could be developed from the provisions of the laws, but the published data do not include the essential figures for applying this formula with a view to making an estimate for each size class. Therefore I mingled the excess-profits tax with the income tax, applied the actual estimating method to total tax (income tax plus excess-profits tax), and thus in effect regarded the excess-profits tax as one of the disturbing elements tending to render total tax a *non*-uniform percentage of statutory net income.

(2) In 1931 (as in several earlier years), a corporation — with certain exceptions — having statutory net income not over $25,000 was allowed a credit of $3000 against net income before computing income tax at the statutory rate (12 per cent in 1931); and a somewhat smaller credit was in effect allowed in cases of net incomes between $25,000 and $25,360. This meant that the effective rate of tax on the full statutory net income of such corporations was below the standard rate — would indeed drop to zero for a corporation having net income of $3000 or under. As amount of net income is not necessarily correlated in high degree with amount of total assets, no basis exists for assurance that some benefit of this credit did not reach to various size classes. Empirical evidence strongly suggests that the bulk of the benefit went to low size classes: this is indicated by the 1931 column — unlike columns for other years — of Table LXVIII, wherein the very low average rate of tax for the bottom size class and the moderately low rates for the immediately higher classes can be ascribed largely to this specific credit. For estimating purposes, no procedure seemed feasible except to let this disturbing element — along

with other such elements — express itself in the general average rate of total tax as a percentage of statutory net income.

(3) For 1931, provisions of the Revenue Act of 1928 with respect to losses of prior years were in effect: a corporation might apply against net income of 1931, before computing

TABLE LXVIII

AVERAGE EFFECTIVE RATE OF TAX, FOR ALL INCOME CORPORATIONS, BY SIZE CLASSES *

Class †	1931	1932	1933	1934	1935	1936 ‡
0	2.885	10.94	14.65	14.44	14.73	11.42
50	5.314	11.82	14.45	14.32	14.67	11.72
100	7.692	12.42	14.38	14.22	14.52	12.14
250	9.651	12.67	14.28	14.16	14.49	12.99
500	10.44	12.83	14.25	14.09	14.42	13.64
1,000	11.18	13.02	14.13	13.97	14.35	14.10
5,000	11.58	13.36	14.02	13.88	14.04	14.09
10,000	11.62	13.52	14.02	13.84	14.07	13.71
50,000	11.90	13.62	14.20	13.83	14.13	13.10
100,000	...	...	...	...	...	13.18

* Stated in per cent. Ratio of Federal taxes (normal plus excess-profits) to net income. Data taken from the source, for numerator and denominator; and they apply to income corporations only.

† Lower limit, in thousands of dollars.

‡ 1936 tax here does not include undistributed profits tax, and is estimated, by special plan described on page 353.

tax liability, a net loss of 1930 and — so far as not exhausted against a net income of 1930 — a net loss of 1929. For 1932, provisions of the Revenue Act of 1932 were in effect: a corporation might apply against net income of 1932, before computing tax liability, a net loss of 1931. The National Industrial Recovery Act of 1933 discontinued this provision of the Act of 1932, and the Revenue Acts of 1934, 1935, and 1936 likewise permitted no carry-forward of losses. For 1933–36, therefore, prior-year loss has no bearing on tax liability. But in 1931, and to a less extent in 1932, prior-year losses might reduce the base against which the income tax was reckoned. Again, we have no feasible means of establishing a formula for estimating this effect in each size class, and this factor also must be treated as one of the elements disturbing the average ratio of taxes to statutory net income.

(4) Beginning in 1932, the rate of tax levied upon the net income of consolidated returns was somewhat above the standard rate. Although the bulk of the consolidated returns probably fall in the high or moderately high size classes, no direct means of allowing for this tax differential seems feasible. It also, therefore, is treated as one of the disturbing elements affecting the average ratio of taxes to net income.

(5) In certain years, when a new revenue law changes the tax rate, some fiscal-year corporations are taxed at two different rates: part of the net income, allocated to the earlier calendar year, is taxed at the old rate; and the remainder is taxed at the new rate. Thus, the 1931 tabulations include certain fiscal-year returns which were taxed in part at the 12 per cent of the 1928 Act and in part at the 13¾ per cent (14½ for consolidated returns) rate of the 1932 Act. The effect of this overlapping of rates may vary from industry to industry and from size class to size class, but available data do not supply a basis for working out a formula. Here also, then, the effect is treated merely as one of the disturbing elements influencing the average ratio of taxes to net income.

Only two of these five elements are likely to have effects upon percentage tax liability differing in any significant way among size classes. These two are the specific credit (exemption) of $3000 against net income, effective only for 1931 (of the period under study), and the loss-carry-forward privilege, effective only in 1931 and to a less degree in 1932. Of the two, probably the first is much more likely to cause differences between size classes. In any case, the method of estimating used amounts to assuming that for each of the five factors — or, strictly, for all five in combination — the differential effects upon the effective rate of tax among size classes are identical for every industrial division and every manufacturing group. In other words, if the five factors tend to make the average rate of tax on reported statutory net income (in any one year) 2 per cent lower for the bottom size class than for the top size class for all lines of industry combined, they are assumed to have the same effect for any particular line.

The theoretical warrant for this assumption is obviously open to question, particularly when we observe that some one of the various factors may operate with greater force in one industry than in another, and for corporations of one size than for those of another. For example, the prior-year-loss factor will presumably be particularly important for those industries, and those size classes in such industries, which felt the force of the great depression early and with exceptional severity. I have seen no way to allow for these theoretical differences, and merely hold the opinion — not supported by empirical evidence — that the errors involved in the basic assumption are probably small. I am especially confident of this opinion for years after 1931, and regard it as tolerably safe even for 1931. But the assumption is manifestly a makeshift, and the liability of the specific tax estimates, by size class by industry, to substantial error is admitted. Nothing short of a full tabulation of these tax figures for each size class in each industrial division and each manufacturing group can fully reveal such errors. Some light on the average magnitude of the errors is given at one stage of the estimating process.

METHOD OF ESTIMATE, 1931–35

The basic assumption on which the estimate rests has already been stated: differences among size classes in the average effective rate of tax on statutory net income, as established from published data for all divisions combined, are assumed to prevail for each separate division and manufacturing group. Obviously, the entire computation pertains only to the income corporations — corporations having in the given year a positive statutory net income. The first operation consists in compiling, for each year, the average effective rate — the ratio of taxes paid (strictly, reported tax liability) to statutory net income — for each size class, on the basis of data published for all divisions combined.[5] These computations for 1935 are shown in the left section of Table LXIX, and the full set of results for all six years has already been presented in Table LXVIII.

The next operation consists in applying these calculated rates for the respective size classes — in line with the basic assumption — to the published figures for statutory net income of each industrial division and manufacturing group in the particular year.[6] In this manner a preliminary estimate of taxes by size classes is obtained; and this process is illustrated, for the manufacturing division in 1935, in the central section of Table LXIX.

The total taxes — for all sizes combined — are known for each division and group.[7] Comparison between this given figure and the total of the preliminary estimates for the nine specific size classes reveals the aggregate error in the preliminary estimates. Thus, comparison of the actual tax of 354,795 thousand dollars with the total preliminary estimate of 351,030 reveals an aggregate error of 3,765 (excess of true over estimate) for manufacturing in 1935. By expressing this error as a ratio to the total estimate of 351,030, applying this ratio to the specific estimate for each size class to yield an adjustment, and adding the adjustment to the preliminary estimate, the series of

[5] For example, Rows 40 and 43 of Table 5 II, pages 62–63, of *Statistics of Income for 1935, Part 2.*

[6] These figures on statutory net income are presented in the size-classification tables for each line of industry. For example, second column from the right of pages 66–83 of *Statistics of Income for 1935, Part 2.*

[7] Thus, in Row 43 of pages 52–59 of *Statistics of Income for 1935, Part 2.*

final estimates is obtained. These operations are illustrated in the right section of Table LXIX.

The process of adjusting the preliminary estimates to the final estimates obviously assumes that the preliminary estimate

TABLE LXIX

ESTIMATE OF TAXES PAID, BY SIZE CLASSES, FOR MANUFACTURING IN 1935 *

	All divisions combined			Manufacturing division			
Class †	Statutory net income (1)	Federal tax (2)	Effective rate (3)	Statutory net income (4)	Preliminary estimate (5)	Adjustment (6)	Final estimate (7)
0	113,602	16,734	14.73	24,084	3,548	38	3,586
50	119,038	17,465	14.67	34,662	5,085	55	5,140
100	267,181	38,806	14.52	97,839	14,206	152	14,358
250	281,569	40,807	14.49	124,950	18,105	194	18,299
500	340,696	49,141	14.42	177,895	25,652	275	25,927
1,000 ...	917,560	131,660	14.35	499,828	71,725	769	72,494
5,000 ...	412,160	57,866	14.04	230,336	32,339	347	32,686
10,000 ..	1,077,725	151,628	14.07	547,791	77,074	827	77,901
50,000 ..	1,539,145	217,415	14.13	731,039	103,296	1,108	104,404
	Sum of preliminary estimates of tax				351,030		
	Total tax of division, from *Statistics of Income*				354,795		
	Discrepancy in aggregate of estimates ..				−3,765		

* Column 3 is column 2 divided by column 1, expressed in percentage.
Column 5 is column 4 multiplied by column 3.
Column 6 is column 5 multiplied by 3,765/351,030.
Column 7 is sum of columns 5 and 6.
All figures, except column 3, are in thousands of dollars.
† Lower limit, in thousands of dollars.

for each size class contributes its proportionate share to the aggregate error for the entire division. As we have no evidence by which to infer how the errors are distributed among the size classes, and though we should indeed admit that some size classes can even have negative errors while others have positive errors, this assumption of a uniform percentage error is the most feasible basis for adjustment. If there were any valid reason for assigning disproportionate shares of the total error to certain size classes, the assumption should of course be modified. The assumption actually used is essentially a corollary of the basic assumption of the method (above, page 342): it recognizes that the average effective rate for an entire division (or group) may differ from the corresponding rate for all divisions combined; but, in addition to allowing for this differential, it maintains the same percentage variation of effective rates among size classes for the particular division (or group) which prevails for all divisions combined.[8]

By the method described above and illustrated in Table LXIX, final estimates of taxes by size classes, in each year 1931–35, were worked out for every industrial division (except the meaningless "division" described in official publications as "nature not given") and every manufacturing group.[9] The re-

[8] This *might* have been accomplished by first adjusting the average effective rates for the several size classes, as determined for all divisions combined, by a percentage factor reflecting the discrepancy of the average effective rate for the entire particular division from that for all corporations combined. In such procedure, computations like the central section of Table LXIX would yield at once final estimates for each size class; and the total of these, except for arithmetic errors, would equal the true tax figure for the division.

[9] In certain groups and divisions, in some years, not all of the nine size classes appear separately in the official tabulations. When a high size class contains only one corporation, Treasury policy of treating tax returns as confidential precludes publishing data for that corporation separately. Under such conditions, the single-return size class is "grouped" with another — usually the next smaller size class — and data are published only for the two grouped classes in combination.

In such cases, also, our tax estimate must pertain to the grouped classes; and the only difficulty presented, in applying the method outlined above, consists in determining the "average effective rate" for the composite size class. In the calculations as carried out, this special rate was obtained by taking a weighted average of the two effective rates pertaining separately to the two combined classes, the weights being the numbers of corporations — for the group or division, and the particular year, in question — in the two classes which were combined. A more painstaking system of weighting might have been suggested, but there is no warrant for great care in weighting for two reasons. One is that cases of classes

sulting final estimates, for every division and group, are tabulated in the Appendix (Table A), along with corresponding figures — obtained by methods presently to be described — for 1936.

TAX ESTIMATE FOR 1936

Several facts explain the greater difficulty of making tax estimates — by size classes, for each division and group — pertinent to income data for the year 1936, and the greater liability to error of the estimates as made. (1) The normal tax on 1936 corporate income was at graduated rates, for the first time.[10] Hence, calculation of an "average effective rate" for an entire division (or group), and application of such rate to specific size classes, may result in error if the share of income subject to higher rates varies — as it probably does — from size class to size class. (2) The fractional taxation of dividends received under the Act of 1936 altered the base for reckoning taxes, in a manner and to a degree not readily allowed for in the estimating process. (3) The imposition of the undistributed-profits tax by the Act of 1936 introduced a new element — highly variable and highly uncertain — into the total tax liability, and special methods for reckoning this tax became necessary. (4) The tabulations of 1936 corporations statistics,

---

grouped always occur high up on the size scale, where changes in effective rate from size class to size class are very slight anyway. The other is that, since a single corporation — rather than several corporations — appears in the higher of the two combined size classes, the role of chance is unusually great: the chance is fairly large that the true tax rate for this single corporation may differ notably from the average effective rate calculated (as in Table LXIX) for the top size class. Nicety of weighting, under such circumstances, is not warranted.

[10] The Revenue Act of 1935 had provided for graduated normal rates; but these did not go into effect for 1935 income (strictly, for corporations with taxable years beginning before January 1, 1936), and were superseded for 1936 income by provisions of the Act of 1936. The specific exemption in effect for 1931 and earlier years (see above, page 339) amounted to a partial "graduation" of the rate, but of very limited applicability.

though in admirably greater detail than previous tabulations, fail to give separately certain items which would render the tax estimates more dependable. (5) In particular, the basic taxable net income figure in the 1936 tabulations is the "net income for excess-profits computation," not the net income upon which normal tax is reckoned. This fact sets a serious obstacle in the way of applying the simple "average effective rate" method used for 1931–35.

An extensive list of assumptions and formulas received consideration in working out the scheme of estimating. Some of these suggested themselves as means of applying various provisions of the law in the estimating process; but all except a few such devices were abandoned. Some were abandoned because the specific provisions of the law were unlikely to have calculable direct effect on the statistics as published. Others were abandoned because actual testing with the available data yielded unfavorable results; several such tests were applied, with different formulas, and yielded results mainly so out of line with known facts as to discredit the formula under test. The method finally adopted is in truth a statistical patchwork, based upon several formulas, resting in some degree on theoretical considerations suggested by provisions of the law and in some degree upon statistical tests which were less unsatisfactory than other similar experiments rather than satisfying in themselves. I repeat that the tax estimates for 1936 are on a distinctly lower plane, as respects their accuracy, than those of 1931–35; but I believe the margin of error in most divisions and groups is not large enough to impair seriously the measured rates of return on equity.

NORMAL TAX ESTIMATE

For all corporate returns (accompanied by balance sheets) tabulated in 1936, the separately stated tax items were: normal, \$982,940,000; undistributed-profits, \$141,154,000; and excess-profits, $20,546,000. Because of its clearly dominating importance, the normal tax was taken as the first item to be estimated by size classes in the several divisions and groups. Because of its slight magnitude (actually, it ran lower in 1936 than in 1935), the excess-profits tax was mingled with the normal tax in this first step of the analysis — a procedure in line with that followed for 1931–35. But the undistributed-profits tax was not only of substantial magnitude in the aggregate but also likely to have widely varying impact upon different industries and upon the several size classes. It was therefore reserved for treatment in a second stage of the estimate (below, page 353).

Two obstacles stand in the way of a direct estimate of the normal tax by a simple formula: (1) the tax is graduated, and (2) the net income figure published in the *Statistics of Income* tabulations is not that upon which the normal tax is reckoned. On the first of these points the estimating process makes no detailed allowance. The process, by its calculation of an average effective normal rate for each size class — which varies somewhat from size class to size class — and application of these rates for each division and group, in effect rests upon the assumption that the greater incidence of the higher normal rates upon larger size classes is characteristic — and equally characteristic — of all lines of industry.[11]

The second obstacle required more careful treatment. The tabulated net income figure is "net income for excess-profits tax computation." This differs from the "base" to which the normal rates are applied in two important respects: (*a*) it in-

[11] Special tabulations published for 1936 (see their description in Chapter XXV) may yield a more precise treatment of this varying incidence of the higher normal rates, but preliminary testing of this new body of data for the present purpose uncovered perplexing difficulties. I therefore abandoned this approach, so far as tax estimates for this book are concerned, but hope to examine the case more intensively later and report my findings elsewhere.

cludes interest on certain government obligations which is subject to excess-profits tax but not to normal tax — such interest was in 1936 about half of total interest received by corporations on government securities; (*b*) it includes all of dividends received from domestic corporations, whereas the normal tax applies to only 15 per cent of such dividends.[12] The income subject to normal tax — called "normal-tax net income" in the tax return — also excludes the excess-profits tax already computed against the basic net income figure; but this deduction, which is relatively unimportant in magnitude, is ignored in our analysis.

As the item "net income for excess-profits tax computation" is the base figure we must use anyway — because it alone is tabulated — in estimating taxes by size classes for each industry, it might be suggested that this figure should be used in calculating "average effective normal rates" by size classes for all divisions combined. This procedure would be analogous to that used for 1931–35. The essential objection is that both items *a* and *b*, mentioned above, arise chiefly in the finance division — over half of item *b* and about seven eighths of item *a*. Hence, for all other divisions and for all manufacturing groups, these items may be taken as relatively unimportant. Therefore, "average effective normal rates" by size classes, calculated from the figures for all divisions combined *as they stand*, would almost surely run too low for all industries except finance, and too high for finance.

The obviously desirable adjustment is to exclude finance from all divisions combined, and then compute average effective normal rates, to be used in estimating normal taxes by size classes for all other industries than finance. A separate calcula-

[12] The 85 per cent credit against dividends received was not allowed to mutual investment companies, for which a different provision with respect to dividends was made in the Act of 1936. This exception is ignored in our analysis.

tion would, of course, be needed for finance. But this procedure is not feasible; for, although we have the "net income for excess-profits tax computation" by size classes separately for finance, we do not have normal tax paid by size classes for finance. This latter figure is, indeed, an object of the scheme of estimating.

An alternative, though less satisfactory, approach consists in reducing the net income (for excess-profits tax computation) of each size class of all divisions combined by the approximate amount of items *a* — interest subject to excess-profits tax — and *b* — corporate dividends received — ascribable to finance. The resulting figures may be expected to reflect more nearly the "base" against which normal tax is reckoned in industries outside finance.[13] Even this approach, however, involves a highly dubious assumption: that the portion of item *a* and of item *b* ascribable to finance is the same in every size class as in all classes combined. After careful examination of the figures, however, I am of opinion that the resulting margin of error, though very substantial, is not objectionably large.

The actual computations (pertaining, of course, to income corporations only) appear in Table LXX. The total of Column 1 is compared with the corresponding figure, 206,252 thousand dollars, for finance; and finance is seen to account for 87.75 per cent of government interest subject to excess profits tax — item *a* of the foregoing discussion. This ratio is applied to the items of Column 1, to yield those of Column 2 (here the assumption noted above is made). In like manner, finance is seen to account for 58.88 per cent of dividends received — item *b* of the foregoing comment. And similarly Column 4 is obtained from Column 3, again using the proportionality assump-

[13] Refinements can indeed be suggested. For example, somewhat less than all of items *a* and *b* for finance should no doubt be deducted, on the ground that the reconstructed finance division — as it appears in the reconstructed all divisions combined — should be assumed to have taxable government interest and dividends to the same extent as other divisions. But the margin of error in the method seems too great to warrant such refinements.

TABLE LXX

Estimate of Average Effective Rate of Tax, Excluding that on Undistributed Profits, by Size Classes, in 1936 *

Class †	Interest, taxable (1)	Same, for finance (2)	Dividends received (3)	Same, for finance (4)	Sum of (2) and (3) (5)	Net income (6)	Same, with finance revised (7)	Taxes (8)	Effective rate (9)
0	139	122	5,330	3,139	3,261	154,148	150,887	17,232	11.42
50	307	269	5,369	3,321	3,590	160,216	156,626	18,354	11.72
100	2,008	1,762	33,512	19,734	21,496	382,848	361,352	43,773	12.11
250	4,922	4,319	32,759	19,287	23,606	406,918	383,312	49,801	12.99
500	8,204	7,198	50,832	29,936	37,134	504,255	467,121	63,725	13.64
1,000	30,745	26,985	224,641	132,266	159,251	1,459,059	1,299,808	183,258	14.10
5,000	15,212	13,349	141,868	83,532	96,881	709,831	612,950	86,405	14.09
10,000	41,088	36,058	425,984	250,820	286,878	1,760,239	1,473,361	202,020	13.71
50,000	16,852	14,790	293,279	172,686	187,476	841,743	654,267	85,719	13.10
100,000	115,559	101,409	1,191,514	701,557	802,966	2,722,716	1,919,750	252,999	13.18
Total	235,036	...	2,405,360	...	...	...	...	...	...
Same, for finance	206,252	...	1,416,478	...	...	...	...	...	...
% in finance	87.75	...	58.88	...	...	...	...	...	...

* All data, except column 9 and bottom row, in thousands of dollars. Columns 1, 3, 6, 8 from source. Column 2 is 87.75% of column 1; column 4 is 58.88% of column 3; column 7 is column 6 minus column 5 and does not strictly leave finance out — only the interest (taxable) and dividend income of finance, Column 9 is ratio, in %, of column 8 to column 7. Column 1 is portion of Government interest subject to excess-profits tax. Column 8 is portion of taxes excluding that on undistributed profits.

† Lower limit, in thousands of dollars.

tion. Column 5, combining Columns 2 and 4, gives the totals of items *a* and *b* ascribed to finance. Deducting these figures from the net income for all divisions combined (Column 6) yields the revised net income figures of Column 7. Division of

TABLE LXXI

ESTIMATE OF TAX, OTHER THAN THAT ON UNDISTRIBUTED PROFITS, FOR THE MANUFACTURING DIVISION IN 1936 *

Class †	Net income (1)	Estimate of tax (excluding undistributed-profits) Preliminary (2)	Adjustment (3)	Final (4)
0	31,828	3,635	121	3,514
50	46,658	5,468	182	5,286
100	134,054	16,274	542	15,732
250	172,610	22,422	747	21,675
500	239,761	32,703	1,090	31,613
1,000	728,596	102,732	3,425	99,307
5,000	357,511	50,373	1,679	48,694
10,000	803,346	110,139	3,671	106,470
50,000	315,585	41,342	1,378	39,964
100,000	1,111,204	146,457	4,883	141,574
Total of preliminary estimates		531,545		
Actual total, from source		513,827		
Discrepancy in estimates		17,718		
Percentage discrepancy		3.3		

* Column 1 is from source. Column 2 is column 1 multiplied by column 9 of Table LXX. Column 3 is column 2 multiplied by .033, and the adjustments are negative. Column 4 is column 2 minus column 3. All figures, except that at bottom, are in thousands of dollars.

† Lower limit, in thousands of dollars.

these into the normal taxes paid (Column 8) yields the desired average effective normal rates of Column 9.

These calculated rates are used to secure preliminary estimates of the amount of normal tax for each size class, separately for every division other than finance and for every manufacturing group. The aggregate error in these preliminary estimates, ascertained by comparing the total of the ten size-class estimates with the tabulated normal tax for the entire division (or group), is then distributed among the size classes on the proportional plan used for 1931–35. The results of this adjustment are the final estimates of normal tax by size classes. The method is illustrated, for the manufacturing division, in Table LXXI.[14]

UNDISTRIBUTED PROFITS TAX ESTIMATE

In calculating the "average effective rates" by size classes for the undistributed-profits tax, the published figures for net income (for excess-profits tax computation) were adjusted by deducting the portion of interest on government obligations which is subject to excess-profits tax and the dividends paid.[15] This adjusted figure was then divided into the stated undistributed-profits tax, for each size class in the table for all divisions combined, to yield the estimated "average effective undistributed-profits tax rates." These appear in Column 4 of Table LXXII.

Application of these rates to the respective size classes, for any one division or group (with exceptions presently noted), then follows; and the operations are illustrated for foods manu-

[14] In cases wherein published data for higher size classes apply only to combined classes the same method of weighting the appropriate effective rates was used as in 1931–35 cases.

[15] The chief of these two deductions is, of course, that for dividends paid. The adjustments do not satisfactorily yield the "undistributed net income," against which the statute levies the undistributed-profits tax — the chief additional adjustment should be deduction of the normal tax. I am not fully content with the adjustments as actually carried out, and the resulting calculation of the average effective rates — the more so as this process is not wholly consistent with that followed in applying the rates to obtain tax estimates by size classes in each industry. But the process adopted rests in part only on provisions of the law; it rests in part also on empirical tests, the application of various test formulas to the actual data. I propose later to reexamine the whole problem, and hope to refine the method of estimating; but, for purposes of the present analysis, I regard the imperfections as coming within a tolerable — though rather large — margin of error.

facturing in Table LXXII. The first operation is the deduction of the final estimate of normal tax from the net income (Column 4 from Column 1, of Table LXXI), and the results appear in Column 1 of Table LXXII. Column 2 gives the dividends paid,

TABLE LXXII

ESTIMATE OF UNDISTRIBUTED-PROFITS TAX, FOR FOODS GROUP IN 1936 *

					Estimate of und. prof. tax		
Class †	Net income, after "normal" tax (1)	Dividends paid (2)	(1) – (2) (3)	Effective und. prof. rate (4)	Preliminary (5)	Adjustment (6)	Final (7)
0	3,445	1,838	1,607	6.26	101	41	142
50	5,281	3,481	1,800	6.89	124	50	174
100	13,849	10,831	3,018	7.20	217	88	305
250	17,389	13,844	3,545	8.01	284	115	399
500	21,327	16,155	5,172	7.62	394	160	554
1,000	57,358	45,064	12,294	7.20	885	359	1,244
5,000	23,229	17,503	5,726	6.92	396	161	557
10,000 ...	78,867	67,267	11,600	5.74	666	270	936
50,000 ...	57,102	48,003	9,099	5.75	523	212	735
100,000 ..	67,013	66,830	183	15.67	29	12	41
	Sum of preliminary estimates				3,619		
	Total und. prof. tax, as given in source				5,087		
	Discrepancy in the estimates				–1,468		
	Percentage discrepancy				40.56		

* All figures, except column 4 and bottom figure, are in thousands of dollars. Column 1 is obtained by deducting — in a table like Table LXXI — column 4 from column 1. Column 2 is from source. Column 4 is explained in text, page 353. Column 5 is column 3 multiplied by column 4. Column 6 is column 5 multiplied by .4056. Column 7 is column 5 minus column 6.

† Lower limit, in thousands of dollars.

which are then deducted from Column 1 to yield Column 3; and this is the approximate estimate of "undistributed net income."[16] Column 4 gives the estimated "average effective rates on undistributed profits"; and then Columns 5, 6, and 7 give —

[16] Wherever column 2 exceeds column 1, the column 3 entry is zero. See provisions in statute concerning carry-forward of a dividends-paid credit.

in the usual manner — the preliminary estimates, the adjustments for error, and the final estimates of the tax. (See next section and footnote 19 for exceptional treatment of certain divisions and groups.)

We should observe that more than mere errors or imperfections in statistical procedure damage the precision of these estimates. There is, of course, a basic assumption like that made in the case of the normal tax: the differences in average effective rates among size classes, as calculated for *all divisions combined*, are assumed to prevail for each division and group (with exceptions noted below, page 357). This assumption is almost certainly less valid here than in the case of the normal tax.

But another, and perhaps more serious, defect is present: we have computed the average effective rate for a *whole class* of corporations — have taken aggregate figures, and attempted to apply to them provisions of law which apply only to single corporations. Thus, if there were five corporations in a class and each had undistributed profits of 15 per cent of its adjusted net income, the total undistributed-profits tax of the class would be less than if the five corporations (assuming they had the same adjusted net income as before) made different distributions of dividends with the result that the ratio of undistributed profits to adjusted net income were under 10 per cent for four but over 40 per cent for the fifth corporation.[17] Thus the variation *among* specific corporations in a size class, as respects the degree to which they distribute dividends, has a vital bearing on the average rate of tax for the class. To be sure, this same argument applies in the case of the normal tax, because it is

[17] To illustrate numerically, suppose each corporation has adjusted net income of $100,000. Under case 1, each pays out $85,000 dividends, and has undistributed profits of $15,000. (Assume also no credit for "contracts restricting" dividends.) Tax on each would then be 7% on $10,000, and 12% on $5,000, or $1,300. In the second case, suppose four corporations

graduated and different corporations in a class may have different levels of net income; but I am confident it has much smaller force in that case. I see no way, with the data available, to make adequate allowances for this factor, and I discuss the matter merely to emphasize its bearing upon the accuracy and appropriateness of the calculated average effective rates, and the implied impairment in the accuracy of our tax estimates.

SPECIAL TREATMENT OF FINANCE

In calculating the normal tax estimates for finance, the "base" to which the estimated rates were applied was arrived at — for each size class — as follows: Deduct from given figure for net income (for excess-profits tax computation) the two items estimated — government interest received, which is taxable (for excess-profits), and 85 per cent of estimated dividends received. Both of these estimated items are described in the second section preceding. The rates applied were the "average effective normal rates" of Table LXX, multiplied by 1.116. The reason for this multiplier is that the "base" for the other divisions and all the groups included full taxable interest and dividends as allocated, and the multiplier was designed to put the finance division on an equivalent basis.[18] In this manner, with the usual adjustment for aggregate error, final estimates of normal tax were found.

---

pay out $95,000 each in dividends, and the fifth pays out $45,000 (total dividends would be as before). Then taxes are:

Four corporations,	7% of	$5,000,	$ 350 each
Fifth corporation,	7% of	10,000,	700
	12% of	10,000,	1,200
	17% of	20,000,	3,400
	22% of	15,000,	3,300

The total tax for the class (five corporations) is $10,000 in this second case, against $6,500 in the first case.

[18] Some other means of accomplishing this purpose might have been used, but a succession of experiments led to the choice actually made.

As respects the undistributed-profits tax, no means was discovered for determining average effective rates for the several size classes in finance. Therefore the rate applied to the "base" — the net income after deduction of estimated normal tax and tabulated dividends paid — was the flat figure of 15.7 per cent, calculated from the published data for the entire division. In all probability no such flat rate applies for all size classes; but no other choice in the practical estimate seemed possible, and we must recognize that the estimated undistributed-profits tax for finance is even less secure than that in various other divisions and groups.[19]

In the usual way, with the base and rate as stated, a preliminary tax estimate was worked out for each size class in finance, adjustments were applied to distribute the aggregate error proportionately, and thus final estimates were obtained.

Net income after taxes. With the two sets of final tax estimates available — one set for normal tax, and the other set for undistributed-profits tax — tabulated figures for "compiled net profits" could be reduced by total taxes, to yield the numerators of our rate-of-return ratios. These operations were carried out, by size classes, for every division and group in 1936.

I remark again that the tax estimates for 1936 stand on a less secure footing than those of earlier years. How large the margin of error may be is uncertain; that in some size classes in some industries it may be very substantial I do not doubt; that in many classes it is large enough to affect somewhat our

[19] In the actual calculation, the errors in preliminary estimates of undistributed-profits taxes were found so large in certain groups and divisions that finally they were treated by the same flat-rate method as finance. These cases are: mining, manufacturing, construction, public utilities, service; tobacco, forest products, printing, miscellaneous, and petroleum. In these cases the flat rate was, after experiment, determined as the ratio of undistributed profits tax (for the entire division or group) to net income after normal tax; and applied to the corresponding figure for each size class.

curves is possible; that in most cases or on the average it is seriously large seems to me unlikely. But, unless and until there is a more detailed tabulation of taxes — particularly those on undistributed profits — in 1936, we must be content with estimates which at best are moderately lacking in precision.

XXVII

EFFECTS OF CONSOLIDATED RETURNS

SOME COMMENTS have already been made (especially in Chapter III) concerning the effects, upon the statistics essential to calculating rates of return, of the changes introduced by the Revenue Act of 1934 with reference to the filing of consolidated returns. In 1933 and earlier years, such tax returns had numbered less than 10,000 — out of a total of about a half-million, for all corporation returns — but this small number of returns accounted for nearly half the total corporate business of the nation, and had therefore an influence, upon the statistics and ratios calculated therefrom, vastly greater than would be indicated by their mere number. The Act of 1934 withdrew the privilege for all corporations except railroads; and the withdrawal took effect in 1934 for most cases, but only in 1935 for certain fiscal-year returns. The result, so far as the statistics are concerned, was a vast shifting of accounting items — among the industrial divisions and manufacturing groups, among the size classes, and between the income and deficit categories — occurring mainly from 1933 to 1934, but appreciably from 1934 to 1935. Different accounting items suffered shifts in different proportions; and hence changes also resulted in ratios, such as the rate of return, calculated from the items separately or in combination.

Furthermore, the change in law resulted in actual changes in the magnitude of certain particular items, as summed into aggregates for all corporations or particular sections (groups, classes, categories) of the entire list. Thus, aggregate figures for such "paired" items as non-tax-exempt investments and securities outstanding, receivables and payables, surplus and deficit, gross sales and cost of goods sold, interest paid and received, rents paid and received, net income and loss, dividends paid and received, were expanded because offsets between the constituent corporations of a consolidated system were no longer in effect. Net income (or loss) and equity, which are residual items in the income account and balance sheet, were exposed to such changes in aggregate magnitude to exceptional degree and in a manner which is exceptionally difficult to trace and explain. Resultant effects upon the calculated rate of return were inevitable: the probability that changes in magnitude were equivalent, in percentage terms, for the net income (or loss) and the equity, is small and perhaps very small. A further difficulty enters because the tax, which enters as a deduction in the numerator, was changed in an uncertain degree by the change in law; a central purpose of changing the law was to increase the tax.

On both counts — because of shifts in classification and of changes in the magnitude of specific aggregate items — the abandonment of consolidated returns probably affected our computed results, and may have affected some of them greatly. To make a satisfactory examination of these effects, one might fairly require full knowledge in all the details used in Treasury tabulations — as to specification of particular accounting items, classification by size, and indication of line of industry — and perhaps other details, not only for each of the approximately 7,000 consolidated returns as they stood in 1933 and perhaps some earlier years, but also for each subsidiary covered by such returns. No such data are available, but the 1934 issue of *Statistics of Income* did present a segregation of 1933 data between the consolidated and non-consolidated lists and a segregation of 1934 data into two lists, separating 1934 corporations which were covered by 1933 consolidated returns from those which were not, and also reclassified (so far as line of industry is concerned) the first of these lists on the 1933 basis.

None of these special tabulations gives any size classification. Moreover, the "reclassification" on the 1933 basis of the 1934 data of corporations which had been covered by consolidated returns in 1933 was in no proper sense a statement of the data as they would have appeared if consolidated returns had been filed in 1934. This is true for two main reasons: the various offsets of inter-subsidiary items were not (probably could not have been) carried out, thus reducing aggregate items; and the shifts between the income and deficit categories, which would have resulted from consolidation of income with deficit subsidiaries, were not accomplished. A third, and minor, reason is that the tax is tabulated as reckoned on the 1934 basis, not as it would have been reckoned for consolidated returns.

Nevertheless, the special tabulations of 1934 are of great assistance, and this chapter reports certain inferences which can be drawn from them. These will be helpful for the present investigation of rate of return, for they serve as a warning and guide in the interpretation of our rates of return, particularly in all cases involving comparisons of 1933 and earlier years with 1934 and later years. A fuller and more incisive determination of the significance of the consolidated returns, and their abandonment under the Act of 1934, must await the completion of an elaborate and complicated examination of the special 1934 tabulations and possibly the realization of hopes that tabulations of the consolidated returns will become available in still greater detail.

THE 1933 SEGREGATION

In order to bring out the different profit experience of the consolidated and the non-consolidated lists, we make first a comparison of these two lists as segregated for 1933 in the 1934 *Statistics of Income*.[1] These 1933 data are better for our im-

[1] Part 2 of the 1934 issue, pages 146–61.

In passing, we observe that the word "consolidated" is used in the

mediate purpose than the 1934 data, even as reclassified, because the reclassification does not — as remarked above — bring out a true reconstruction of the tabulations as they would appear if consolidated returns were filed in 1934.

As already noted, no classification of these data according to size of corporation is available. The source does give a classification into divisions and groups, and between income and deficit categories. Table LXXIII shows rates of return as calculated for the consolidated and non-consolidated lists separately, for each division and group; and the calculation was made in all respects on the same basis as in earlier chapters. Shown also are the 1933 rates, as worked out in previous chapters, covering both consolidated and non-consolidated lists in combination.

Considering first the figures for both categories — income and deficit — combined, we find notable differences between rates for consolidated and non-consolidated corporations in most divisions and groups, although the figures for all divisions combined are very close to each other. Some differences in sign appear — for example, in agriculture, manufacturing, trade, paper, and chemicals — but these are not necessarily more significant than differences in level where signs are the same. Generally, in cases of like sign, the consolidated rate is nearer zero (is smaller numerically) than the non-consolidated; but even this characteristic is not systematic, as instanced by the figures for all divisions combined. The most striking difference, in view of its magnitude and of the size of the division concerned, is for manufacturing: an average loss rate of .32 per cent for consolidated corporations, and a profit rate of 1.89 per cent for non-consolidated. But in numerous other cases differences are

sense defined by the revenue laws — see above, Chapter III. In ordinary discussion of corporate problems, other systems of corporations, not even formerly permitted to file consolidated returns, are sometimes called "consolidated."

sufficiently large to suggest the likelihood of significant changes in the rates of return studied in previous chapters whenever any substantial shift occurs in the industrial classification of companies making up the consolidated list.

Comparisons are even more striking when the income and deficit categories are considered separately. With very few exceptions the rates for the consolidated list stand closer to zero — run numerically smaller, whether positive or negative — than corresponding rates for the non-consolidated list. And many of the differences are strikingly large, for each category (income and deficit); for example, consolidated rates are less than half of non-consolidated rates for manufacturing, much less than half for chemicals, and only moderately above one half for all divisions combined. This set of comparisons is particularly informing with reference to the problem which confronts us.

Why should the consolidated rate run numerically smaller — a smaller positive figure for the income category and a smaller negative figure for the deficit category — than the corresponding non-consolidated rate? The essential reason is that, in a consolidated return, the numerator of the rate figure is reduced (numerically) by the offsetting of deficits of some subsidiaries against profits of others. How great the magnitude of these offsets may be, we have no direct means of knowing; but a rough indirect estimate shows them very large. Two other important factors bear upon the relation between consolidated and non-consolidated rates. The equity of a consolidated system is generally smaller, and sometimes much smaller, than the aggregate equities of its constituent companies (parent and subsidiaries) would be if these subsidiary equities were stated on a non-consolidated basis. This is because, in consolidation, some equity securities of subsidiaries are offset against investments of the parent. This factor would clearly tend to raise consolidated rates (numerically, that is, ignoring sign) above

TABLE LXXIII

RATES OF RETURN IN 1933 FOR EACH DIVISION AND GROUP, SEPARATELY ACCORDING AS CONSOLIDATED RETURNS WERE OR WERE NOT FILED *

	Consolidated (1)	Not consolidated (2)	All (3)
Divisions			
All	**−.89**	**−.74**	**−.81**
	3.96	7.20	5.77
	−3.81	*−7.27*	*−5.48*
Agriculture	**.76**	**−4.20**	**−2.91**
	3.86	4.20	4.03
	−2.74	*−6.16*	*−5.57*
Mining	**−.54**	**−1.93**	**−2.39**
	3.12	6.11	5.29
	−3.42	*−5.28*	*−4.17*
Manufacturing	**−.32**	**1.89**	**.68**
	3.76	8.62	6.19
	−3.98	*−7.46*	*−5.35*
Construction	**−1.65**	**−6.39**	**−5.18**
	2.69	10.22	9.19
	−2.23	*−12.06*	*−9.25*
Public utilities	**−.46**	**2.80**	**.45**
	3.63	5.68	4.52
	−2.94	*−5.43*	*−3.21*
Trade	**.32**	**−.42**	**−.25**
	6.41	7.84	7.49
	−7.38	*−9.74*	*−9.23*
Service	**−8.46**	**−8.54**	**−8.52**
	6.31	7.61	7.30
	−12.52	*−14.12*	*−13.66*
Finance	**−3.19**	**−3.36**	**−3.32**
	6.51	5.87	5.95
	−4.69	*−6.40*	*−5.97*
Groups			
Foods	**2.34**	**5.00**	**3.84**
	4.75	9.79	7.54
	−4.82	*−7.21*	*−6.23*
Liquors	**6.82**	**10.49**	**9.35**
	10.44	19.67	16.30
	−10.67	*−6.91*	*−7.61*

TABLE LXXIII (*Continued*)

	Consolidated (1)	Not consolidated (2)	All (3)
Tobacco	**4.98**	**5.93**	**5.87**
	12.44	8.41	8.54
	−2.56	*−14.96*	*−12.20*
Textiles	**.73**	**3.33**	**2.80**
	6.09	8.23	7.86
	−6.76	*−8.38*	*−7.94*
Leather	**2.15**	**4.27**	**3.69**
	6.85	10.32	9.51
	−5.41	*−14.07*	*−10.90*
Rubber	**.05**	**2.74**	**.59**
	1.76	6.81	3.13
	−1.44	*−6.16*	*−2.05*
Forest products	**−3.56**	**−3.91**	**−3.77**
	3.91	4.84	4.57
	−5.14	*−7.49*	*−6.46*
Paper	**−.90**	**2.64**	**.83**
	3.79	7.92	6.76
	−2.29	*−5.53*	*−3.35*
Printing	**.56**	**1.48**	**1.09**
	1.84	8.70	5.46
	−3.30	*−10.41*	*−8.06*
Chemicals	**−.05**	**6.04**	**1.28**
	2.26	10.48	4.38
	−4.25	*−12.45*	*−5.34*
Stone	**−1.09**	**−1.55**	**−1.40**
	3.10	5.96	5.03
	−4.42	*−7.45*	*−6.47*
Metals	**−.97**	**−1.03**	**−.95**
	5.55	6.33	5.91
	−3.47	*−5.76*	*−4.24*
Miscellaneous	**−3.34**	**−2.03**	**−2.58**
	7.56	8.86	8.30
	−12.25	*−10.44*	*−11.20*

* Boldface type, both categories combined; ordinary type, income category; italics, deficit.

non-consolidated, and the evidence of the table indicates that this factor may be less effective than that considered above.

The other clearly important factor is the comparative sizes of the typical consolidated and non-consolidated corporations. Although no size classification of either list is available, the average size of consolidated companies runs much higher than that of non-consolidated. We may therefore assume that a greater proportion of all consolidated companies than of non-consolidated companies falls in high size classes. Abundant evidence in earlier chapters shows that rates of return are closer to zero — much closer and very systematically for deficit companies, somewhat closer but less systematically for income companies — in high size classes than in low. It may be urged that this is merely a reflection of the dominant place of consolidated returns in the high size classes, that the very fact now under examination — of consolidated rates closer to zero than non-consolidated — accounts for the findings of earlier chapters. But this point of view seems not to hold in the face of the systematic way in which income and deficit rates converge toward zero all along the size scale, and in widely different lines of industry, and in the face of the smallness of the number of consolidated returns available for scattering along the size scale in various divisions and groups. I conclude that the earlier findings tend to explain the present relationship — rates converging toward zero for higher size classes tend to explain rates nearer zero for consolidated than for non-consolidated returns — rather than the reverse. This conclusion is strengthened by the persistence of the relationship earlier found after abandonment of consolidated returns in 1934.

Quite apart from the foregoing argument, the disparities observed between the rates of return for consolidated and non-consolidated companies, when income and deficit categories are considered separately, emphasize the necessity of giving separate attention to the two categories in our examination of the classification problem resulting from abandonment of consolidated returns. Within a particular consolidated system, as it stood in 1933, there may have been various subsidiaries with positive rates — perhaps one or more of them large — and several with negative rates — perhaps one or more of them large — but the position of the system as between income and deficit categories depends upon the net result of combining all of these. If there had been no such consolidated return, and if in consequence thereof no changes had been made in the accounting data of the subsidiaries, some of those subsidiaries would have fallen in one category and some in the other. This shift, in classification by category, is quite as important for our purpose as the shift in industrial classification which resulted from abandoning consolidated returns.

THE 1934 SEGREGATION

Accordingly, the special tabulation of 1934 which shows aggregate 1934 figures for those companies which had been covered by consolidated returns in 1933 does not shift numerous corporations from one category to another as they would in effect have been shifted had consolidated returns actually been filed in 1934.[2] Likewise the special tabulation which shows aggregate 1934 figures for those companies which had been covered by consolidated returns in 1933 "classified on business reported on the consolidated returns for 1933" does not make shifts between categories, but only shifts among industrial divisions and manufacturing groups.[3] These reservations are essential in examining the first four columns of results in Table LXXIV. In studying the two categories separately, comparisons

[2] *Statistics of Income for 1934, Part 2*, pp. 162–69. That no such shifts have been made is apparent by checking the sum of the item in Row 9 of the first column of p. 162 and the corresponding item on p. 170 with the corresponding item on p. 66 (and likewise for other columns).

[3] *Ibid.*, pp. 186–93. If such shifts had been made, offsets of net income against loss would have occurred and the figures of all divisions combined

TABLE LXXIV

RATES OF RETURN IN 1934 FOR EACH DIVISION AND GROUP, SEPARATELY ACCORDING AS CONSOLIDATED RETURNS WERE OR WERE NOT FILED IN 1933, AND AFTER RECLASSIFICATION ON 1933 BASIS *

	Returns consolidated in 1933		Returns not consolidated in 1933	All 1934 returns	
	As classified in 1934 (1)	As classified in 1933 (2)	(3)	As classified in 1934 (4)	On revised classification (5)
Divisions					
All	**1.76**	**1.76**	**1.67**	**1.72**	**1.72**
	5.81	5.81	7.68	6.75	...
	−1.61	*−1.61*	*−5.22*	*−3.13*	...
Agriculture †	**.78**	**2.04**	**−4.47**	**−3.21**	**−2.85**
	4.75	5.49	4.95	4.88	...
	−5.17	*−2.92*	*−9.50*	*−8.80*	...
Mining	**.46**	**.98**	**.91**	**.63**	**.95**
	4.27	4.03	7.19	5.62	...
	−1.63	*−1.04*	*−3.41*	*−2.36*	...
Manufacturing ..	**2.33**	**3.39**	**2.78**	**3.01**	**3.10**
	7.36	7.29	8.99	8.31	...
	−2.49	*−.56*	*−7.20*	*−4.34*	...
Construction ...	**−3.94**	**−1.51**	**−2.64**	**−2.95**	**−2.39**
	4.50	4.24	9.83	8.56	...
	−8.90	*−4.62*	*−10.10*	*−9.82*	...
Public utilities ..	**.88**	**.79**	**3.10**	**1.47**	**1.28**
	4.68	3.97	6.01	5.13	...
	−3.05	*−1.80*	*−4.49*	*−3.30*	...
Trade	**4.60**	**4.07**	**2.52**	**3.05**	**2.92**
	9.49	8.62	8.50	8.77	...
	−7.57	*−3.33*	*−8.89*	*−8.60*	...
Service	**−4.99**	**−3.96**	**−5.92**	**−5.52**	**−5.29**
	7.38	6.95	8.96	8.38	...
	−20.63	*−11.72*	*−13.84*	*−15.09*	...
Finance	**2.38**	**.34**	**.31**	**1.41**	**.32**
	5.24	8.71	6.38	5.76	...
	.79	*−2.41*	*−2.85*	*−.94*	...
Groups					
Foods	**6.14**	**7.81**	**6.13**	**6.13**	**7.03**
	8.15	8.38	9.36	8.84	...
	−3.35	*6.94*	*−7.83*	*−6.01*	...

TABLE LXXIV (*Continued*)

	Returns consolidated in 1933		Returns not consolidated in 1933 (3)	All 1934 returns	
	As classified in 1934 (1)	As classified in 1933 (2)		As classified in 1934 (4)	On revised classification (5)
Liquors	**14.10**	**16.55**	**10.77**	**11.46**	**12.58**
	20.12	20.93	19.24	19.43	...
	−4.86	*7.25*	*−9.83*	*−8.96*	...
Tobacco	**10.76**	**9.01**	**10.49**	**10.50**	**10.38**
	14.14	10.73	11.06	11.18	...
	−2.87	*−3.75*	*−6.41*	*−5.59*	...
Textiles	**−1.78**	**−1.65**	**.95**	**.38**	**.37**
	4.90	4.49	6.95	6.64	...
	−6.68	*−6.14*	*−8.39*	*−7.91*	...
Leather	**1.54**	**1.52**	**3.17**	**2.82**	**2.78**
	4.91	5.53	9.01	8.08	...
	−9.03	*−20.07*	*−11.00*	*−10.63*	...
Rubber	**3.46**	**3.31**	**.07**	**2.75**	**2.67**
	2.27	3.13	6.08	3.22	...
	4.59	*3.50*	*−9.35*	*2.26*	...
Forest products .	**−2.20**	**−1.61**	**−3.34**	**−2.92**	**−2.62**
	4.88	5.20	5.05	5.00	...
	−4.41	*−3.59*	*−7.60*	*−6.32*	...
Paper	**.49**	**.63**	**5.49**	**3.06**	**2.66**
	5.22	5.05	9.67	8.11	...
	−2.73	*−1.71*	*−5.12*	*−3.53*	...
Printing	**−.24**	**2.38**	**5.68**	**3.68**	**4.22**
	7.47	7.67	10.49	9.62	...
	−12.66	*−1.84*	*−10.90*	*−11.72*	...
Chemicals	**1.80**	**3.48**	**8.61**	**3.73**	**4.45**
	6.95	7.80	11.45	9.22	...
	−.77	*.37*	*−8.33*	*−1.37*	...
Stone	**2.72**	**3.40**	**1.06**	**1.64**	**1.92**
	5.69	5.98	7.14	6.55	...
	−5.11	*−1.37*	*−6.74*	*−6.34*	...
Metals	**2.59**	**2.90**	**1.86**	**2.27**	**2.53**
	7.66	6.62	7.06	7.39	...
	−3.10	*−2.35*	*−5.52*	*−4.07*	...
Miscellaneous ...	**3.37**	**5.24**	**2.25**	**2.71**	**3.74**
	12.28	13.64	9.72	10.67	...
	−6.05	*−4.37*	*−9.27*	*−7.77*	...

* Boldface type, both categories combined; ordinary type, income category; italics, deficit.

† See third footnote to Table IX.

among the columns are distorted by the category shifts just discussed. All but one of the four columns, that for which consolidated returns were not previously filed, are affected by such shifts; for even the fourth column, which combines both lists, is affected by shifts in category — from the basis used in 1933 to that used in 1934 — for the very reason that it includes some formerly consolidated corporations. To be sure, a direct comparison between Columns 3 and 4 has some significance even with respect to the rates for the categories separately, but not the same significance as the comparison between Columns 2 and 3 of Table LXXIII wherein the data of Column 3 do reflect allocation to categories of the consolidated returns (making up part of the list covered by Column 3) on a strict consolidated basis.

The changed basis of determining equity in 1934 must also be remembered: for the consolidated returns of 1933, equity is a consolidated equity and probably runs less than the sum of the equities of the subsidiaries; for the 1934 returns which had been consolidated in 1933, the equity is not a consolidated equity but is the sum of the (now separately reported) equities of the subsidiaries.[4] For this reason also, the rates are not comparable with those of Columns 1 and 3 of Table LXXIII. The extent of this change in the basis of equity, and the degree of its effect upon the calculated rates, do not apparently admit of quantitative determination from the data now available.

---

for net income and loss would have been reduced: items in the first two columns of Row 39 on p. 186 would have been numerically smaller than the two corresponding items on p. 162. In fact, they check exactly; and therefore no inter-category shifts were made in the table of p. 186.

[4] I neglect the fact here and elsewhere in this chapter that this list contains some returns which were still filed in 1934 on a consolidated basis — the railroads, and those other (fiscal-year) companies which did not give up consolidated returns until 1935. This is a substantial, but not seriously large, fraction of the list.

PARTIAL RECONSTRUCTION OF 1934 DATA

The analyses reported in earlier chapters of this book, so far as they concern comparisons between 1933 and 1934, are based on data corresponding to Colunm 3 of Table LXXIII and Column 4 of Table LXXIV.[5] It is now evident that such comparisons are distorted, in some cases seriously, by the abandonment of consolidated returns in 1934. The differences between Columns 1 and 2 of Table LXXIII, while not fully measuring the effects under study, indicate that they may be of large magnitude. The lack of parallelism between the 1933–34 changes for the non-consolidated list (Column 2 of Table LXXIII and Column 3 of Table LXXIV) and those for the consolidated list (Column 1 of Table LXXIII, and — though neither is strictly comparable with 1933 — Columns 1 and 2 of Table LXXIV) also emphasizes the probability of distortion. That these distortions may be even more serious for some of the size classes may be taken for granted: the tendency for the consolidated companies to be large implies that the effects under study would be particularly evident in high size classes, if a size classification were available.

It might be suggested that one way to avoid the difficulty is to rest 1933–34 comparisons upon the non-consolidated returns (Column 2 of Table LXXIII and Column 3 of Table LXXIV), on the ground that these figures are free of any distortion due to the change in law. But these figures cover less than two thirds (in terms of importance) of the entire corporation list, and less than half in certain lines of industry; and they run on the average much smaller than the consolidated corporations, and therefore smaller than (on the average) all corporations. A hurried comparison of appropriate columns (confining chief

[5] Such analyses cover also the size classes; but separate size-class data for consolidated returns are not available, with the result that the work of this chapter is limited to classification on an industrial basis.

attention to rates for both categories combined) in the two tables shows that this procedure would deeply alter the indicated 1933–34 changes (as reported in previous chapters) for most lines of industry.[6] But, significant as these indicated alterations may be, the complete elimination of the consolidated returns is no answer to our problem: the consolidated returns constitute too large and too peculiar a section of corporate industry to warrant treating the non-consolidated returns as a representative sample of the entire corporate list.

An alternative suggestion is that the 1934 results (Column 4 of Table LXXIV) be modified by using the classification basis of 1933, and this yields the results shown (for combined categories only, as separate categories are less trustworthy) in Column 5. The figures for net profit (or loss) after tax for 1934 returns not consolidated in 1933, and for those which were consolidated in 1933 classified on the 1933 basis, were added — separately for each category and each line of industry — and the same addition was made for equity.[7] The result was a new set of figures for net profits after tax and equity, differing notably (except for all divisions combined, of course) from those on which Column 4 rests. From these new figures the rates of Column 5 were computed.

That this is only a partial reconstruction of the 1934 results on a basis comparable with 1933 must be emphasized. The two great defects have already been noted, by implication, in earlier pages of this chapter. The reclassification of 1934 data on the 1933 basis refers only to the industrial classification, and does not make the shifts between categories which actual consolidated returns would make.[8] This defect damages the reconstructed

[6] And, if size classifications were available, we should find without doubt notable alterations in the curves relating rate of return to size of corporation.

[7] Data in the source at pages 170–77 and 186–93.

[8] Other possible offsets between items in the income account of a consolidated return are here ignored.

rates for the separate categories, but not for both categories combined (Column 5). The second defect is the basis of reckoning equity: the reclassification of 1934 data did not reconstruct the equity as it would have appeared on a consolidated basis. Hence the denominators used in getting Column 5 are not on a basis comparable with 1933, generally running larger than they would be if strictly consolidated; and this defect damages the rates (not shown) for the separate categories and those for both combined.[9] As already suggested, these two defects may not (probably do not, in many specific consolidated corporations) operate in the same direction, and we may hope that in many cases they partially offset each other.

In any event, it is clear that the results of Column 5 are not a complete reconstruction of 1934 rates on a basis comparable with 1933, and we can not even be sure that they afford an unmistakably better means of comparison than the figures of Column 4. But the very fact that we are uncertain whether Column 4 or Column 5 yields better comparisons with 1933 adds importance to the differences between them: if two equally good — so far as we know — estimates of a single unknown magnitude are available, the presence of a wide discrepancy between them warns us against making precise inferences. Here the differences (except for all divisions combined, figures for which of course were not changed by industrial reclassification) are numerous and in some cases substantial. The one very large difference is for the finance division; but substantial differences appear for such groups as foods, printing, and chemicals. In general, however, the differences are not large; and, if it were not for the two defects of unknown magnitude out-

[9] I neglect here a joint consequence of the two defects. By the method used for reckoning average equity for the year, the net profit or loss shares in determining the actual equity figure used in the denominator of the rate. Hence the rates for separate categories in Column 5 suffer further damage on this account.

lined above, we should infer that Column 5 largely substantiates Column 4 and suggests the validity of 1933–34 comparisons based upon Column 4.

Nevertheless, the possibility that the two defects noted above — really only the second defect, that in the equity, is significant for the rates for income and deficit categories combined — may influence the calculated rates in serious degree must not be overlooked. While the results of Column 5 strengthen my confidence that 1933–34 comparisons, as reported in previous chapters for entire divisions and groups, are tolerably trustworthy, the reader is cautioned that concealed errors of significant magnitude may exist in such comparisons. This applies also, of course, to comparisons of years after 1934 with 1933 and earlier years. I further believe that the danger of error is even greater for separate size classes, because it seems probable that the defects noted may work with particular force in certain size ranges. How extensive these errors are will perhaps never be determined, because the compilation of needed information seems very improbable; and we must continue to regard the time comparisons of the profits data as subject to a break, and possibly a serious break, in homogeneity in 1934.

MAGNITUDE OF THE SHIFTS

As a final batch of evidence in this chapter, some indications can be given of the size of the changes in make-up of different divisions and groups, resulting from the legal change in 1934. *Statistics of Income* publishes an informing table indicating the number of corporations gained or lost by specific divisions or groups, as a result of the 1934 abandonment of consolidated returns, and giving specifically the divisions and groups in which the corporations of a particular division or group in 1934 had been classified in 1933.[10] Inferences from this table as to gains or losses, in number of corporations, for particular

[10] Part 2 of 1934 issue, pp. 25–27.

divisions or groups are clear: because the table gives the actual number of corporations in each division or group as they were classified on each basis, that for 1934 and that for 1933. But a general difficulty limits any interpretation of these figures: the *number* of companies is no fair index of importance; and, although the consolidated systems are generally large, the subsidiaries of such systems may differ widely in size. Any satisfactory study of the importance of the shifts which took place must therefore rest upon a more informing figure than mere number of corporations.

Selection of such a figure from the accounting items is not easy; for 1933–34 was a time of extensive and diverse cyclical and irregular changes in industry, and any reconstruction of 1934 data according to 1933 classification would give no trustworthy indication of the 1933 levels — actual or comparative — of those data. Moreover, certain accounting items were subjected to actual changes by the abandonment of consolidated returns. Thus, investments other than tax-exempt were about 26 billion dollars for the consolidated returns in 1933, but over 47 billions in 1934 for the corporations which had been covered by consolidated returns in 1933. While some of this change may have reflected actual purchases (partially offset by sales) of securities by these corporations, the great bulk of the change reflects merely the listing as investments of intercorporate holdings of securities formerly offset in the consolidated returns. Similar, but perhaps less striking, changes appear in numerous other items; and the aggregate effect of such changes is a large change in total assets, and net effects appear also in such residual items as equity.

If we ignore the implied 1933 levels, however, numerous accounting items are available for testing the importance of shifts in classification (only according to industry, however) in 1934. Such an item is total assets, and the shifts in terms of this figure are shown in Table LXXV. Here the results are reported only for both categories combined because, as previously noted, the "reclassification" applied to 1934 data reassigned them (on the 1933 basis) by industrial lines but did not reassign them as between income and deficit categories. Very large absolute changes appear in the manufacturing and finance divisions and

TABLE LXXV

ESTIMATED NET REDUCTION (−) OR INCREASE (+) IN TOTAL ASSETS DUE TO THE RECLASSIFICATION OF 1934 FOLLOWING ABANDONMENT OF CONSOLIDATED RETURNS *

Divisions:		Groups (*continued*):	
Agriculture	33,601	Tobacco	−58,822
Mining	198,267	Textiles	−69,599
Manufacturing	−14,103,027	Leather	−70,476
Construction	75,987	Rubber	−175,956
Public utilities	−15,529,668	Forest products	−156,632
Trade	782,683	Paper	−496,885
Service	−131,830	Printing	−523,592
Finance	28,766,673	Chemicals	−5,163,086
Groups:		Stone	−77,339
Foods	−1,432,508	Metals	−5,374,232
Liquors	−123,219	Miscellaneous	−380,663

* In thousands of dollars.

in several manufacturing groups, and important percentage changes appear in numerous other divisions and groups. The indicated relative changes differ somewhat according as the base figure for the ratio is taken from the assets figure for the "consolidated" list or from that for the total list of all corporations whether consolidated or not. Manifestly the abandonment of consolidated returns caused a heavy loss of assets to the manufacturing division, and a heavy gain to finance. Such a statement must be qualified, however, by remembering the points raised above: the 1934 assets, classified on the 1933 basis, are not comparable with the 1933 assets. Moreover, these figures showing changes are *net* figures: a much greater shifting of assets probably occurred, but some shifts into a single division (or group) were matched by shifts outward. Only the unmatched shifts contribute to the changes shown in the table.

In this sense, the present figures (and those reported later in this chapter) are less satisfactory than the published figures on number of corporations affected by the shifts. Moreover, unlike the special tabulation of corporations by number, these figures give no key as to specific shifts: they do not show from what divisions (on the 1933 basis) the 1934 increase in assets of a particular division came. Thus, we may not infer that because manufacturing lost heavily in assets, and finance gained heavily, the bulk of the shift was from manufacturing to finance. The figures might have resulted if a huge shift from manufacturing to trade, and one from trade to finance, had occurred. Without doubt, a substantial shift did occur from manufacturing to finance, but no clear evidence of the magnitude of this shift can be secured from the data.[11]

In case we desire comparisons, similar to that of Table LXXV, which are free or tolerably free from the actual changes in accounting items — such as the change in non-tax-exempt investments — caused by the abandonment of consolidated returns, no accounting figure like total assets is acceptable. Several items, in either the balance sheet or the income account, may be suggested as tolerably free from the offsets incident to consolidated returns. Several such items were examined: net capital assets, inventories, tax-exempt investments, compensation of officers, depreciation, depletion, and taxes (other than Federal). Some of these may in very small degree be affected by offsets; but all of them are nearly free of such influences,

[11] In a limited way, however, much can be accomplished in this direction by studying some of the other accounting items. Thus, shifts into the mining division can be traced in part, but by no means precisely, from the depletion figures; and, less satisfactorily, rent paid supplies a helpful key for trade. But, broadly speaking, we can make no satisfactory appraisal of the "origin" and "destination" of the corporations which were shifted.

and some of them completely so. But nearly all of these figures do have another flaw for the present purpose: each of them, perhaps without exception, is of greater significance in

TABLE LXXVI

ESTIMATED NET REDUCTION (−) OR INCREASE (+) IN NET CAPITAL ASSETS AND IN INVENTORIES DUE TO THE 1934 RECLASSIFICATION *

	Net capital assets	Inventories
Divisions:		
Agriculture	68,997	5,373
Mining	652,668	−26,248
Manufacturing	−2,438,540	−292,718
Construction	77,295	12,257
Public utilities	−28,639	−100,211
Trade	26,064	494,233
Service	358,872	−2,075
Finance	1,318,612	3,916
Groups:		
Foods	−169,767	−44,613
Liquors	−2,213	−14,453
Tobacco	−4,186	−1,065
Textiles	11,275	5,866
Leather	−18,515	−12,393
Rubber	−40,754	−9,682
Forest products	−44,521	−3,706
Paper	−64,720	−4,954
Printing	−64,908	−1,724
Chemicals	−789,968	−141,455
Stone	18,797	4,068
Metals	−1,222,923	−71,113
Miscellaneous	−46,139	2,508

* In thousands of dollars.

some lines of industry than in others. Such figures are therefore not satisfactory measures of importance as among industries,[12] though each such figure may be definitely better than the mere number of corporations. The various results of these

[12] On a percentage basis, these difficulties are somewhat reduced.

tests are not reported in full; but Table LXXVI gives the figures for the two most satisfactory tests, net capital assets and inventories. Both series show heavy losses for the manufacturing division and most of its groups. Inventories show a far more important gain for trade, on a percentage basis, than does net capital assets; and the reverse statement applies to finance. Perhaps some composite of these various items, which are not affected by offsets in consolidated returns, could be worked out, and would provide a test of the comparative importance of shifts among divisions not distorted by the peculiar significance of such composite to any one line of industry. I see no satisfactorily simple or logically sound way of developing such a composite, and am content to neglect it because its availability would still leave unanswered the crucial questions as to where a shift started and where it ended and as to the degree to which net figures conceal gross shifts some of which are matched in opposite directions. I leave the evidence in this incompletely digested form with the single conclusion, supported by all the evidence, that the 1934 change in tax law brought a huge shift among industries, in assets and indeed in various items of the balance sheet and income account.

XXVIII

TECHNICAL POINTS

THE PRESENT CHAPTER includes descriptive and explanatory remarks on several technical points raised in the general treatment of foregoing chapters. Less general points have been discussed from time to time as they arose.

AVERAGE EQUITY FOR THE YEAR

The denominator figure is a somewhat imperfect estimate of the average equity for the year. It rests upon one item which is known from the published tabulations, the equity at the end of the year, and one item which is estimated, the equity at the beginning of the year. Even if the beginning-year equity were not subject to errors in estimating, taking average equity as the simple mean of the beginning-year and end-year figures would not be entirely satisfactory. The course of change in equity during the year may not be along the straight line from the beginning-year to the end-year level which this simple average implies; it may in fact depart notably from such a line, particularly in cases involving issuance or retirement of stock. No evidence exists permitting an adequate allowance for this non-linearity; and the method used is the best available makeshift, but is subject to a considerable possible error.

In any case, the beginning-year equity is merely an estimate, and is liable to particularly important errors in years when issuance or retirement of stock bulks large or revaluations of assets are numerous and substantial. The estimate of beginning-year equity has admittedly taken account of only two factors which can change the equity during the year — net earnings (or loss) after taxes, and dividends paid. The former is an addition to, and the latter a subtraction from, the beginning-year equity in passing to the end-year figure. No satisfactory estimate could be made for the other factors — chiefly changes in amount of stock outstanding through issuance or retirement, and revaluations of assets — which may change equity during the year. These factors manifestly are likely to operate with different force in different years. Particularly with reference to revaluations, much evidence exists that the early years of the six-year period under study must have been marked by extensive changes.

If allowance could have been made for these factors, the calculated rates of return would certainly have been more precise. That significant changes in the indicated cyclical course of rates of return might have resulted seems entirely likely; and probably indicated differences in level of rate, especially between 1936 and 1931, would have been altered. That significant changes in the indicated relation between the rate of return and size would have appeared seems less likely. To establish a probability of such changes, we should have to premise that the factors not allowed for are more influential in certain size classes than others. If, for example, downward revaluations of assets were more important relatively in high size classes than in low, the beginning-year estimates of equity would run too small in both sizes but more so for the high than for the low. Hence, our rates of return run too large for both sizes, but more so for the high than for the low. This implies that our rates of return show too great an increase with increase of size. No clear evidence exists, however, on the question concerning unequal importance of revaluations in different size classes. We may suspect the differential is as suggested above, but our opinion is perhaps prejudiced by the accident that revaluations by prominent companies get into the financial news.

So far as the two adjustments which *were* made in estimating beginning-year equity are concerned, the clear effect was to reduce the indicated increase of rate of return with size. In other words, if we had used end-year equity as the denominator of the rate of return, the indicated increase of rate with size would have been greater than that shown in the charts. The chief reason for this, of course, is that the aggregate net loss of the corporations of the lowest size class is so considerable a fraction of the equity that its application to the end-year equity, in getting the beginning-year figure, necessarily produces a large change. The dividends-paid adjustment seems to have had less bearing on the outcome, though even this factor produced in some cases a comparatively greater change in equity for small corporations than for large.

It may be suggested that comparison of the actual equity for the end of one year with the estimated equity for the beginning of the following year would disclose the extent of the effects upon equity due to the factors for which no allowance was made. At best, this device is clearly effective only for all divisions combined (with both categories combined), and even in this case possible error enters because of the entrance of new corporations and disappearance of old corporations (in the tabulations) from one year to another. For the separate divisions and groups, the comparison is still less trustworthy, because of shifts in industrial classification. This is emphatically clear in comparing 1933 with 1934, because of classification shifts resulting from the abandonment of consolidated returns. Comparisons limited to specific size classes are even less useful because of shifts of corporations, between one year and the next, from size class to size class. Finally, such comparisons for either income or deficit category separately are practically worthless, because of the very large annual shifts of corporations between the categories.

Ignoring therefore the classification by size and category, we present in Table LXXVII the tabulated end-year equity for comparison with the estimated equity at the beginning of the following year, in the cases of all divisions combined and each division and each group. Only five comparisons are available in each case, as no figure for the end of 1930 was tabulated and none for the beginning of 1937 could be estimated.

The record for all divisions combined shows the end-year equity higher than the estimated equity of the next year in every case except 1933. In that case, the excess of the beginning-year equity of 1934 over the end-year equity of 1933 can be ascribed entirely to the abandonment of consolidated returns in 1934. That legal change, through the elimination of offsets formerly made among the subsidiaries of a consolidated system, greatly increased the reported equity for 1934. We can not be sure that beginning-year equity of 1934, if it had been reported on the former basis, would have been below the end-year equity of 1933; but very strong reason exists for believing so. Similarly, the smallness of the indicated difference between the 1934 end-year and the 1935 beginning-year figures may be ascribed to the change in the law: abandonment of consolidated returns did not go into effect until 1935 for certain fiscal-year companies. The three other comparisons show substantial differences all in the same direction: estimated beginning-year equity is below the actual end-year figure of the preceding year. Waiving changes in coverage of the tabulations — new corporations entering and old corporations leaving the list — these facts indicate clearly that our estimating method neglected in these years factors which together would have *raised* the beginning-year estimates. The most probable explanation is in downward revaluations of assets — omission of allowance for such revaluations in our estimates would render those estimates too low.

Consideration of the similar figures for various divisions and groups reveals mainly like tendencies, although irregularities in particular years appear in certain groups and divisions. In general, the indications for separate divisions and groups are

TABLE LXXVII

Comparison of Equity at End of Each Year with Corresponding-Class Equity at Beginning of Following Year *

	End of year	Beginning of next year		End of year	Beginning of next year
	All divisions combined			Agriculture	
1931	143,262	141,215	1931	1,348	1,430
1932	133,569	131,725	1932	1,339	1,248
1933	127,578	143,947	1933	1,206	1,455
1934	141,586	140,049	1934	1,384	1,344
1935	138,931	134,157	1935	1,322	1,299
	Mining			Manufacturing	
1931	7,340	7,283	1931	47,640	46,868
1932	6,988	6,755	1932	43,976	44,204
1933	6,506	7,360	1933	43,341	38,577
1934	7,141	6,764	1934	38,155	37,656
1935	6,557	6,585	1935	37,611	38,284
	Construction			Public utilities	
1931	1,259	1,252	1931	36,875	36,885
1932	1,124	1,078	1932	35,828	35,027
1933	997	956	1933	34,192	34,623
1934	905	857	1934	33,915	33,131
1935	826	819	1935	32,363	30,520
	Trade			Service	
1931	11,446	11,158	1931	3,472	4,240
1932	10,174	10,124	1932	3,790	3,245
1933	9,886	10,569	1933	2,940	2,980
1934	10,498	10,339	1934	2,758	2,901
1935	10,285	10,425	1935	2,716	3,534
	Finance			Foods	
1931	33,750	31,994	1931	5,133	5,148
1932	30,253	29,977	1932	4,930	4,484
1933	28,448	47,407	1933	4,465	4,067
1934	46,813	47,041	1934	4,064	3,881
1935	47,242	42,692	1935	3,905	3,971
	Liquors			Tobacco	
1931	...	...	1931	950	917
1932	...	...	1932	942	939
1933	566	563	1933	898	872
1934	605	644	1934	867	841
1935	666	773	1935	847	841

TABLE LXXVII (*Continued*)

	End of year	Beginning of next year		End of year	Beginning of next year
	Textiles			Leather	
1931	3,848	3,799	1931	1,033	699
1932	3,463	3,445	1932	636	622
1933	3,479	3,460	1933	626	562
1934	3,375	3,343	1934	556	561
1935	3,306	3,263	1935	573	570
	Rubber			Forest products	
1931	822	790	1931	2,065	2,120
1932	739	750	1932	1,907	1,882
1933	747	776	1933	1,799	1,695
1934	781	650	1934	1,613	1,582
1935	659	648	1935	1,535	1,542
	Paper			Printing	
1931	1,778	1,802	1931	1,961	2,006
1932	1,717	1,681	1932	1,909	1,888
1933	1,666	1,592	1933	1,861	1,627
1934	1,593	1,551	1934	1,605	1,602
1935	1,555	1,509	1935	1,609	1,655
	Chemicals			Stone	
1931	11,424	10,888	1931	1,674	1,638
1932	10,549	10,233	1932	1,516	1,497
1933	9,997	7,832	1933	1,452	1,449
1934	7,776	7,995	1934	1,428	1,450
1935	7,892	8,225	1935	1,446	1,458
	Metals			Miscellaneous Manufacturing	
1931	15,770	15,573	1931	1,502	1,490
1932	14,319	14,951	1932	1,347	1,298
1933	14,552	12,970	1933	1,237	1,114
1934	12,788	12,492	1934	1,102	1,065
1935	12,555	12,729	1935	1,066	1,100

* Unit: millions of dollars. End-year figure compiled from source, beginning-year figure estimated.

less consistent than for all divisions combined; and this probably follows in part from changes in industrial classification.

LOGARITHMIC SCALE OF THE CHARTS

The horizontal scale of every chart shown in the book, except where that scale is a time scale, is logarithmic. This choice was made for a mechanical reason: the size classes are very narrow at the low end and very wide at the high end, and a scale which would show the desired detail at the low end without stretching too far to the right therefore had to be chosen. The result is to give a different appearance to the curves from that which would appear on an arithmetic scale: in general, the curvature is decreased at the low end of the size scale and increased at the high end. Moreover, the change in level of the curve per lateral inch of chart is less at the low end and more at the high end than it would appear on an arithmetic scale in a chart of equal width. In other words, a visual examination of the chart, without careful attention to the scale, is likely to give a false impression of the change in level of rate per unit (say $50,000) of size — an impression of change too small at the low end and too great at the high end. It must be concluded that most of the charts imply only an exceedingly gradual change of rate of return with size above some intermediate level, say above $500,000.

In the actual plotting, of course, no zero of the horizontal scale could be shown; and the left boundary of the charts is therefore not the bottom (zero) of the lowest size class, but was taken at $1000. In any one class interval, except the top class, the rate pertinent to that class was assumed to apply to the arithmetic mid-point of the class — the simple mean of the two boundaries of the class. In the actual chart, such a point appears slightly to the right of the apparent mid-point of the interval, because of the progressive compression of the logarithmic scale toward the right. The assumption that the class rate applies to the arithmetic mid-point of the class is generally not valid, especially as most of the evidence indicates that these frequency distributions of corporations according to size of assets are skewed so greatly as to be practically if not precisely *J*-shaped. For such a distribution the arithmetic mid-point is too high an estimate of the "center of gravity" of a class. It might have been preferable to calculate, for each class, the average assets in the class — dividing the total assets of the class by the number of corporations. These averages would undoubtedly have differed from industry to industry, from year to year, and between the income and deficit categories; and in general the result would have been a small and irregular shift of the curves toward the left. Although this would undoubtedly have yielded a more nearly accurate picture, certain disadvantages in having the corresponding points for different industries, years, and categories fall at different points on the horizontal scale led to the adoption of the cruder method.

The single exception pertains to the top size class. Here, as no upper boundary is known, the simple scheme used for other classes could not be used.[1] Instead, in all these cases, the point of the horizontal scale to be used in plotting was taken as the average per corporation of the aggregate assets in the top class. This explains why in many of the charts, even where none of the high size classes are grouped together in the official tabulations, the horizontal position of the right end of the curve varies from year to year. In 1936, of course, another factor enters: in that year the over-50-million class is broken into two new classes, one up to 100 millions, the other above 100 millions. The plotted point for the latter is necessarily

[1] Strictly, the maximum value of the upper limit can be determined in each case. Thus if six corporations fall in the 50-million-and-over class, and have aggregate assets of 365 millions, no one of the six can have above 115 millions. But to assume one of them is that large is to imply a degree of *J*-shapedness perhaps even greater than that suggested by most of the data.

farther right than would be the single point for the two classes combined on the former basis.

In all cases in which the Treasury tabulations group together two or more high classes to conceal the data of a single corporation the same rule applies. The "and over" class then reaches down to the bottom, on the size scale, of the classes thus grouped; and, for this compound "and over" class, average assets per corporation determined the horizontal location of the plotted point. This explains why the right ends of some of the curves for smaller divisions and groups appear at irregularly located points well below the top of the size scale.

GROUPED SIZE CLASSES

The combination, in official tabulations, of two or more high size classes in order to conceal the accounting data of a single company is a fairly common defect in the data for our purposes. Such combinations occur chiefly in the smaller divisions or groups, for all larger divisions or groups generally have two or more companies in each category in the top size class. The combinations, even for a particular group or division, vary from year to year and between categories. Thus, data for one year may contain a classes-grouped case while data for another year may not, in a particular division or group. And the income category may contain a classes-grouped case while the deficit category does not, in any one year.

Broadly speaking, we have made the maximum possible use of the data. A category which had no grouping, whereas the other category did, was studied with respect to the given classes separately; and the summary tables of rates (see, for example, Table XVII) give the full detail. Figures for both categories combined, however, must carry classes-grouped as far down the size scale as the grouping extends in either category. Hence, in the summary tables, the classes-grouped figure for the combined categories in any one year reaches as far down on the size scale as that for the category (among the two) which reaches farther down. Generally, in such cases, a classes-grouped figure does not appear for the other category; but for that category rates pertinent to the separate classes are shown. Where a classes-grouped figure appears for each category, it may be assumed that it reaches down to the top of the highest size class showing a separate rate figure in that category.

In a few cases, no corporation appeared in the top size class, for one category or the other; and, although these cases probably cause no false impressions in the tabulations, they can be identified by inference or by examining the source tabulations.

In a very small number of cases, the official tabulations skip a class in reaching back to make up the classes-grouped combination. Thus, separate figures may be tabulated for the 10–50-million-dollar class, whereas the 5–10-million-dollar class and the over-50-million-dollar class are grouped. In such cases, the only satisfactory procedure has been to include the isolated class in "classes grouped" — in the illustration given, the entire range above five million dollars is called a grouped class. This sacrifices slightly the detail which might be presented from the available record, but such presentation would be misleading because the isolated class is *within* the size range of the two grouped classes.

Finally, in making up six-year averages of rates, grouping of classes had to be carried as far down the scale in every year as it reached in any year, for each particular division or group. The result is that such charts obscure considerably the detail available annually near the right ends of the curves. An example appears in Chart XXVI.

SIX-YEAR AVERAGES OF RATES

In showing summary comparisons between divisions and between groups in Chapter III, a single curve for each division and group — to be fairly typical of all six years — was desired. After some experimentation, simple averaging of the six annual rates of each size class was chosen as the means of securing the typical figure. This same method was used also in the summary comparisons (like Chart IV) of income and deficit categories with each other and with both combined. The warrant for this procedure is open to examination.

In effect, the procedure accepts the corporations actually in a size class (each category separately) in a particular year as a sample of corporations in that size class, and treats the six annual samples as equally good in yielding "observations" on the rate of return for the class. As the year-to-year variation in rate is wide in many cases, the six observations have rather wide dispersion, and the average figure is therefore not highly trustworthy as a typical summary number. This defect is probably greater for the separate categories than for both combined, and for low size classes than for high.

An alternative procedure might have rested upon weighted averages of the six annual rates: the six figures for profits after taxes might have been summed, and divided by the sum of the six equity figures. In general, this would result in giving low weight to low (or high negative) rates, and high weight to high rates; because equity tends to run larger as profits run larger. This effect, again, would be most noticeable when the categories are considered separately. This technical bias in the weighting was regarded as adequate reason for abandoning the weighted averages in favor of simple means of the six annual rates.

The simple means are admittedly, however, not highly precise typical figures; and the inferences drawn from the six-year average curves should accordingly be carefully qualified. The summary figures do, in many cases, largely eliminate the irregularities appearing in individual size classes in particular years, and yield accordingly a fairly smooth curve giving a simplified impression of the relation between rate of return and size.

Such smoothness is nevertheless merely a helpful guide, and probably does not portray reality.

SPECIAL SUMMARY DEVICES

Examination was made of several analytical devices which might summarize the findings along lines apparently more simplified, and perhaps more readily seen if not understood. The outcome of these tests was not sufficiently satisfying to justify their systematic use in the main chapters, but two of them are mentioned here as mere suggestions of possible further technical steps — apart from economic interpretation — in the analysis of rates of return.

TABLE LXXVIII

COMPARISON OF RATES OF RETURN FOR ALL DIVISIONS COMBINED, IN 1935, WITH LOGARITHMS OF LOGARITHMS OF CENTERS OF SIZE CLASSES

Lower limit of class * (a)	Center of class † (b)	Log of b (c)	Log of c (d)	Rate of return ‡ (e)
0	25	1.3979	.1455	−10.77
50	75	1.8751	.2730	−1.24
100	175	2.2430	.3508	.70
250	375	2.5740	.4106	1.81
500	750	2.8751	.4587	2.07
1,000	3,000	3.4771	.5412	2.87
5,000	7,500	3.8751	.5883	2.90
10,000	30,000	4.4771	.6510	4.29
50,000	211,000	5.3243	.7262	4.33

* In thousands of dollars.

† Averages of lower and upper limit, except in top class where it is average assets per corporation, in thousands of dollars.

‡ From Table II.

The shape of the typical curve on the logarithmic scale (for example, any curve of Chart I, except those for 1933 and 1936) suggested that plotting on a log-log scale (this, be it noted, is different from a so-called double-log chart) might convert the curve nearly to a straight line. Considering the 1935 case for all divisions (and both categories) combined, we have the pertinent facts in Table LXXVIII. Plotting a chart with Column *d* measured horizontally and Column *e* vertically (both scales arithmetic) will show that linearity is not yet even approximately realized. Similar tests applied to certain divisions and groups also failed to produce linearity, although the curvature shown in the main charts of the book was of course generally reduced.

TABLE LXXIX

RATES OF RETURN FOR CLASSES CUMULATED FROM THE BOTTOM, ALL DIVISIONS COMBINED, IN 1935

Upper limit of cumulated classes *	Cumulative net profits after taxes †	Cumulative equity †	Rate of return
50	−200.1	1,857	−10.77
100	−227.3	4,059	−5.60
250	−194.5	8,773	−2.22
500	−103.7	13,804	−.75
1,000	25.3	20,050	.13
5,000	567.4	38,959	1.46
10,000	852.4	48,738	1.75
50,000	1,902.5	73,234	2.60
None	4,778.1	139,540	3.43

* Unit: $1,000.
† Unit: $1,000,000.

The second device tested consisted in calculating rates of return for cumulative classes, beginning with the bottom. Thus, the lowest class and the next were combined by adding their figures for profits after taxes and for equity; and the corresponding rate of return was calculated by dividing the first of these sums by the second. Then the third class from the bottom of the size scale was added in, and so on. These computations are illustrated, for all divisions combined in 1935, in Table LXXIX. The final column shows, in each figure, the average rate of return for *all* corporations *below* the size limit shown at the left. The possibility that rates calculated on this cumulative basis, when appropriately plotted, might conform to some simple type of curve — possibly a nearly straight line — or suggest some other simple relationship was not realized in this case. The test has not been applied to other years for all divisions combined, or to separate divisions and groups in any year; and I merely notice the method here as one of the possible devices worthy of further examination.

APPENDIX

Certain tabulations which bear upon the foregoing analysis in general, or upon particular parts thereof, are brought together here to avoid inserting them at particular points in the main treatment. Table A presents the basic estimates of Federal taxes by size classes, which were needed in order to derive the numerator of our rate-of-return figure from the published data on profits or losses. The method of securing these estimates is explained in Chapter XXVI.

Table B presents the six-year averages of rates of return, which were used in making the series of charts (like Chart IV) which compare income and deficit categories with each other and with both combined.

Table C presents 1936 rates of return for the two new groups into which each of three old groups — metals, chemicals, and textiles — was divided for the first time in that year.

TABLE A

FINAL TAX ESTIMATE, TO BE DEDUCTED FROM COMPILED NET PROFIT OR LOSS TO OBTAIN NUMERATOR OF RATE-OF-RETURN RATIO *

I. INDUSTRIAL DIVISIONS

Size Class †	1931	1932	1933	1934	1935	1936 Und. prof.	1936 Other
			AGRICULTURE				
0	35	40	98	134	181	24	164
50	40	40	82	144	199	37	255
100	127	86	211	429	450	81	586
250	144	80	155	361	436	67	520
500	147	96	211	335	494	94	777
1,000	...	141	...	805	1,658	222	1,898
5,000	...	...	...	549	850	117	1,003
10,000	...	...	...	...	...	...	...
50,000	...	...	...	...	...	...	...
100,000	...	...	...	...	...	...	...
Grouped	666	164	1,362	1,430	1,784	313	2,583
Error §	54	77	−37	2	78	§§	901
			MINING				
0	92	261	440	683	614	67	630
50	116	242	287	678	641	58	562
100	421	531	891	1,566	1,453	141	1,416
250	640	599	791	1,723	1,756	167	1,815
500	792	845	1,113	1,999	1,994	174	2,000
1,000	1,861	1,718	2,539	4,520	4,559	514	6,115
5,000	443	817	1,104	2,094	1,817	292	3,468
10,000	2,265	1,668	...	5,910	6,033	688	7,928
50,000	433	662	...	2,355	2,987	374	4,099
100,000	...	...	...	...	...	462	5,110
Grouped	...	...	2,727	...	...	...	...
Error §	−8	690	−38	−66	295	§§	4,264
			MANUFACTURING				
0	588	897	1,980	3,232	3,586	607	3,514
50	1,167	1,143	2,858	4,406	5,140	887	5,286
100	3,936	3,167	8,190	11,404	14,358	2,536	15,732
250	5,741	4,082	10,638	14,739	18,299	3,235	21,675
500	8,064	5,476	14,505	19,703	25,927	4,461	31,613
1,000	23,342	14,685	38,386	52,805	72,494	13,477	99,307
5,000	13,694	9,577	20,025	26,561	32,686	6,618	48,694
10,000	33,032	19,070	45,510	54,228	77,901	14,933	106,470
50,000	74,538	41,432	63,627	75,466	104,404	5,907	39,964
100,000	...	...	...	...	...	20,779	141,574
Grouped	...	...	...	...	...	...	...
Error §	−2,031	809	−689	−355	−3,765	§§	17,718

NOTE. For footnotes, see p. 404.

TABLE A (*Continued*)

Size Class †	1931	1932	1933	1934	1935	1936 Und. prof.	1936 Other
			CONSTRUCTION				
0	153	149	173	333	475	140	559
50	261	161	183	328	526	163	672
100	897	356	346	578	893	292	1,256
250	1,107	441	336	736	804	298	1,383
500	1,275	343	349	472	814	297	1,461
1,000	2,497	1,017	907	1,340	2,817	520	2,659
5,000	262	...	119	396	...	149	758
10,000	...	...	621	286	...	119	589
50,000	...	...	...	...	...	...	...
100,000	...	...	...	...	...	...	...
Grouped	1,010	1,006	...	...	996	...	...
Error §	−69	292	−89	−78	−384	§§	9
			PUBLIC UTILITIES				
0	226	451	779	1,075	1,226	64	1,007
50	315	425	624	878	1,156	58	947
100	780	968	1,089	1,933	2,581	140	2,365
250	1,086	1,032	1,108	1,977	2,592	131	2,397
500	1,249	1,518	1,558	2,997	3,367	184	3,559
1,000	4,345	5,104	5,373	10,769	11,316	546	10,954
5,000	4,366	3,752	3,943	6,704	6,285	395	7,926
10,000	14,852	14,859	14,501	29,664	30,807	1,634	31,746
50,000	77,213	69,151	63,070	69,820	66,234	832	15,361
100,000	...	...	...	...	...	4,400	81,786
Grouped	...	...	...	...	...	...	...
Error §	−1,104	−2,599	552	604	2,551	§§	16,538
			TRADE				
0	1,033	1,346	3,679	5,669	6,003	2,072	6,602
50	1,340	1,078	3,191	5,165	6,226	1,734	7,109
100	2,917	2,031	5,780	9,566	11,273	2,801	14,140
250	2,877	2,144	5,401	8,117	9,886	2,387	13,393
500	2,788	2,270	5,751	8,834	9,563	2,313	14,186
1,000	6,907	4,542	11,041	17,664	20,728	5,279	31,053
5,000	3,491	2,777	4,078	7,873	7,795	2,380	1,630
10,000	5,890	4,350	7,128	12,730	14,327	1,265	24,752
50,000	17,951	9,777	15,657	17,659	21,666	562	10,383
100,000	...	...	...	...	...	3,760	19,604
Grouped	...	...	...	...	...	...	...
Error §	−156	−57	−217	−307	1,068	−7,168	−7,527

NOTE. For footnotes, see p. 404.

TABLE A (*Continued*)

Size Class †	1931	1932	1933	1934	1935	1936 Und. prof.	1936 Other
			SERVICE				
0	406	622	933	1,845	2,277	562	2,329
50	444	453	683	1,114	1,539	392	1,667
100	1,097	907	1,094	2,020	2,549	645	2,857
250	1,433	979	1,144	1,681	2,234	555	2,652
500	1,351	978	859	1,474	2,034	558	2,819
1,000	2,393	1,680	1,843	3,987	4,875	1,458	7,651
5,000	1,039	710	625	808	861	211	1,106
10,000	...	...	...	738	...	...	...
50,000	...	...	...	1,202	...	...	...
100,000	...	...	...	...	...	...	...
Grouped	2,713	1,871	1,363	...	1,439	941	4,762
Error §	−552	−193	−33	−4	163	§§	3,566
			FINANCE				
0	534	930	1,230	1,614	2,311	365	2,716
50	972	1,033	1,245	1,765	2,002	423	2,098
100	2,954	2,331	2,874	3,777	5,215	836	6,489
250	3,513	2,435	2,517	3,373	4,818	961	6,696
500	3,658	2,427	2,836	3,665	5,036	1,374	8,088
1,000	10,301	5,801	6,907	9,979	13,561	6,921	19,837
5,000	4,976	3,011	2,763	5,332	6,975	2,890	13,028
10,000	10,017	6,049	7,239	14,325	20,390	7,617	29,743
50,000	15,672	10,760	5,912	15,291	20,319	652	18,860
100,000	...	...	...	...	...	1,533	5,041
Grouped	...	...	...	...	...	...	...
Error §	3,789	996	530	229	40	§§	−12,243
			II. MANUFACTURING GROUPS				
			FOODS ‡				
0	150	268	298	474	432	142	428
50	314	317	435	735	618	174	677
100	987	693	1,141	1,834	1,826	305	1,847
250	1,332	990	1,544	2,215	2,255	399	2,505
500	1,801	1,317	1,685	2,538	2,792	554	3,249
1,000	3,896	2,826	4,642	7,150	9,347	1,244	9,080
5,000	2,932	1,914	2,480	4,356	4,576	557	3,674
10,000	6,949	5,584	8,836	9,631	11,957	936	12,087
50,000	18,329	11,229	16,239	13,235	11,124	735	8,305
100,000	...	...	...	...	...	41	9,814
Grouped	...	...	...	...	...	...	...
Error §	−466	1,376	−93	−313	−102	−1,468	1,634

NOTE. For footnotes, see p. 404.

TABLE A (*Continued*)

Size Class †	1931	1932	1933	1934	1935	1936 Und. prof.	1936 Other
			LIQUORS				
0			213	381	464	69	488
50			191	407	371	83	527
100			624	767	897	174	1,022
250			844	1,210	1,429	297	1,448
500			1,775	2,054	1,826	556	2,317
1,000	NO DATA	NO DATA	3,622	4,937	5,684	2,121	7,184
5,000			645	1,400	1,791	828	2,332
10,000			2,565	1,943	3,242	...	...
50,000			...	...	...	...	...
100,000			...	...	...	...	...
Grouped			...	...	...	788	7,347
Error §			−208	−151	−308	−1,496	327
			TOBACCO				
0	3	7	21	5	6	...	9
50	3	5	11	22	26	...	9
100	40	43	41	44	44	2	44
250	18	16	6	32	29	2	46
500	46	11	14	14	27	1	52
1,000	661	466	433	508	670	20	727
5,000	257	517	452	416	192	7	256
10,000	1,640	1,949	1,776	2,460	2,811	99	3,543
50,000	14,395	16,038	6,187	9,722	9,884	...	...
100,000	...	...	...	...	...	...	...
Grouped	...	...	...	...	...	385	13,048
Error §	−248	−267	228	83	340	§§	−833
			TEXTILES **				
0	88	106	377	360	420	74	186
50	146	153	584	555	608	102	325
100	439	400	1,570	1,349	1,592	318	1,084
250	702	604	2,298	1,823	2,296	401	1,719
500	987	694	3,135	2,510	3,009	682	3,078
1,000	2,607	1,645	8,863	6,347	7,658	1,856	9,111
5,000	535	425	2,760	...	1,844	779	3,581
10,000	...	...	...	4,450	5,678	983	8,672
50,000	...	...	...	...	1,350	135	1,895
100,000	...	...	...	...	...	...	...
Grouped	1,809	1,006	9,143	2,220	...	...	...
Error §	479	258	32	38	46	−1,158	−163

NOTE. For footnotes, see p. 404.

TABLE A (*Continued*)

Size Class †	1931	1932	1933	1934	1935	1936 Und. prof.	1936 Other
			LEATHER				
0	16	20	71	58	63	16	59
50	39	52	122	131	118	21	94
100	130	127	443	312	463	70	394
250	146	122	368	370	522	111	458
500	95	114	563	489	651	139	809
1,000	625	355	1,940	1,365	2,126	382	2,038
5,000	185	162	896	221	680	148	983
10,000	...	...	...	...	...	...	...
50,000	...	...	...	...	...	...	...
100,000	...	...	...	...	...	...	...
Grouped	2,079	1,446	2,342	2,091	2,137	85	1,906
Error §	−67	70	−25	6	51	58	79
			RUBBER				
0	4	6	11	78	22	7	20
50	5	11	35	42	29	5	32
100	15	24	90	103	135	26	135
250	61	32	136	197	234	58	287
500	18	...	155	83	173	45	308
1,000	270	107	639	536	868	225	1,447
5,000	...	...	...	108	323	115	806
10,000	...	...	345	...	1,797	196	1,184
50,000	...	...	...	...	884	...	...
100,000	...	...	...	...	...	...	...
Grouped	994	144	505	885	...	452	3,150
Error §	170	59	−31	−22	−191	−24	−90
			FOREST PRODUCTS				
0	21	21	99	113	184	37	180
50	51	39	184	150	244	57	281
100	190	94	448	504	773	194	1,012
250	167	85	432	629	866	249	1,388
500	253	102	530	545	872	271	1,594
1,000	600	...	838	1,240	1,489	534	3,281
5,000	67	...	253	300	306	231	1,439
10,000	25	...	...	...	...	...	...
50,000	...	...	...	...	...	...	...
100,000	...	...	...	...	...	...	...
Grouped	...	315	470	310	698	336	1,976
Error §	26	6	−38	20	20	§§	387

NOTE. For footnotes, see p. 404.

TABLE A (*Continued*)

Size Class †	1931	1932	1933	1934	1935	1936 Und. prof.	1936 Other
				PAPER			
0	11	10	53	60	82	22	77
50	25	34	94	167	168	33	141
100	149	121	453	624	668	141	600
250	250	164	609	793	927	210	806
500	502	319	742	1,369	1,364	276	1,433
1,000	1,473	804	2,262	3,294	3,887	1,137	4,971
5,000	576	426	1,123	1,843	1,934	393	2,529
10,000	...	...	...	...	...	421	4,223
50,000	...	...	...	...	...	...	...
100,000	...	...	...	...	...	...	...
Grouped	1,204	332	2,059	3,110	3,851	130	577
Error §	−180	−72	−17	−33	205	−772	298
				PRINTING			
0	101	150	216	489	553	109	516
50	167	138	219	535	656	122	595
100	522	447	577	1,174	1,443	268	1,355
250	799	581	761	1,281	1,501	325	1,779
500	1,258	826	880	1,651	2,049	399	2,306
1,000	2,828	1,610	2,273	3,901	4,630	937	5,632
5,000	2,483	1,870	1,988	2,764	3,717	701	4,200
10,000	...	...	...	...	...	966	5,618
50,000	...	...	...	...	...	...	...
100,000	...	...	...	...	...	...	...
Grouped	4,588	2,040	2,938	4,385	5,098	190	1,048
Error §	−638	−104	68	81	262	§§	1,817
				CHEMICALS **			
0	55	122	205	431	310	65	240
50	96	137	330	467	594	60	397
100	498	525	937	1,347	1,434	253	1,317
250	721	731	1,301	2,123	1,947	305	1,756
500	1,079	1,119	2,100	2,828	3,719	422	2,724
1,000	4,297	4,007	5,777	8,392	8,884	1,035	8,856
5,000	3,190	2,707	4,790	5,489	5,555	246	4,665
10,000	7,826	5,096	10,627	13,295	15,518	1,105	18,148
50,000	11,192	8,051	11,790	9,324	13,006	605	3,873
100,000	...	...	...	...	...	2,457	14,504
Grouped	...	...	...	...	...	...	...
Error §	−928	−287	−234	−75	691	−1,157	6,445

NOTE. For footnotes, see p. 404.

TABLE A (*Continued*)

Size Class †	1931	1932	1933	1934	1935	1936 Und. prof.	1936 Other
			STONE				
0	15	19	34	73	76	45	126
50	53	33	58	100	194	54	229
100	117	110	140	284	424	132	660
250	174	74	265	386	584	167	752
500	288	160	332	592	743	234	1,149
1,000	741	406	665	1,302	2,063	358	3,090
5,000	362	210	622	1,312	1,517	455	2,770
10,000	2,332	...	...	2,547	3,961	330	6,743
50,000	445	...	...	1,791	3,024	...	...
100,000	...	...	...	...	...	...	...
Grouped	...	748	2,792	...	...	811	4,489
Error §	−21	−19	−9	42	−76	−731	226
			METALS **				
0	77	98	264	549	800	265	759
50	178	146	426	872	1,200	328	1,369
100	584	359	1,209	2,435	3,764	1,050	4,493
250	1,006	495	1,656	2,991	4,577	1,475	6,335
500	1,345	570	1,970	4,017	7,033	2,269	9,056
1,000	3,811	1,358	5,294	11,834	21,066	6,513	33,436
5,000	2,299	937	3,006	5,626	8,266	2,627	15,895
10,000	7,425	2,226	5,051	10,934	21,166	3,513	31,357
50,000	23,735	3,365	22,030	35,008	60,339	1,260	11,023
100,000	...	...	...	...	...	4,760	34,287
Grouped	...	...	...	...	...	...	...
Error §	−112	−134	−244	6	−4,261	−5,784	−59
			MISCELLANEOUS MANUFACTURING				
0	43	64	123	167	212	46	168
50	83	68	173	226	293	66	246
100	263	212	535	624	858	178	694
250	343	160	435	694	1,084	280	1,181
500	383	229	660	1,024	1,599	324	1,444
1,000	1,495	839	1,183	2,024	4,167	1,050	4,851
5,000	850	340	960	1,365	1,851	378	1,745
10,000	...	...	...	...	...	...	...
50,000	...	...	...	...	...	...	...
100,000	...	...	...	...	...	...	...
Grouped	2,646	1,359	3,395	3,668	5,066	1,489	6,641
Error §	−161	−88	−172	−34	−305	§§	1,813

NOTE. For footnotes, see p. 404.

TABLE A (*Continued*)

III. GROUPS SUB-DIVIDED IN 1936 **

Size Class †	Clothing		Petroleum		Motor vehicles	
	Und. prof.	Other	Und. prof.	Other	Und. prof.	Other
0	57	218	2	13	6	26
50	72	318	3	21	10	41
100	158	852	18	115	19	151
250	191	968	23	152	24	147
500	198	1,140	45	315	125	816
1,000	411	2,257	149	1,092	332	3,013
5,000	96	926	229	1,674	139	965
10,000	39	692	96	683	546	4,916
50,000	...	...	169	1,137	5	3,238
100,000	...	...	2,157	14,672	4,483	51,409
Grouped	...	...	...	...	...	...
Error §	253	86	§§	8,855	−365	−7,832

* Unit; $1,000. Calculation of estimates described in Chapter XXVI.

† Lower limit of size class, in unit of $1,000. For 1931–35, $50,000,000 class has no upper limit; for 1936, $100,000,000 class has none. Row marked "Grouped" covers cases in which two or more high size classes are combined in the source tables.

§ Not the error in *final* estimates. Aggregate discrepancy, between preliminary figures and tabulated figure, distributed proportionately among preliminary figures to obtain final estimates. Error stated positive if preliminary estimate exceeds final estimate.

‡ Includes beverages in 1931–32.

** 1936 data subdivided, see final section of Table A. The 1936 data given in sections of Table A for textiles, chemicals, and metals pertain to those groups *after* exclusion of clothing, petroleum, and motor vehicles, respectively.

§§ The "error" here is zero, because a special undistributed-profits tax calculation, necessarily showing no *aggregate* error, was used for these divisions and groups.

TABLE B

SIX-YEAR AVERAGE RATES OF RETURN, FOR EACH DIVISION AND GROUP AND ALL DIVISIONS COMBINED *

Class †	All divisions §	Agriculture §	Mining	Manufacturing §	Construction	Public utilities
0	**−16.34**	**−16.79**	**−33.01**	**−17.24**	**−22.14**	**−15.07**
	10.79	9.38	24.50	11.11	12.17	12.68
	−34.52	*−29.67*	*−74.70*	*−33.46*	*−36.19*	*−71.28*
50	**−4.73**	**−8.22**	**−6.24**	**−5.22**	**−8.74**	**−1.85**
	8.45	6.61	11.59	9.38	11.20	11.26
	−14.26	*−14.16*	*−16.93*	*−16.53*	*−18.84*	*−21.39*
100	**−2.68**	**−5.42**	**−2.95**	**−2.36**	**−4.92**	**.60**
	7.98	5.27	10.51	9.38	10.84	9.72
	−11.79	*−10.70*	*−11.13*	*−12.99*	*−13.40*	*−15.06*
250	**−1.40**	**−3.22**	**−1.38**	**−.33**	**−1.79**	**−.51**
	8.06	4.85	8.67	9.36	11.80	8.94
	−9.63	*−7.38*	*−8.59*	*−9.74*	*−10.33*	*−19.67*
500	**−.80**	**−2.85**	**−1.52**	**.80**	**−1.17**	**.15**
	7.90	4.46	7.39	9.50	10.47	8.01
	−8.70	*−6.04*	*−6.96*	*−9.25*	*−9.78*	*−15.20*
1,000	**−.05**	...	**−.57**	**1.56**	**3.26**	**1.00**
	7.46	...	5.52	8.84	13.48	6.88
	−6.81	...	*−3.96*	*−7.32*	*−5.25*	*−10.76*
5,000	**.38**	...	**−.05**	**2.54**	...	**1.14**
	7.30	...	4.09	9.26	...	5.69
	−6.20	...	*−2.99*	*−6.02*	...	*−7.28*
10,000	**1.44**	...	...	**2.47**	...	**2.22**
	7.25	...	...	8.16	...	5.98
	−4.92	...	...	*−5.36*	...	*−6.11*
50,000	**2.59**	...	...	**3.58**	...	**1.52**
	6.01	...	...	7.11	...	4.68
	−1.01	...	...	*−2.01*	...	*−2.15*
Classes grouped ‡	...	**−.30**	**−.33**	...	**1.49**	...
	...	4.17	4.35	...	8.98	...
	...	*−4.69*	*−2.51*	...	*−3.36*	...

NOTE. For footnotes, see p. 408.

TABLE B (*Continued*)

Class †	Trade	Service	Finance	Foods §	Tobacco	Textiles
0	**−12.53**	**−21.63**	**−19.37**	**−11.08**	**−14.58**	**−23.86**
	8.96	17.76	9.51	10.66	15.64	8.22
	−26.40	*−52.76*	*−41.47*	*−27.08*	*−24.51*	*−41.89*
50	**−3.86**	**−7.59**	**−4.72**	**−2.71**	**−3.04**	**−7.64**
	7.39	11.58	6.20	8.99	10.05	8.00
	−13.40	*−20.52*	*−12.29*	*−14.10*	*−10.99*	*−20.46*
100	**−1.92**	**−3.88**	**−3.76**	**−.79**	**.48**	**−3.73**
	7.31	9.68	6.28	8.85	9.54	8.31
	−10.92	*−13.59*	*−10.47*	*−12.14*	*−9.11*	*−15.60*
250	**−.29**	**−2.58**	**−2.88**	**2.08**	**−1.68**	**−.73**
	8.76	9.59	5.46	9.20	5.16	8.41
	−9.03	*−10.87*	*−8.21*	*−8.93*	*−8.79*	*−10.86*
500	**.55**	**−3.82**	**−2.50**	**3.22**	**−1.07**	**.01**
	7.93	7.92	5.22	9.53	4.78	7.65
	−8.70	*−11.93*	*−7.50*	*−8.00*	*−7.32*	*−9.26*
1,000	**1.87**	**−4.37**	**−1.63**	**3.44**	...	**.38**
	8.09	7.86	5.46	9.16	...	6.84
	−7.99	*−10.80*	*−5.95*	*−7.55*	...	*−6.89*
5,000	**3.24**	**−5.83**	**−1.66**	**5.48**	...	...
	9.04	8.27	5.75	10.39	...	...
	−6.64	*−11.94*	*−6.34*	*−5.76*	...	...
10,000	...	...	**.63**	...	...	...
	...	...	7.66	...	...	...
	...	...	*−4.14*	...	...	...
50,000	...	...	**4.51**	...	...	...
	...	...	10.82	...	...	...
	...	...	*.53*	...	...	...
Classes grouped ‡	**5.48**	**−4.47**	...	**6.22**	**11.75**	**.69**
	9.74	6.24	...	8.45	12.92	5.89
	−5.54	*−13.24*	...	*−2.40*	*−4.64*	*−6.33*

NOTE. For footnotes, see p. 408.

TABLE B (*Continued*)

Class †	Leather	Rubber	Forest products	Paper	Printing	Chemicals
0	**−22.80**	...	**−20.08**	−13.34	−13.85	−15.48
	9.77	16.72	8.68	9.28	10.33	15.40
	−40.96	...	*−34.34*	*−30.11*	*−28.50*	*−36.60*
50	−7.43	−2.85	−11.61	−1.64	−3.49	−1.44
	9.52	12.32	7.37	8.71	8.34	11.09
	−21.65	*−18.53*	*−20.14*	*−14.03*	*−14.55*	*−13.37*
100	−2.44	−1.16	−7.14	1.41	−.34	1.37
	9.51	10.98	6.97	10.40	9.05	11.40
	−14.25	*−12.23*	*−14.76*	*−12.33*	*−12.48*	*−11.08*
250	−1.89	3.23	−5.40	2.88	2.36	3.68
	8.36	10.37	6.11	9.89	9.57	11.94
	−12.24	*−9.53*	*−11.43*	*−8.27*	*−11.76*	*−9.19*
500	−1.57	...	−3.83	3.36	3.22	5.00
	8.47	...	5.88	9.89	9.54	12.96
	−10.66	...	*−8.94*	*−8.78*	*−17.92*	*−8.52*
1,000	...	...	...	2.30	4.77	6.13
	...	...	...	8.10	9.26	11.36
	...	...	...	*−6.74*	*−8.67*	*−7.19*
5,000	...	...	...	...	8.33	8.46
	...	...	...	...	10.36	14.02
	...	...	...	...	*−7.63*	*−5.22*
10,000	...	...	...	...	...	5.22
	...	...	...	...	...	10.26
	...	...	...	...	...	*−7.29*
50,000	...	...	...	...	...	2.27
	...	...	...	...	...	4.87
	...	...	...	...	...	*−1.30*
Classes grouped ‡	3.18	2.00	−2.46	1.14	4.50	...
	6.16	3.90	4.54	5.41	7.60	...
	−10.35	*−3.60*	*−5.17*	*−2.41*	*−3.20*	...

NOTE. For footnotes, see p. 408.

TABLE B (*Continued*)

Class †	Stone	Metals	Miscellaneous manufacturing			
0	**−17.32**	**−19.17**	**−21.28**	...	...	...
	8.47	10.52	10.72	...	...	...
	−27.18	*−34.30*	*−37.24*	...	...	...
50	**−6.67**	**−5.85**	**−7.34**	...	...	...
	8.54	9.37	9.63	...	...	...
	−13.78	*−15.85*	*−17.94*	...	...	...
100	**−4.99**	**−3.19**	**−2.97**	...	...	...
	8.41	8.75	9.45	...	...	...
	−11.67	*−12.07*	*−13.76*	...	...	...
250	**−3.36**	**−1.65**	**−1.00**	...	...	...
	7.64	8.60	9.32	...	...	...
	−9.26	*−10.48*	*−10.25*	...	...	...
500	**−1.06**	**−.39**	**−.56**	...	...	...
	7.31	8.66	9.51	...	...	...
	−9.81	*−8.55*	*−10.68*	...	...	...
1,000	**−1.01**	**.30**	**1.18**	...	...	...
	6.24	8.17	9.62	...	...	...
	−6.20	*−7.47*	*−7.94*	...	...	...
5,000	**1.15**	**.89**	...	...	...	...
	7.55	8.01	...	...	...	...
	−5.69	*−6.46*	...	...	...	...
10,000	...	**.56**	...	...	...	...
	...	7.66	...	...	...	...
	...	*−5.79*	...	...	...	...
50,000	...	**3.16**	...	...	...	...
	...	7.94	...	...	...	...
	...	*−2.02*	...	...	...	...
Classes grouped ‡	**3.62**	...	**3.25**	...	...	...
	6.90	...	11.13	...	...	...
	−3.59	...	*−7.22*	...	...	...

* Boldface type, both categories combined; ordinary type, income category; italics, deficit. All data for liquors, and part of lowest class for rubber, missing.

† Lower limit, in thousands of dollars.

‡ For each category, grouping reaches down to lowest class grouped in category in any year. For both categories combined, grouping reaches down as far as for either category.

§ See footnotes to Chart I, and Table IX.

TABLE C

Rates of Return in 1936, for New Groups into which Former Groups were Separated in that Year *

Class †	Formerly in metals		Formerly in chemicals		Formerly in textiles	
	Motor vehicles	Metals	Petroleum	Chemicals	Clothing	Textiles
0	**−25.62**	**−3.87**	**−27.28**	**−9.62**	**−11.48**	**−12.42**
	14.94	13.86	18.94	17.12	8.01	10.01
	−258.86	*−24.45*	*−107.76*	*−35.51*	*−30.54*	*−33.75*
50	**1.40**	**5.45**	**−2.28**	**4.90**	**1.55**	**−.53**
	12.09	13.38	14.52	14.01	8.62	9.60
	−19.54	*−13.31*	*−167.28*	*−9.96*	*−12.35*	*−19.41*
100	**3.34**	**7.44**	**11.23**	**7.89**	**5.77**	**3.10**
	14.30	13.19	21.79	14.30	10.53	10.50
	−11.77	*−9.41*	*−14.65*	*−9.45*	*−9.30*	*−11.62*
250	**3.94**	**9.00**	**10.61**	**10.07**	**8.19**	**3.82**
	11.93	13.37	24.92	13.43	10.64	9.39
	−28.97	*−9.08*	*−16.08*	*−5.02*	*−8.18*	*−9.48*
500	**14.79**	**9.18**	**8.71**	**10.86**	**9.82**	**5.23**
	22.07	12.86	17.55	15.57	11.45	9.25
	−7.90	*−6.98*	*−19.75*	*−8.25*	*−3.74*	*−7.93*
1,000	**12.44**	**11.01**	**10.48**	**11.75**	**8.48**	**4.73**
	23.26	13.93	13.05	13.84	10.17	7.77
	−21.22	*−6.52*	*−11.75*	*−7.43*	*−18.38*	*−6.02*
5,000	**7.66**	**10.44**	**18.57**	**13.42**	**10.89**	**4.32**
	13.68	12.35	27.41	15.79	10.89	7.70
	−5.31	*−4.99*	*−2.32*	*−1.79*	...	*−5.92*
10,000	**8.71**	**9.24**	**.94**	**12.85**	**8.11**	**7.31**
	11.97	9.97	4.25	13.36	8.11	8.39
	−7.25	*−5.92*	*−12.38*	*−2.45*	...	*−2.45*
50,000	**15.78**	...	**2.47**	**13.38**	...	**8.65**
	15.78	8.16	3.49	13.38	...	8.65
	...	...	*−1.11*	...	...	...
100,000	**15.77**	...	**3.25**	**14.39**	...	...
	15.77	7.75	3.64	14.39	...	...
	...	...	*−2.19*	...	...	...
Classes grouped ‡	...	**6.73**	...	...	...	...
	...	...	...	...	...	...
	...	*−1.03*	...	...	...	...

* Boldface type, both categories combined; ordinary type, income category; italics, deficit.

† Lower limit, in thousands of dollars.

‡ Deficit category only is grouped. Both categories grouped for the combined (boldface) figure.

INDEX

INDEX

Symbols attached to page numbers have the following meanings: c, chart; Ch, chapter head; n, foot-note; t, table. References to *industries* apply to the following list of index items: agriculture, all industries combined, chemicals, clothing, construction, finance, foods, forest products, leather, liquors, manufacturing, metals, mining, miscellaneous manufacturing, motor vehicles, paper, petroleum, printing, public utilities, rubber, service, stone, textiles, tobacco, trade.